MEASURING
AND ASSESSING
ORGANIZATIONS

Wiley Series On
ORGANIZATIONAL ASSESSMENT AND CHANGE

Series Editors:
Edward E. Lawler III and
Stanley E. Seashore

Assessing Organizational Change: The Rushton Quality of Work Experiment
by Paul S. Goodman and Associates

Measuring and Assessing Organizations
by Andrew H. Van de Ven and Diane L. Ferry

Organizational Assessment: Perspectives on the Measurement of Organizational Behavior and Quality of Work Life
edited by Edward E. Lawler III, David A. Nadler, and Cortlandt Cammann

SCHEDULED BOOKS

Work and Well-Being
by Robert L. Kahn

The New Plant
by Dennis N. T. Perkins, Veronica F. Nieva, and Edward E. Lawler III

Employee Productivity and the Quality of Work Life
by Richard E. Walton and Leonard Schlesinger

The Bolivar Quality of Work Experiment: 1972-1978
by Barry A. Macy, Edward E. Lawler III, and Gerald E. Ledford, Jr.

PROSPECTIVE BOOKS

Observing and Measuring Organizational Change: A Guide to Field Practice
edited by Stanley E. Seashore, Edward E. Lawler III, Philip H. Mirvis, and Cortlandt Cammann

MEASURING AND ASSESSING ORGANIZATIONS

ANDREW H. VAN DE VEN

The Wharton School
University of Pennsylvania

DIANE L. FERRY

Department of Business Administration
University of Delaware

A WILEY-INTERSCIENCE PUBLICATION

JOHN WILEY & SONS, New York
Chichester • Brisbane • Toronto

Library of Congress Cataloging in Publication Data

Van de Ven, Andrew H
  Measuring and assessing organizations.

  (Wiley series on organizational assessment and change)
  Bibliography: p.
  Includes indexes.
  1. Organizational effectiveness.   I. Ferry, Diane
L. II. Title. III. Series.
HD58.9.V35   658.4   79-20003
ISBN 0-471-04832-1

Printed in the United States of America

10 9 8 7 6 5 4 3 2 1

*. . . To the managers, employees, and associates of the Job
Service Division in the Wisconsin Department of Industry,
Labor, and Human Relations—in particular:*

James F. Brown	*Philip E. Lerman*
Brian B. Carlson	*Steven J. Reilly*
Virginia B. Hart	*Stanley R. Spencer*
George A. Kaisler	*Mary Joan (Treis) Young*
Edwin M. Kehl	*Janet M. Van Vleck*
Martin Kestin	*Francis J. Walsh*

*These practitioners committed themselves and their organiza-
tions to improving the theory and practice of management.
They constructively accepted the often frustrating trial-and-
error process involved in developing Organization Assessment.
It is only because of their foresight, courage, perseverance, and
trust over the years that new ideas, methods, and learning
experiences can be offered here for measuring and assessing
organizations.*

Series Preface

The ORGANIZATIONAL ASSESSMENT AND CHANGE SERIES is concerned with informing and furthering contemporary debate on the effectiveness of work organizations and the quality of life they provide for their members. Of particular relevance is the adaptation of work organizations to changing social aspirations and economic constraints. There has been a phenomenal growth of interest in the quality of work life and productivity in recent years. Issues that not long ago were the quiet concern of a few academics and a few leaders in unions and management have become issues of broader public interest. They have intruded upon broadcast media prime time, lead newspaper and magazine columns, the houses of Congress, and the boardrooms of both firms and unions.

A thorough discussion of what organizations should be like and how they can be improved must comprehend many issues. Some are concerned with basic moral and ethical questions—What is the responsibility of an organization to its employees? —What, after all, is a "good job"? —How should it be decided that some will benefit from and others pay for gains in the quality of working life? —Should there be a public policy on the matter? Yet others are concerned with the strategies and tactics of bringing about changes in organizational life, the advocates of alternative approaches being numerous, vocal, and controversial; and still others are concerned with the task of measurement and assessment on grounds that the choices to be made by leaders, the assessment of consequences, and the bargaining of equities must be informed by reliable, comprehensive, and relevant information of kinds not now readily available.

The WILEY SERIES ON ORGANIZATIONAL ASSESSMENT AND CHANGE is concerned with all aspects of the debate on how organizations should be managed, changed, and controlled. It includes books pertaining to the basic moral and ethical issues, the assessment of organizational effectiveness, and the study of organizational changes that represent new approaches to organizational change and process. The volumes in the series have in common a concern with work organizations, a focus on change and the dynamics of change, an assumption that diverse social and personal interests need to be taken into account in discussions of organizational effectiveness, and a view that concrete cases and quantitative data are essential ingredients in a lucid debate. As such, these books consider a broad but integrated set of issues and ideas. They are intended to be read by managers, union officials, researchers, consultants, policy makers, students, and others seriously concerned with organizational assessment and change.

The present volume, by Andrew Van de Ven and Diane Ferry, is addressed to issues of conceptualization and measurement in the assessment of organizations. We believe it represents the first contribution to such issues that is comprehensive in topical coverage, firmly grounded in organizational theory, and supported by a sophisticated methodology. The areas of measurement include the environment of an organization, gross structural features, aspects of the core work technology, certain aspects of the design of sub-parts and activity processes, and performance outcomes. In each area, the leading theoretical and operational contributions are incorporated, with preference for measures that are generally applicable and potentially useful for comparison between organizations and for the detection of changes over time. The intent is to promote the assessment of an organization as a whole, and to match the concerns of managers and of most researchers. The volume is sufficiently detailed to serve as a manual of procedures for those who wish to apply, or adapt, the instruments and methods to their own purposes. The work reported is an exemplary model for the development of improved measurement methods, with admirable attention given to the sequential stages of field trial, quality assessment, revision, and validation.

EDWARD E. LAWLER III
STANLEY E. SEASHORE

Ann Arbor, Michigan
August 1979

Preface

This book, *Measuring and Assessing Organizations,* is written for organizational researchers, consultants, and practitioners who diagnose, evaluate, and take action to solve problems in the design and performance of organizations. It is concerned with the development of a scientifically valid and practical approach for assessing the performance of a complex organization in relation to how it is organized and to the environments in which it operates. It is based on the results of a longitudinal research program called *Organization Assessment* (OA), which has been in progress since 1972. This book describes, evaluates, and proposes a revised *framework,* a *set of measurement instruments,* and a *process* for conducting ongoing assessments of complex organizations.

Based on a synthesis of the organizational literature and findings from the OA research program, the *OA framework* identifies the organizational and environmental characteristics that are important for explaining the effectiveness, efficiency, and quality of working life of organizations, work groups, and jobs. Using the framework as the conceptual guide, this book focuses on an evaluation and revision of the *OA instruments* (OAI), which measure the context, structure, and behavior of an overall organization and of work groups and individual jobs. The OAI are intended to be used for basic and applied research and evaluation. For basic research, the OAI provide a set of measures that can be used to develop and evaluate theories on how the contexts and designs of organizations, work groups, and jobs are interrelated and how they effect organizational performance. For applied research, the OAI provide a set of survey procedures and measurements that can be used to diagnose strengths and weaknesses in the structure and behavior of organizations, particularly when the OAI surveys are conducted regularly and used as part of an ongoing program of organizational development. In order to properly use the OA Framework and Instruments for these purposes, this book also offers a *process model* for designing and conducting assessments of organizations. The OA process model emphasizes the need to involve organizational participants in each phase of the assessment process—design, data collection, and feedback—in order to identify relevant criteria of organizational performance and to obtain the practical benefits available from longitudinal assessments of organizations.

Seven years of intensive research have been conducted to initially develop, revise, and improve on three versions of the OA framework and instruments in two major organizational settings. Three versions of the OAI were developed and administered, in 1972, 1973, and 1975, in the Wisconsin Job Service Division (which contains 30 local offices, 334 organizational units, and about 1700 employees). In addition, portions of the revised OAI versions were administered four times between 1972 and 1977 in 14 Texas child-care organizations to measure and assess inter-organizational coordination. Although such a setting is limiting to the generalizability of the OAI evaluations, it provided the opportunity for the multiple trials necessary in constructing measurement instruments. Much progress has been made over the years in developing the OAI. Whereas many changes were found necessary in the 1972 version, progressively fewer and less drastic revisions were needed in the 1973 and 1975 versions of the OAI.

This book focuses on an evaluation of the 1975 version of the OA framework and instruments and proposes a fourth version for use in other organizations. As the evaluations will indicate in detail, most of the measures in the 1975 OAI show good indications of reliability and validity. The OAI measures explain large variations in the efficiency, effectiveness, and job satisfaction of different types of organizations, work units, and jobs. The results also show substantial support for the theories underlying OA and suggest specific areas where improvements can be and are made in the framework. Finally, the OAI data are found to be useful for addressing many practical problems and questions raised by managers about organization design and the consequences of alternative reorganization decisions. When used on a longitudinal basis, the OAI can be useful as a core management information system to help managers monitor, explain, and improve the design and performance of their organizational units.

These evaluation results suggest that with the revisions made here, the OA framework and instruments have reached a developmental stage that warrants their publication so they can be available to others. Further administrations of the OAI in other organizations are needed to test their generality and to establish norms on OAI indices across organizations. In addition, more experimental adoptions of the OAI by organizations are needed to realize their practical uses and applications. In return for making the new version of the OA framework and instruments publicly available, we hope that users will communicate to us (the authors) the findings from their applications and evaluations of the OAI. In this way we can continue to revise and extend the OAI to further their development and generality for measuring and assessing organizations.

The purposes of this book then, are to describe our approach to measuring and assessing organizations and to provide the basic information needed to make choices on using the OA framework and instruments for basic and applied research purposes. To achieve these purposes, this book will: (1) describe the conceptual framework underlying the OAI; (2) evaluate both the measurement properties of all indices in the OAI and the theories in the OA framework; (3) propose a revised OA framework and instruments for use in other organizations; and (4) suggest specific procedures and guidelines for designing and conducting assessments of organizational design and performance.

Throughout the book, attempts were made to minimize technical obtuseness in describing the statistical methods used in evaluating the OA framework and instruments. Although it is assumed the reader is familiar with basic statistical methods—for example, correlations and regressions—the reader is not expected to be a psychometrician or a statistician to understand the evaluation methods and results. In addition, the conclusions of each chapter restate in nontechnical terms the major substantive findings obtained from the empirical testing of OA in that chapter.

This book represents the tip of an iceberg of effort, commitment, and important contributions to the development of OA over the years by so many people that it would be impossible to recognize them all.

First and foremost, we owe a great debt of gratitude to the practitioners in the Job Service Division of the Wisconsin Department of Industry, Labor, and Human Relations—to whom this book is dedicated. It was out of the principal author's ongoing work with the managers and employees in this state agency from 1972 to 1977 that the basic ideas and goals for OA emerged. As discussed in Chapters 2 and 3, these practitioners courageously committed themselves, their organizations, and their resources to the development of OA and subjected themselves to the often frustrating trial-and-error process involved in creating and revising the OA framework, instruments, and process model over the years. In short, OA owes its existence largely to these practitioners, and it is a tribute to them that new ideas, methods, and learning experiences can be offered here for measuring and assessing organizations.

In addition to the help of these practitioners, we have been greatly assisted by many other organization theorists and researchers through three major day-long reviews session and countless informal discussions conducted over the years. In particular, we must recognize the many critical but constructive suggestions on OA's development offered by the following colleagues: Howard Aldrich, Cornell University; David Bowers and Cortlandt Cammann, University of Michigan; Larry Cummings and Richard Schoenherr, University of Wisconsin—Madison; Andre Delbecq, University of Santa Clara; Benjamin Dowell and Arlyn Melcher, Kent State University; William Evan, Jay Galbraith, Lawrence Hrebiniak, Giorgio Inzerilli, William Joyce and Marilyn Morgan, University of Pennsylvania; Terry Gleason, Bell Laboratories; Richard Hackman and John Kimberly, Yale University; Richard Hall, State University of New York—Albany; Pradip Khandwalla, Indian Institute of Management; Robert Miles, Harvard University; Ian Mitroff, University of Pittsburgh; Johannes Pennings, Noel Tichy, and Michael Tushman, Columbia University; Charles Perrow, State University of New York—Stony Brook; Steven Shortell, University of Washington; William Starbuck, University of Wisconsin—Milwaukee; Fremont Shull, University of Georgia; Roland Warren, Brandeis University; and David Whetten, University of Illinois.

Based on the learning experiences obtained in developing OA in the Wisconsin agency, we expanded the research program into a number of other organizations. A longitudinal assessment of organization design and inter-organizational coordination of Texas child-care organizations was initiated in 1973 and is still in progress. This study is sponsored by the Early Childhood Development Division of the Texas Department of Community Affairs. We particularly appreciate the help of Jeannette Watson, Bruce Esterline, Jennie Liston, Richard Orton, and Doyal Pinkard of this agency in designing and conducting this longitudinal study. With regard to OA's development, this study provided a particularly useful comparison for developing the OA process model and also provided opportunities for testing alternative versions of the OAI dealing with inter-unit coordination.

During 1975 and 1976 the OAI were also administered in twenty California employment service, unemployment insurance, and vocational rehabilitation offices—consisting of 250 work units and about

1300 employees. This study was conducted with David Roberts and John Mitchell, now with Teknekon, Inc., and The Urban Institute, respectively. This cross-sectional study provided the opportunity to replicate and test the generality of the OAI in another set of employment security organizations which are structured very differently from those in Wisconsin. Unfortunately, time pressures prevented us from incorporating the results of this study in this book. However, a replication of the evaluations of the OAI presented in Chapters 4 to 8 is now nearly complete, and the results are closely similar, with no major exceptions, to those presented here on the Wisconsin agency. These findings greatly increase our personal confidence in the OA evaluation results presented here.

The OA research program has also expanded into a number of other public and private organizations as the result of other researchers who have requested part or all of the OAI for use in conducting their organizational studies. These researchers and organizations include: (1) Mark Chadwin, The Urban Institute, to conduct a national evaluation of the WIN Program; (2) Charles Perrow, SUNY—Stony Brook, to study the organization of municipal departments; (3) Noel Tichy, Columbia University, to conduct a longitudinal assessment of industrial organizations; (4) Jerald Hunt and Richard Osborn, Southern Illinois University, to study United Way and military organizations; (5) Steven Shortell, University of Washington, to conduct a survey of western hospitals; (6) Jay Galbraith and Thomas Gilmore, University of Pennsylvania, to evaluate merger possibilities of state bureaus of probation and corrections; (7) John Brian, Manchester Polytechnic Institute, to assess business organizations in England and Japan; and (8) Joseph Setzer, La Salle College, to conduct an evaluation of the organization of secondary schools. Most of these early adoptions of the OAI are still in the data collection stage.

As we request of other users, these researchers have agreed to provide us information on the measurement properties of the OAI. By accumulating this information from a wide variety of organizations, we intend to test the generality of the OAI and to establish norms—averages, standard deviations, correlations—on OAI measures for different classes of organizations. These norms will be made available and will be particularly useful for comparing the OAI data from one organization with those obtained in others. The validation of any measurement instrument is an ongoing and never-ending process—and so it is with the OAI. With continued research and the cooperation of OAI users, this book will hopefully be the first of a series of editions.

Throughout the history of the OA research program, we have been blessed with graduate student assistants who have contributed immeasurably to the effort. In chronological order of their involvement as members of the OA research team, they are: Stanley Mendenhall, 1972; Dennis Emmett, 1972–1974; Richard Koenig, Jr., and David Hoffman, 1973–1975; Diane Ferry, 1974–1977; Martin Katz, 1974–1975; Carol Cheu, 1975–1977; Ann Siukola, 1976–1979; Robert Drazin, 1977–1978; Jeff Marusin, Gregory Uchimura, and Peter Spitalieri, 1977–1979; Marcel Genet, 1978–1979; and Antonio Infante, beginning in 1979. Their combined contributions included on-site data collection and coding, computer data set construction and editing, data analysis, preparation of tables and reports, literature searches, and reviewing and editing various OA working papers.

Following her involvement as research assistant, Diane Ferry has continued to make substantial contributions to the OA research program by collaborating with the principal author in preparing this book. In addition, in her doctoral dissertation (Ferry, 1979), she develops an innovative way to view structural–contingency theories of organizations and tests this view with data obtained in the OA research program.

Funding to support the OA research program over the years has been provided by grants from: (1) the Wisconsin Job Service Division, Department of Industry, Labor, and Human Relations; (2) Regions V, Chicago, and IX, California, of the Employment and Training Administration, Department of Labor; (3) the Early Childhood Development Division of the Texas Department of Community Affairs; (4) the Comparative Administration Research Institute, Kent State University; and (5) the Center for the Study of Organizational Innovation at the University of Pennsylvania.

Actual preparation of this book began in January, 1975, and since then has occupied most of the working time of the authors and the OA research team. Initially, our intention was to limit the book to an evaluation of the OAI. However it soon became apparent that one cannot evaluate and revise a measurement instrument without simultaneously evaluating and revising the theory underlying the instrument. Indeed, when errors were detected in the OAI, the source of the problems could often be traced back to omissions in the OA framework. As a consequence, we became involved in an iterative process of evaluating and revising the OA framework and instruments simultaneously, a process that far exceeded our initial predictions of time and effort. The process has been very rewarding, however, because it has permitted; (1) a closer linkage between the revised OA framework and instruments; (2) a synthesis and application of the work and thought of others; and (3) a broadening of our initial perspective on organization design. Obviously, future evaluation of the revised OA framework and instruments will be necessary to verify the revisions made.

An earlier draft of this book was reviewed by Mark L. Chadwin, The Urban Institute; Edward Lawler, III, University of Southern California; Jon L. Pierce, University of Minnesota, Duluth; and Stanley E. Seashore, University of Michigan. Their comments and suggestions were very helpful in preparing this final draft. Melinda Brunger and Robert Freeland have been instrumental in editing the draft to improve its readability and to detect errors. We are also particularly thankful for the excellent typing of repeated draft versions by Cindi Buoni, Susan Shaw, and Chris Stennis.

Last, but certainly not least, we are indebted to our families and loved ones. They have shared most in this undertaking, and made it an exciting, growing, and enjoyable experience—both personally and professionally.

ANDREW H. VAN DE VEN
DIANE L. FERRY

Philadelphia
January 1980

Contents

MEASURING
AND ASSESSING
ORGANIZATIONS

CHAPTER ONE

An Introduction to Organization Assessment

PROBLEMS AND NEEDS IN ASSESSING ORGANIZATIONS

Management theorists and practitioners generally agree that the ways in which organizations are designed and the environments in which they operate make a difference in affecting organizational performance. Given this general agreement, it is quite amazing that so little systematic effort has been taken by theorists and practitioners to develop reliable and valid ways for measuring and assessing organizations.

Most organization theorists and researchers have dwelt upon trying to describe the functioning of an organization as a sociological entity. This means that much of what is commonly thought of as current organization theory consists of an examination of the relationships between Weberian elements of bureaucratic structure and how they are influenced by the larger social system of which the organization is a part. Although we do not question the usefulness of viewing an organization as a sociological entity, we do question why organizational researchers have generally ignored the criterion that apparently matters most to managers—the performance effectiveness or efficiency of alternative organizational designs. The absence of performance criteria by which organizational structures can be assessed under varying environmental conditions has been one of the major blocks to putting organization theory and research into practice.

On the other hand, in practice most organizations tend to dwell on their performance and ignore their sociological nature. That is, most organizations invest great sums of money and effort in management

1

information systems that routinely measure and distribute data throughout the organization on the performance effectiveness and efficiency of various cost centers, departments, and individual jobs. Information and problems about the designs of jobs, work groups, and the organization are generally left for managers to figure out—after all, that is their job, isn't it?

Unfortunately, most of the information systems used in practice and those created by organizational researchers for their studies are not designed to provide a clue on *why* or *how* a given level of performance was achieved. *What does a manager or consultant do when performance is unsatisfactory?* Equally important, but too often ignored, *How and why did a work group or the entire organization exceed its performance expectations?* These questions are basic if managers hope to improve the functioning of their organizations, and if one hopes to train others in the management of organizations. However, those who work with or observe managerial behavior quickly recognize that practitioners at all levels of organizations are hard-pressed to provide logical and supportable answers to these questions. For that matter, if organizational consultants and analysts are honest with themselves, they too are unable to answer these questions adequately.

Although many explanations can be given for this unfortunate state of affairs, three reasons are basic: (1) inadequate theories about how organization design affects performance under varying environmental conditions, (2) lack of reliable and valid measures of organization structure and behavior, and (3) incomplete management information systems used by organizations.

Many of the principles and prescriptions that either exist in management literature or are implicit in managerial explanations about how organizational and environmental characteristics influence performance lack sound theoretical and empirical support. More than 30 years ago, Herbert Simon (1946) recognized this predicament by pointing out that many of the principles of classical management literature are nothing more than proverbs. He suggested that if a science of administration is to develop, there is a need to go beyond the superficial and oversimplified principles on division of labor, hierarchy of authority, span of control, and centralization. A valid approach to the study of administration, Simon argued, requires that all relevant dimensions of organization structure and environment which may affect performance be identified; that each administrative situation be analyzed in terms of the entire set of dimensions; and that research be instituted to determine how weights can be assigned to the various organizational characteristics that may explain organizational performance. Simon concluded that until administrative description reaches this higher level of sophistication and until analysts are willing to undertake the tiresome task of conducting the systematic research that this entails, there is little reason to hope that rapid progress will be made in identifying and verifying valid administrative principles.

A second basic reason why so little is known about how organization design and environment influence performance is that our capability to *measure* (and thereby investigate) some basic characteristics of the structure and behavior of organizations, work groups, and jobs has been very limited. As a consequence, little data are available on the relationships of organizational structure and function to performance, or on the effectiveness of alternative organizational designs under varying environmental conditions. Without reliable and valid ways to measure the context and designs of organizations, work groups, and jobs, one cannot come to know in any objective sense how these factors interrelate and affect the efficiency, effectiveness, or quality of working life in organizations.

Finally, while most managers will assert that organizational and environmental factors are important for explaining performance, the fact is that organizations typically do not do much to obtain or provide periodic data on these factors with their management information systems. Indeed, the so-called "management information systems" used by most organizations are more appropriately labeled "performance information systems" because they only tend to provide information on various indicators of performance outcomes (quantity, quality, cost of outputs, efficiency, and effectiveness). We believe one basic reason why most practitioners find their information systems of little or no help in making basic managerial decisions is because these systems only include the performance side of the equation and do not provide information on the organizational and environmental conditions that managers deal with on a direct and daily basis in efforts to influence performance.

Equally important, Pfeffer and Salancik (1978:74) point out that the information collected in an information system focuses organizational energy, attention, and demand on that information. The distribution of that information in periodic reports and tables throughout the organization means not only that it can be used, but also that it is more likely to be used in making decisions because its existence and prominence conveys the impression that the information is important. Unless information is regularly available to managers about organizational and environmental factors, it is not likely they will consider or place much emphasis on these factors when attempting to explain (and thereby coming to understand) how and why a given level of organizational performance was achieved.

THE ORGANIZATION ASSESSMENT RESEARCH PROGRAM

This book attempts to respond to these problems by describing and evaluating the findings of a longitudinal applied research program called *Organization Assessment* (abbreviated, OA), which has been in progress since 1972. The major goal of the OA research program has been to develop a *framework*, a set of *measurement instruments*, and a *process* that are scientifically valid and practically useful for assessing organizations on an ongoing basis. Although much work lies ahead to achieve this ambitious goal, the results presented in this book will demonstrate that much progress has been made.

The *OA framework* attempts to follow Simon's (1946) advice by identifying the dimensions of context, structure, and behavior that are important for explaining the performance of organizations, work groups, and individual jobs. This conceptual scheme is a synthesis of the extensive literature on organizations and represents our current thinking. It is our third statement on the subject as the result of evaluations and revisions of earlier frameworks presented in Van de Ven and Delbecq (1974) and Van de Ven (1976a). This book includes empirical tests of the main theories included in the current OA framework. The results show substantial support for the theories underlying OA and suggest specific areas where improvements and extensions of the framework can be and are made. As Lewin (1947) aptly stated, "Nothing is quite so practical as a good theory." Such a framework is needed not only to direct the development and evaluation of the OA measurement instruments, but also to provide a conceptual foundation to guide a systematic assessment of complex organizations.

The *Organization Assessment Instruments* (OAI) consist of a set of questionnaires and survey procedures for measuring the dimensions included in the OA framework, i.e., various characteristics of the context, structure, and behavior of the overall organization, work groups, and jobs. A description and evaluation of the third version of the OAI will be the major focus of this book, while evaluations of two previous versions of the OAI are available in Van de Ven et al. (1975, 1977). As the evaluation results will show in detail, most of the measures in the OAI are found to have good indications of reliability and validity. Further, it will be demonstrated that the OAI measures explain large variations in the efficiency, effectiveness, and job satisfaction of different types of employment security and child care organizations, work units, and jobs.

The evaluations of the OAI also identify specific areas where improvements and revisions are needed. These modifications are incorporated in a fourth version of the OAI, which is proposed for use in other organizations for basic and applied research purposes. For basic research, the OAI provide a set of measures that can be used to develop and evaluate theories on how the contexts and designs of organizations, work groups, and jobs are interrelated and influence organizational performance. For applied purposes, the OAI provide a set of survey procedures and measurements that can be used to diagnose strengths and weaknesses in the structure and behavior of organizations, particularly when the OAI surveys are conducted regularly and used as part of an ongoing program of organizational development. Adoptions of the new version of the OAI for either basic or applied purposes require that users conduct a pilot study to test the applicability of the OAI in the organizations under investigation because the development and testing of the OAI are limited to employment security and child care organizations.

The *process* component of the OA research program is concerned with developing ways to apply and use the OA framework and instruments in organizations. Although the OAI can be used to obtain a cross-sectional snapshot of organizational design and practices, their practical usefulness to an organization is greatly enhanced when OAI surveys are conducted periodically over time. Longitudinal assessments greatly facilitate learning and managerial development because: (1) they permit one to identify trends and examine how changes in organizational and environmental conditions affect changes in performance, (2) they can stimulate managers and analysts to take an experimental role in evaluating survey feedback by developing and implementing alternative interventions in areas where improvements are found needed, and (3) feedback from subsequent surveys can provide an understanding of the consequences of interventions taken in the previous cycle of the ongoing assessment process. It has been our experience that if organizations are to implement an ongoing organization assessment and obtain these potential benefits, there is a need to integrate the OAI with an organization's regular information systems and to incorporate it into a data-based program of organizational development. If OA is kept separate from an organization's core information systems for decision making and developmental practices, there is little likelihood that organizations will use or continue to commit the resources and effort needed to maintain OA over time.

In practical terms, the OAI represent an attempt to develop an *organizational* information system which is analogous to the existing *performance* information system within most organizations. Once developed and implemented, data obtained periodically with the organizational and performance information systems are linked together as an overall *OA Management Information System*. By examining data in such an OA MIS, one can come to learn over time what the relationships are between characteristics of organization context, structure, and performance. When incorporated as part of an ongoing program of data-based management and organizational development (as suggested in Chapter 2), we believe that managers and analysts can begin to obtain the benefits outlined previously from longitudinal organizational assessments. In addition, they can learn to systematically answer basic questions about the performance of their organizations on the bases of how they are structured and the environments in which they operate. This, then, is the practical objective of the OA research program.

AN OVERVIEW OF THE OA FRAMEWORK AND INSTRUMENTS

Any measurement instrument is based upon a conceptual scheme of how one views the world, in this case, the structure and functioning of organizations over time. Obviously, different organizational theories evoke different filters for measuring and observing organizational behavior. Therefore, it is important to understand the basic theory of organization underlying the OAI before proceeding with a description of the instruments and procedures used for measuring and assessing organizations.

Definitions and Theoretical Premises

Basic to the framework is the definition that a complex organization is an open social action system consisting of many different forms of structures and processes. The action system consists of an iterative series of choices made regarding the organization's environment, people, money, and work by decision makers (March and Simon, 1958; March and Olsen, 1976) and a repetitive cycle of procuring, transforming, and distributing inputs into outputs (Katz and Kahn, 1978). The design of the action system is constrained by environment and economic factors to the extent that the organization must input resources (i.e., raw materials or clients, money, technology and equipment, and labor) from its factor markets, and deliver outputs (i.e., products or services) to its product markets. Because choices are made with purposes in mind and because inputs are processed to yield outputs, organizational behavior consists of a series of goal-directed events, and there are cause-and-effect relations among the events (Parsons, 1962). These events are segmented by like functions and activities to achieve the benefits of process specialization (Thompson, 1967). Each event, in turn, has its own cyclical pattern of subgoal-directed activities and choices and is therefore a subsystem (Katz and Kahn, 1966). These subsystems are exhibited in complex organizations as vertically and horizontally differentiated components (departments or units) and positions (jobs). Depending upon the nature of its work and the function it contributes to the larger organization, each component adopts a particular program, or modus operandi, for organizing its cyclical activities into a predictable pattern of behavior (Van de Ven and Delbecq, 1974; Parsons, 1962). Thus, the structure of an organizational component is found in the program that it uses to govern the behavior of its members (March and Simon, 1958). The development and maintenance of relationships within and between organizational components are exhibited in the flows of information and resources (money, work, personnel) among positions. Instrumental and maintenance processes in an organization are found in the transactions of information and resources among positions. Overall, then, the complex organization consists of many differentiated but interdependent subsystems, each with its own program for structuring its cyclical activities. These subsystems are linked together as an overall organizational system through information and resource flows.

Implicit in this definition is the assumption that a thorough assessment of a complex organization requires an operational theory and methodology that cuts across and links the overall organization, unit, work group, and individual job levels of analyses. It is not obtained by focusing on just a small set of variables or issues at one particular level of organizational analysis, particularly given our limited current state of knowledge about organization design and performance. Instead, *what is needed is a framework that*:

1. *Identifies the relevant properties of context, design, and performance at the macro-organization, unit, and job levels of analyses,*

2. *Examines the unique design patterns of units and jobs which are differentiated vertically and horizontally within the complex organization, and*

3. *Determines how these different units and jobs are integrated and what functional contributions they make to the overall performance of the organizational system.*

Specifically we propose that a comprehensive assessment of an organization focus on the different levels of analyses illustrated in Figure 1-1 in terms of the dimensions outlined in Figure 1-2. This premise and proposed framework for measuring and assessing organizations are elaborated as follows. Detailed discussion of the theory and instruments are deferred to subsequent chapters when each component of the OA framework is examined.

Levels of Analyses and Modules in the OA Framework and Instruments

As Figure 1-1 illustrates, the OA framework examines an organization at four different levels of analyses: the overall organization, work

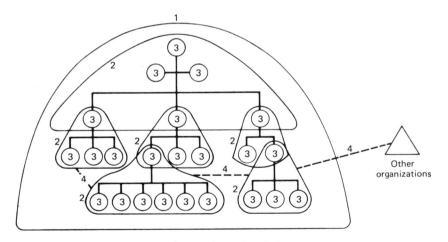

Key to Numbers: 1 = Overall organization focus of analysis
2 = Organizational unit focus of analysis
3 = Individual job or position focus of analysis
4 = Relations within and between units focus of analysis

Figure 1-1   Illustration of levels of analyses involved in conducting an in-depth organization assessment.

groups or units, individual jobs, and relationships between jobs and units within the organization and with other organizations. At each of these four levels of analyses, Figure 1-2 outlines the different dimensions of context, design, and performance on which one should focus in conducting a comprehensive assessment of organizations. The various factors listed in Figure 1-2 are measured with five different modules or component instruments in the OAI. They consist of the following.

1. *A performance module,* which consists of obtaining measures from organizational records on the performance efficiency and effectiveness of the total organization and its work units and jobs that are included in the assessment.

2. *A macroorganizational module,* which focuses on the overall structural configuration of an organization, its history, scale of operations, and domain. These factors are measured in the OAI with organization charts and records, interviews, and questionnaires.

3. *An organizational unit module* uses questionnaires and existing organizational records to measure various characteristics of the task, structure, and process of all organizational units or work groups.

4. *A job design module* measures with questionnaires the way in which individual jobs or positions are structured, the background characteristics of job incumbents, the organization's technical and functional requirements of jobs, and employees' affective responses to their jobs.

5. *An interunit module* provides an assessment of the structure of interdependence, coordination, and control among organizational units and positions. Questionnaires are used to measure various characteristics of the pair-wise relationships each organizational unit has with other units both within and outside of the organization.

These OA modules constitute the basic outline for this book. Specifically, each chapter makes an in-depth description and evaluation of the OA theory and measurement instruments for one of these modules. Therefore, it is appropriate to summarize here the basic perspective taken in each OA module and to indicate how they add up to provide a comprehensive assessment of an organization.

1. Measuring Organizational Performance and Design. Organizational performance is the ultimate criterion and starting point in an assessment of organizations. Performance is a complex construct

1. MACROORGANIZATION FOCUS OF ANALYSIS

Macroorganization Context

1. Organization Demographics
   —History, Age, Growth Stage
2. Organizational Domain (Strategy)
   —Type, Uncertainty, Complexity, Restrictiveness
3. Projected Demand and Supply for Period
   —Production/Service Quota
   —Resources (budget, personnel) Available

Macroorganization Design

1. Structural Configuration
   —Vertical, Horizontal, & Spacial Differentiation
   —Forms of Departmentation (by function, program, geography, matrix)
   —Administrative Intensity
2. Distribution of Power and Authority among Corporate Decision Makers

Macroorganization Outcomes

—Value judgments on criteria used to evaluate the overall effectiveness of the organization. For example:

1. Attainment of Goals in Organization's Domain
2. Market Share in Product Lines
3. Profitability, Return on Investment

Figure 1-2

2. ORGANIZATIONAL UNIT OR GROUP FOCUS OF ANALYSIS

Organizational Unit (Department) Context	Design of Organizational Units (Work Groups)	Organizational Unit Outcomes
1. Macroorganization Context and Design —Functional Contribution of Unit to Organization —Vertical & Horizontal Location of Unit in Organization Chart 2. Nature of Work Performed by Unit —Task Difficulty and Variability 3. Size of Unit (number of personnel)	1. Unit Specialization —# Different Tasks Assigned Unit —# Different Job Titles in Unit 2. Personnel Composition —Heterogeneity of Personnel Skills —Interchangeability of Roles 3. Unit Standardization —Automation of work Methods —# & Detail of Unit Rules, Procedures 4. Unit Decision Making —Centralization of Decisions in Spv. —Decision Strategies Used (computational, judgmental, bargaining, heuristic) 5. Unit Performance Norms & Standards —Quality/Quantity-Control Emphasis —Group/Individual-Based Incentives —Group Pressures to Conform (Soldiering)	—Value judgments on criteria used to evaluate effectiveness of organizational unit. For example: 1. Percent of Unit Performance Goals Attained 2. Unit Efficiency —Cost per unit of output 3. Unit Morale —Cohesiveness of work unit —Turnover rate 4. Unit Adaptiveness —Responsiveness to changing demands

Figure 1-2—continued

3. INDIVIDUAL JOB OR POSITION FOCUS OF ANALYSIS

Individual Jobs or Positions Context

1. Organizational Requirements of Job
   —Role of Job in Unit and Organization
   —Level in Hierarchy of Job or Position
   —Difficulty and Variability of Tasks
   Performed in Job

2. Characteristics of Person in Job
   —Job Career History or Promotion
   Sequence
   —Tenure in the Organization
   —Growth Need Strength
   —Age and Sex

Design of Individual Jobs or Positions

1. Job Specialization
   —# Different Tasks Performed
   —Scope of Tasks Performed

2. Job Expertise
   —Education
   —Length of Job-Entry Orientation
   —Time in On-The-Job Training

3. Job Standardization
   —Detail of Job Description
   —# & Detail of Job Rules, Procedures

4. Job Discretion
   —Latitude in Making Job-Related
   Decisions
   —Closeness of Supervision

5. Job Incentives
   —Feedback from Work, Supervisor,
   Peers
   —Job Contingent Rewards &
   Sanctions

Individual Job or Position Outcomes

—Value judgments on criteria used to
evaluate effectiveness of individual jobs
or positions. For example:

1. Percent of Job Performance Goals
   Attained (MBO)

2. Job Efficiency
   —Cost per unit of individual output

3. Job Satisfaction
   —Satisfaction with work, supervisor,
   co-workers, pay, and career in
   organization

4. Work Motivation
   —Effort put into job

Figure 1-2—continued

4. RELATIONSHIPS BETWEEN ORGANIZATIONAL UNITS FOCUS OF ANALYSIS

Interunit Coordination Context

1. External Unit Dependence
   —Job Dependence on other units
   —Resource Dependence
   —External Interventions affecting unit

2. Awareness of Other Units
   —Knowledge of Services, Goals, Resources
   —Personal Acquaintance

3. Consensus/Conflict with other Units
   —Agreement on unit services and goals
   —Conflict over terms of coordination

4. Domain Similarity of Units
   —Sameness of unit goals, services, staff skills, clients, and technologies

Design of Interunit Relationships

1. Intensity of Relationships
   —Amounts of Interunit Resource Flows
   —Amounts of Interunit Information Flows

2. Formalization of Relationships
   —Voluntary to Mandatory Forms of Coordination
   —# & Detail of Rules over Terms of Relation
   —Standardization of Interunit Contacts

3. Complexity of Interunit Relationships
   —# Units, Parties Involved in Network
   —# Different Resources Transacted

4. Centralization of Relationships
   —Centrality of Interunit Communications
   —Distribution of Power & Influence among units involved in the relationship

Interunit Coordination and Control Outcomes

—Value judgments on criteria used to evaluate effectiveness of interunit relationships. For example:

1. Percent of Goals for Interunit Relationships Attained

2. Costs of managing transactions across units within organization relative to across organizations or the market

3. Perceived Effectiveness of Coordination
   —Extent parties involved believe relationships are equitable, worthwhile, productive, and satisfying

Figure 1-2—continued

13

which reflects the criteria and standards used by decision makers to assess the functioning of an organization. As this definition suggests, performance is a *value judgment* on the results desired from an organization at different levels of analyses. Decision makers in different organizations and in different units and positions within complex organizations strive to attain unique performance goals. In addition, value judgments on desirable performance outcomes often change over time. These changes jeopardize the applied relevance of longitudinal assessments of organizations and units and jobs within them. What were initially considered by decision makers as necessary and appropriate measures of performance may soon become irrelevant. Finally, in varying degrees, decision makers disagree on a given set of performance criteria to evaluate the effectiveness of the organization, units, or jobs. However, a measurement of performance does not require that different people agree on effectiveness goals, criteria, and standards. Consensus may in fact be an unrealistic euphemism to attempt to achieve. An organization assessment simply requires that the unique and conflicting definitions of performance be made explicit and that the organization analyst determine at the outset whose value judgments and criteria will be operationalized and measured.

Chapter 2 deals with these complexities of organization performance. Based upon our own successes and failures, we suggest a process for defining and operationalizing organizational effectiveness and for conducting all the phases involved in an organization assessment.

The basic argument presented in Chapter 2 is that the first steps in the assessment of any organization should be a series of meetings with people in the host organization (1) to identify the stakeholders and interest groups who are the decision makers that will use the findings from such an OA, and (2) to ask each user group through a series of meetings what goals, criteria, and standards they consider relevant for judging the effectiveness of the organizations, units, and jobs that will be investigated in the organization assessment. Subsequent steps in the OA process include involving user groups in developing specific performance measures, the overall design of the data collection process, and the methods for providing feedback on OAI survey data. The involvement of user groups throughout the assessment process is critical for finding practical and useful ways to implement OA on an ongoing basis in organizations.

Chapter 3 describes the historical evolution of the OAI and the considerations that were taken into account to develop, evaluate, and revise them over the years. Our goal in developing the OAI is relatively straightforward: to develop a reliable and valid set of instruments for measuring the factors listed in Figure 1-2 in a wide variety of organizations. To make the OAI widely applicable, we describe the decisions made to create instruments that are: (1) simple to understand, (2) inexpensive to administer, (3) standardized, to facilitate comparisons from unit to unit and organization to organization, and (4) clear in providing an explicit and consistent frame of reference for respondents. In addition, Chapter 3 describes the activities undertaken over the years to establish the content validity of the OAI, as well as the quantitative methods used to estimate and evaluate their reliability and validity. Results from using the psychometric methods are reported in subsequent chapters.

It should be recognized that one of our major gaols cannot be achieved here; that is, to test the generality of the OAI. Data upon which the OAI are evaluated are narrowly limited to employment security organizations and a study of interorganizational relations among child care organizations. Much further work in testing the OAI in other types of organizations is needed before we can confidently address the generality of the OAI.

2. Macroorganizational Design. The design of an organization is neither a naturally nor deterministically occurring condition for given states of nature. Rather, the structure and functioning of organizations are the result of strategic choices made either implicitly or explicitly by management or by people who are the key decision makers in an organization. The basic premise underlying the macroorganization context and structure dimensions in the OAI and listed in Figure 1-2 is that management must make at least three key sets of interrelated decisions for an organization to operate on an ongoing basis.

a. Choose the domain in which an organization operates, in terms of the functions it performs, the products or services it renders, and the target populations and markets it serves.

b. Solve the organization's production function problem, which is concerned on the one hand with making decisions on production quotas that a firm hopes to deliver to selected markets during an operating period, and on the other hand in securing and allocating the necessary resources (i.e., money, personnel, and technologies).

c. Solve the organization design problem, which is concerned with (1) the division of labor and available resources among organizational units and positions, (2) the interdependence and suboptimization thereby created among organizational units, and (3) the structure of authority and reporting relationships established to manage interdependence and conflict.

Chapter 4 argues that an understanding of the domain chosen by an organization requires an assessment of the organization's history, age, and growth stage because past choices constrain and provide the context to explain future choices. Further, implied in the type of domain chosen by an organization are various degrees of uncertainty, complexity, and restrictiveness of environments that it chooses to live with, which in turn significantly influence the alternatives available in solving the production function problem and designing the overall structural configuration of an organization. Although the economic production function problem has too often been overlooked in organizational studies, it is critical for understanding the scale of operations of an organization during a specific period in terms of the amount of products or services to be produced and the resources needed to produce them. At the overall organizational level, the organization design problem consists of making decisions on how to divide the labor (vertical and horizontal differentiation), what form of departmental structure to adopt (functional, program, geographical, and matrix arrangements), what span of control is appropriate for managers at each level (administrative intensity), and how power and authority should be distributed among organizational units.

Chapter 4 goes further to describe and evaluate the indicators used in the OAI to measure these macroorganizational factors and then examines their interrelationships and effects on the overall efficiency, effectiveness, and job satisfaction of employees in employment security offices. Once an analyst understands the overall context and structural configuration of an organization, then he or she can begin to systematically examine the structural design of organizational components or units within it.

3. The Design of Organizational Units. The organizational unit or work group represents the basic and smallest source of collective behavior within organizations and is defined as consisting of a supervisor and all personnel reporting directly to that supervisor. As Figure 1-1 illustrates, Likert's (1967) concept of "linking pins" is used to operationally identify work units at all supervisory levels in an organization. The basic perspective taken in Chapter 5 is that a focus on organizational units is needed to examine the different patterns of structure and process that exist within organizations. By definition, a complex organization consists of many differently structured units within it, each dealing with a different relevant environment and making a different functional contribution to the total organization. As a result, these units adopt different structures to perform their unique tasks and functions. Attempts to examine these different units from a macroorganizational perspective inherently present a distorted assessment because whereas some organizational units may be highly structured, others may be very organic, and any overall average profile of these differently structured units is an inaccurate summary of both.

Organizational units are the product of the division of labor within the organization by like functions and tasks. These tasks, which vary in difficulty and frequency of exceptions encountered, are delegated to organizational units in the forms of work programs. Programs are strategies for organizing the work of a unit into a predictable pattern of recurring activities. These programs are assessed in the OAI in terms of: (1) *specialization*, the number of different tasks assigned to a unit, (2) *personnel composition*, the heterogeneity of personnel skills and the interchangeability of roles among personnel within the unit, (3) *standardization*, the procedures and pacing rules that are to be followed in task performance, (4) the *centralization* of decision making on work-related matters by the supervisor or unit employees, and (5) the *performance norms and incentives* that are provided to unit personnel to work as a group in achieving its goals. In addition, the work program used to structure an organizational unit also requires a consideration of the interdependence among unit personnel and the processes of coordination and control that are used to manage this interdependence.

Chapter 5 describes and evaluates how the OAI measure these dimensions inherent in the work program used by an organizational unit to govern its behavior. In addition the patterns of correlations among these dimensions are presented, as well as their abilities to predict significant variations in the performance efficiency, effectiveness, and job satisfaction of employment security units. Based upon the evaluation, several changes are recommended in future assessments of organizational units.

4. Job Design. At the most micro level of analysis, the job or position that individuals occupy is the core element of any in-depth assessment of organizations and represents a major attempt to expand our initial OA framework and instruments (Van de Ven, 1976a). As Figure 1-1 illustrates, complex organizations consist of numerous units, and a unit, in turn, is composed of identifiable jobs or positions. The job design dimensions included in the OAI (shown in Figure 1-2 and evaluated in Chapter 6) represent member-level counterparts to the dimensions of work unit design. That is, the following five pairs of core job and unit design characteristics tap similar conceptual domains but from a different level of analysis: unit and job specialization, unit personnel composition and job expertise, unit and job standardization, unit centralization and job discretion, and unit and job incentives.

Although these counterpart dimensions of units and jobs have clearly different meanings, different reference points, and require different measurement procedures, Chapter 6 argues that their parallel communalities are important for identifying what options and tradeoffs may exist between the design of jobs and units.

The job design dimensions included in the OA framework and instruments lean heavily on the major conceptual and empirical contributions of Hackman and Oldham (1975) and their foretrekkers. Whereas the Hackman and Oldham job dimensions focus more heavily on the attitudinal aspects of jobs, the five OA job factors instead tend to emphasize their behavioral aspects. The reason we lean toward a behavioral description of jobs is because behaviors are more objective and easier for analysts and practitioners to observe, control, and change than the more subjective attitudes of people regarding their jobs.

5.   Interunit Relationships.   Once an understanding has been obtained of the overall context and structural configuration of an organization and of the different design patterns of units and jobs within it, then one can begin to examine how these units are linked together, so that the organization can act as an integrated system. Chapters 7 and 8 describe and evaluate the measures used in two versions of the OAI to examine coordination patterns between employment security units (Chapter 7) and between child care organizations (Chapter 8). Although different levels of analyses apply in studying relationships between organizational units and between organizations themselves, the same basic conceptual framework is examined in Chapters 7 and 8. Interunit and interorganizational relationships are examined in the OAI in terms of the direction, frequency, and amounts of resources and information that are transferred among the parties involved. The reasons the OA framework and instruments focus on resource and information flows are: (1) they are argued to be the basic elements of processes in organizations; (2) they are indicators of task-instrumental and pattern maintenance functions necessary for any organized system to survive; (3) they provide a way to operationalize sociotechnical theory; and (4) they provide a sociometric mapping of the network of relationships among units within an organization or among organizations as a service delivery system in a community or industry. In addition, a focus on resource and information flows avoids the value-laden concepts of cooperation, conflict, and other attitudinal impressions associated with coordination that have plagued many previous efforts at assessing relationships among organizational units. Although these concepts are important to examine in their own right and are included in the OAI, they are not used as the measures of coordination.

The assessment of interunit and interorganizational coordination in Chapters 7 and 8 suggests that various dimensions of resource and information flows in the OAI are importantly related to the performance of employment security units, are useful for addressing practical managerial questions, and provide a systematic way for explaining how and why relationships among organizations develop and grow over time. However, the evaluation of the OAI resource and information flow dimensions also indicates several areas where improvements are needed to make the measures useful for research in other organizations.

The Revised Organization Assessment Framework and Instruments

This book concludes with a revised framework and set of instruments to measure the dimensions outlined in Figure 1-2. Although most of the measures in the revised OAI are the same as those included in the previous version, the evaluations conducted in Chapters 4 to 8 identify several instances where the OAI can be improved. In addition, new indices have been added to measure dimensions not previously included in the OAI because of conceptual revisions in the OA framework.

Chapter 9 presents revisions and extensions made in the OA framework to guide the analyst in diagnosing the different patterns of structure and behavior that exist within complex organizations. In addition, Chapter 9 describes the conceptual basis for the revised OAI. A glossary and the actual questionnaires included in the revised OAI are presented in the Appendices.

Practical Uses of the OAI

Although the OAI have been used by the authors and several other researchers to conduct cross-sectional studies of several complex organizations in the public and private sectors, the most challenging and practically useful applications of the OAI have come in those organizations who have adopted the OAI on a longitudinal basis and attempted to incorporate OA as part of an ongoing organizational development or management improvement program.

For example, within the employment security agency in which the OAI were developed, OAI surveys were conducted throughout the organization every year or two and results were fed back to unit supervisors after each survey to stimulate organizational evaluations and performance improvements.

Four basic kinds of statistical analyses were conducted to interpret and use the OAI data for applied purposes.

1. For each data collection period, descriptive summaries by individual units within the organization were developed to provide specific feedback to unit managers on the OA factors and performance over time.

2. The relationships between the situational, structural, and performance factors were examined and presented to show how much variation in performance was explained by the OAI dimensions.

3. The high- and low-performing Employment Service jobs, units, and offices were classified and compared to determine what their different patterns are on the situational, structural, and process factors.

4. Over time, the OAI data were analyzed further to examine how changes in situational and organizational design characteristics affect changes in performance. The objectives here were to identify trends and to examine cause-and-effect relationships among the OA factors and performance.

The findings from the latter three forms of analysis were documented in reports and discussed in a series of day-long feedback sessions to help unit managers understand and interpret their individual feedback reports. Further suggestions for conducting feedback sessions and incorporating them as part of a data-based organizational development program are sketched out in Chapter 2 and discussed at length in Nadler (1977) and in Dunham and Smith (1979).

Of course, data collected with the OAI can be analyzed in many ways on a wide variety of administrative decisions. For example as discussed in Chapters 4 to 8 in the employment security agency, the OAI data have been used for the following special applied projects: to determine the implications of a reorganization of the entire agency or specific functional areas, to monitor and evaluate the decentralization of specific decisions, and to identify how the OAI dimensions relate to performance criteria used to allocate resources.

Thus, it should be kept in mind throughout that the OAI are designed for *measuring* and *diagnosing* organizations, units and jobs, especially on a *regularly scheduled ongoing basis*. The OAI are *research and evaluation* tools aimed at measuring and assessing the effects of changes in situational and organizational factors upon performance. When periodic OAI surveys are conducted in an organization, the findings can be fed back regularly to managers at all levels in the organization. In this way managers can obtain information useful for learning more systematically how to explain and plan for the performance of the units for which they are responsible.

In this regard (as discussed further in the next chapter), it is important to clarify what we believe is the proper role of the OA framework and instruments in practice. Our experiences suggest that the *processes* followed in designing and conducting organizational assessments are far more important in obtaining their acceptance and use than the specific framework or instruments that are used to conduct such assessments. Obviously, we consider it important to have a good theory and a reliable set of measurement tools to conduct quality assessments of organizations (they are, after all, the technical core of any organization assessment). However, the OA framework and instruments are precisely that: they are *tools* that can be used constructively for management and organizational improvements or misused with destructive consequences. When used properly within the context of an overall process of assessment tailored to the needs of a specific organization, as suggested in Chapter 2, we believe that the OAI tools can provide substantial opportunities for learning about and improving the design and performance of organizations, work groups, and jobs.

CHAPTER TWO

A Process for Assessing Organizations

INTRODUCTION

Chapter 1 has outlined a framework for assessing the design and performance of a complex organization. This OA framework identifies characteristics of the context, structure, and behavior of organizations, work units, and jobs which one can focus on to measure and evaluate an organization. In addition, as is shown in subsequent chapters, this framework is useful as a guide for predicting and explaining under what conditions certain patterns of organization, work unit, and job designs should result in higher performance than others. However, as any researcher who actually conducts an organizational study quickly learns, such an OA framework provides few process guidelines on what steps are involved in assessing an organization.

The *process* of conducting an evaluation of organization design and performance remains a form of art or craft which each researcher or analyst is forced to learn by apprenticeship or reinvent by trial and error. Most research methodology texts assume that the researcher is the sole decision maker and user of the results of a study in question. In practice, assessments of complex organizations occur in contexts where the interests and value judgments of many stakeholders need to be taken into account. As a result, people who are commissioned to conduct an organization assessment are confronted with three problems that are largely ignored by organization theorists and research methodologists. (1) Who should decide what measures should be used as the criteria for evaluating an organization? (2) Whose conceptual model or framework should be used to guide the assessment? (3) How can one facilitate learning and use of results within the organization being assessed?

This chapter delves into these problems by attempting to (1) clarify some of the conceptual confusion on goals, values, and facts regarding measures of organizational effectiveness, (2) suggest a process model that may be useful for designing and conducting studies to assess organization design and performance, and (3) report our learning experiences in using the process model to guide two longitudinal assessments of organizations.

CONCEPTUAL PROBLEMS OF ORGANIZATION EFFECTIVENESS

Three Uses of Goals

Scott (1977) recently pointed out that goals are employed in at least three ways in organizations: (1) to motivate people, (2) to provide direction and set constraints on behavior, and (3) to provide criteria for identifying and appraising selected aspects of organizational functioning.

> These conflicting views of goals as factors that (do or do not) motivate and direct behavior of participants are reviewed here primarily so that they may be set aside as largely irrelevant to our present topic. . . . We must analytically distinguish between goals employed to motivate or direct participants' behavior, on the one hand, from goals which are used to set criteria for the evaluation of participants' or the entire organization's behavior on the other.   (Scott, 1977:66)

Scott's perspective allows us to clarify the perspectives of some analysts who have disassociated themselves from the conventional goal models. For example, Yuchtman and Seashore (1967) have proposed that an organization is effective if it manages to survive. If one views survival as a direction or constraint on organizational behavior, then their approach seems reasonable because a firm cannot obviously continue to operate if it does not maintain a sufficient inflow of essential resources from its environment. However, if Yuchtman and Seashore intended to use survival as a criterion of effectiveness, then it is clear that the third meaning of goals is being used (that is, survival is itself a goal in that it reflects the aspirations of managers to continue the firm in existence). However, survival may not be a criterion of effectiveness for many organizations. *The Wall Street Journal* provides daily examples in which firms are considered more effective by their owners when they are liquidated, dissolved, or taken over than when they survive.

The effectiveness models proposed by other theorists provide additional examples of the different but often-masked uses of the goals concept. Blake and Mouton (1969) state that an organization is effective if its managers exhibit a high concern for people and work (the 9-9 cell of the Managerial Grid). Likert (1967) defines an effective organization as one that approached his "System 4" style. Finally, Beckhard (1969: 10-11) defines a healthy organization as one that is aware of, open to, and reactive to change. It searches for new forms and methods of organizing. Employees are entrusted with work responsibilities that are satisfying and increase their self-actualization. An atmosphere of trust prevails among people; conflicts are confronted rather than avoided, and communications occur freely and openly.

We interpret these models as applications of the first two ways goals are used, that is, as attempts to motivate and direct the behavior of organizations in ways that are implicitly hypothesized by the authors to lead to effectiveness. However, if these models are interpreted as the criteria of an effective organization, then these theorists are simply revealing their value judgments on what effectiveness means to them, which others may not agree with. For example, Karl Weick (1976) has presented an equally good case for believing that an effective organization is garrulous, clumsy, haphazard, hypocritical, monstrous, octopoid, wandering, and grouchy. Although these opposing views are not necessarily mutually exclusive and may often exist within the same organization, they are reviewed here to illustrate that effectiveness is a value judgment, and that the goals set to motivate, direct, and constrain organization behavior are often not the same as those which specify the criteria by which an organization's performance is appraised.

In practice we should, of course, expect the effectiveness criteria to interact over time with the goals set to motivate, direct, and constrain behavior. Hrebiniak (1978) states that this interaction can be observed particularly when assessments are made of organization performance against goals; these assessments represent important learning exercises for those who assign tasks and those who evaluate effectiveness.

> It forces a response to the question of where the organization is versus where it should have been, and why this is the case. But goal-setting is done not only to commit (motivate or direct) the organization to getting from A to B (on a scale of effectiveness). Another purpose is to discover where the organization is, and where it might go next (i.e., to select new effectiveness criteria), given an understanding of A and B. (Hrebiniak, 1978:11)

In summary, we begin with Scott's suggestion that it is useful to distinguish between goals set to motivate, direct, or constrain behavior and those set to define effectiveness. This distinction clarifies many of the intended meanings of goals and permits one to discuss their inter-relations. However, since our main purpose is to identify and opera-tionalize effectiveness, the remainder of this chapter focuses attention on the use of goals to supply criteria for assessing organization effective-ness. In this context, the next issues that require clarification are mat-ters of values and facts regarding goals and criteria of organization effectiveness.

Matters of Values and Facts

John Campbell (1977) emphasizes the importance of distinguishing between matters of values and facts. Although the distinction is seldom clear-cut and should not be exaggerated, value judgments revolve around questions of what goals, criteria, and standards should be chosen to assess the effectiveness of an organization, and why an assess-ment should be made.

> Neither the people in organizations nor the outsiders studying them can avoid the value judgment of what the goals of the organization should be, even though everyone seems to try. . . . Well, the obvious moral here is that the value judgment of what goals the organization should adopt must precede everything else and how the judgment is made (e.g., by default) can induce wide variation in the way organizational effectiveness is assessed.   (Campbell, 1977:16)

Once these value judgments are made, it becomes possible to consider more factual matters, which focus on the framework for organization assessment, the reliability of measures, the cost of alternative data collection methods, and the data analysis and reporting procedures.

We concur with Campbell's opinion that "most discussions of organi-zational effectiveness and most research studies attempting to measure it jump to the factual domain much too soon" (p. 16). Furthermore, it is our opinion that organizational goals and effectiveness criteria have continued to evade organizational theorists for the following reasons. (1) It makes little sense to search for "objective" and universal measures of a concept that is inherently subjective—and is generalizable only to the unique set of decision makers who make the same value judgments in choosing effectiveness criteria. (2) Organization theory and logic of the mind is of little help in defining a concept that reflects the basic values,

Table 2-1 Characteristics of Questions Requiring Answers to Understand Organization Effectiveness

	What is the desired result?	How does one measure the desired result?	What produces or causes the desired result?
Nature of Question	Normative, Subjective	Positive, Methodological	Positive, Analytical
Nature of Solution	Value judgments on goals, criteria, and standards for evaluation	Descriptive set of measures and data collection methods	Theory, hypotheses, or data which treat effectiveness as the dependent variables
Knowledge Base of Solution	Introspection, intuitions or "gut" feelings	Psychometric theory, and discipline of operationalizing a concept	Organizational theories, observations, and practical experience
Process Followed to Obtain Solution	With the help of the analysts, decision makers articulate: 1. Reasons for evaluation 2. Goals for organization 3. Criteria to evaluate goals 4. Standards on criteria which they will use to judge satisfactory goal attainment	Analysts and Technicians: 1. Operationalize goals criteria and standards in terms of concepts, constructs, and variables 2. Develop preliminary draft of measurement instruments. 3. Conduct pilot test and revise measures 4. Outline procedures for data collection	Analysts and Decision Makers: 1. Develop conceptual model to explain effectiveness 2. Design and conduct research study 3. Analyze and evaluate data to test model 4. Select and implement most appropriate action
Criteria to Evaluate Internal Validity of Solution	Decision makers' ability and honesty in articulating goals, criteria, and standards	Quantitative and qualitative indications of reliability and validity of measures (see chapter 3)	Satisfy criteria threatening internal validity Type I and II errors
Criteria to Evaluate External Validity of Solution	Generality is limited to the decision makers and groups who either participated in process above or have values and beliefs similar to those presented in the solution	Technical quality and social acceptability of measurement instruments and procedures by decision makers	Satisfy criteria threatening external validity Type III error Willingness of decision makers to take action based on the results

or simply, the "gut" feelings of people on "what they really want" and "what is important to them". (3) The *processes* by which people in organizations do, don't, and can articulate answers to these questions have been ignored.

Basic Questions in an Organization Assessment

The Webster dictionary defines "effective" as producing a desired result. An operational understanding of this concept requires answers to the following three questions in the order specified. (1) *What is the desired result?* (2) *How does one measure the desired result?* (3) *What produces or causes the desired result?* The first two questions deal with the matters of values and facts, respectively, regarding effectiveness. The third question is not necessary to conceptualize and operationalize organization effectiveness; this is provided by answers to questions 1 and 2. However, question 3 is included here because organization analysts and practitioners are generally unwilling to go through the effort needed to answer the first two questions explicitly and stop there without an answer to the third question. Indeed, answers to all these questions are necessary to conduct an organization assessment.

What is more important to recognize is that the nature of these three questions is very different, and different paradigms are required to answer each (see Table 2-1). The first question is normative and must necessarily rely on the introspection of decision makers to obtain a solution that is a value judgment on goals, criteria, and standards of effectiveness. The second question presumes that an answer is available to the first, and is positive and methodological. It can be answered in a rather factual way by applying psychometric theory and the discipline of operationalizing a concept into a set of variables and measures. The third question presupposes answers to the first two questions which are used as the dependent variables in an analytic search for what produces or causes effectiveness. Theories, observations, and practical experiences are relied upon to select those organizational factors that are believed to explain variations in effectiveness.

Table 2-1 indicates that the process steps generally followed to answer the three questions are also very different. Although the procedures for answering questions 2 and 3 are quite well known and codified in most research methodology texts, little is known about how decision makers in organizations can come to some resolution about the value judgments needed to define effectiveness. The next section of this chapter suggests a specific process that can be used to help decision makers answer the first question, as well as a sequence of phases and steps for iteratively answering questions 2 and 3 when conducting an organization assessment.

Finally, the criteria often used to assess the internal and external validity of solutions obtained to the three questions are also very different. The internal validity of an answer to question 1 is a function of how well and how honestly decision makers articulate their values, whereas the internal validity of answers to questions 2 and 3 hinges on the psychometric properties of the measures and how well a research design satisfies the criteria threatening internal validity (Campbell and Stanley, 1963).

The generality of the solution to question 1 is limited to the people who either participate in developing the solution or have values and beliefs similar to those reflected in the solution. This necessarily implies that a universal operational definition of organization effectiveness is highly unlikely, if not impossible to obtain. Instead, one will more likely obtain many different and often conflicting definitions, criteria, and standards of effectiveness which reflect the unique value judgments of various decision makers. Further study of effectiveness in terms of questions 2 and 3 does not require that different people agree on effectiveness goals, criteria, and standards. It simply requires that the unique and conflicting definitions of effectiveness be made explicit. Further, it requires that the organization analyst determine at the outset whose definitions of effectiveness will be operationalized and addressed in questions 2 and 3.

The limited external validity of any definitions of effectiveness also suggests the futility of attempts to compare different types of organizations in terms of effectiveness. Such comparisons seem reasonable only when the organizations under investigation have similar tasks, products, or services (e.g., firms within the same industry). For such organizations, there is a strong probability that some common definitions and criteria of effectiveness are shared and can be used for comparative purposes. Overall, given the external validity problems of effectiveness definitions, we concur with Scott's conclusion that more limited criteria which:

(1) make explicit the normative basis for our choice,

(2) call attention to those who support or share and those who oppose it, and

(3) allow us to make more specific comparisons among organizations performing similar work

will prove to be more useful, at least at the present stage of theoretical development, than continuing the search for universal criteria for assessing organizational effectiveness.   (Scott, 1976:20)

The external validity of solutions to the second and third questions in Table 2-1 is based on technical psychometric and research design considerations on the one hand and on the acceptability of solutions by decision makers on the other hand. Because of the sequential dependence among the three questions, this implies that the external validity of solutions to questions 2 and 3 are ultimately based on the acceptability of answers to question 1. John Campbell (1977:18) aptly summarizes this point:

> If the people won't use a particular kind of criterion, there is no sense in collecting it. Why build indicators of organizational health if these are going to be ignored? Why develop new measures of performance if no one trusts them?

These questions are being raised with increasing frequency by other social scientists and action/evaluation researchers concerned with the relevance of applied research (Clark, 1976) and have been developed more formally as Type III errors. Mitroff and Featheringham (1974) define this third type of error as the probability of having solved the wrong problem with the right methods. Type III error occurs when the initial problem (in this case, the definition of organization effectiveness) is inadequately represented or formulated. As is discussed in subsequent text, Type III errors are easy to detect after the fact when users are unwilling to act upon the solutions obtained to question 3. However, they are very difficult to prevent unless explicit review sessions with users are conducted at key points in the organization assessment process.

In effect, an assessment of organizations requires that researchers place themselves into a larger intervention context than what the narrow definition of research often implies (i.e., to measure, analyze, and report results of a study designed on the bases of the researcher's own value judgments and conceptual model). It requires a process that responds to the concerns of a greater number of users (only one of which is the researcher), makes explicit the multiple and conflicting values underlying any definitions of organization effectiveness, and facilitates learning among users by having them become a part of the model building and applied research process.

For this to happen when assessing an organization, Suchman (1971) has suggested that at least five key steps be performed before the study is undertaken:

1. The researcher must *identify the users* of the evaluation study. The users are those individuals or groups who desire to use the results of a study for making decisions or taking a concrete set of actions.

2. Tangible *effectiveness goals must be identified* which are considered desirable or have some positive value. These goals must be specified *by the users* of the study.

3. The specific *organizational components* to be evaluated need to be *identified*. The selected organization components should be held accountable for, and capable of, achieving the desired goals.

4. A set of *criteria are to be subjectively chosen* by the users that represent the bases upon which they will judge the extent to which effectiveness goals are attained as a result of the organizational components being evaluated.

5. A decision is made to *use the scientific method* to design and implement measurement procedures that determine the extent to which the effectiveness goals (step 2) are attained by the selected organizational components (step 3) in terms of the users' criteria (step 4).

As the five steps suggest, organization assessment, like evaluation research, is an applied problem-solving process. It attempts to make decision makers' goals, criteria, and concerns explicit and to use these explicit value judgments as a basis for assessing selected organizational components. A never-ending concern of the researcher should be the relevance of the study to the users. Unlike pure or theoretical research (where the researcher is also the user and decision maker), in applied evaluation research the *user is the decision maker* or stakeholder, and the *researcher is the technician* and *process consultant* who explicitly identifies and incorporates the value judgments of users to conduct the study.

A PROCESS MODEL FOR ASSESSING ORGANIZATIONS

Figure 2-1 proposes six phases of activities that often recycle and overlap for conducting an organization assessment designed to answer the three questions in Table 2-1. The overriding objectives of the process model are to suggest a set of task phases and activities that (1) guides a researcher or analyst in dealing with matters of values and facts while designing and implementing an evaluation of organization effectiveness, and (2) maintains a balanced concern for the technical quality and social acceptance of effectiveness definitions, measures, and explanations that are developed. The process model relies heavily on

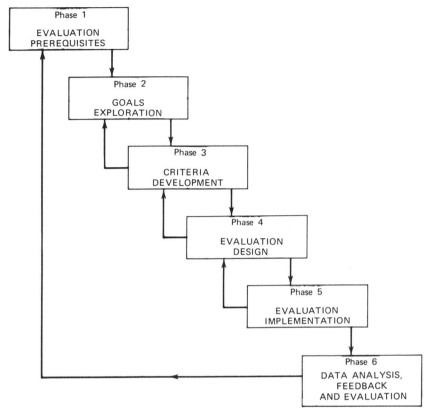

*Figure 2-1   A process model for evaluating organization effec-
tiveness.*

the evaluation/action research and organization development literature
and is an adaptation of the Program Planning and Evaluation Model
originally developed by Delbecq and Van de Ven (1971), extended by
Van de Ven and Koenig (1976), and empirically tested and found
largely supported (Van de Ven et al., 1976a,b). Activities within each
phase of the process model are now discussed.

Phase 1, Evaluation Prerequisites

At the outset, the analyst and the commissioners of the study establish
their working contract and clarify their roles by answering the following
questions:

1. What are the reasons for conducting an organization assessment?
2. How will the results of the study be used?
3. What organizational components or issues are to be assessed?
4. What individuals and groups will be the users of the study?
5. Who should conduct the evaluation study?
6. To what extent is there a commitment to using the methods and knowledge of science to design and conduct the study?
7. What resources are available to conduct the study?

Answers to these questions are crucial for determining whether an evaluation study is worthwhile, what the nature of the working relationships between the analyst and the users will be, and how to tailor the process and content of the evaluation to specific user needs. In varying degrees, the decision to undertake an organization assessment represents a significant commitment of resources and human energy on the part of the analysts and the users involved in the process, as well as all the organizational employees affected by it. It should also be recognized that the involvement of users in the evaluation process may heighten their expectations that the study itself will increase organization effectiveness in terms of the ways they define it. Furthermore, individuals within complex organizations have multiple, conflicting, and sometimes dishonest personal motives for and uses of an evaluation study.

These realities imply that the negative side effects from naively undertaking an evaluation study without establishing a clear understanding of its process and content can easily outweigh its positive and intended consequences. Thus, the decision on whether or not to undertake an organization assessment should not be considered lightly. As discussed subsequently, it has been the authors' experience that most problems encountered in later phases of an evaluation study can be traced back to the initial absence or misunderstandings of answers to the prerequisite questions.

With regard to the decision on who should conduct the assessment, Suchman (1967) suggests there are benefits and costs to only using outside evaluators or inside evaluators. The arguments for using an outside evaluator include those of increased objectivity and the ability to see things that persons connected with the organization might simply take for granted. The outside evaluator has less ego involvement in the outcome of the evaluation and will feel less pressure to make compromises in the research design or in the interpretation of the results. On the other hand, the outside evaluator is likely to be less sensitive to either the program being evaluated or to the possible disruption caused by the evaluation study—as well as to the practicality of the recommendations that stem from the evaluation. As an outsider he also represents a threat to the staff of the organization.

Evaluation by an "insider" has counter advantages and disadvantages. On the positive side, an inside evaluator is more informed about the organization and is in a better position to know which aspects require evaluation. He is also more readily accepted by the staff, especially if the staff considers the study a self-evaluation for self-improvement. Such an evaluation is also likely to generate more staff involvement and result in a greater application of the results. On the negative side, it is extremely difficult for an insider in a self-evaluation to maintain objectivity. There is an almost irresistible tendency to focus upon the successful aspects of the program and to overlook the "minor" weaknesses or failures. Certain procedures that have a time-honored validity will rarely be brought to question. As a result, evaluation studies by insiders are often considered less credible. From a technical point of view, it is also less likely that the program staff will possess the required research knowledge and skills to conduct a professional evaluation study.

The joint collaboration of insiders and outsiders in conducting an evaluation study, however, has many advantages in a kind of division of labor. The inside evaluator performs the major process role to obtain user involvement in defining and formulating the goals and criteria (Phases 2 and 3) in consultation with the outside evaluator, who is encouraged to raise questions. Then, the inside and outside evaluators collaborate in Phase 4 to design evaluation procedures that are scientifically acceptable. Data collection (Phase 5) is conducted by the collaborated efforts of the insiders and outsiders due to the manpower needs during that period. In Phase 6, the outside evaluator performs the initial data analysis and reporting role, with the inside evaluator serving as a co-author by reacting to and editing the initial reports. The inside and outside evaluators work as a team in conducting the evaluation feedback workshops with users. Throughout the process, the inside and outside evaluators serve as cross-checks upon one another to insure that the organization assessment remains on target to users' needs, is sensitive to practical concerns, and maintains scientific standards of objectivity and quality.

Phase 2, Goal Exploration

Obviously, organizations do not have goals; instead, people have goals for an organization. Therefore, in Phase 2 the evaluators conduct a series of meetings with various groups of users to identify the effectiveness goals they have for the organizational components being assessed. Users were defined previously as people within and outside the organization who have a stake in the organization assessment. If the dominant coalition of decision makers within an organization are chosen in the prerequisites phase as the only users of an OA, then it is quite likely that the effectiveness goals developed in Phase 2 will narrowly reflect internal managerial and organizational values and tend to ignore issues of who benefits from the organization, whether the organization should exist at all, or what the contributions of the organization to society or the public should be. These latter issues tend to be questioned only if the user groups involved in Phase 2 represent not only the organization's dominant coalition, but also outside organizational clients or customers, funders, community interest groups, and employees within the organization. Including a wide cross section of users to identify effectiveness goals for an organization (1) minimizes the tendency for assessments or organizations to be myopic, (2) brings out the different and often conflicting goals various stakeholders expect of an organization, and as a consequence (3) tends to produce the information needed to stimulate creative problem solving and conflict resolution in choosing effectiveness goals that are responsive to the multiple expectations people make of an organization.

As discussed previously, these effectiveness goals are value judgments. Rand (1964) states that all values have two attributes: (1) *content*, or what desired results users want an organization to attain, and (2) *intensity*, or how important each of these desired results are to the users. An individual's desired results ranked by intensity represent his or her goal priorities, and the goal priorities of a group would be the sum of the members' intensity ratings for each goal (Locke, 1976).

It is presumptuous to expect users to be able or willing to articulate completely the content and intensity of their effectiveness goals for an organization. That would be analogous to expecting an individual to verbalize completely the personal goals for his or her life. However, it is even more presumptuous for an analyst to impose his or her own value judgments on an organization by selecting the effectiveness goals and criteria on which an organization will be evaluated without consulting the people who are the principal users of the study. We simply assume and have found that users can and will articulate in an operational form *some* of their value judgments about effectiveness goals when asked to do so, particularly when users are provided a process to make repeated estimations of their value judgments in a nonthreatening manner. For example, the authors have found it useful to conduct a series of meetings over time, with users performing different roles at each meeting, offering repeated opportunities for users to "second guess" their prior judgments. First, Nominal Group meetings could be conducted to develop a preliminary list of effectiveness goals with each group of users. (For explanation of the Nominal Group technique, see Delbecq et al., 1975, and Van de Ven, 1974.) In subsequent meetings the preliminary goals can be classified, ranked, discussed, modified, and reranked to identify goal priorities.

The effectiveness goals users cite can often be classified and operationalized further in the following categories: (1) the quantity and quality of inputs (means) and outputs (ends), (2) efficiency (the ratio of outputs to inputs), (3) employee morale (job satisfaction and absenteeism), and (4) impact (growth, market share, and contributions to the larger environment or community of which the organization is a part). Another nominal group representing a cross-section of users may meet to clarify and rank goals in these categories.

The goal exploration phase concludes with an evaluation session in which user representatives review the unique sets and priority rankings of effectiveness from each user group, confront disagreements, and agree to proceed to the next phase with an explicit awareness of the goals on which there is consensus and conflict among user groups.

Phase 3, Criteria Development

The evaluators obtain the value judgments of users on the criteria they will use to assess the extent to which each goal priority is attained. Whereas goals are desired end states, criteria are operational dimensions or continua representing the degree to which goals are met. The process of criteria development requires that users make three normative decisions: (1) Select *concrete observable characteristics or dimensions* that are to be measured and used as indicators of goal attainment; (2) specify *standards* or cutoff points on the dimensions above which users believe goals are attained and below which goal attainment is considered unsatisfactory; and (3) in the usual case of multiple criteria, determine the *weights of importance* to be assigned to the dimensions in order to understand hierarchical relations among the criteria and to develop an aggregate or composite measure of goal attainment (Scott,

1977; Campbell, 1977). The evaluators assist users in making these decisions incrementally through a series of group meetings, discussions, and workshops as in Phase 2.

Of course, the raw data obtained in the criterial development workshops do not automatically become useful for developing operational measures of effectiveness. A necessary intermediate task between the generation of criteria and the development of effectiveness indicators is a content analysis of the qualitative data. Three search and two screening decision rules are proposed as follows to guide evaluators in choosing measurable criteria of effectiveness.

1. Search for criteria of each goal priority that are observable over wide variations in the organizational components being evaluated. Criteria on which there are little or no variations are of limited use for comparative evaluation because they do not discriminate between the organizational components being evaluated (Hage, 1971).

2. Search for criteria of each goal priority that seem to capture or explain a large number of related criteria. It is impossible to measure all criteria that may be considered relevant indicators of goal attainment. Thus, parsimony is an important decision rule for content analysis.

3. Search for criteria that are easiest to measure in a reliable and valid way and lowest in measurement cost.

4. Classify criteria into those which are considered *means* and *ends* of organization effectiveness. That is, determine whether each criterion is a dependent variable in its own right (an end), or whether it is an independent or moderating variable (a means) that is believed to influence some more terminal outcome or end.

5. Classify criteria by levels of organization analyses, that is, those that pertain to individuals, work groups, sections, divisions, and the total organization.

If the overall definition of organization effectiveness is the degree to which the goals and criteria judged to be "ends" are attained, then a direct assessment of effectiveness is possible by operationalizing and measuring only the ends criteria. It is tempting to simply measure all key criteria and empirically establish the pattern of means–ends relations among the criteria. However, it is important to recognize that the classification of criteria as means or ends is not a methodological but a theoretical question that requires careful consideration of what goals the users consider ends or outcomes. The classic example is the conflicting empirical evidence on whether job satisfaction causes performance or the latter causes the former, or whether both are ends in their own right (Cummings and Schwab, 1973). Ultimately, the question must be resolved by what outcomes users want to include as measures of effectiveness.

The question of which criteria are means or ends is largely a function of the level of organization analysis. Means criteria for the total organization are usually ends criteria for specific sections, units, or individuals within the organization. However, the aggregation of effectiveness criteria for all individuals, groups, and sections generally do not add up to total organization effectivenesss (Hannan and Freeman, 1977). The classification of effectiveness criteria by levels of organization analysis requires matching the objectives with the individuals or units held accountable.

A substantial proportion of the classification bias that necessarily enters the content analysis of the data can be detected and corrected in a rigorous review session with users at the conclusion of the criteria development phase. At this review session, the evaluators present the major effectiveness criteria developed by each user group and present their content analysis of the criteria. In addition, conflicting priorities among the effectiveness criteria of various user groups are outlined. User representatives at the evaluation session then review this material, are encouraged to confront disagreements, and are asked if the evaluators can proceed to the design phase with an explicit understanding of the varying degrees of consensus among users on effectiveness goals and criteria.

Phase 4, Evaluation Design

Given the goals and criteria chosen by the user groups, the evaluators work with technical staff within the organization to develop and pilot test a set of effectiveness measures. In addition, they conduct a workshop with user representatives to develop an overall conceptual model for explaining organizational effectiveness (question 3 in Table 2-1).

In ongoing organizations, many effectiveness measures that directly reflect users' criteria may already be available in existing performance reporting systems. However, although performance reporting is omnipresent in organizations, almost every system has something wrong with it (Haberstroh, 1965:1182). A so-called "objective" measure of effectiveness in a reporting system is a subjective measure once removed (Campbell, 1976:53). Many kinds of work occur under circumstances which render inspection impossible, and many performance-reporting systems are so complex that even experienced employees find it difficult to determine what proportions of their working time or completed tasks should be assigned to what standardized time and work output codes designated in the reporting systems. Thus, a search for effectiveness measures from existing information systems requires the same amount of careful investigation and validity checking as would be required in designing and testing a new system for measuring effectiveness. A good starting point is to conduct an intensive series of meetings with the technical staff responsible for maintaining and analyzing data from the information systems of an agency. By systematically reviewing each effectiveness criterion selected by users, the technical staff can suggest specific measures for each criterion from the existing system. These staff members are generally very knowledgeable about the major problems with each measure in the organization's performance reporting systems.

To incorporate the in-depth knowledge of the organization that users have and to facilitate their ultimate use of the evaluation results, we have found it helpful to involve users in the formal development of a conceptual model for explaining organization effectiveness. For example, this can be achieved by conducting a Nominal Group meeting with users in which selected effectiveness measures are presented, and users are asked, "What situational or organizational factors predict or explain effectiveness (as defined)?" Such a Nominal Group will not result in a complete conceptual scheme, nor does it replace the need for the analyst to have a systematic theory of organization and effectiveness. Instead, such a meeting provides evaluators the information needed to modify their theoretical terminology into the argot and jargon comfortable to users, and to extend or modify their theory to include the factors of concern to practitioners. Indeed, when there is a prevailing consensus among practitioners on the conventional wisdom for including or excluding factors in a conceptual scheme, how can a conscientious evaluator justify ignoring them?

User involvement in developing the conceptual model is also important for identifying those factors and organizational units that influence effectiveness. Users can identify which organizational units and components are held accountable for each effectiveness measure; supraorganizational and environmental factors which are beyond the control of the organizational components being evaluated should be measured but controlled for when explaining organizational effectiveness.

Once the evaluators have (1) identified acceptable effectiveness measures in existing reporting systems and (2) obtained user input to develop and evaluate a conceptual model for answering question 3 in

Table 2-1, they proceed to develop the operational research design for assessing an organization. The process involves the technical tasks described in most research methodology texts for developing a good research design—including selection procedures, sample size, measurement, and procedures for data collection, analysis, and feedback.

With regard to measurement and instrument construction, the evaluators develop or select measures of organization design factors included in the conceptual model and additional effectiveness measures not available in existing information systems. Measures of many situational and organizational factors included in the model can be obtained from published measurement instruments. Indeed, the major purpose for the remaining chapters of this book is to present and evaluate a set of indices in the OAI that may be useful for precisely this purpose. However, just as in the case of using effectiveness measures from existing information systems, the selection and use of published scales and instruments requires a careful evaluation of their measurement properties. This requires that the evaluators review the studies where the selected measures have been used, and also contact the developers of the measurement instruments directly to determine the strengths and weaknesses of each measure and what changes they suggest to avoid past mistakes. Finally, no measurement instrument is applicable to all organizations. Modifications in the wording of some questions and data collection procedures will be necessary. A pilot test of any instrument should be conducted in the organizations being evaluated before it is used in Phase 5, even for those measures found to be highly reliable and valid in other studies. This is because evaluations of any measurement instrument are situation specific and limited to the sample or organizations in which the instruments were tested.

The work in this phase concludes with a review session with user representatives to evaluate the research design, to revise it where necessary, and to obtain a decision to proceed to Phase 5. Given the knowledge and resource constraints in constructing an ideal design, the evaluators present the limitations of the proposed effectiveness study in terms of the desired information that cannot be provided and the factors threatening the internal and external validity of the research results (Campbell and Stanley, 1963). The users then judge whether and how to proceed with the evaluation, with a clear understanding of its limitations.

Phase 5, Evaluation Implementation

The evaluators and technical staff implement the study by following the procedures outlined and approved in the Phase 4 evaluation design.

The principal concerns during this phase are (1) maintaining integrity and controls on the uniformity of data collection procedures, (2) tracking of organizational units and respondents, particularly with a longitudinal study, (3) recording of unanticipated events which may influence results of the experimental or quasi-experimental study, and (4) responding to feelings of threat and sensitivities of respondents and users.

Phase 6, Data Analysis, Feedback, and Evaluation

The evaluators process the data to construct computer data files and analyze the data following procedures set forth in the evaluation design (Phase 4). The major process concerns during this phase are to provide users opportunities to participate in analyzing, interpreting, and learning from the results of the evaluation study. Although the most appropriate ways for doing this are unknown, we have relied upon a series of one- and two-day workshops with users in which preliminary and interim findings on initial questions and problems are presented verbally, in writing, and with illustrations.

These workshops begin with a review of the purposes for the study, the effectiveness goals and criteria selected by users, and the design and conduct of the study. The scores and standards on the effectiveness criteria of each user group are presented. These highlight the alternative outcomes that are obtained given the conflicting criteria of different users. In addition, simple descriptive and analytic statistics are presented that show the alternative organizational design profiles that are obtained for high and low effective organizational units under alternative criteria of effectiveness. When these findings are presented, users quite naturally raise a host of questions and issues. They become embroiled in group discussions and debates as they review and evaluate the data—and learning has begun. Some of the questions can be answered by reanalyzing the data, and these become part of the agenda for the next workshop. Some of the questions raised can be clarified and answered directly with the data at hand and require that users make some decisions to change existing organizational patterns. Finally, some new issues and effectiveness goals are raised which cannot be resolved with the current evaluation data and become the inputs for conducting the next assessment cycle of Phases 1 to 6.

Subsequent assessment cycles generally require less effort because only marginal revisions are made in each phase from the preceding cycle. However, with each recycling of the evaluation phases, there are significant increases in the amount of information and knowledge available for predicting and explaining organization effectiveness with longitudinal analyses of the data. Moreover, an ongoing process of organization assessment permits users to determine objectively, and thereby learn, the consequences of their decisions to implement changes in the organization based on problems identified in previous evaluation cycles.

DISCUSSION

The process described here for assessing organizations may appear to the reader as being too structured, requiring so much involvement of users in each evaluation phase that it stretches out to be an endless series of conflict-ridden meetings and potential veto decisions. Admittedly, the OA process model will not provide speedy solutions, and deviates considerably from conventional notions of what is involved in conducting an organizational study. This is because the OA process model is intended to avoid many of the unintended consequences that result from the ways research and evaluation studies are traditionally conducted.

Argyris (1968) points out that in efforts to achieve traditional criteria of "rigorous" research (establish experimental controls, minimize contamination, standardize observations, replicate procedures, etc.), the researcher places organizational participants (aptly called "subjects") into a world where their "behavior is defined, controlled, evaluated, and reported to a degree that is comparable to the behavior of workers in the most mechanized assembly-line conditions" (p. 186). Argyris goes on to argue convincingly that since the temporary conditions established by traditional research methods are very similar to those found in highly authoritarian organizations, then the unintended consequences found in these organizations are in varying degrees similar to those found in temporary research settings. These unintended consequences of traditional field studies (which parallel those found in formal organizations) include: not responding to questionnaires or physically withdrawing from interviews (absenteeism and turnover), fudging or lying in answers to questions (sabotage), second-guessing the research design and trying to circumvent it in some fashion (soldiering), participating in the study for a price (emphasis on monetary rewards), and ignoring or rejecting study findings (apathy and nonresponsibility).

We view the OA process model as a realistic attempt to: (1) avoid these unintended consequences of traditional research methods, (2) identify and confront the different and conflicting values held by various groups of users regarding any organizational assessment, and

(3) cope with the lack of knowledge about what factors and issues are critical for investigating the specific questions and problems requiring solutions. In even moderately complex and changing organizations, these "crises of values and knowledge" (Friedmann, 1973) are beyond the cognitive and physical limits of any single central evaluation or planning unit. The proposed solution is to portray the OA process as a participative form of learning between users and evaluators who collaborate to design and conduct a study that incorporates their value judgments and conceptual perspectives. This portrait is very consistent with Lewin's (1947) original model of action research, which called for repeated cycles of data gathering, analysis, planning of action, implementation of action, and measurement of the impact of the action. More specifically, the OA process model relies on theory and research which suggests that *learning, technical quality,* and *social acceptance* of solutions to complex problems can be enhanced in four important ways.

First, the proposed process divides the entire evaluation effort into an adaptive but structured set of stages which are similar to the basic phases of creative decision making or problem solving (Thompson and Tuden, 1959; Maier, 1964; Bales and Strodtbeck, 1967; Delbecq and Van de Ven, 1971). The evaluation process begins with extended explorations of users' value judgments on effectiveness goals and criteria in Phases 2 and 3 before jumping to more factual matters of evaluation design, implementation, and analysis in Phases 4 to 6. In this way the evaluation process clearly distinguishes and addresses matters of values and facts regarding organization effectiveness as Campbell (1976) proposes. Of course, no one evaluation phase deals solely with matters of values or facts. Instead, it is more correct to say that each phase includes varying degrees of factual and value-laden tasks.

Second, the proposed evaluation phases should be viewed as a continuous process of incremental action, review, and adaptation over time and not as a discreet, one-shot go/no-go decision. Emphasis is placed on taking and assessing small, tentative, and consecutive steps in evaluation, with each step being subject to review, modification, and reiteration on the basis of experience and knowledge gained during the intervening period. In this way, users can second-guess their initial value judgments, and tangible effectiveness goals and alternative conceptual schemes of organizations become apparent during the process. The design and use of an organization assessment thereby become fused during the course of the action itself (Suchman, 1971; Friedmann, 1973).

Third, the proposed assessment process emphasizes the participation of users, technical staff, and other interest groups in each phase on problems relevant to their functional expertise, experience, and organizational position. Participation not only brings out differing user values and the technical complexities of an evaluation study, it also legitimates and builds support and use of the study. Indeed, there is extensive research evidence to suggest that active self-assessment and development of corrective adjustments by users facilitates their adoption of a program (e.g., Bennis et al., 1962; Delbecq et al., 1975; Filley et al., 1976). Bass (1971), for example, found that performance, satisfaction, and motivation of individuals in implementing their own plans are higher than when they carry out someone else's plan. Applying the concept of participation to the design and conduct of an organizational study, Argyris (1968:194) reports the following.

> In our experience the more subjects are involved directly (or through representatives) in planning and designing the research, the more we learn about the best ways to ask questions, the critical questions from the employees' views, the kinds of resistances each research method would generate, and the best way to gain genuine and long-range commitment to the research.

Finally, the OA process model attempts to address the pluralistic nature of organizations that continually change over time. In most organizations, there are multiple evaluative and monitoring efforts that occur simultaneously. Each of these efforts is conducted with limited knowledge on behalf of those doing the evaluation. Each has its own distinct sets of users, yet each also overlaps with other sets of users. This implies that, at any one point in time, no one evaluation unit nor any one set of users has sufficient knowledge, control, or power to conduct a comprehensive evaluation of organization effectiveness. However, over time coordinated evaluation efforts can be enhanced (1) by involving other evaluation units in formulating flexible "working" evaluation designs, and (2) through an ongoing process of diffusing evaluation findings to other evaluation units and users of the social system.

LEARNING EXPERIENCES IN APPLYING THE OA PROCESS MODEL

In conclusion it is appropriate to outline some of our experiences and impressions in attempting to implement the process model for organization assessment at two different stages of its development in two large state government organizations. The two longitudinal studies—

conducted to explain organizational effectiveness—met with varying degrees of success. One of the assessments was conducted in the head-quarters bureaus and 30 local offices of the state employment security agency (hereafter Agency A). The second study was conducted in a state office of early childhood development and 14 local community child care programs (hereafter Agency B). In both studies the principal author contracted with the state agencies to be the outside evaluator, and worked directly with a professional staff person assigned full time to the evaluation study as the inside evaluator.

The later stages of the Agency A evaluation yielded an explicit evaluation process that was applied nine months later in the study of Agency B. Although no formal attempts were made to evaluate the evaluation processes themselves, the following impressions emerged from a review of our research diaries.

Phase 1, Evaluation Prerequisites

As stated above, most of the difficulties encountered in later phases of organizational assessments can be attributed to not adequately address-ing the Phase 1 prerequisite questions with users. As such, it is important to obtain clear answers to these questions. However, we learned four things in attempting to get answers to the prerequisite questions.

1. Agency administrators and users prefer to treat the prerequisite questions in a general way to avoid becoming embroiled in con-flicts and debates among themselves in developing definitive answers.

2. It is not correct to assume that agency administrators and users can provide definitive answers to the prerequisite questions at the onset of an organization assessment, even when hard pressed to develop answers.

3. Preliminary answers to the prerequisite questions, which are suf-ficiently operational to begin the assessment process, are possible when developed *jointly* by the users and the outside analyst through Nominal Group meetings. Joint participation establishes a working relationship between evaluators and users.

4. Either by plan or default, further clarifications and revisions of answers to the preliminary questions emerge during the course of the evaluation study.

In Agency A only cursory responses were obtained to the prerequisite questions, and the clearest answers were obtained to the procedural and administrative questions (e.g., what is the evaluation budget? who will be the inside and outside evaluators? how much staff time is involved? and when will the evaluation begin and end?). The more important substantive questions such as, what is to be evaluated? why is the study to be conducted? and how will the results be used? received only cursory attention. The reason, we think, is because we did not press enough nor provide a process to answer the questions with users. In addition, there was little agreement among users on these substantive questions, and it was hoped that these questions would become clear once the evaluation process was set in motion. It turned out that these questions never were addressed adequately. Answers were obtained either by default or through conflict-ridden meetings between and among the evaluators and users at critical review points in the evaluation process when operational decisions on effectiveness measures, research design, data collection, and feedback had to be made. To date, there is little evidence that the practical findings and recommendations emerging from the evaluation study have been used or implemented in Agency A.

In Agency B, where the evaluation process model was followed more closely, a two-day workshop was conducted with agency administrators and users to address the prerequisite questions. This workshop began by presenting and discussing an overview of the basic phases and tasks in the evaluation process model. The remaining day and a half of the workshop was spent developing answers to the prerequisite questions. The Nominal Group process was used to address the major substantive questions first, and preliminary answers to the procedural questions became apparent from discussions of the substantive issues. The decisions reached during the workshop were recorded, distributed to participants, and used to initiate goal exploration as well as subsequent evaluation phases. This repeated review of the reasons for the evaluation study was found particularly useful for keeping the evaluation process on track, as well as in clarifying and modifying the process as it evolved.

Phases 2 and 3, Goals and Criteria Development

The major learning experiences here were that:

1. It is not correct to assume that users have a clear understanding in their own minds of the specific goals and criteria of effectiveness for an organization or its components.

2. In the process of developing tangible goals and specific criteria, it is important to provide users opportunities to second-guess their own statements of goals and criteria.

3. In developing tangible goals, it is helpful to have users break down their goal statements into specific time periods and to identify what organizational components are responsible for each goal.

4. Once tangible goals are developed, it is relatively easy for users to specify the criteria they use to assess goal attainment.

5. It is important that users distinguish between goals and criteria and perform a proactive role in developing them.

6. We tend to grossly underestimate the amount of time required for users to develop tangible goals and criteria.

As the OA process model suggests, the choice of effectiveness goals and criteria are basic value judgments that users must make if the results of an assessment are to become relevant and useful for their needs.

In Agency B the process of having users articulate effectiveness goals and criteria in Phases 2 and 3 was more iterative than sequential, which itself constitutes an important lesson. Initial attempts in Phase 2 resulted in users articulating intangible goals because users had not operationalized their value judgments in their own minds. Without recognizing the intangible nature of the goals, we (the evaluators) led the users into Phase 2 to develop criteria. As might be expected, users found it impossible to formulate criteria they would use to measure intangible goals. The users were then forced to reevaluate their goals and specify tangible objectives. This was facilitated by identifying specific time periods for each objective and the organizational components or actors responsible for achieving each objective.

In this process of developing effectiveness goals and criteria, it is important to provide users opportunities to make repeated estimations of their value judgments. These opportunities tend to be threatening to users and require a process that does not force users to "eat their own words" but permits them the freedom to reconsider their previous efforts. An approach found useful in Agency B was to conduct a series of meetings, with users performing different roles at each meeting. First, Nominal Group meetings were conducted to develop initial lists of goals and criteria. Then the initial goals and criteria were synthesized and categorized by areas. In subsequent sessions the users reacted to the preliminary lists of goals and criteria, modified them, and selected priorities. Throughout this period, the evaluators repeatedly asked the users if the goals statements were "really what they wanted," and if they would use the criteria as the bases for evaluating goal attainment. This allowed the users to second-guess their prior value judgments.

In Agency B, where the preceding process was followed, it took four months of intensive and repeated meetings with users to develop tangible goals and criteria, when one month had been originally allotted. As a result, the evaluation timetable was pushed back.

In Agency A no distinction was made between effectiveness goals and criteria. Instead, attention simply focused on identifying effectiveness measures that were considered relevant to users and could be used as the dependent variables for assessing the organization. The evaluation steering committee of users in Agency A (to whom the evaluators reported for administrative and policy decisions) directed the evaluators to work with technical staff in the agency's performance-reporting section to develop a list of valid effectiveness measures and to submit them to the committee for selection and priority ranking. This appeared as a logical way to proceed at the time but, in retrospect, was a fatal mistake that lead to making a Type III error.

We (the evaluators) joined forces with the technical staff to embark upon an intensive, full-time, three-month investigation of the information systems jungle of the agency. The investigation exposed many problems in the accuracy of "objective" performance measures in the information systems and produced a number of recommendations for improving the systems, as well as a list of effectiveness measures that the technical staff and evaluators agreed upon as sufficiently accurate to include in the evaluation study.

The list of effectiveness measures was then presented in a series of review sessions to the user committee and to all the directors of local offices and headquarters bureaus. In these review sessions the users were asked to (1) react by evaluating the list of measures, (2) proact by suggesting additional effectiveness measures not included on the list, and (3) choose priorities from the total list of measures presented and developed during the sessions.

Reflecting on these sessions, it is now painfully clear that (1) the measures presented were the major ones used for resource allocation and did not reflect the effectiveness criteria considered relevant to most of the organizational participants, (2) users could not break out of their reactive role and proact by generating new effectiveness measures, even when asked to do so but not provided with a process for doing so, and (3) there was little consensus among users on priorities among effectiveness measures (a Phase 3 design task) because goals and criteria had not been developed. In effect, Phases 2 and 3 were skipped. As a result, the user steering committee selected effectiveness measures after the fact—indicating, however, that these measures were valid only for the study and were not *the* criteria of agency effectiveness. The Type III error had been committed.

Phase 4, Evaluation Design

During this phase in Agencies A and B, one key insight was obtained that seems to facilitate learning on the part of users and to increase the applied relevance and eventual use of the evaluation results.

- It is important for users to develop their own conceptual model on what factors influence or explain effectiveness rather than to simply react to the evaluator's model.

In both Agencies A and B the evaluators had a relatively operational theoretical model already developed for predicting or explaining effectiveness before the research design phase began. However, the manners in which the evaluators' conceptual models were presented and used during the research design phase created very different dynamics for users in Agencies A and B.

In Agency A Phase 4 began with presentations of the evaluators' theoretical model to a host of user groups as well as outside organization researchers and theorists. These review sessions were especially helpful to the evaluators in sharpening the model, adding a variable here and there to the model, modifying terminology to the argot more comfortable to users, and in evaluating the content validity of the theory and proposed measures. All these factors improved the internal consistency and generality of the evalutors' model. However, in retrospect, the users were again placed in a reactive mode and, in essence, required to work within the evaluators' framework for explaining what situational and organizational factors were likely to influence effectiveness. They were not given a proactive opportunity to learn and create their own conceptual model.

In Agency B Phase 4 began with a two-day workshop in which the evaluators participated with the users to develop a conceptual model through nominal and conventional group discussions, as well as heated but constructive debates. The fact that the evaluator had already developed a model before the workshop was simply an indication that he had done his homework, just as other user participants had been asked to do to prepare for the workshops. It turned out that the conceptual model that emerged from the workshop was significantly different, more comprehensive, and more precise—in terms of the specification of arrows among variables in a path-analytic sense—than that which the evaluators had developed prior to the workshop. Moreover, model building did not stop with the conclusion of the workshop. Users and evaluators continued to reformulate the model through written correspondence and whenever opportunities for get-togethers presented themselves—even to today, now six years after the original model-building workshop. In effect, the evolving model had become the communication code and working guide for both evaluators and users in Agency B. In Agency A, this degree of use of the conceptual model has not diffused beyond the inside and outside evaluators.

Phase 5, Evaluation Implementation

The conventional problems of data collection discussed in most research methodology texts were encountered in Agencies A and B during Phase 5. However, two learning experiences merit further attention.

1. The establishment of an efficient, standardized system for data collection permits the evaluator flexibility to pursue and probe new ideas and unanticipated problems encountered during the data collection period. It also minimizes the dysfunctional consequences of conflicts of interests in the study by the evaluator.

2. Quality control procedures during data collection are imperative and seem to be most appropriately monitored by a person on the outside evaluator's staff who is not directly involved in field data collection activities.

Once the conceptual model, hypothesis, and measures have been developed in Phase 4, the scientific method demands that researchers shift from a developmental to a systematized mode (Van de Ven and Delbecq, 1974) in Phase 5 to measure the variables of interest in a highly consistent and standardized way across all observations. However, no set of measurement instruments, no matter how well developed, will capture all the unanticipated factors encountered during data collection which are considered important extensions of the conceptual model. In addition, as a result of the active involvements with users in Phases 1 to 4, by the time data collection begins the principal outside evaluator has in many respects become an "insider" who is increasingly called upon to consult users on other problems, participate in various staff and policy meetings, deal with individual concerns and feelings of threat often unrelated to the evaluation study, and yet manage a data collection process that attains the standards of consistency and objectivity in measurement. Although these digressions embroil the evaluator in a host of conflicts of interest, they are a necessary part of an organization assessment and provide rich qualitative insights for analyzing and understanding research results in Phase 6.

In Agencies A and B these multiple and conflicting roles were managed by establishing a standardized set of measurement instruments and data collection procedures, schedules, and programs in advance of data collection. Extensive training sessions were conducted with the data collection teams. Pilot studies provided opportunities not only to make final adjustments in the measurement instruments, but also to "debug" the data collection and monitoring systems. Once the data collection systems were set in place and implemented, the evaluator simply dealt with the exceptions, and had the freedom to pursue and probe new ideas and unanticipated directions encountered during the period of data collection.

Critical to the data collection systems were quality control procedures for insuring that evaluation documents and instruments were being properly completed while the data were being collected. A person on the outside evaluator's staff was assigned full-time responsibility to monitor incoming data because the task was one that could not wait while the data became old. The important learning experience here is that a substantial fraction (approximately 15 percent) of the instruments contained items that were either incorrectly completed or not completed at all. These instruments were returned to the individuals for completion whenever possible. As a result, we avoided a significant portion of missing data that was unintended and would have been unnecessary.

Phase 6, Data Analysis and Feedback

During this phase, the major challenges are translation and utilization of research knowledge. Essentially the same processes as described in Phase 5 above were followed in Agencies A and B. However, our subjective impressions are that users in Agency B understood the results more clearly when the feedback workshops were conducted than did Agency A users. To date, utilization of evaluation results has been more widespread among users and has concerned more significant policy and administrative issues in Agency B than in Agency A. From these comparative impressions we can only speculate that *active user involvement during evaluation Phases 1 to 5 in the manner described for Agency B facilitates the translation and utilization of evaluation results* in Phase 6. User involvement in early evaluation phases represents an important period of learning for users (as well as evaluators) and increases their receptivity and motivation to see and use evaluation results.

CONCLUSION

This chapter has addressed some of the process problems in conducting an organization assessment. It was argued that effectiveness is inextricably tied to the concept of organization goals. However, to study effectiveness systematically, it is important to distinguish goals for motivating and directing behavior from effectiveness goals and to understand matters of values and facts of the latter. Specifically an understanding of organization effectiveness requires answers to: (1) What are the desired results? (2) How should they be measured? and (3) What produces or causes them? The first question primarily requires a value judgment, whereas the latter two are mostly factual.

A process model for conducting an organization assessment was developed for answering these questions. The model emphasizes that user involvement in each phase is necessary for making value judgments on effectiveness goals and criteria and for enhancing the understanding and utilization of research knowledge. The theoretical justification for the evaluation process model was presented, as well as the learning experience obtained in using the model at different stages of its development in two state agencies. Of course, these learning experiences are simply subjective and restrospective impressions and certainly do not constitute a test of the model.

However, we are increasingly using the process model to guide the conduct of future assessments of organizations. The model highlights critical issues in conducting action/evaluation research and provides guidelines for interfacing users and evaluators on matters of values and facts that must be dealt with in any kind of research endeavor. It further suggests group processes and agenda formats to conduct each evaluation phase. Finally, the general character of the process is consistent with current research on the dissemination and utilization of research knowledge (e.g., Rogers and Schoemaker, 1971; Havelock, 1973; Clark, 1976).

CHAPTER THREE

Methodology in Constructing and Evaluating the OAI

HISTORICAL DEVELOPMENT OF THE OAI

Seven years of work have been performed to develop and test the OAI in a large state government employment security agency. Although such a research setting limits the generalizability of the OAI test results, it does provide the opportunity for multiple trials that are very necessary in test and instrument construction.

In 1972 an initial OAI was developed and data were collected in a sample of 16 local offices and 249 work units. The measurement properties of this initial OAI were evaluated to identify strengths and weaknesses and to develop an improved OAI. In 1973 a second survey was conducted with the revised OAI in all 30 local and administrative offices and 318 units of the employment security agency. Another psychometric evaluation was then performed on data collected with the 1973 OAI (see Van de Ven et al., 1975). From this analysis grew the awareness that although significant improvements were made over the 1972 version, further improvements in some questionnaire items and answer scales were needed before the OAI could be considered acceptable for the basic and applied research purposes stated in Chapter 1. The changes that were believed necessary in the 1973 OAI were therefore made by developing a "third generation" of instruments. This new version of the OAI was used in 1975 to conduct a third survey in 30 offices and 334 units of the same employment security agency.

Throughout its development, revisions of the OAI were based on both qualitative and psychometric considerations. The major qualitative concerns in designing and evaluating drafts of the OAI included its applicability and utility in a wide variety of organizations, the frame of reference of the measures, and its content validity. Psychometric methods were used primarily to evaluate statistical properties of reliability and validity of each OAI version to determine where improvements were necessary in succeeding versions. This chapter describes the procedures used to address these qualitative and psychometric considerations.

QUALITATIVE CONSIDERATIONS IN DEVELOPING THE OAI

As Chapter 1 described, our goal is relatively straightforward: to develop a reliable and valid instrument for measuring the factors listed in Figure 1-2 in a wide variety of organizations. To make the OAI widely applicable, we attempted to create measures that were: (1) simple to understand, (2) inexpensive to administer, (3) standardized, so they were comparable from unit to unit and organization to organization, and (4) explicit and consistent in their frame of reference to guide respondents in interpreting and answering the questions.

Simplicity, Efficiency, and Standardization of the OAI

By definition, complex organizations contain multiple levels and units, each with a unique pattern of structure and behavior to achieve its subgoals. An appreciation of these different structures and behaviors in various organizational units is generally beyond the information-processing capabilities of any central evaluation unit, let alone an outside observer. As a result, studies of organizations by researchers have tended to rely on observations of a few selected organizational functions or relied on the perceptions of a limited number of top or middle-level managers. Yet, it has been amply demonstrated in previous research that the observations or perceptions of a few managers are not generalizable to the functioning of the entire organization (Dearborn and Simon, 1958; Porter, 1958). In developing the OAI, we began with the assumption that the most knowledgeable informants about the patterns of task, structure, and process within various organizational levels and units are the people who work daily in the levels and units under investigation. These people occupy various positions and roles in performing their jobs, and as informants they can provide differentiated perceptions of the structure and behavior within and between the organizational units being assessed. When these perceptions of informants throughout the organization are aggregated in specific ways, it is believed we can obtain measures of organizational design that are a closer reflection of reality than would be obtained through observations or perceptions of only top- or middle-level managers.

Since all personnel in the organizational units being studied are included in an OA survey, wide applicability of the OAI requires that the verbal level of the measures be low enough that they can be responded to by almost any potential worker. Therefore, in developing the OAI measures, we attempted to use words that were simple enough to be understood by almost any English-speaking adult and which are relevant to almost any organizational setting. This requirement rules out long complicated statements or case illustrations to which informants are asked to respond. It also rules out job or organization specific items, and requires the use of simple generic terms. These terms often need to be defined initially and used consistently throughout the instrument. For example, in the OAI a *work unit* is defined and consistently referred to as a supervisor and all subordinates who report directly to that supervisor. It was found that other closely related terms (e.g., work group, department, section, subdivision, team, gang) took on different connotations from organization to organization. However, the simple generic terms used in the measures must also be specific enough so that the frames of reference of each question are unambiguous to informants and consistently reponded to across informants (see the following section on frames of reference).

Wide applicability also implies that the OAI should be inexpensive in terms of time, money, and staff hours required, not only to collect data but also to analyze and feed back data collected with the OAI. This latter requirement is particularly important if the OAI is to be used on a longitudinal basis and incorporated as part of an ongoing applied program of organization assessment and development. Efficient data collection requires that the OAI measurement devices be short, require a minimal amount of effort, and be administered to a large number of people at a time, and yet maintain acceptable standards of reliability and validity. From this perspective, questionnaires and organizational records were chosen over personal or group interviews, participant observation, or other forms of time, motion, or interaction scoring procedures to measure the variables of interest.

Of course, data collection efficiency was not the only criterion for selecting a measurement device. It was also a function of the researchers' conceptual clarity of the constructs to be measured. When we embarked on this research in 1972, there were a number of organizational constructs that were not understood well enough to know how to formulate questions to measure them. Either we were unsure of how respondents would interpret our questions or what the range of alternative answers to questions might be. Preliminary measures of these constructs (e.g., workflow interdependence, coordination and control mechanisms) were included in an interview schedule that was administered to all unit supervisors, whereas measures of constructs that were more clearly understood were included in a questionnaire for unit supervisors and members. Although the 1972 OAI survey was extremely time consuming (particularly the 250 interviews, each of which averaged two and a half hours) it provided much conceptual and methodological clarity in the organizational constructs we attempted to measure. As a result, most of the constructs measured in the interviews in 1972 were revised and included in questionnaires in the 1973 and 1975 OAI versions.

Questionnaires not only provided a more efficient and standardized method of measurement, they also eliminated some of the basic problems of interview surveys, including the loss of information that occurs in the transmission of verbal responses into written answers, and variability in responses due to interviewer styles, personalities, and skills. Of course, questionnaires, like interviews, are subject to a host of other kinds of measurement errors. Indeed, one purpose of this book is to detect and evaluate the various sources of measurement error in the OAI. However, in developing each version of the OAI, attempts were made to avoid predictable sources of measurement errors by developing an explicit frame of reference for the measures in the OAI questionnaires.

FRAMES OF REFERENCE

Smith, Kendall, and Hulin (1969:11–30) and Guilford (1954:299–337) have reviewed the research evidence that shows that perceptual selectivity in determining human judgments is dramatic. An individual selects and interprets certain aspects of a situation or question and responds according to those aspects. When two persons with different frames of reference are exposed to the same objective situation or stimulus, they will select different aspects as pertinent to their judgments and provide different summary evaluations of that situation. Frames of reference are the internal standards or cognitive filters a person uses in describing or evaluating a situation (Helson, 1964). For purposes of instrument construction and evaluation, it is useful to examine at least three interlocking issues that influence a respondent's frame of reference: (1) the immediate characteristics of the stimulus or situation a person is exposed to, and (2) the systematic, and (3) the unsystematic individual differences and biases that respondents bring to bear to a stimulus or situation as a result of their prior experiences, predilections, expectations, and personalities.

The first issue requires an examination of how a respondent's frame of reference is influenced by the composition of the measurement instrument itself and the setting in which respondents complete it. Specifically, the nature, complexity, referent, and time perspective of questions and the anchor points on an answer scale have been found to significantly influence a respondent's frame of reference at the point of measurement (Smith et al., 1969). To the extent that a measurement instrument takes these factors into account explicitly, one can control one of the major sources of variation in respondents' frames of reference and thereby have a better understanding of the judgments made by people about the organizational phenomena of interest. Therefore, the next section describes in greater detail how each of these factors were considered, to structure an explicit frame of reference into the OAI.

In addition to the effects due to composition and administration of the measurement instrument itself, there are systematic and unsystematic effects on frame of reference due to the position, past experiences, and predilections of the respondent. The systematic effects include those individual differences in respondents that are known, as a result of previous theorizing or research, to influence respondents' judgments in predictable ways. For example, judgments about individual and group behavior in organizations have been found to differ systematically when respondents occupy different positions and levels in an organization (Porter, 1958; Ghiselli, 1973; Bouchard, 1976). Indeed the systematic differences in judgments about organizational behavior between respondents in different organizational positions provide the ultimate justification for the method used to aggregate individual responses on various measures in the OAI to obtain organizational and unit scores.

In studies of job satisfaction and other attitudinal characteristics of organizations (e.g., climate and morale), perceptions have been found to differ systematically among respondents of different age, sex, education, social background, and job tenure in the organization (Smith et al., 1969; Dunnette, 1976). These individual difference factors are commonly used as stratification variables in reporting norms for instruments measuring various attitudinal dimensions of jobs and organizations. The reason for this strategy is to statistically control or correct for the frames of reference of respondents when evaluating a measurement instrument.

Finally, unsystematic effects on frame of reference include a host of unknown predilections, personality orientations, and contextual factors within respondents that influence their individual judgments of a given stimulus in different ways. For example, a sickness in the family, a recent extremely happy or sad incident, and the psychological or physiological mood or health of a respondent at the time of data collection undoubtedly influences his or her answers to questions (Guilford, 1954). However, these kinds of influences on frames of reference are unsystematic in the sense that they are expected to be randomly and normally distributed among the sample of respondents or informants and will therefore cancel out statistically when judgments are averaged together. These kinds of unsystematic disturbances on frames of reference are the basis of the argument for obtaining the perceptions of many judges or informants on a given organizational phenomenon. Classical test theory has extensively demonstrated that reliability of a measure increases by increasing the number of judges (Lord and Novick, 1968). This is one of the major reasons why we have continued to develop and administer various components of the OAI for all employees of an organization and then aggregate individual scores to obtain summary measures of organization and work unit behavior.

Frame of Reference in OAI Questionnaires

As the preceding discussion implies, a better understanding of the judgments made by individuals can be obtained if the intended frames of reference of questions in the OAI questionnaires are made explicit and unambiguous for respondents. In developing and revising the OAI, the following factors were taken into account because they are importantly related to the frame of reference taken by respondents at the point of measurement.

1. Time perspective of questions (short to long term).

2. Nature of the measures, in terms of: descriptive versus evaluative and behavioral versus attitudinal questions.

3. Absolute versus relative anchor points and the number of alternatives on an answer scale.

4. Referent of the measures, in terms of questions pertaining to individual, group, or organizational phenomena.

Although these factors are not necessarily independent, we describe how each is individually related to frame of reference and clarify how each factor is dealt with and structured into the OAI.

1. Time Perspective of Questions. When making judgments about the functioning of an organization, the frame of reference of a respondent may range from a consideration of the historical evolution of organizational policies and practices over the past five years or longer to the minute-by-minute activities of a particular task. In addition, the respondent's evaluation may vary greatly if he or she focuses on organizational practices occurring during a normal operating period or on a time episode of exceptions, crises, or chaotic events. Obviously, the time frame of questions in a measurement instrument depends upon whether the investigator wishes to examine organizational behavior from a long- or short-term perspective and during normal or exceptional operating periods. However, when the time frame is *not* made explicit in a question, the respondent is left to self-select whatever period of time she or he chooses to focus on in answering the question, and as a result, the answer is often uninterpretable to the investigator. As a general rule, an explicit consideration of the time period covered in a question enables the investigator to interpret the respondents' answers with a greater degree of accuracy and rationality than if the time frames of questions are left implicit or unspecified (Guilford, 1954:295).

Although the time frames of measures in the OAI vary depending upon the specific organizational constructs examined, most range between three to six months and focus on normal patterns of behavior during these time periods. For example, most questions in the OAI questionnaire, include a phrase such as *"During the normal course of work or events in the past three (or six) months,* how often, how much, or to what extent did some organizational practice or activity occur?" (See subsequent chapters for specific time periods and measures for each construct in the OAI.) There are two reasons for selecting an intermediate time frame of three to six months for measures in the OAI.

First, the constructs in the OAI are intended to *describe* (not project) patterns of behavior in an organization, that is, to measure existing rather than future activities and conditions. Recognition of a normal pattern of behavior necessarily requires an historical (rather than a futuristic) account over a time period sufficiently long to observe the existence of a repetitive cycle of activities (which by definition is a normal pattern of behavior). However, descriptions of historical events become increasingly unreliable over time due to loss of memory (Gregson, 1975), and the recency effect (i.e., the tendency to rationalize and distort accounts of past behavior in terms of subsequent and more recent events and conditions). We believe that three to six months is long enough to recognize normal patterns of behavior on the organizational dimensions examined in the OAI, but short enough to avoid significant distortions in judgments of historical behavior.

The second reason for choosing a three to six month time frame for measures in the OAI is to clearly segment each data collection wave when conducting longitudinal research. Ideally, the slice of time examined should account for all variations in OAI scores measuring the same dimensions over time. The clear delineation of these "slices of time" clarifies an assessment of trends and correlates of change and also decreases the problem of correlated disturbance terms which plagues statistical attempts to test causal models on longitudinal data in the social sciences (Borgotta and Bohrnstedt, 1970).

2.   Objective versus Subjective Measures. Recently, much (and in our opinion, ill-directed) effort has been spent in comparing the reliability and validity of objective versus subjective measures of organizations. "Objective" measures are defined as those that require only "a direct assessment of organizational properties without any conceptual transformation" (Payne and Pugh, 1976:1128). Here informants simply provide information from available measurement instruments such as an organization chart or staffing and performance records. "Subjective" measures require an "indirect assessment of organizational properties by instruments which measure group perceptions; here a member is a respondent to instruments with statements such as, 'The jobs in this organization are clearly defined . . .' or 'The employees here are constantly checked for rule violation'" (Payne and Pugh, 1976:1128).

Payne and Pugh go on to review studies that compare subjective and objective approaches to measuring dimensions of organization structure and conclude that little convergent validity has been found. For example, Pennings (1973) collected data in ten organizations on centralization, formalization, and complexity using the "objective" Aston (Pugh et al., 1968) and "subjective" Hall (1963) instruments. He obtained low correlations between the objective and subjective measures, and "calls into question the assumption that the different instruments tap identical structural attributes."

Given the embryonic state of development of organization measurement, there is clearly a need for more construct validation efforts by comparing parallel measures of organizational dimensions. Unfortunately most of the construct validation efforts reviewed by Payne and Pugh are based on conceptually weak assumptions and definitions. Why should one assume that indicants of structure from organizational records and archives are the same as the perceptions of structure in the minds of organizational members? It becomes difficult to argue, for example, that an objective measure of "the number of pages or words in an organization's procedure manual" taps the same conceptual domain as the subjective question, "How many written rules and operating instructions are there for workers?" The former taps rule codification while the latter taps awareness of rule codification. Obviously, the selection of an objective versus subjective measurement procedure should be a direct reflection of how constructs are defined. Unfortunately, when constructs of interest are loosely defined, these important conceptual distinctions are not recognized and often result in selecting inappropriate parallel measures to establish construct validity.

Another popular myth about objective versus subjective measures is that the former are more valid than the latter. In this regard, we concur with John Campbell's (1977) stance, "Any objective measure is a subjective measure once removed." Documents, records, and archives can be very useful to measure objective properties of organizations. However, the belief that they are generally more reliable or valid than subjective measures is patent nonsense, particularly when one considers the sloppy ways many organizations score or keep track of their reporting systems, the fudging of data that occurs daily, the shifts in administrative reporting directives, the need to look good to higher executives and funding sources, and the need to prevent law suits. These practices reflect the fact that a variety of different frames of reference and intentions are involved when organizational members enter data into organizational records that may be functional for some organizational purposes but not for basic or applied evaluation research purposes. Indeed, there are many instances where subjective measures that ask respondents directly and in confidence what goes on within the organization may yield more accurate data than objective measures obtained from records compiled by the organization being assessed. Dalton (1959), Madge (1965), and Webb, et al. (1966) go into greater length to describe the serious limitations of various kinds of organizational documents. The major conclusion is that data in organizational records can never be taken at face value until a detailed investigation of their accuracies and inaccuracies has been conducted. The problems with such an investigation are compounded by the lack of knowledge of record-keeping rules and practices within an organization by an outside investigator and the limited utility of classical psychometric methods in conducting such an investigation.

In selecting and evaluating objective measures of organization and performance for the OAI, we obtained the help and direction of technical staff within the agency and embarked upon an intensive, full-time, three-month investigation of the organization's information systems jungle. The investigation exposed problems in the accuracy of many objective organization and performance measures in the information systems. It did, however conclude with a list of measures that the technical staff and the evaluators agreed upon as sufficiently accurate for purposes of the organization assessment. (See "Selection of Organization Performance Criteria" following for further description.)

   3. Descriptive and Evaluative Measures. Measurements of organizations can range along a continuum from being descriptive to evaluative in nature. Descriptive measures are positive or value-free, and focus on the factual characteristics and behaviors that actually exist or occur in the organization. Evaluative measures are normative or value-laden, and ask a respondent to provide an opinion about the strengths, weaknesses, likes, or dislikes of characteristics and behaviors in the organization. For example, in measuring task variability, at the descriptive end of the continuum one might ask, "What proportion of your tasks are the same from day-to-day?" At the evaluative end of the scale one might ask "To what degree do you feel there is enough variety in your work from day-to-day?" In the middle of this continuum one might ask a question that requires some description and evaluation: "From day-to-day what proportion of the time do you feel there is too little variety in your work?" Measures that vary along this descriptive–evaluative range yield systematically different results because they differently affect a respondent's frame of reference and because they clearly tap different conceptual domains (they ask different questions).

   Based on Helson's (1948, 1964) research on adaptation level theory, Smith, Kendall, and Hulin (1969:17) point out that evaluative questions are more susceptible to varying frames of reference by respondents than are descriptive questions. For example, two respondents may descriptively report that three-fourths of their tasks are the same from day-to-day (although there is some adaptation to even these kinds of questions). However, one may evaluate this job as providing "far too little" variety and the other as providing "too much" variety. Descriptive measures tend to be less affected by an individual's frame of reference because descriptive questions are usually framed in terms of an external or observable standard or norm. Evaluative questions, on the other hand, ask respondents to invoke their individual standards, norms, or values to make an assessment. As stated previously, these individual standards are a function of all previous experiences and conditions to which the respondent has been exposed (Helson, 1964). As a result, one should expect to observe greater differences in norms on evaluative than descriptive measures when scores are stratified by individual background variables (e.g., age, sex, education, and job tenure in the organization).

Ultimately, the decision to use evaluative or descriptive measures should be influenced not only by frames of reference but also by the operational definitions of the constructs to be measured. In developing the OAI, an attempt was made to define and measure all organizational context and design dimensions in descriptive terms, whereas organizational performance, morale, and job satisfaction (the outcome criterion variables) were intended to be evaluative. This strategy is consistent with the basic approach that we take in conducting an organization assessment. This approach consists of three basic steps: (1) to measure along various descriptive dimensions the actual ways in which jobs, units, and the total agency are organized and the contexts in which they operate, (2) to obtain subjective and objective measures of performance along various evaluative dimensions, and (3) to statistically analyze how existing patterns of organizational design and context (obtained in step 1) are related to evaluations of performance (obtained in step 2). These distinctions between descriptive and evaluative measures are made explicit to minimize the confounding of relationships in step 3. Achieving this enables us to learn the degrees to which organization context and design factors are practically important for predicting, explaining, and eventually improving organization performance.

4. Number of Points on Answer Scales. Another factor that significantly influences respondents' frames of reference is the number of alternative categories or points on a rating scale used to answer questions which can range along continua from low to high, little to much, and so on. The effects of the number of scale points on the reliability of measures (the operational criterion of varying frames of reference) has received considerable attention and much empirical investigation.

In selecting the number of points on a rating scale, Guilford (1954:289–291) suggests several logical considerations. If too few scale points are used, the answer scale is obviously a coarse one, and much information is lost because the scale does not capture the discriminatory powers that respondents are capable of making. On the other hand, by adding too many scale points, the scale can become graded so finely that it is beyond the respondents' limited powers of discrimination. Indeed, Miller (1956) argues that the average individual can process seven, plus or minus two (the "magical number") bits of information at a time.

Conflicting research conclusions have been drawn on the question of how many scale points are optimal. Conklin (1923) concluded after analysis of some 23,000 ratings that for untrained respondents the maximum number of points should be *five* for a single (unipolar) scale and *nine* for a double (bipolar) scale. Starting from the empirical observation that the average of interrater correlations is .55 to .60, Symonds (1924) concluded that *seven* points is optimal. At this level of reliability, more than seven scale points increases reliability by an amount that is so small that it does not pay off for the extra effort involved. Symonds (1931:79) advised that fewer scale points may be desirable if the question is rather obscure, if the respondents are untrained and only moderately interested, or if a number of ratings of different aspects of the construct are to be combined. Champney and Marshall (1939) questioned Symond's conclusion and suggested that when respondents are trained and motivated, the optimal number of scale points may be as many as three times seven. Symonds' conclusion was partially based on the fact that interrater reliabilities on scales with a few broad categories tend to be higher than those on fine (many-point) scales. However, the effect of grouping errors on the correlation coefficient is a percentage change, and the fewer the scale points, the greater the percentage of reduction. The smaller the correlation with many fine scale points, the smaller is the net change. Thus, when reliabilities of ratings (from a fine scale) are relatively low, one could well tolerate the loss that coarse grouping involves (Guilford, 1954:290).

Other researchers have found that reliability is generally independent of the number of scale points for Likert-type items (Bendix, 1954; Komorita, 1963; Komorita and Graham, 1965; Matell and Jacoby, 1971). However, Jahoda, Deutsch and Cook (1951) and Ferguson (1971) state that the reliability of a scale increases as the number of scale points increases, particularly when the instrument measures relatively homogeneous items. Comparability and reconciliation of these results has been difficult because of the variety of methodological approaches and test instruments used in these studies.

More recently Lissitz and Green (1975) conducted a Monte Carlo study in an effort to reconcile the differences by examining the effects of the number of scale points and test homogeneity (item variance–covariance structures) upon reliability. Figure 3-1 graphically portrays the effects obtained upon coefficient alpha of changes in the number of scale points (from 2, 3, 5, 7, 9, to 14) and three different item variance–covariance structures (.8, .5, and .2) on a 10-item test. The graph shows that for each covariance structure, coefficient alpha increases as the number of scale points increases. Lissitz and Green obtained similar curves for other indices of reliability (i.e., Spearman–Brown test–retest reliability and the squared correlations

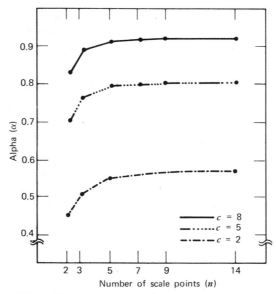

Figure 3-1   The effect upon coefficient alpha (α) of changes in the number of scale points (n), and the amount of covariance (cj). Source: Robert W. Lissitz and Samuel B. Green, "Effect of the Number of Scale Points on Reliability: A Monte Carlo Approach," Journal of Applied Psychology, Vol. 60, No. 1 (1975), p. 12.

between true and observed scores). It was also found that the standard deviations of scores decrease as the number of scale points increase with a particular variance–covariance structure, but the standard deviations are generally larger for the smaller covariance structures.

Most of the past studies indicated that either one particular number or no particular number of scale points yielded maximum reliability. Lissitz and Green (1975:12) state that these results are due to the sizes of the standard deviations in comparison to the difference between the reliabilities from one particular number of scale points to another. The Lissitz and Green study also gives strong support for rejection of 7 scale points as an optimal number. Figure 3-1 shows that the increase in reliability levels off after 5 scale points and that the utility of having more than 5 points will generally be little. These Monte Carlo study findings assume that respondents have perfect perception. Since respondents are fallible, Lissitz and Green conclude that even fewer than 5 scale points may be necessary.

Our qualitative experiences in varying the number of scale points in the OAI support the conclusions drawn by Lissitz and Green. In the early 1972 and 1973 versions of the OAI questionnaires, 10 points were used for the answer scales. However many respondents (particularly nonprofessional clerical workers) expressed ambiguities in discriminating between fine points while answering the questionnaires (e.g., with questions, "What is the difference between an 8 and a 9?"), and dissatisfaction with the numbers on the scales they selected to represent their answers when they handed their completed questionnaires to the researchers. Guided by the literature reviewed previously, 5-point Likert-type scales were constructed for most questions in the revised 1975 OAI questionnaires. Five-scale points not only reduced the complexity of answering questions for respondents by one-half, it also permitted us to develop clearly distinguishable anchors or cues to represent the intended meaning of each number on the 5-point scales. For the earlier 10-point scales we found it impossible to develop commonly meaningful adverbs and cues to distinguish each point on the scale. Therefore five cues were placed on every other point on the 10-point scales. In retrospect, we should have recognized then that our 10-point scales had in effect five meaningful categories interspersed with five meaningless categories. Furthermore, if we (the investigators) could not provide meaningful cues to discriminate each of the ten points on the answer scales, we should not have expected or assumed that respondents could make these fine discriminations. After the 1975 OAI questionnaires were completed, many respondents (who also completed the earlier versions of the OAI) commented that the revised 5-point scales were easier and more meaningful to answer than the earlier 10-point answer scales.

   5. Anchors or Cues on Answer Scales. It has been known for a long time that the precision and validity of measures can be increased significantly if the physical or psychological cues to be used in making judgments are made clear to the respondent (Smith et al., 1969:25). Cues on each point of an answer scale have the double purpose of supplementing and reinforcing the definition of the continuum and of providing anchors or mileposts to guide the respondent in making quantitative judgments (Guilford, 1954:293). However, an extensive body of literature has shown that judgments along a continuum or series of stimulus cues tend to shift somewhat systematically with the phenomena being assessed and the norms or adaptation levels of respondents with regard to that phenomena (see reviews in Guilford, 1954:302–340; Helson, 1948; 1964; and Smith et al., 1969). For example, a 4-ounce fountain pen is heavy, but a baseball bat to be heavy must weigh over 40 ounces. So also, weekly communications among members of a traveling sales force may be judged by its members to be "very frequent," whereas weekly communications are judged "very infrequent" among secretaries in a steno pool. Furthermore, these judgments are likely to vary among members of the same unit who may have experienced widely differing occupational and organizational careers.

Given that these differing norms and adaptation levels exist, the basic practical problem becomes one of tying down the answer scales so that the meanings of particular cues or anchors are relatively general and fixed. As the preceding examples suggest, the problem is more acute for psychological cues than physical cues. Cues in physical units (e.g., the number of times per week people communicate or specific events occur in a specified period of time) are less subject to varying norms and adaptation levels than are psychologically based cues (e.g., subjective expressions of frequency, amount, and extent). Scores in physical units tend to approximate a ratio scale more nearly than those obtained in psychological units. However, Guilford (1954:343–344) cautions that although physical measurements enable one to make neat statements about behavioral activities and performance, these statements remain in the realm of physical discourse and do not permit sure psychological conclusions. If one intends to measure a psychologically based construct, then psychological measures are needed, whereas physical units are appropriate for those constructs that are defined in terms of physically observable events or phenomena. Although most psychological measures have neither equal units nor a meaningful zero point, psychological equality of definitions and measures "is essential if we are to establish the correct kind of functional relationship between the *psychological* variable in which we are interested and some other variable" (Guilford, 1954:344). Of course, not all psychological (and for that matter, physical) measures evoke the same degrees of variations in adaptation levels as the discussion so far implies. Some psychological traits are more easily observed and judged than others. In particular, descriptive measures are more objective and different judges are more likely to agree upon them than they do upon other more subjective evaluative traits (Smith et al., 1969).

Consistent with these prescriptions, response scales in the OAI were constructed in physical units wherever possible to measure the occurrence of activities, events, and behaviors in organizations, whereas psychological cues were used for psychologically based constructs. With varying degrees of success, we also attempted to attain the following criteria for constructing good cues that have been offered by Champney (1941) and restated in Guilford (1954:293).

a. *Clarity.* Use short statements in simple, unambiguous terminology.

b. *Consistency.* The cue should be consistent with the question and its definition as well as with other cues. Avoid bringing into a cue any implications of other questions. Such a slip is all too easy to make without realizing it.

c. *Precision.* A good cue applies to a point or very short range on the continuum. There should be no doubt about its rank position among other cues, and if possible it should not overlap them in quantitative meaning. This implies our being able to localize the cue at a point on a scale.

d. *Variety.* The use of the same terms in all or many of the cues may fail to differentiate them sufficiently. Vary the language used at different scale levels.

e. **Objectivity.** Stay clear of terminology implying ethical, moral, or social evaluations, unless dealing specifically with such types of questions. Cues with implications of good or bad, worthy or unworthy, and desirable or undesirable should generally be avoided.

f. *Uniqueness.* The cues for answering each question should be unique to that question. Avoid using cues of a very general character, such as "excellent," "superior," "average," "poor," and the like. Use cues that are more specific and pinpoint the realistic alternatives that are available to respondents in answering the questions.

Attaining these criteria for good cues should help tie down the answer scales so that the meanings of particular anchors are relatively general and fixed.

 6. *Individual and Collective Levels of Analysis.* Two final factors were considered in structuring the OAI: changing levels of analysis (individual, group, or organizational) and the aggregation of individual data to measure collective properties. In measuring various dimensions of job design, satisfaction, and other microorganization factors as covered in Chapter 6, the individual is the unit of analysis and no aggregation of the data to group or organizational levels is performed. Here, the individual, as a "respondent," answers questions

that pertain directly to his or her background, behavior, or value judgments. However, when collective properties of structure and behavior of groups (Chapter 5), between groups (Chapter 7), between organizations (Chapter 8), or of the total organization (Chapter 4) are of interest, then we must deal with the problem of how to obtain reliable information from individuals to measure the collective phenomena.

Most of the literature on aggregating individual scores to obtain measures of group and organization structure has focused on ecological and individualistic fallacies (e.g., Hannan, 1970; Scheuch, 1969; Galtung, 1967). The ecological fallacy is described as erroneously making inferences about individuals from results obtained for the group of which the individuals are members. In contrast, the individualistic fallacy (which is the major concern here) is the error created by incorrectly drawing inferences about the group or organization based on the responses obtained from individual members. Hannan (1970) points out that underlying these fallacies of disaggregation and aggregation are, respectively, the conceptual problems of the degree to which microproperties of individuals are the same as macroproperties of groups and organizations and the extent to which one can make inferences from results at one level to other levels. Homans (1961:379–380) summarizes quite well the polar positions of theorists on whether there are continuities or discontinuities in changing units of analysis of social systems:

> Some sociologists were once inclined to think of the small informal group as a microcosm of society at large: they felt that the same phenomena appeared in the former as in the latter but on a vastly reduced scale—a scale that incidently made detailed observation possible. And no doubt there are striking resemblances between the two. . . . But to say that the two phenomena have points in common is not to say that one is a microcosm of the other, that the one is simply the other writ small. . . . The reason lies. . . . in the fact that, in the institutions of societies at large, the relations between the fundamental processes are more complex.

Presently, most theorists have adopted the perspective that there are enough discontinuities in structure and behavior between different levels of analysis to alert the investigator of possible aggregation and disaggregation problems when changing units of analysis. Galtung (1967:45), for example, states:

> The "fallacy of the wrong level" consists not in making *inferences* from one level of analysis to another, but in making direct *translations of properties or relations* from one level to another, i.e., making too simple inferences. The fallacy can be committed working downwards, by projecting from groups or categories to individuals, or upwards, by projecting from individuals to higher units.

Much of the literature on the aggregation problem has subsequently focused either on detecting bias in aggregated variables or in examining changes produced in empirical relations by shifts in the unit of analysis. For example, in a study of structural and individual effects of control, power, performance, and satisfaction, Bachman, Smith, and Slesinger (1966) found that correlations on aggregated organizational scores were much larger than the same correlations on nonaggregated individual scores. Of course, these results are not surprising since as early as 1939 Thorndike pointed out that measures of association between pairs of variables increased in value as the size of the units used increased (Thorndike, 1939).

Most aggregation problems found in examining relationships across levels of analysis stem from the construction of the measurement instruments themselves. Lazarsfeld and Menzel (1969) and Seidler (1974) suggest that at the point of measurement aggregation problems can be largely controlled if the investigator (1) clarifies the distinct types of collective properties she or he is attempting to measure, (2) makes explicit the individual, group, or organizational referent to which the measures pertain, and (3) defines the roles to be performed by individuals from whom information is obtained.

Lazarsfeld and Menzel (1969) develop a typology of distinct properties of groups which is useful for clarifying how data obtained from individuals can be aggregated to measure characteristics of groups or the total organization. At the point of measurement, three types of data are obtained with the OAI for measuring group or organizational characteristics: member, relational, and global data. These data are then transformed through mathematical operations to examine various properties of work units and the organization.

Member data include characteristics of members which are obtained without reference to collective characteristics. *Relational* data examine the linkages of members to each other, and are obtained from information about the substantive relationships each member has with other members in the collective. *Global* data are macrocharacteristics of the collective which are not based on any information about individual members. For example, in measuring the design of work units in Chapter 5 individual employees are the members and the work unit is the collective. Member data include measures of task difficulty and variability, educational level, length of job training, and amount of discretion exercised by unit members. Relational measures include the interdependence and frequency and communications and conflict among unit members. Finally, measures of unit size, specialization, and interchangeability of jobs are global measures. In Chapter 4 global data are obtained to measure all the dimensions of environment and the structural configuration of the organization, whereas relational data are obtained to measure all the dimensions of interunit and interorganizational relations in Chapters 7 and 8.

Although global data are not aggregated because they are obtained on the collective itself, Lazarsfeld and Menzel (1969) describe a number of ways in which member and relational data can be aggregated to obtain *analytical* and *structural* properties of collectives. Analytical properties of collectives are obtained by performing some mathematical operations upon member data, whereas structural properties are computed from relational data. For example, from member data on the amount of education and training of each unit member, one can compute analytical properties of the heterogeneity of skills of personnel in an organizational unit or the distribution (i.e., the standard deviation) of education and training among members. From relational data on the frequency of communications between each member and others in a group, one could compute structural properties of the total (sum) communications among members or construct a sociogram of the centrality of communications in the unit.

A basic source of errors in aggregating data from individuals to groups is in not being clear about whether group properties are intended to have parallel meaning with individual properties. In the preceding examples, the average amount of participation by unit members and the total communications among members are analytical and structural properties of groups which have a similarity of meaning to the member and relational data on which they are based. However, heterogeneity of skills and centrality of communications apply only to the unit collective and have no parallel meaning on the level of the individual. In general, Lazarsfeld and Menzel (1969:507) state that:

> Whereas correlations, standard deviations, and similar measures always have a meaning peculiar to the group level, averages, proportions, . . . [and sums] . . . may or may not have a parallel meaning on the individual level. Lack of parallel meaning is perhaps most clearly illustrated in the concept of a "hung jury," that is, a jury rendered indecisive by its inability to reach the required unanimity. Such a state of affairs is most likely when the individual jurors are most decisive and unyielding in their convictions.

Hannan (1970) clarifies that the difference between constructing measures of dispersion and association and constructing measures of central tendency is that the latter are linear combinations of individual values whereas the former are not. Neither Lazarsfeld and Menzel

(1969) nor Hannan (1970) suggest an overall prescription for avoiding troublesome measurement and aggregation issues in moving from individual variables to collective variables. These issues are better dealt with on a specific variable-by-variable basis in which the intended and observed meanings of each variable at the individual and group levels are evaluated and made explicit. It should be clear that underlying any mathematical aggregation of data are assumptions on how the micro- and macrovariables are functionally related, that is, in what specific ways properties of individuals and collectives have similar and dissimilar meanings. To the extent that these functional relations are made conceptually explicit, one can better detect and correct aggregation errors and know more concretely the meanings of the data when they are analyzed.

7. Respondent versus Informant Roles of Subjects. Closely related to the collection of member, relational, and global data are the roles performed by people from whom data are obtained. In the OAI subjects act as *respondents** to obtain member and relational data, whereas they act as *informants* to collect global data. With member and relational data the emphasis is on information about the individual, and as a respondent the individual is asked to provide information strictly about his or her personal behavior and perceptions, or personal relations with other individuals or parts of the organization (Seidler, 1974:817). On the other hand, global data pertain to the collective as a whole and have no meaning for any particular member—consequently it would be inappropriate for the subject to act as a respondent. Instead, "informants" are used to measure global characteristics of a unit or an organization. The use of informants means asking the persons contacted to act as reporters by giving information about the group or patterns of behavior which exist outside of the persons giving the information (Zelditch, 1962).

Seidler (1974) describes in greater detail how organization researchers have used both respondent and informant approaches to measure their concepts. For example, Aiken and Hage (1968) obtained member data on participativeness by asking staff employees of welfare organizations to act as respondents in answering questions on how often they participated in making various decisions. Lawler et al. (1968) used the respondent approach to obtain relational data when they asked managers to report on their own communication patterns. On the other

---

* Thus far, the term "respondent" has been used loosely to define a person's relationship to an interview or questionnaire. In this section "respondent" refers strictly to persons who provide information about themselves as the subjects of the study.

hand, researchers have also requested people to act as informants to obtain global data. For example, Inkson et al. (1970) asked the chief executives of forty organizations where the authority lay for deciding various issues, to construct a measure of concentration of authority. In addition, executives and technical staff people were informants when they asked for information about documents, from which they derived an index of formalization. Blau and Schoenherr (1971) also relied upon informants within employment security agencies to construct their organization charts, from which they derived a number of structural configuration measures.

Sometimes researchers ask the subjects to alternate roles in the same study. For example, Georgopoulos and Mann (1962) used the same nurses as respondents when collecting data on hospital communications, and as informants when requesting ratings on the overall care received by patients. More important, Seidler (1974:818) points out that many researchers implicitly ask subjects to switch roles while answering questions in the same conceptual index. For example, among the five items used by Aiken and Hage (1968) to measure hierarchy of authority, three requested summary ratings of organizational authority patterns and two requested responses about one's own personal relations with his boss. Unless the subject is made explicitly aware of such role changes, they may confuse the person, especially when she or he is unsure of how much weight to give to judgments about behavior of self or of others. For these reasons, in the OAI we avoid switching subjects' roles while answering questions in the same conceptual index. Instead, questions pertaining to member, relational, and global data are divided into separate sections of the questionnaires, and the introduction to each section clarifies the specific types of data being asked and whether subjects are to act as respondents or informants.

The distinction between using respondents and informants also has implications for sampling. In using the respondent approach for measuring member and relational characteristics, the investigator should obtain information from a representative sample or all the individuals in each segment of the organization(s) under investigation. From this information the investigator can compute appropriate measures of analytical and structural properties with considerable confidence that they reflect the distributions of perceptions of members in the collective upon which they are based. With the informant approach one relies on a limited selective sample of people who are the most knowledgeable of the global properties of interest, or who have direct access to documents and records needed to obtain objective global data.

To the extent that little agreement (or low interrater reliability) is expected when attempting to measure certain global properties, a larger stratified sample of informants occupying different organizational positions will be necessary to obtain a balanced perspective by averaging informants' perceptions (Seidler, 1974:822).

For example, in obtaining global data on work units within organizations, the unit supervisor was used as the key informant in the OAI. For objective global characteristics of each unit (i.e., the arrangements of work flows in the unit, unit size, and specialization) only the perceptions of the unit supervisor were used. However, for global measures that were more subjective (e.g., the interchangeability of jobs among unit personnel), the perceptions of the supervisor and nonsupervisors were obtained and averaged together. To measure objective global characteristics of the total organization, we rely heavily on technical staff in the information-reporting sections of the organization to supply documents and records. However, more subjective characteristics of organization environment and the vertical and horizontal distributions of authority rely upon the perceptions of all supervisors in the organization. An assessment of the reliabilities of these alternative data collection strategies is presented in subsequent chapters.

Summary

This section has reviewed some of the literature on the multidimensional facets that influence a person's frame of reference and hence his or her judgments in response to questions about individual and organizational behavior. The underlying assumption made is that a better understanding of the judgments made by individuals can be obtained if one can specify as clearly as possible what frame of reference individuals are to take when they complete the OAI. In structuring a frame of reference into the OAI we attempted to clarify our positions on the following factors:

1. On the average, a three- to six-month historical time perspective is taken for measures in the OAI.

2. Objective measures are used for physical constructs, subjective measures for psychological constructs. This is done without reflection on the reliability or validity of either—both are highly subject to measurement error.

3. In developing the OAI, an attempt was made to define and measure all organizational context and design dimensions in

descriptive terms, whereas organizational performance, morale, and job satisfaction (the outcome criterion variables) were intended to be evaluative.

4. Five scale points with cues or anchors on each point are used as the standard response scale for questions in the OAI questionnaires.

5. The OAI obtain measures of member, relational, and global data. Member data are aggregated to obtain analytical properties and relational data are aggregated to obtain structural properties of work units and the total organization.

6. Individuals providing information of member and relational data perform a "respondent" role, whereas global data are obtained from individuals acting as "informants."

These considerations in structuring an explicit frame of reference into the OAI were not clearly specified by us when we initially embarked on this work in 1972. Instead, they became apparent through trial and error over the years in repeated attempts to evaluate and improve the content validity of the measurement instruments. A brief historical overview of the qualitative considerations in developing and evaluating the content validity of the OAI is therefore appropriate at this point.

DEVELOPING AND EVALUATING CONTENT VALIDITY OF THE OAI

The first step in development of the OAI was to operationalize theoretical constructs into measures. The sole criterion for including measures in the original 1972 OAI was their content or face validity, that is, the extent to which items appeared to be logical and understandable indicators of the constructs under consideration. Indicators were developed to relate the theoretical abstractions of each construct with everyday work situations.

The content validity of any instrument ultimately rests with the degree of consensus that can be obtained from a heterogeneous group of reviewers. As a result, many review and evaluation sessions were conducted with other organization researchers and staff (both professional and nonprofessional) from the employment security agency to assess the content validity of the OAI throughout its developmental period. Three day-long review sessions with 18 organization researchers from 13 universities were conducted between 1972 and 1976 to obtain expert judgments and evaluations of the OA theory, methodology, and measures.* Thirteen formal review sessions with at least 70 staff personnel from all program areas in the employment security agency were conducted over the years to determine whether the content of questions and items in each index were meaningful and relevant indicators of each construct.

These review sessions generally began with an overall presentation of the Organization Assessment framework and methods. Then participants were handed a paper that defined each OA construct and presented the questions or items for measuring each construct. Participants were then asked to discuss two questions: (1) "How can these questions or items be improved to measure this construct as defined previously?" (2) "Can you suggest a more efficient way to measure this construct in a reliable and valid way?" Often following the Nominal Group technique format (see Delbecq, Van de Ven, and Gustafson, 1975), reviewers were provided a short period of time to think and respond to the questions in writing. Then a general discussion ensued to obtain group opinions. The qualitative written comments from these review sessions were especially helpful in modifying the OAI in each successive version.

Before each new version of the OAI was administered throughout the agency, pilot studies were conducted on the revised OAI in a local office and an administrative bureau. Each time, about fifteen process validation interviews were conducted to determine whether respondents interpreted the questionnaire items in the way that was intended. Although no empirical data were collected on the content validity of the OAI from these review sessions and pilot studies, the researchers made every reasonable effort to continually assess the qualitative feedback, identify problems, and improve the OAI at each stage of development.

The feedback of the 1973 and 1975 OAI results by individual work units to unit supervisors provided another opportunity to assess the

* We are grateful for the many useful suggestions in developing the OAI over the years from the following: Howard Aldrich (Cornell University), Elmer Burack (Illinois Institute of Technology), Larry Cummings, Andre Delbecq, and Richard Schoenherr (University of Wisconsin—Madison), Jay Galbraith and Terry Gleason (University of Pennsylvania), Arlyn Melcher and Anant Negandhi (Kent State University), Johannes Pennings (Columbia University), Charles Perrow (State University of New York at Stony Brook), Stanley Seashore and Cortland Cammann (University of Michigan), William Starbuck (University of Wisconsin—Milwaukee), David Whetten (University of Illinois), Jon L. Pierce (University of Minnesota—Duluth), Richard Hall (State University of New York at Albany), and Richard Koenig (Temple University).

content validity of the OAI. From December 1973 to May 1974, six day-long feedback and training sessions were conducted to report the results of the 1973 OAI to all office and bureau managers. OAI scores for each of the 318 work units were detailed in individual reports and presented to office managers and unit supervisors. From November 1975 to April 1976, ten day-long feedback and training sessions were conducted to report the results of the 1975 OAI survey to all office managers and unit supervisors. Again, individual reports summarizing the OAI scores for each of the 334 work units were prepared and distributed to the unit supervisors and managers responsible for those units.

During these 1973 and 1975 OAI feedback sessions each manager and unit supervisor spent a full day analyzing and interpreting the descriptive scores on the OAI dimensions for their own work units. After the feedback sessions supervisors were asked to conduct similar feedback sessions with their respective unit employees by presenting and discussing their unit OAI scores. In addition they were asked to report back to the agency administrators on a series of issues which included a question on the validity of the unit OAI descriptive reports. The results of these reports were rewarding. Appropriate challenges to the validity of certain items in the OAI were reported to exist in about ten percent (30 of the 318 units) of the 1973 OAI units and less than three percent (9 of the 334 units) of the 1975 OAI unit summary reports.

PSYCHOMETRIC PROCEDURES FOR EVALUATING THE OAI

Measurements of organizational and human behavior are not error-free. Therefore, generalizations from such measures to theories of behavior are subject to uncertainty in a measurement paradigm. Hence, uncertainty can provide an indication of the level of explanation and prediction possible. The reader is referred to Cronbach and Gleser (1965), Cronbach, Gleser, Nanda, and Rajaratnam (1972), and Lord and Novick (1968) for a more sophisticated treatment of current models of measurement error and models of reliability, and to Campbell (1976) and Nunnally (1967) for a general treatment of psychometric theory. Finally, the American Psychological Association provides standards (1974) for designing and evaluating tests and measurement instruments.

The concepts of reliability and validity form the basis for evaluating the OAI. In the most general sense, reliability concerns the consistency, stability, or dependability with which an instrument measures a set of dimensions. Validity refers to whether or not an instrument accurately measures what it is intended to measure. The two criteria are highly interdependent mathematically (Lord and Novick, 1968), and from a practical standpoint Campbell (1976) observes that the concept of reliability becomes indistinguishable from that of validity. As a consequence, it is not surprising that there is much confusion and debate among methodologists on operational definitions and procedures for estimating various forms of reliability and validity of a measurement instrument.

To avoid becoming caught up in this debate on terminology, we have chosen to evaluate the OAI from two basic perspectives that are equally important in judging the merits of any measurement instrument, intrinsic and extrinsic validity. The *intrinsic validity* of an instrument refers to how well it measures what it is intended to measure in a consistent way, while *extrinsic validity* focuses on the practical usefulness of the instrument in addressing the basic research or applied problems with which it was intended to deal. The remainder of this chapter describes the psychometric procedures used to evaluate the intrinsic and extrinsic validity of the OAI. Results using these procedures on various components of the OAI are presented in subsequent chapters.

Intrinsic Validity

The procedures used to evaluate the intrinsic validity of the OAI are factor analysis, indices of internal consistency, discriminant validity, and correlations of selected dimensions with parallel measures.

Factor analysis is commonly used in test and instrument construction as a heuristic procedure for identifying orthogonal scales, selecting the best items within each scale, and thus imputing a *post hoc* theoretical meaning and definition to each scale. Although such a procedure is intuitively useful for identifying constructs and selecting items, it magnifies chance error and promotes a *post hoc* interpretation that is consistent with the data.

An alternate use of factor analysis, and the one adopted here, is hypothesis testing (Kerlinger, 1973:687). The questions being addressed using this procedure are: (1) How well do items designed to measure a construct converge by loading together as a single factor? and (2) How well do items designed to measure other constructs discriminate by breaking out as different factors? As described previously, the OAI constructs are based on a theoretical framework, and the indices designed to measure each construct evolved into their present form from previous administrations, evaluations, and revisions of the 1972 and 1973 OAI.

A principal components factor analysis was performed on various parts of the OAI discussed in subsequent chapters. Principal factors were extracted from the correlation matrix with unities as diagonal elements. The factors with eigenvalues or characteristic roots greater than one were extracted and obliquely rotated with an oblimin procedure to final solution. Eigenvalues equal to or greater than one are a convention established by Kaiser for identifying the number of factors that are "necessary, reliable, and meaningful for the explanation of the correlations among variables" (Harman, 1967:168). Oblique rotation was used because the indices included in each factor analysis are hypothesized to be interrelated as the theory suggests.

The factors in each final solution were then evaluated in terms of the hypothesized structure. Departures from the hypothesized structures were identified by observing where indices broke apart into different factors and where individual items were confounded by loading highly (above a conventional .40 cutoff level) on more than one factor. In addition, the eigenvalues and percent of common variance accounted for by each factor were used to evaluate the "explanation" of unit or organization design. As in previous evaluations of the 1972 and 1973 OAI, departures from expected structures in 1975 OAI become one source of information for identifying where further improvement in the OAI is necessary. The reader is referred to Gorsuch (1974) for a more complete discussion of these factor-analytic procedures.

The factor-analytic results from each analysis were examined with three further procedures to evaluate different criteria of the intrinsic validity of the OAI indices:

1. coefficient alpha to estimate the internal consistency of each index,

2. median correlations of items within an index with items in all other indices to determine how well each index discriminates from others, and

3. correlations with parallel measures to evaluate the criterion-related validity for some of the indices. These procedures are discussed in the following sections.

1. Coefficient Alpha. The internal consistency of items within each index was evaluated by obtaining reliability estimates from the average correlation among items in an index with coefficient alpha: $\alpha = (k\bar{r})/(1 + (k - 1)\bar{r}$, where k is the number of items and $\bar{r}$ is the average intercorrelation among all items in an index (Cronbach, 1951). Coefficient alpha is concerned with detecting measurement error due to a lack of internal consistency in responses to items within an index. If coefficient alpha is low for an index, the items in the index are probably not operational referents of the same construct. Nunnally (1967) notes that coefficient alpha provides a good estimate of reliability in most situations because (1) the major source of measurement error is normally due to sampling content, and (2) the reliability estimates based upon internal consistency actually consider other sources of error such as those based upon sampling situations.

Although coefficient alpha is commonly used and reported in the literature as an indicator of the internal consistency of an index, no standards or guidelines exist on what magnitudes of the coefficient are adequate for alternative measurement scales. Therefore, a set of standards was developed for evaluating the internal consistency of the OAI indices.

The major criterion in developing a standard for coefficient alpha was the sampling scope of a construct. The scope of a construct refers to the number of conceptually distinct terms (Kaplan, 1964) or elements (Kerlinger, 1973) necessary to define the breadth of meaning of a construct. For example, in Chapter 5 task variability is defined as a narrow construct because it includes only one conceptually distinct term, the number of exceptions encountered in the work by an organizational unit. Task difficulty, on the other hand, is a moderately broad construct because it is defined by two terms, the analyzability and predictability of a unit's work. As exemplified here, the conceptual scopes of all constructs in the OAI were classified according to whether their definitions were narrow, moderately broad, or broad (or whether they consisted of one, two, or three or more conceptually distinct terms, respectively). The following criteria were then used to establish standards on the expected ranges of coefficient alpha for indices measuring constructs of varying domain breadth.

	Breadth of Construct Measured by Index		
	Broad Construct (3 or more terms)	Moderately Broad Construct (2 terms)	Narrow Construct (1 term)
1. Number of items in index (k)	3	3	3
2. Expected average correlation among items ($\bar{r}$)	.10–.25	.30–.45	.50–.65
3. Expected range of coefficient alpha for index (α)	.35–.55	.55–.70	.70–.90

Beyond $\alpha = .90$ we believe the items in a three-item index become too redundant and inefficient for the kind of measurement scales being developed here.

The preceding standards were set on the basis of only three items in an index. Coefficient alpha is not only determined from the average correlation among items but also the number of items in an index. This is clearly shown in Figure 3-2, which plots values of coefficient alpha as a function of the number of items in an index (k) and the average correlation among items ($\bar{r}$). Therefore, appropriate modifications to the standards preceding need to be made for using coefficient alpha to evaluate the internal consistency of indices varying in length. The decision rules on expected ranges on coefficient alpha should not be considered an iron-clad rule for evaluating the internal consistency of measurement scales. Instead they are intended as a rough rule of thumb for making coefficient alpha a useful criterion for evaluating the internal consistency of measurement indices that may vary in sampling domain and number of items.

    2. *Median Correlation with Other Index Items.* One indication of the discriminant validity of items used to measure a construct is the median correlation between the items designed to measure a construct with all other items designed to measure other constructs included in the instrument (Hackman and Oldham, 1975). When viewed in conjunction with estimates of the internal consistency reliability, they provide another indication of the degree to which items are measuring a single construct. An indication of discriminant validity for an index is shown when the median correlation of items in that index with items in other indices is low (and smaller than the average intercorrelation of items within the index).

    3. *Parallel Measures* were developed for a number of constructs in the OAI to determine the criterion-related validities of selected indices. Here, two different approaches were developed to measure the same construct. The correlation between these parallel measures provides an indication of how well a selected OAI index measures what it is intended to measure.

Extrinsic Validity

Equally important as the intrinsic validity of the OAI is its extrinsic validity or its practical utility in achieving the basic and applied organizational research objectives described in Chapter 1. For each of the four major parts of the OAI (i.e., macroorganization design, work unit design, individual job design, and interunit relations) extrinsic validity

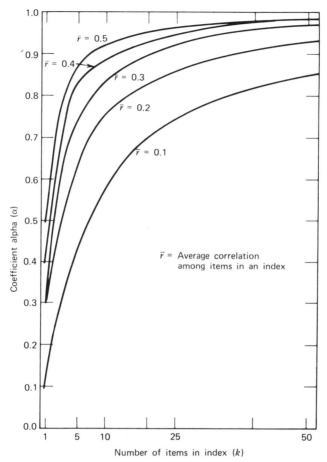

Figure 3-2 Plot of coefficient alpha as a function of the number of items in an index and the average intercorrelation of items. (We are grateful to our colleague Professor Terry C. Gleason, who developed this figure and gave permission to present it here.)

was evaluated in three basic ways. First, the OAI indices were interrelated to determine how well observed correlations corresponded with the theoretically expected pattern of relationships among the dimensions. Second, analyses of variance on the OAI indices were computed to determine how well the OAI indices detect and discriminate between different types of organizational units, jobs, and interunit relationships. Third, correlation and multiple regression analyses were used to determine the percentage of variation in performance that was explained by the OAI indices. Indices that measure macroorganizational constructs were related to overall organizational indicators of efficiency, effectiveness, and job satisfaction. The OAI indices measuring work unit design were related to the unique measures of performance efficiency and effectiveness for which different types of units in employment security offices were held accountable. Finally OAI measures of job design were correlated with job satisfaction and work motivation. These relationships between the OAI indices and various measures of performance provide an indication of concurrent validity (APA standards, 1974), or the ability of the OAI indices to explain the ultimate criterion variables in the assessment of organizations.

Criterion measures of organization and unit performance were obtained from existing performance reporting systems used by the employment security agency in which the OAI was developed and is being tested. As described in greater detail in Chapter 2, performance is a value judgment that reflects the criteria used by decision makers to judge how well an organization and its units achieve their operating objectives. The problems of operationalizing performance are compounded by the fact that different units within complex organizations strive to attain and are held accountable for different effectiveness goals. In developing the performance criteria, we first asked the administrators of the employment security agency to indicate what measures from their reporting systems could be used as "relevant" criteria for evaluating the efficiency and effectiveness of each of the basic types of units in district employment security offices. The administrators suggested five efficiency and four effectiveness measures (one for each type of unit) that are used as the major criteria by the Federal Department of Labor for allocating resources to state and local employment security agencies.

Efficiency is defined as the ratio of the quantity of output divided by the number of personnel positions (or working hours) used to produce the output. The efficiency measures used for five basic kinds of units in ES offices are as follows:

1. Intake and claims processing units—the number of initial and continued unemployment claims taken and processed per position, and the number of new job applicants processed per position time spent on these functions;

2. Adjudication units—the number of disputed unemployment compensation claims determined and resolved per position time spent on this function;

3. Placement and employer relations units—the number of job seekers placed into jobs per position time spent on this function;

4. Employment counseling units—the number of individuals given unemployment counseling and special employment development services per position time spent on these functions; and

5. Work incentive units (WIN)—the number of WIN clients placed into jobs per position time spent on this function.

Effectiveness is defined as the percentage of attainment of production goals. The effectiveness measures selected by the ES managers for evaluating the different kinds of ES units are as follows:

1. Intake claims processing units—no measure of the percent of goal attainment was available in the ES agency performance reporting system;

2. Adjudication—the percentage of decisions (or determinations) to resolve unemployment compensation claims disputes that were not appealed by employers or claimants to higher judiciary decision-making bodies;

3. Placement and employer relations units—the percentage of all available job openings or orders from community employers which were filled by placement of job applicants from the ES office;

4. Employment counseling units—the percentage of all individuals who were placed into jobs after counseling by ES employment counselors; and

5. Work incentive units—the percentage of all WIN clients who were deregistered or taken off public welfare roles (AFDC) after they were placed into jobs that provide yearly salaries higher than the poverty level.

The third criterion that is used for evaluating the concurrent validity of the OAI indices is the average level of job satisfaction of unit personnel, which was measured in the same way for all ES units in the OAI supervisory and employee questionnaires. The job satisfaction index was adopted from the Survey of Organizations (Taylor and Bowers, 1972) and was computed as the average response obtained to six questions that asked how satisfied employees were with their job, supervisor, pay, co-workers, career progress up to now, and chances for career advancement in the future.

Table 3-1 reports the correlations among the different unit efficiency, effectiveness, and job satisfaction measures, as well as their means and standard deviations. The table shows that the various unit performance measures are either unrelated or positively correlated with two exceptions. The exceptions are the substantial negative relationships between the efficiency and effectiveness criteria of adjudication units with the efficiency of counseling units. Pragmatically, these are not important exceptions because the number of job applicants counseled per position was ranked the least important of the six efficiency measures by the ES agency administrators. Overall then, the data suggest that enhancing efficiency is not at the expense of either effectiveness or job satisfaction for a given unit. Similarly, increasing the efficiency, effectiveness, and job satisfaction of personnel in one unit does not occur at the expense of decreasing the performance of other units (with the exception noted) or of ES offices as a whole. Thus, the problem of suboptimization often found in other studies does not exist in this sample of ES offices (that is, where the optimal performance of a given unit is at the expense of other units or the overall performance of the organization).

As Table 3-1 shows, large variances on the raw fiscal year scores were obtained on these efficiency and effectiveness measures. To examine their interrelations as well as their correlations with the OAI dimensions, a z-score transformation of each efficiency and effectiveness measure was computed, which yielded means of zero and standard deviations of one. This provided a common metric for comparing the relative efficiency and effectiveness of different units.

The z-score transformations of the efficiency and effectiveness measures were also used to compute overall composite scores of the efficiency and effectiveness of ES offices to evaluate the concurrent validity of the macroorganization indices in the OAI. These overall composite office efficiency and effectiveness measures also permit one to examine which characteristics of each unit contribute to overall office performance. Such an analysis is needed because units within employment security offices, like units in most organizations, are interdependent, and the optimal performance of a given unit in an office may be at the expense of reducing performance for the overall office.

Based upon the composite office efficiency measure, the 29 district offices in the state were classified into low, medium, and high levels of efficiency and effectiveness. Table 3-2 shows the average raw scores of the top third and bottom third performing offices on the five efficiency and effectiveness criteria during fiscal year 1975. The middle third performing offices were excluded to minimize classification error. The

Table 3-1 Means, Standard Deviations, and Correlations among Unit Efficiency, Effectiveness, and Job Satisfaction for 269 Units in 29 District Employment Security Offices

	Mean[a]	SD	1	2	3	4	5	6	7	8	9	10
Unit Efficiency Measures												
1. # Job Applicants Received & Processed/Position	2,470.0	983.3										
2. # UC Claims Processed/Position	19,263.7	2447.9	.19									
3. # UC Disputes Determined/Position	2,615.6	884.0	.09	.06								
4. # Job Placements/Position	560.9	226.1	.23	.50	.16							
5. # Job Applicants Counseled/Position	754.9	306.2	.19	.24	-.54	.20						
6. # WIN Placements/Position	123.9	69.1	.33	.19	.34	.39	.26					
Unit Effectiveness Measures												
7. % UC Determinations Not Appealed	92%	.04	.15	.20	.64	.34	-.43	.45				
8. % Job Openings Filled	63%	.10	.00	.47	.22	.62	.19	.26	.18			
9. % Clients Placed after Counseling	17%	.08	.17	.45	.23	.28	-.03	.04	.38	.54		
10. % WIN Clients Taken off Welfare	48%	.17	.33	.32	.50	.25	-.05	.46	.79	.38	.45	
11. **Job Satisfaction of Unit Personnel**	3.56	.55	.02	.16	.12	.19	.05	.20	.30	.15	.16	.20

[a] The actual fiscal 1975 year-end means and standard deviations on the efficiency and effectiveness measures are reported here for the units included in the sample. However, the correlations are based upon z-score transformations of each measure (yielding means of zero and standard deviations of one), to avoid spurious effects in correlations among variables with widely differing distributions.

Table 3-2 Percentage Differences between High and Low Efficient District Employment Security Offices

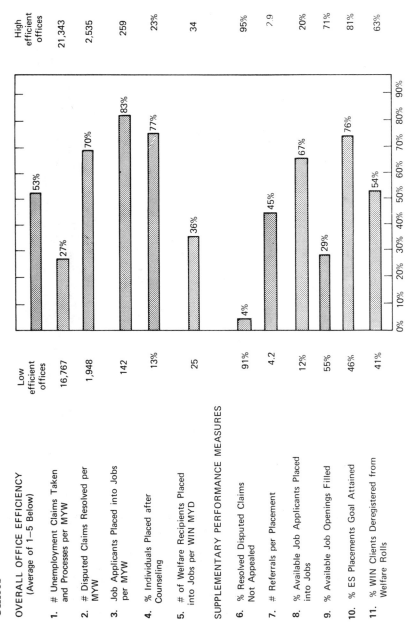

	Low efficient offices		High efficient offices
OVERALL OFFICE EFFICIENCY (Average of 1–5 Below)			
1. # Unemployment Claims Taken and Processes per MYW	16,767		21,343
2. # Disputed Claims Resolved per MYW	1,948		2,535
3. Job Applicants Placed into Jobs per MYW	142		259
4. % Individuals Placed after Counseling	13%		23%
5. # of Welfare Recipients Placed into Jobs per WIN MYD	25		34
SUPPLEMENTARY PERFORMANCE MEASURES			
6. % Resolved Disputed Claims Not Appealed	91%		95%
7. # Referrals per Placement	4.2		7.9
8. % Available Job Applicants Placed into Jobs	12%		20%
9. % Available Job Openings Filled	55%		71%
10. % ES Placements Goal Attained	46%		81%
11. % WIN Clients Deregistered from Welfare Rolls	41%		63%

Bar chart values: 53%, 27%, 70%, 83%, 77%, 36%, 4%, 45%, 67%, 29%, 76%, 54%

table shows that there are substantial percentage differences between the low and high performing offices.

However, the composite office efficiency measure is not directly appropriate for assessing the concurrent validity of the OAI indices at the work unit level of analysis. Unfortunately, the performance reporting systems in the employment security agency only records performance by office and does not break it down by work units or individuals. Therefore, to directly relate OAI indices of work unit design to work unit efficiency, an assumption was made that allocated units' time to the performance of the specific functions listed. Although there is some overlapping of functions between units in local offices, in the main it was observed that this assumption is supportable. However, a further complication exists in those local offices that have a number of the same kinds of units (e.g., two or more placement units) because different OAI unit design scores would be related to the same single measure of efficiency in the respective functional area that is available for that office. (This problem is most severe in one large metropolitan ES office in this sample (Milwaukee). This office was therefore excluded from the analysis when evaluating the concurrent validity of the OAI unit design indices). It must be recognized, however, that the absence of a unit performance reporting system to relate unit design with unit performance does limit our evaluation of the concurrent validity of the OAI unit indices in this study.

CONCLUSION

This chapter has described the historical evolution of the OAI, and the considerations taken into account over the years to develop, evaluate, and revise it. To make the OAI applicable in a wide variety of organizations, we described the qualitative considerations and decisions made to create a set of measurement instruments that: (1) are simple to understand, (2) are inexpensive to administer, (3) are standardized, so results are comparable from unit to unit and organization to organization, and (4) include an explicit and consistent frame of reference to guide respondents and informants in interpreting and answering questions. Activities undertaken over the years to establish and evaluate the content validity of the OAI were also described. Finally, we reported the quantitative methods that were used for evaluating the statistical properties of reliability and validity of the OAI indices. Results from these psychometric methods can now be reported in subsequent chapters.

CHAPTER FOUR

Overall Organization Context and Structure

A discussion or analysis of an organization invariably begins with a description of its general context and an illustration of its organization chart. This common practice is not just a formality or habit. It is necessary to provide the uninitiated with an overview of the social and economic domain in which the organization operates and a simple "picture" of the structural configuration of the organization as a whole. The organization chart provides useful background information for in-depth assessment of an organization, and comparative studies across organizations have shown that much of the variation in overall organization structure is explained by organizational context or domain.

This chapter examines the selected dimensions of organization context and structure listed and briefly defined in Figure 4-1. At the macroorganizational level, we define structure in terms of the skeletal division of labor and authority in an organization illustrated by the organization chart. Its underlying dimensions are the degrees of vertical, horizontal, and spacial differentiation; the forms of departmentation; and the allocation of administrative overhead. The organization chart, when supplemented with the perceptions of informants on the question which Rossi (1957) asks, "Who makes what decisions where?" also provides an overall understanding of the structure of authority in an organization. The reason why we focus on these structural dimensions is because they are basic to solving the organization design problem at the overall organizational level of analysis. As we discuss more fully in this chapter, the organization design problem is principally concerned with (1) the division of labor in terms of degrees of differentiation and forms of departmentation, (2) the interdependence and suboptimization among organizational components that

CONTEXTUAL FACTORS

DOMAIN FACTORS

Organization Age and History*
–No. of years in existence
–Description of origin and history
Organization Domain Type*
–Types of functions performed
–Types of products/services rendered
–Populations and markets served
Domain Uncertainty
–Agreement on goal priorities
–Clarity of knowing how to respond to
  events occuring in domain
Domain Complexity
–No. of different products/services,
  markets, and territories organization
  operates in
Domain Restrictiveness*
–Degree of external mandates and
  regulations
–Slack and transferability of resources
–Specificity of domain statement

$\longleftrightarrow$

**STRUCTURAL
CONFIGURATION FACTORS**

Vertical Differentiation
–No. of supervisory levels
Horizontal Differentiation
–No. of sections, units, and job titles
Spacial Differentiation
–No. of geographical operating sites
Forms of Departmentation*
–By function, program, geography,
  matrix at upper levels of
  organization
Administrative Intensity
–Supervisor–staff ratio
–Manager's span of control
Distribution of Power and Authority
–Relative amounts of influence in
  making specific decisions by
  different supervisory levels,
  organizational units, and other
  interest groups

$\updownarrow$

ECONOMIC FACTORS

$\longleftrightarrow$

Demand for Products or Services
–Production quota for period
–Projected no. clients/customers
Supply or Size of Resources Available
–No. of employees in period
–Production/service capacity
–Operating budget for period

*Figure 4-1   Conceptual scheme for examining overall organiza-
tion context and structural configuration. Dimensions marked
with an asterisk (*) are new additions to the Organization
Assessment Framework and were not included in the 1975 OAI.
Hence, their measurement properties cannot be evaluated here.*

division of labor creates, and (3) the structure of authority and reporting relationships established to manage interdependence and conflict. Once an analyst understands this skeletal resolution to the organization design problem at the macro level, then he or she can begin to systematically examine the designs of organizational components as well as their relationships with their respective environments, as is discussed in subsequent chapters.

Conventionally, organization context refers to all the conditions and factors external to the organization or unit under consideration (Blau and Schoenherr, 1971:206). In this sense, context is closely related to earlier definitions of the environment as the set of constraining phenomena that exist external to the organization but within which the organization must function (Van de Ven et al., 1974). These definitions imply, however, that organizations have no choice or control over their environment or context. Expanding upon the definition provided by Pugh et al., (1969), we define organization context as the social and economic setting in which an organization chooses to operate. In other words, context is defined as those dimensions within the control of an organization that create the setting for the development of organizational structure. The contextual factors examined in the OAI focus on two clusters of dimensions: (1) the nature of the domain chosen by organizational decision makers and (2) economic factors of demand and supply that designate the resources available (the budget) and the production goals of products or services. After a discussion of the conceptual bases for these macroorganizational context and structure dimensions, operational definitions and measures developed to date in the OAI are presented and evaluated.

CONCEPTUAL PERSPECTIVE ON ORGANIZATION CONTEXT AND STRUCTURE

The design of an organization is neither a naturally nor deterministically occurring condition for given states of nature. Rather the structure and functioning of organizations are the result of strategic choices made either implicitly or explicitly by coalitions of people both within and outside the organization (Child, 1972; Galbraith, 1977; Pfeffer, 1978). In Chapter 2 these coalitions of people were called users or stakeholders. In practice, management is usually considered the dominant coalition, although organizational employees, board members, funders, suppliers, and customer groups should also be considered as important coalitions who have a stake in the way an organization is structured.

However, to argue that organizations are designed by strategic choice does not suggest what kinds of decisions are made and what criteria are used as the bases for making strategic decisions. The basic premise underlying the macroorganizational context and structure dimensions listed in Figure 4-1 is that management must make at least three key sets of inter-related decisions for an organization to operate on an ongoing basis.

1. Choose the domains in which the organization will operate.

2. Solve the economic production function problem to determine the budget and the level of production or services for an operating period.

3. Solve the organization design problems.

Although these three sets of decisions are highly interdependent and are made iteratively, it is instructive to examine each separately first and then look at how they are related.

Choice of Organizational Domain

The prevailing thought today is that organizations act to create their own environments by choosing the domains in which they operate (Weick, 1969; 1977; Child, 1972; Pfeffer, 1978; Miles and Snow, 1978). *Domain* refers to the specific goals of an organization in terms of the functions it performs, the products or services it renders, and the target populations and markets it serves. In this sense, domain is similar to what Chandler (1962:13) defines as *strategy*, or "the determination of the basic long-term goals and objectives of the enterprise and the adoption of courses of action and the allocation of resources necessary for carrying out these goals." (We view the allocation of resources as more a part of the economic production function problem than of domain choice, as described below.)

Past choices and behavior constrain future choices and behavior. Therefore, the choice of organizational domain tends to be more visible in younger organizations because they can be more flexible in exploring various opportunities and in experimenting with new management philosophies, goals, and alternative organizational techniques (Miles and Snow, 1978). In contrast, older organizations have learned from and made significant commitments to past decisions or sunk costs on the domain, scale of capital and financial operations, and organization structure. Unless confronted with major financial or external crises, practice has shown that the dominant coalitions within organizations tend to rationalize their past decisions and resist changes in organizational structures because structure largely reflects the outcomes of past power struggles among coalitions within organizations (Pfeffer, 1978). Therefore, with increasing organizational age, we should expect increasingly marginal adjustments to be made in domain choices and an increasing tendency for goals and the meaning of organizational action to be inferred retrospectively, or after the action has occurred.

Weick (1969), Pfeffer (1978), and others have come to the conclusion that goals and other "purposive" statements for an organization are really attempts to make sense out of actions that have already occurred, rather than plans for the future. The implication is that the concept of goals or purposive organizations is of little use in understanding organization behavior. Without historical understanding of the evolution of domain choice, such a conclusion is seductively appealing. We counter this conclusion by simply asking: What produced the actions that have occurred in the first place? Although one can quickly become embroiled in a chicken-or-the-egg controversy, we submit that if this question is traced over time, much of the subsequent action in a given organization is based on the implicit or explicit statements of purpose, mission, or domain for the organization by a succession of founders, entrepreneurs, and dominant coalitions.

The choice of a domain (a line of business or services for a target population and set of markets) powerfully influences other choices that organizations make. For example, a firm's decision to retail hardware, market drugs, or publish a newspaper for a local, state, or international market implies great differences in the financing and capitalization needed (the economic production function problem) and the kinds of structures and processes it will employ (the organization design problem). Indeed, without a domain choice there is little point in making these other choices.

To systematically assess these implications, we examine three dimensions underlying the type of domain chosen by an organization: uncertainty, complexity, and restrictiveness (see Figure 4-1). Although these dimensions have been used extensively by other researchers to characterize organization environments, we apply them to the domain of an organization to emphasize the point that in varying degrees organizations create their own environments by their choice of domain.

1. Domain Uncertainty. Implied in the type of domain chosen by an organization is the level of uncertainty with which it chooses to live. At the idealized pole of domain uncertainty, decision makers can easily understand and analyze the mission and goals of the organization and the means for achieving them. Operationally, this means that they agree on operating goals and priorities and that they can predict and respond consistently to events and issues.

Defined in this way, domain uncertainty is the basic dimension underlying most conceptions of organizational *rationality*. March and Simon (1958) and Thompson (1967) point out that rational action is rooted on the one hand in *known or agreed upon outcomes* or ends, and on the other hand in *certainty about cause–effect relationships*. To the extent that people agree on the outcomes desired of an organization and the activities performed are believed or judged to produce the desired outcomes, one can speak of rational behavior. Thus, rational decision-making about an organization's domain, resource allocation, and structural design is based on: (1) defining and agreeing upon the organization's domain and (2) determining cause–effect relationships among means and outcomes.

More correctly, when these dimensions of uncertainty are dichotomized according to Thompson and Tuden's (1959) well-known typology of decision strategies (see Figure 4-2), it becomes apparent that rational behavior assumes known and agreed-upon goals or ends, and rationality varies directly with the extent to which means to given ends are known or understood (i.e., the left column of Figure 4-2). Where the means to achieve given ends are readily known, decisions can be programmed using a computational strategy that Thompson and Tuden (1959) indicate is most efficiently performed in a bureaucracy by specialists, with one specialist for each computational problem. When the means to a desired end are unclear or unknown, however, nonprogrammed decisions are required and can be dealt with in a rational

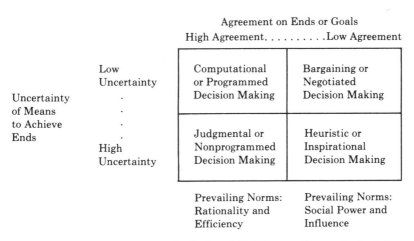

Figure 4-2   Thompson and Tuden (1959) typology of decision-making strategies under varying conditions of agreement on ends and uncertainty of means.

way by reducing them to a series of programmed decisions (Simon, 1977:40). Alternatively, Thompson and Tuden (1959) and Shull, Delbecq, and Cummings (1970) have proposed an organizational structure and strategy for judgmental or collegial decision making among experts or professionals. These variations in rational decision making strategies are quite well known because most theories of organization and management assume organizational decision makers and participants agree on the desired outcomes or ends.

However, when there is little or no agreement on the domain or goals of an organization, the rational model is replaced with organizational structures and strategies for bargaining and inspiration (Thompson and Tuden, 1959). Central to nonrational theories of choice are the concepts of power, social influence, and conflict among coalitions within the organization—each attempting to achieve its own ends. Pfeffer (1978) goes into greater detail, indicating that when there are substantial disagreements on the domain or ends of an organization, coalitions within the organization are in a continual contest for power and a continual process of conflict and negotiation.

> Individuals enter and leave the contests as their strength and interests dictate, but some level of change and negotiation does continue as a process in the organization. Conflict is uncomfortable to most organizational participants, and moreover, to undertake long struggles over each decision would be too time consuming. Consequently, precedent becomes very important in organizational decision-making. Once an acceptable basis for resource allocation is achieved or once a set of policies (or a structure for the organization) is adopted, precedent becomes the guide to future organizational decisions. This avoids reopening negotiations, which might reactivate the conflict and involve a lot of time and effort . . . and precedent will operate as long as the existing balance of influence remains relatively stable. When, however, the distribution of influence within the organization shifts dramatically from what it had been when the initial set of bargains was reached, it is likely that those who have gained influence will attempt to re-open the negotiation, seeking to throw away precedent and to establish a new basis for future organizational actions.   (Pfeffer, 1978:14)

2. Domain Complexity is the diversity and range of products, markets, and geographical territories that decision makers choose for the organization. Domain complexity is the dimension that underlies much of the theory and research on how diversification strategies affect organization structure. For example, based on the historical work of Chandler (1962), Wrigley (1970) and Rumelt (1974) examined how the following four different types of diversification strategies were related to departmentation: single-product, dominant, related, and unrelated businesses. Underlying this typology are increasing degrees of domain complexity.

Managing a complex domain requires more information processing and mutual adjustments among interdependent functions and activities than does dealing with a simple domain (Dill, 1958; March and Simon, 1958; Child, 1972; Duncan, 1972; Osborn and Hunt, 1974; Galbraith, 1977). Since the human brain has a limited capacity for retaining conscious information, as domains become more complex, organizations will increasingly segment their domains into homogeneous functions, products, markets, or territories, and adopt unique strategies and structures for coping with each (Thompson, 1967; Jurkovich, 1974). By developing separate structural divisions within the organization to manage each major distinctive component of the domain, each organizational division in effect manages a simple domain.

Differentiation creates problems of coordination and control among organizational components because complex domains can seldom be divided into a set of *independent* simple domains. In addition, personnel within organizational divisions managing different domain components are likely to develop different norms about interpersonal behavior, organizational goals, structuring of activities, and time span of attention (Lawrence and Lorsch, 1967). Thus, with increasingly complex domains, there is likely to be decreasing interdivisional agreement on organizational goals, but increasing agreement on subgoals (March and Simon, 1958). In response, the top management of the organization will seek integration by (1) using a sophisticated management information system to keep track of the operations and performance of each division, (2) implementing throughout the organization those standard operating procedures and rules that seem to work well in a variety of situations (Khandwalla, 1977:338), and (3) relying upon hierarchy, boundary spanners, and group meetings to deal with exceptions and mutual adjustments. To secure cooperation of the various divisions, the decision-making process among central administration and top levels of each division will be characterized by a participative style of bargaining and negotiation to resolve disagreements on ends. Computational and judgmental decision styles will tend to be used more within divisions where greater agreement on ends is likely to exist.

3. Domain Restrictiveness. Thus far we have argued that organizations are free to choose their domains. However, as Child (1972), Khandwalla (1977), and Miles and Cameron (1978) point out, some organizations are more restricted or constrained than others to choose and alter their functions, the products and services they render, and the populations and markets that they serve. Miles and Cameron

(1978) state that the major sources of restriction on domain choices arise from external mandates and regulation, the generalizability and amount of slack in the organization's internal resources, and the specificity of the formally stated domain of an organization.

The basic dimension that distinguishes public from private sector organizations is that the former are issued or mandated with a specified domain by federal, state, or municipal laws, whereas the latter can select and alter their own domains (e.g., product line, target market, capital investment decisions). But even in the private sector, organizations choose domains whose markets or industries vary in degrees of governmental regulation, economic competition (e.g., competitive, oligopolistic, monopolistic), barriers to entry, and unionization of the labor force. Domain restrictiveness also increases with the absence of internal organizational slack, in terms of low cash reserves and many distinctive specialized personnel skills and core technologies that are difficult to generalize or use elsewhere. Miles and Cameron (1978:87) state that a final factor that influences domain restrictiveness is the manner in which organizations define and redefine their domains. The degree to which formally stated organizational domains are narrowly or broadly defined becomes particularly salient during the birth of an organization. When the founders are choosing and negotiating an initial domain and when organizations have accomplished the mission for which they were created, they must decide whether to discontinue operations or move into a new domain.

> For example, when William Ruckelshaus took over the newly formed Environmental Protection Agency (EPA), he defined the initial goal of the organization with great care. He observed that the founders of two agencies similar in nature to the EPA had defined their statutory goals either too narrowly or too amorphously, thereby threatening the life of both agencies. The National Aeronautics and Space Administration (NASA) goal had been framed very narrowly as "let's get to the moon in ten years." When they did they almost put themselves out of business. In contrast the Office of Economic Opportunity (OEO) defined its goals very amorphously as "let's do something about poverty," and consequently had difficulty demonstrating to its constituencies that it was making progress toward this objective.   (Miles and Cameron, 1978:87–88).

Although domain restrictiveness has received very little attention in previous organizational research and theory, Miles and Cameron conclude that this dimension emerged as the dominant force behind the behaviors of the Big Six tobacco companies in coping with the antismoking campaign over the past quarter century.

In the final analysis, then, it may come down to the degree of domain choice flexibility offered the organization that ultimately determines its fate and constrains the strategic choices it can make. . . . The Big Six exploited domain choice flexibility in a variety of ways. . . . First they attempted to squeeze out the existing demand for cigarette products from the existing domestic market by partitioning that market into segments based on different consumer tastes and tailoring cigarette brands and brand promotions to particular segments. Next, they responded to the smoking-and-health threat with two distinctive waves of product innovations, each producing a mix of cigarette brands which was much lower, because of advanced filtration systems and reduced tobacco content, in tar and nicotine content than the preceding generation. Third, the Big Six, in varying degrees, expanded into foreign markets in order to exploit markets not so sensitive as the domestic one to the smoking-and-health controversy. Finally, member firms diversified their domestic domains, moving into new markets for which their traditional expertise in consumer goods marketing could be used to its full potential or "young industries" which showed great promise but required capital, plentiful in the cash rich tobacco industry.   (Miles and Cameron, 1978:84–85)

In his study of 103 Canadian firms, Khandwalla (1977) examined how restrictiveness of organizational domains is related to the planning and decision-making styles of top management. He found that the degree of domain restrictiveness was significantly correlated with more planning and controlling of operations and an optimization-oriented style (or a fact- and research-based scientific approach) to decision making. This was particularly true for the firm where restrictions on domain were largely legal in nature and imposed on the organization because of its monopoly nature or because it served vital public interests. Khandwalla also found that as the domains of organizations become more restrictive, at first there is an increase and then a decrease in the coercive orientation of top management. He provides the following explanation for these findings.

Apparently, when there are few constraints, there may be little need for management to be coercive. As constraints increase, the traditional patterns of decision-making may need to be changed drastically by top management fiat in order to take into account the new constraints. However, the organization is simultaneously getting technically trained staff and installing a sound control system to deal more effectively with the constraints. If constraints should continue to increase, decision-making then relies increasingly on technocratic advice rather than on power plays by managers. In other words, organizations in highly constraining environments must rely on systems rather than on personal power to ensure that constraints are not violated and operations are efficient.   (Khandwalla, 1977:340)

The Production Function Problem

The process of choosing and redefining an organization's domain is seldom, if ever, completed. However, temporary "working solutions" are necessary for an organization to operate in a given period. They are generally reached when commitments of resources are made and an organizational structure is set in place or rearranged to achieve specific objectives relative to the overall domain. This section presents a conceptual perspective of how the domain choice of an organization is operationalized with the commitment of resources and the development of the organization's budget, whereas the next section discusses the choice of organization structure.

Under idealized conditions of low domain uncertainty and restrictiveness, the commitment of resources to selected products and markets is primarily based on *economic* considerations of *demand* and *supply*. Demand refers to the projected amounts of each line of products or services that an organization can sell or will provide during a specified operating period. Supply is the amount of resources an organization needs to produce the output with its existing technology during the operating period.

Customer (or product market) demand for an organization's outputs and the factor market's cost of inputs for supplying them are the classic elements of microeconomic theory of the firm (Samuelson, 1948). **The determination of the best level and combination of input resources for the provision of a particular level of outputs is the economic production function problem** (Henderson and Quandt, 1958:44). Under conditions of perfect certainty and competition (i.e., low domain restrictiveness), it is solved by equating marginal costs with marginal revenues. An economist's production function assumes total rationality (i.e., consensus on organizational goals and perfect knowledge of means to achieve ends) and efficiency in the design of an organization. In other words, classical microeconomic theory assumes an optimal solution to the **organization design problem, defined as the most appropriate use and transformation of a particular combination of inputs to achieve the projected levels of output.** Although these assumptions are unrealistic, they permit a starting point for integrating and understanding where microeconomic theory of the firm leaves off and where organization theory begins. Specifically, a strategic economic decision by management to solve the production function problem for a given period is prerequisite to an analysis of the structure and functioning of an organization. Without a determination of the production quota or of the land, labor, and capital available to a firm to achieve its output quota, there is no organization design problem because there is no *raison d'etre* for organizing. Thus, although the production function problem is trivial in the case of perfect certainty and competition, this case underscores that its solution is a parameter for solving the organization design problem.

1. Effects of Domain Uncertainty and Complexity. We now relax the assumption of perfect certainty of means to achieve organizational ends but maintain the assumption of agreement on ends and low domain restrictiveness (specifically a firm operating in a perfectly competitive market). Under conditions of increasing uncertainty of means to ends or events in an organization's domain, bounded rationality is introduced, and the classical economic argument shifts from maximizing to satisficing the production function problem.

Bounded rationality refers to human behavior that is "intendedly rational, but only limitedly so" (Simon, 1961:xxiv). Bounded rationality involves neurophysiological and language limits. The physical limits refer to the limited powers of individuals to receive, store, retrieve, and process information without error. Simon observes that "it is only because individual human beings are limited in knowledge, foresight, skill, and time that organizations are useful instruments for the achievement of human purpose" (1957:199). Language limits refer to the inability of individuals to articulate their knowledge or ideas through words, numbers, or graphics in ways that permit them to be understood by others. March and Simon (1958:164) indicate that language is generally well developed for describing concrete objects and things that can be classified, but poorly developed to communicate objects that are nonstandardized and not well understood.

Bounds on rationality apply, of course, only to the extent that the preceding limitations are reached, that is, under conditions of uncertainty and complexity. Moreover, domain complexity refers to the number of different actors and issues in the product and factor markets that decision makers must take into acount in solving the production function problem. In the absence of either domain uncertainty or complexity, the set of contingent actions by decisions makers can be fully specified at the outset. Thus, as Williamson (1975:22) points out, it is the joint conditions of uncertainty and complexity that occasion the economic problem. Given a highly complex but certain domain, decision makers "engineer" a solution to the production function problem through whatever degree of complexity needs to be dealt with. Similarly, given a simple but moderately uncertain domain, bounded rationality constraints are seldom reached and the production function problem can be optimized. However, under joint conditions of uncertainty and complexity it is very costly, perhaps impossible, to achieve an optimal solution because (1) the complete decision tree cannot be specified, (2) neither the alternative paths to a solution nor the rules for generating them are available, and (3) the consequences of alternatives are difficult, if not impossible, to estimate (Feldman and Kanter, 1965:615). As a result, approximation must replace exactness in reaching a decision.

Where bounded rationality but low restrictiveness prevails, the projected demand for an organization's products or services (e.g., the number of clients to be served; the quantity, quality, and mix of products to be produced) represents the opportunities open to the organization. This product market potential is generally determined by forecasting methods or consumer surveys to estimate the quantity and kind of services demanded of the firm in the next year or some other period in the future. On the basis of such projections, management determines the quantity and cost of input resources (e.g., money, raw materials, and plant or equipment) necessary for producing at projected output levels (Baumol, 1965). Under norms of rationality, firms simultaneously establish output and variable input quotas for an operating period where the marginal cost of inputs roughly approximates the marginal revenue or value of outputs.

Where there is little or no consensus among decision makers on the domain or goals for an organization, (1) norms of economic rationality are replaced with norms of social power, influence, and bargaining among conflicting coalitions (in the same way as discussed previously in selecting an organizational domain under conditions of uncertainty), and (2) the power of decision makers as reflected in the existing structure of the organization becomes the parameter to solving the production function problem. These two issues imply a complete reversal of our argument developed thus far in solving the production function problem. The first issue implies that the production function problem is no longer based on economic considerations of demand and supply but on social considerations of power and influence. The second issue implies that a solution to the production function problem is no longer a prerequisite or parameter to solving the organization design problem, but that the former is a consequence of the latter.

There is some empirical support for this alternative "nonrational" and noneconomic basis to solving the production function problem. Based on their study of budget allocations to departments in a university, Salancik and Pfeffer (1974) noted that goal statements and objective economic criteria were selectively chosen and outwardly expressed by department heads to achieve their personal or departmental self-interests. They found statistically that even after controlling for objective factors, social influence accounted for a significant amount of the variation in resource allocation (Pfeffer and Salancik, 1974). In a survey of business executives, Stagner (1969) reported that the executives said that strong subunits within the organization were frequently able to get their way without regard for the goals of the total organization. However, Pfeffer (1978:12) states that social power and influence are more likely to affect resource allocation decisions when the resources are scarce (i.e., under conditions of increasingly restrictive organizational domains).

> There is no point contending when the decision is not critical. And there is not a decision problem or a problem of allocation unless there is some element of scarcity. If every person can get all he wants, or what he wants, then there is no need to use social power and influence, because everyone can be satisfied simultaneously.   (Pfeffer, 1978:12)

We maintain that the production function problem as developed here is general for public, private, profit, or nonprofit organizations—whether it is solved rationally or nonrationally, on economic or social grounds. Normally, management makes the production function problem decision on a yearly basis; optimal—or even satisfactory—solutions are rarely, if ever, obtained. In the employment security agency, for example, the production function problem decision is made yearly through a management-by-objectives system. Local office managers negotiate with headquarters to jointly establish output quotas and resource input levels (primarily personnel positions). A satisfactory solution is reached when the budget level is believed sufficient to attain the plans of service, assuming the agency is efficiently organized and managed.

Once this strategic decision is made, then the input and output quotas become thought of by managers and employees as the *short-run goals* for an organization in a given period. The output quota becomes the operational measure of *instrumental goals*, or the intended production output and impact of the organization upon society. The input resource quota (or the budget) becomes the operational indicator of internally oriented *maintenance goals*, which are defined as the intended impact of what the organization does to maintain itself. Because both input and output quotas must be attained jointly to solve the production function problem, the instrumental and maintenance goals of an organization are equally important. "Each may be viewed both as a limitation upon and a subgoal of the attainment of the other" (Mohr, 1973:476).

2. Effects of Domain Restrictiveness. Now we relax the assumption of an unrestricted organizational domain and admit to conditions of increasing economic, governmental, and social constraints, as well as scarce internal organizational resources. Under these conditions, organizational decision makers have less freedom in solving the production function problem. We infer from Thompson (1967) that organizations with increasingly restrictive domains have three available strategies for solving the production function problem.

One strategy for obtaining closure on the production function problem is to decrease a firm's dependence on the factor markets by limiting, smoothing, or rationing outputs to the product market. This reactive set of strategies largely limits an organization's production quotas to the quantity of resources it controls during an operating period. We would expect these reactive strategies when an organization faces a highly restrictive environment and when decision makers are willing to sacrifice personal motivations for uncertainty reduction.

A second basic strategy is for organizations to decrease their dependence on any single source (while maintaining or even increasing their total dependence on the environment) by seeking additional alternative sources of supply and customer markets. In effect, this second strategy suggests that a firm can decrease its domain restrictiveness by increasing its domain complexity and diversifying its dependence, thereby reducing its uncertainty or risk. We would expect this strategy to be employed with firms operating in relatively competitive markets; if the environment contains not only many alternative sources of supply but also many product markets with the requisite demand, then we are at or near the point that economists describe as perfect competition (Thompson, 1967:32).

A third basic set of strategies for an organization to obtain the resources needed to solve its production function problem is to expand control over its domain (i.e., decrease domain restrictiveness) by seeking prestige, contracting, co-opting, and coalescing or merging with other organizations that represent critical contingencies for the organization. Thompson indicates that these proactive methods, in order, increasingly expose an organization to its environment (thereby increasing domain uncertainty), and tend to be employed with increasingly restrictive domains.

The second and third strategies are analogous to the markets and hierarchies framework proposed by Williamson (1975). He argues that the decision over whether resource transactions are executed across markets (strategy 2) or within the hierarchy of a firm (strategy 3) depends on the degree of opportunism of the decision makers involved and the perceived uncertainty and restrictiveness of an organization's domain. Given a constant level of opportunism or self-interest motives by decision makers, the greater the domain uncertainty and restrictiveness, the more strategy 3 is preferred over strategy 2.

Of course, combinations of the three strategies discussed previously may be employed simultaneously by organizations. This is especially true of large organizations with complex domains. Under norms of rationality, organizations facing heterogeneous environments will segment their markets and adopt unique strategies for coping with each (Thompson, 1967).

In summary, the production function problem is concerned on the one hand with making decisions on the projected quantity and mix of products or services that an organization will produce and deliver to selected markets and territories during an operating period. On the other hand, it is concerned with securing the necessary resources (land, labor, and capital) and allocating them among various divisions and components within the organization. We discussed how variations in domain uncertainty, complexity, and restrictiveness significantly affect the ways this problem is solved. Under conditions of low domain uncertainty and restrictiveness it can be solved rationally, according to microeconomic principles of supply and demand. Bounded rationality and satisficing behavior are introduced when there are joint increases in domain uncertainty (particularly disagreement on goals) and restrictiveness. The bounded rationality model based on economic criteria is increasingly replaced with a bargaining model of decision making based on social power and influence among conflicting coalitions and individuals. With increasingly complex domains, organizational decision makers are likely to be involved in all these processes simultaneously by attempting to optimize in those parts of their domains that are clear-cut, satisfice in those areas that are not well understood but generally agreed upon, and be involved in power struggles and bargaining over those components of an organization's domain where there is little agreement.

Whatever the processes used, it is clear that solutions to the production function problem are periodically and regularly necessary for an organization to continue to function. Witness, for example, how Pennsylvania state government agencies in 1977 came to a near standstill and were forced to temporarily lay off thousands of civil servants because the state legislature was in a deadlock over passing the state's budget (or solving its production function problem). A solution to the production function problem will designate the organization's production quota, which becomes the operational indicator of the organization's instrumental goals for the period. In addition, the budget, which defines the land, labor, and capital size of the organization, becomes the operational indicator of the firm's maintenance goals for the period. Given these parameters or solutions to the production function problem, one can then begin to address the organization design problem.

The Organization Design Problem

At the macro level, the organization design problem tends to be operationalized in terms of making decisions on how to divide the labor (vertical and horizontal differentiation), what forms of departmental structures to adopt (functional, program, geographical, and matrix arrangements), what span of control is appropriate for managers at each level (administrative intensity), and how power and authority are to be distributed among organizational units.

As organizations increase in size, they divide the labor (tasks and functions to be performed) and available resources (personnel, money, and technologies) and allocate them to different organizational units and positions. The division of labor makes specialization possible and enables an organization to overcome the limited information-processing capabilities and the limited set of skills of any one individual (March and Simon, 1958). Specialization has the dual benefits of (1) promoting efficiency and economy of scale by reducing a complex task into simple tasks, standardizing them, and using machines and low-cost unskilled personnel to perform them, and (2) attaining quality and successful performance of highly difficult tasks by assigning them to professional experts, who by definition and necessity tend to be trained in depth in narrow areas of inquiry (Blau, 1974). Either form of specialization permits each organizational unit to focus its effort on attaining its assigned subgoal and to filter out or ignore other problems, information and tasks related to other organizational goals. March and Simon (1958:152–153) review the research that shows that this focus of attention by each unit is reinforced by the selective frames of reference and time spans of attention within individuals, the filtering of information that occurs with in-group communications among members in a common profession, and the selective environmental information to which a unit is exposed in carrying out its assignments.

However, the benefits obtained from specialization that comes with the division of labor are limited, particularly for labor-intensive organizations. First, increasingly subdividing tasks among units implies that interdependence among units increases because each unit performs a smaller fraction of the total task. Second, each unit becomes more homógeneous internally and more different from other units in the orga-nization. The latter reinforces in-group solidarity and suboptimization (the persistence of a unit to optimize its subgoals at the expense of or in conflict with goals of the larger organization) and also increases the dif-ferentiation of values, orientations, and subgoals between units when they are becoming more interdependent. These factors explain why the incremental benefits of specialization become quickly outweighed by the costs of coordination.

Thompson (1967) offered a series of propositions for explaining how organizations will cope with these offsetting benefits and costs produced by the division of labor. Under norms of rationality organizations will minimize coordination costs by grouping together the most highly (reciprocal) interdependent units first under a common supervisor, and next, by linking the serially dependent units into adjacent sections. Thereafter, coordination costs are minimized by grouping the least interdependent units into separate divisions and allocating from a common pool the resources necessary for each division to operate in a quasi-autonomous fashion. The logical conclusion drawn from Thompson's propositions is that one can largely predict the levels of interdependence between units from an organizational chart; this is illustrated in Figure 4-3. As one moves down the vertical levels in an organization chart, there tends to be an increase in the amount of inter-dependence between the horizontally adjacent units (Van de Ven, 1976a).

Thus, the rational response to managing interdependence between segmented organizational units is to structure additional levels of supervision and to increase administrative overhead. With increases in horizontal and spacial differentiation come increases in vertical division of labor and administrative overhead to coordinate and control interde-pendence. However, as Pfeffer (1978) points out, this solution to the macroorganization design problem does not take into consideration how power and influence within the organization affect, and are affected by, the division of labor, interdependence, and integration.

Vertical differentiation may provide increased orderliness and review of organizational processes, but by providing more levels between the top and bottom of the organization, it may cause so much distortion of information that control may be lost rather than enhanced. And hori-zontal differentiation, obtained through having a large number of depart-ments, may also lead to different outcomes. On the one hand, greater integration and control efforts may be required as subunits develop subgoals and separate identities. On the other hand, creation of parallel units may lead to decreased reliance on any single one, thereby lessening its influence within the organization.

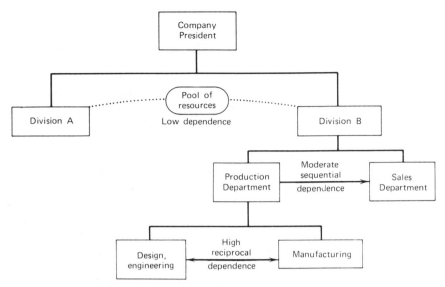

Figure 4-3 Dependencies in a divisionalized organization. The arrows point to the dependencies.

It is clear, then, that a solution to the organization design problem involves not only division of labor, interdependence, and integration, but also the distribution of power and authority within the organization. Pfeffer points out that virtually no studies have systematically examined what most practitioners clearly recognize: Organization design choices are undertaken with a consideration of the power and control of various units and positions within the organization. Although we do not propose to suggest such a systematic framework, we clearly concur with Pfeffer (1978) and Child (1972) that there is a need to begin to examine the question of power and conflict as critical components of organization design choices.

Summary

This section has presented a conceptual framework for assessing macroorganization context and structure by pulling together and making operational a number of ideas that have recently emerged but remained scattered in the literature. From a theory-building perspective, we believe that the framework makes the following contributions to the literature.

1. The framework expands the currently held view that organizations are designed by choices and not simply by natural or deterministic conditions occurring outside the organization (e.g., Child, 1972; Galbraith, 1977; Pfeffer, 1978). Our basic premise is that decision makers make choices regarding the organization's domain, the production function, and the organization design problems, and over time simultaneously live with the consequences of these choices and make adjustments in these choices for the future.

   a. The choice of a domain refers to the specific goals an organization chooses to pursue in terms of the functions it performs, the products or services it delivers, and the target populations and markets it serves. Past choices and behavior constrain future choices and behavior. Therefore, an historical assessment of the evolution of domain choices is necessary to avoid drawing the incorrect conclusion that organizations are not purposive, or goal directed, simply because goals and the meaning of actions are increasingly inferred retrospectively by organizational participants as organizations grow older.

   b. The production function problem is concerned on the one hand with making decisions on production quotas that an organization will deliver to selected markets during an operating period, and on the other hand in securing and allocating the necessary resources (i.e., money, personnel, and technologies). In an extensive review of the literature on organization size, Kimberly (1977) concluded that there is strikingly little theoretical understanding of the definition and origin of the concept of organization size. The reason, we believe, is because organization theorists have generally ignored the contributions of microeconomic theory of the firm. Specifically, it is in the solution to the economic production function problem that organization size, as a concept, originates. The number of employee positions (along with other specific line items in the organization's budget for an operating period) is one of the vital input resources that is determined or chosen by a solution to the production function problem.

   c. Central to most formulations of the organization design problem are (1) the division of labor (the degrees of horizontal and spacial differentiation and the forms of departmentation), and (2) the structure of authority and vertical reporting relationships that are established to manage the interdependence and suboptimization among organizational units. The solution to the problem is one of choosing a structure that balances the benefits of specialization against the costs of coordination and control. However, as Pfeffer (1978) points out, this is only a partial solution because it does not take the power structure of an organization into account. Thus, at the present stage of conceptualization, our framework for solving the macroorganization design problem remains incomplete.

2. We underscored the importance of three dimensions of the types of domains chosen by organizations: domain uncertainty, complexity, and restrictiveness. Our contribution here is not to suggest three new dimensions (they have existed in the literature for quite some time), but rather to synthesize and explore how they individually and jointly affect the processes and outcomes of choosing the production function and organization design problems.

   a. Domain uncertainty is the basic dimension underlying most conceptions of organizational rationality and explains the degrees to which choices regarding organizational domain, the production function, and structure are made on the bases of rationality and efficiency versus social power, influence, and bargaining.

   b. Domain complexity is the dimension that underlies most typologies of diversification strategies in the strategy–structure literature, and largely explains the degree to which organizations carve up or differentiate their production function and design problems into quasi-independent, simpler problems.

   c. Domain restrictiveness distinguishes public from private sector organizations and varies according to governmental regulation, economic competition, barriers to entry, and unionization of the labor force. Domain restrictiveness explains the extent to which organizations are free to choose their domains and to flexibly react and proact to changing social and economic conditions.

3. In addition to these main effects of domain uncertainty, complexity, and restrictiveness, we suggested a few possible interaction effects of these three dimensions on the decision-making processes used by organizations to solve the production function and organization design problems.

   a. Under idealized conditions of low domain uncertainty, complexity, and restrictiveness, the production function problem can be solved according to classical microeconomic principles of equating marginal costs with marginal revenues. With moderate increases in domain complexity, restrictiveness, and uncertainty of means to ends, bounded rationality is introduced, and the classical economic argument shifts from maximizing to satisficing the production function problem. In both perfect and bounded rationality cases, a solution to the production function problem is prerequisite to solving the organization design problem, and the application of organization theory begins where microeconomic theory of the firm leaves off.

b. However, with further increases in domain uncertainty (particularly on goals) and restrictiveness: (1) the bounded rationality model based on economic criteria is increasingly replaced with a bargaining model of decision making based on social power and influence among conflicting coalitions and individuals, and (2) a solution to the production function problem becomes decreasingly a prerequisite to, but increasingly a consequence of, the way the organization design problem (in particular, its structure of authority) is solved.

c. In addition, by examining joint variations in domain uncertainty, complexity, and restrictiveness, we were able to derive some of the basic strategies proposed by Thompson (1967) and Williamson (1975) which organizations employ to both isolate themselves from their environment and to gain control over their environments.

d. Although our theory-building efforts are far from complete, we believe that the preceding insights are sufficiently interesting to suggest that domain uncertainty, complexity, and restrictiveness provide a rich point of departure for developing a systematic framework for assessing macroorganization context and structure.

DEFINITIONS AND OAI MEASURES OF ORGANIZATION CONTEXT AND STRUCTURE

This section operationally defines and describes the measures used in the OAI (Organization Assessment Instruments) for some of the dimensions listed in Figure 4-1. The dimensions asterisked in Figure 4-1 were not included in the 1975 OAI survey of employment security organizations. Hence, we cannot evaluate here the measurement properties of the following factors: organization age, domain type, domain restrictiveness, and forms of departmentation. These factors were not measured in the 1975 OAI for two reasons: First, our conceptual scheme for assessing macroorganization context and structure had not developed to the present state, and instrument construction must necessarily lag theory building. Second, there is very little or no variation on these factors across the sample of employment security offices in which the OAI was developed over the years. As is reported in the following results section, all the offices included in the sample operate within the same governmental restrictions, resource allocation channels, and administrative structure at the state, regional, and federal levels of the Department of Labor. In addition, within each local office, the same form of functional departmentation is used, although wide variations exist in the degrees of differentiation.

Operational definitions and measures for the remaining dimensions in Figure 4-1 are now presented. However, it should be recognized at the outset that measures of the contextual dimensions are necessarily idiosyncratic to the types of organizations under investigation. Therefore, measures of the four contextual factors following should be viewed by the reader as only examples of how one might operationalize these factors because they do not generalize to other kinds of organizations. This problem, however, does not exist in the measurement of the structural dimensions; the procedures suggested are intended to apply to a wide variety of organizations.

1. Service Demand. Service demand refers to the number of products or services that are forecast to be produced or delivered by an organization for an operating period. For employment security offices, service demand is estimated from the number of clients needing services for Employment Service, Unemployment Compensation, and Work Incentive Programs.

Service demand was measured from the existing reporting systems of the agency by adding: (1) the number of ES applicants or job seekers enrolled with the agency, (2) the number of initial claims for unemployment compensation, and (3) the number of people registered at the Department of Public Welfare for entry into the Work Incentive Program. All measures of demand were based on fiscal year total figures.

2. Operating Budget for Fiscal Year (Number of Personnel Positions). The budget is the dollar value of resources used by an organization to operate for a fiscal year. The budget includes *fixed* costs (capital expenses for land, office space and buildings, and equipment), and *variable* costs (salaries, office supplies, travel, and programmatic expenses).

In very labor-intensive organizations such as employment security offices, the budget is operationalized primarily in terms of the number of personnel positions paid in an office. The Fiscal Bureau in the headquarters office of the state agency maintains and reports monthly on the number of personnel positions paid by each office.

*3. **Domain Uncertainty***. Domain uncertainty is a broad construct that refers to the degree to which decision makers clearly understand the *mission or goals* of their organizations and the *means* for achieving them. Operationally, domain uncertainty is reflected in the degree of agreement on the operating goals and priorities of the organization and the perceived clarity in predicting and knowing how to respond to events and issues occurring within and outside the organization that are relevant to the organization's domain. Therefore, two indices were constructed to measure domain uncertainty in employment security offices: consensus on operating goals, and clarity of operating strategies.

The *consensus on operating goals index* consists of eight goal statements for an employment security office, which all supervisors in each office were asked to rank in order of importance. The goal statements were developed in collaboration with the in-house management analysts and administrators of the agency, and they summarize the basic functions employment security offices are commissioned to perform. Goal consensus was computed at Kendall's coefficient of concordance on responses to the following rankings of goal statements among all supervisors within each office.

Listed below are sets of functions which may vary in importance over time for the Job Service Division. Although the roles are not mutually exclusive, *we want to know what you think is the order of importance of performing these roles or functions in the Wisconsin Job Service Division this year.*

Please *rank-order the relative importance of the following roles* by writing a "1" next to the most important role, "2" next to the second most important role, etc.

RANK-ORDER
OF IMPORTANCE
THIS YEAR
(1 = MOST IMPORTANT)
.
.
.
(8 = LEAST IMPOR-
TANT)

a. Place people into available job openings which
    match their existing qualifications and interests.   a. _____

b. Provide intensive job services to upgrade the
    qualifications and chances for people to find
    better jobs.   b. _____

c. Obtain job orders from employers and fill their
    job openings with the most suitable available job
    seekers.   c. _____

d. Promptly take and process claims and special
    program allowances in order to help people while
    they are unemployed.   d. _____

e. Provide assistance or information to employers
    on the application of the UC Law.   e. _____

f. Ensure that all employers are properly charged
    for the costs resulting from reduced earnings of
    claimants.   f. _____

g. Coordinate manpower needs and services with
    other public and private agencies in the
    community.   g. _____

h. Develop and obtain resource grants and
    contracts for job services.   h. _____

Clarity of operating strategies focuses on the extent to which office
managers clearly know how to deal with events that occurred in different domain sectors of local employment security offices during the
past year. For employment security offices the domain sectors
examined in the OAI were: (1) the local community labor market, (2)
the headquarters or administrative offices of the agency, (3) other
public and private sector organizations in the community, and (4)
internal organizational events within the office (e.g., labor union relations, client complaints, personnel grievances). The index of perceived
clarity of operating strategies was measured as the average quantitative
responses to the following questions by office managers.

IN VARYING DEGREES, THE INTERNAL OPERATIONS OF YOUR IMMEDIATE
UNIT WERE AFFECTED BY FACTORS AND EVENTS WHICH OCCURRED DURING
THE PAST YEAR WITHIN YOUR OFFICE, IN THE LABOR MARKET, AT THE
MADISON ADMINISTRATIVE OFFICE, AND IN OTHER COMMUNITY AGENCIES.
THIS SECTION ASKS QUESTIONS ABOUT HOW YOU AND YOUR IMMEDIATE
SUBORDINATES COORDINATED WORK ACTIVITIES IN YOUR OFFICE WITH
THESE PLACES.

First, we would like to know what specific factors or events (if any) have
affected the internal operations of your immediate unit during the past
year, and what strategies you have available to deal with them.

Under the headings below, *list the one or two major events* (if any) *that affected or changed the internal operations of your immediate unit* during the past year.	To what *extent* do you *have a clearly developed strategy* to deal with each event?				
	WE HAVE NO IDEA HOW TO DEAL WITH THIS	A PRELIMIN-ARY STRATEGY HAS BEEN DISCUSSED BUT IS STILL UNCLEAR	WE HAVE A GENERAL STRATEGY BUT DON'T KNOW IF IT WILL WORK	WE HAVE A PRETTY CLEAR STRATEGY FOR DEALING WITH THIS	WE HAVE A VERY CLEAR TRIED AND TESTED STRATEGY TO DEAL WITH THIS
a. Events in the Economic Conditions of the Labor Market					
(1)	1	2	3	4	5
(2)	1	2	3	4	5
b. Events at the Administrative Office in Madison					
(1)	1	2	3	4	5
(2)	1	2	3	4	5
c. Events in Other Public or Private Community Organizations					
(1)	1	2	3	4	5
(2)	1	2	3	4	5
d. Events that Happened within Your Own Office					
(1)	1	2	3	4	5
(2)	1	2	3	4	5

4. Domain Complexity. Domain complexity is defined as the diversity and range of activities in which an organization is engaged.

Operationally, domain complexity is reflected in the number of different products or services of an organization, the number of different markets and geographical territories in which it operates, and the heterogeneity of client or customer populations that it attempts to serve. Obviously, different characteristics constitute the relevant indicators of domain complexity for different types of organizations. For employment security offices, the measures used were: (1) the number of different service programs provided by an office, (2) the number of counties served by an office, (3) the average monthly unemployment rate in the community, and (4) the percentage of community population on welfare rolls.

The local employment security offices included in the sample vary from being limited-service to full-service operations in terms of the number of programs they offer (which may include employment services, unemployment compensation, the work incentive program, as well as a host of special manpower training and development programs administered by the Department of Labor). A count of the number of these different programs offered by a local office was the first indicator of domain complexity.

The number of counties served indicates the geographical spread of the communities to which a local office is mandated to provide services. This measure is strongly associated with the percentage of the population that lives in rural areas.

The unemployment rate is a key indicator of the *raison d'etre* for employment security offices: to provide unemployment compensation for people laid off from work under the law, and to find jobs for job-seekers. When measured over time, increases or decreases in the monthly unemployment rate greatly increase the difficulty of staffing and managing employment security offices. For example, in the 1974–1975 recession, when unemployment rates rose to record highs in the offices sampled, demand for services greatly exceeded the supply of staff, office space, and management capability in most offices.

The percent of population on welfare rolls is a relevant indicator of the complexity of special client service programs (Work Incentive Program, food stamps, and various manpower training programs offered by local offices.) These programs are legislated particularly for people on welfare and those disadvantaged socially and economically.

Data on the number of programs provided and counties served were obtained from organizational records, whereas measures of unemployment and the percent of population on welfare were obtained from county and metropolitan census tract records.

Definitions and Measures of Organization Configuration

With the exception of the distribution of authority, all measures of macroorganization structure were obtained from organization charts which were constructered by the researchers for each employment security office in the sample. The organization charts maintained by the employment security offices were not sufficiently precise and up-to-date for our data collection purposes. For organization charts to be useful in making an organization assessment, it is necessary that they be timely and developed in a consistent way, according to a detailed set of standards and conventions.

Appendix A describes the OAI standards for constructing organization charts, which we believe are sufficiently general to apply to all kinds of organizations. Figure 4-4 presents an example of an organization chart for a local employment security office. The circled numbers in the figure represent the ten standards that were developed and followed in constructing tables of organization, and these are described in detail in Appendix A. From these charts the following key measures of the structural configuration of the employment security offices were obtained:

1. Organization size: a parallel measure of the number of personnel positions budgeted

2. Vertical differentiation: number of supervisory levels;

3. Horizontal differentiation: number of sections and job titles;

4. Spacial differentiation: number of geographical operating sites;

5. Administrative intensity: average supervisory–staff ratio, office managers' spans of control, and the percentage of supervisors above the bottom level unit supervisors.

These indicators of structural configuration are particularly relevant for the kinds of organizations examined here; these same indicators were measured by Blau and Schoenherr (1971) in their national survey of employment security organizations. Although these indicators apply to organizations in general, additional indicators of structural configuration may become salient in studies of other kinds of organizations. For example, the number of divisions and the form of departmentation (functional, project, product, or matrix forms) have been used extensively to describe the division of labor in large industrial and multinational corporations (Galbraith, 1977; Galbraith and Nathanson, 1978). What is important to recognize is that these and other indicators of structural configuration can be obtained directly from organization charts constructed according to the standards described in Appendix A. Definitions and measures of the indicators examined here are now described.

1. ***Organization Size.*** The number of equivalent full-time salaried employees in an organization is one of the vital input resources that is determined by a solution to the production function problem, as described previously. The most conventional approach to measure size is to count the number of people in the organization chart (e.g., Blau and Schoenherr, 1971; Hickson et al., 1971; Hall et al., 1967). In this study, size was measured by adding up and weighting each full-time employee as 1 and each part-time employee as ½. The correlation between this organization chart measure of size and the budgeted number of personnel positions paid is .97. However, if one only counts the number of full-time employees from the organization charts and does not include part-time employees, the correlation drops to .81. This suggests that it is important to include and weight by ½ the part-time employees in a measure of size of employment security offices.

2. ***Number of Supervisory Levels.*** The number of supervisory levels refers to the different strata that are manifest in the reporting relationships between formal positions in an organization. The major formal indicator of vertical differentiation is the number of hierarchical levels. The concept of hierarchical or supervisory levels derives from the principles stated by Weber (1947:197): "The principles of office hierarchy and of levels of graded authority mean a firmly ordered system of super- and subordination in which there is a supervision of the lower offices by the higher ones." Fayol (1959:34–35) called it the scalar chain principle. The number of levels of authority refers to links in the chain of command, not to skill gradations or salary grades (Blau and Schoenherr, 1971:404).

The number of supervisory levels is measured by counting the longest chain of command in the organization chart. In other words, the number of levels is obtained by finding the deepest or longest division in the organization chart and counting the number of supervisory boxes in the chain of command from top manager to the first-line unit supervisor. For example, Figure 4-4 illustrates three hierarchical levels of supervision.

3. ***Number of Job Titles.*** The number of different job titles is an indicator of the overall division of labor among formal positions in an organization. The number of civil service classifications, not counting different grades within a classification, was used as the measure of the number of job titles in this governmental agency. The official roster of job classifications maintained by the personnel section in the state's Department of Administration describes in detail the duties for all positions as well as the qualifications and entry tests necessary for an individual to obtain a given civil service classification. The employment security agency typically determines the job classes that it needs but must have them authorized by the personnel section. Grades within job classifications (e.g., manpower specialist I, II, or III) indicate differences in skill or experience and are counted as one job title in the measure.

The objection may be raised that differences in civil service classifications do not accurately reflect differences in actual tasks or functions performed. We observed that employees in the same classification often perform quite different tasks and that those in different classifications often do similar work. Therefore, we also asked employees to describe the tasks they perform in a normal working day. The unit specialization measure described in Chapter 5 is a count of the number of different tasks performed by unit personnel. Within work units the correlation between the number of civil service classes and the number of tasks performed in ES units is .77. From this we infer that civil service classifications are a valid indication of the division of labor in an office. We concur with Blau and Schoenherr (1971:17) that on the whole the job to which an employee is appointed largely governs the tasks assigned to him or her. Typists are not hired to counsel applicants or to make employer contacts, although they may be assigned to do a host of typing-related activities such as filing, record keeping, and reception.

The original source of the civil service classification recorded on the organization charts was the fiscal bureau in the administrative office of the employment security agency.

4. Number of Sections. "Sections," a generic term synonymous with Blau and Schoenherr's (1971:401) "major subunits," is used as the other indicator of horizontal division of labor in an organization. In employment security district offices the major subunits or sections are most often the employment service, unemployment compensation, and work incentive program sections.

The director of a section always reports directly to the top manager. By definition, a section must have a section supervisor. Nonsupervisory personnel reporting directly to the top manager are not counted as a section. Thus, in the Figure 4-4 organization chart, there are three sections (UC, ES, and WIN). The secretary or the individuals dispensing food stamps do not constitute independent sections. As in the case of

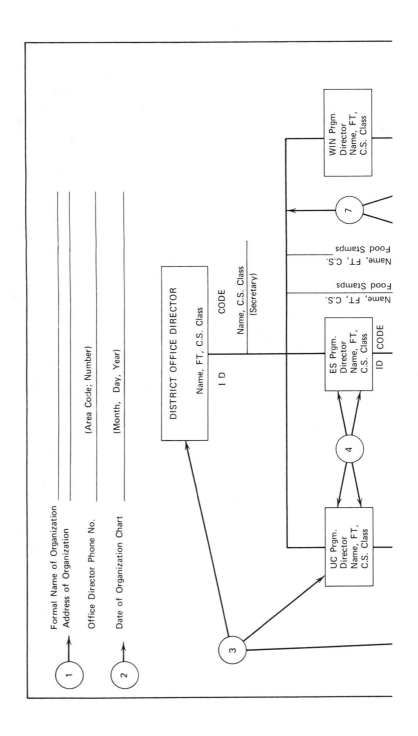

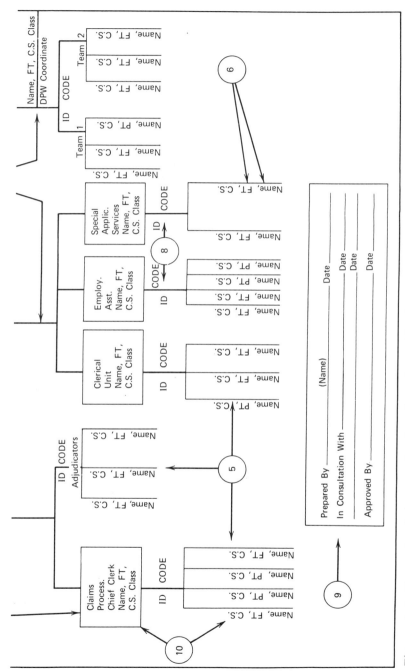

Figure 4-4 *Example of an organization chart for a district employment security office. (See Appendix A, pages 419–423, for key to numbers which refer to standards in constructing organization charts.)*

119

the UC and ES sections, section directors are generally middle-level supervisors who have subordinate supervisors reporting to them. As in the case of the WIN program, a section director can also be a bottom (or first) level unit supervisor who reports directly to the top manager. In the very small offices or organizations there may be no sections, because no supervisory personnel report to the top manager. The number of sections will be the same as the number of first-line units only when all section directors have no supervisory staff reporting to them.

5. *Number of Geographical Operating Sites.* The number of different geographical locations where an organization operates is an indicator of spacial differentiation. Unlike increases in horizontal differentiation, which provide benefits of increased process specialization, increases in geographical division of labor decrease the potential for process specialization and increase administrative overhead costs in each operating site. However, spacial differentiation increases the accessibility and adaptability of an organization to its diverse suppliers, consumers, or clients.

From the organization charts, geographical differentiation was measured by counting the number of different locations in the communities where the employment security office provides services through satellite offices or outstations. These locations were written into the organization charts according to the standard for constructing the charts described in Appendix A.

6. *Supervisor–Staff Ratio.* One indicator of administrative intensity is the supervisory ratio, computed as the total number of supervisors divided by the total number of nonsupervisory personnel in an organization. The supervisory ratio is an overall indicator of the shape of the pyramid of an organization chart. The higher the supervisory ratio, the taller the pyramid, and the higher the administrative overhead.

7. *Top Manager's Span of Control.* A second indicator of administrative intensity is the top manager's span of control. Blau and Schoenherr (1971:193) prefer to use span of control over supervisory ratio since it has no mathematical nexus with the number of levels and sections in an organization. Using a span of control measure made it possible for Blau and Schoenherr to examine the empirical influences of structural differentiation on administrative intensity independent of this mathematical connection.

The office manager's span of control was computed by counting all personnel reporting directly to the office manager or the deputy office manager. This measure differs from the number of sections in that the latter does not include the nonsupervisory employees often under the direct supervision of the top manager.

8. Percentage of Supervisors above Bottom-Level Unit Supervisors. A supplementary indicator of administrative intensity or overhead is the percentage of all supervisors in an organization who are located hierarchically above bottom-level unit supervisors. This indicator reflects the proportion of supervisors who are middle- and upper-level managers and who are not directly supervising production and line operations of nonsupervisory workers. In terms of Parson's (1962) distinctions between technical, managerial, and institutional functions performed at different subsystem levels of complex organizations, this indicator measures the proportion of managerial and institutional-level supervisory positions to technical/instrumental supervisory positions in an organization.

The proportion of middle- and upper-level supervisors is obtained from the organization charts by dividing the total number of supervisory positions into the number of supervisors above the first-line unit supervisors. First-line unit supervisors are most easily identified by approaching the organization chart from the bottom and looking upward to the lowest level supervisors. By definition, there will be as many bottom-level supervisors as there are first-line units. Figure 4-4 illustrates six bottom-level supervisors, that are subtracted out of the total number of supervisory positions to obtain the numerator of the number of middle- and upper-level supervisors. In Figure 4-4, 25 percent of all supervisors exist above the bottom-level unit supervisors.

Measurement of the Distribution of Power and Authority in Organizations

In the literature, *power* is often defined as the ability of A to get B to change in some manner (Filley et al., 1976:92). Many attempts have been made to operationalize this broad definition of power. The most well-known are Etzioni's (1961) coercive, remunerative, and normative forms of power and French and Raven's (1959) five bases of power: reward, coercive, legitimate, referent, and expert. Whereas power is the ability to act, *authority* is the right to act. According to Weber (1947), authority, or legitimate power, is obtained in three ways: (1) by tradition, (2) by bureaucratic or rational–legal means in which authority is vested in a position, and (3) by charismatic qualities of an individual. Finally, *influence* is defined as the capacity of A to get B to do something (without resorting to manipulation of rewards and punishments) which B would otherwise not have done (Presthus, 1962:138). Filley, House, and Kerr (1976:94) attempt to clarify the overlap and confusion among these definitions by stating that "whenever a power relationship exists, an influence relationship is also present; whenever an authority relationship exists, both power and influence are present; influence, however, may be present where neither power nor authority exist."

Although these fine conceptual distinctions among power, authority, and influence may be useful for theoretical purposes, we treat these terms as being synonymous for practical and empirical reasons. Based upon extensive interviews and discussions over the years with supervisors and employees in the employment security organizations, we have encountered only a few people who distinguish between the concepts of power, authority, and influence—or behave differently if they do make these conceptual distinctions. In other words, our observations suggest that people pragmatically treat these concepts synonymously. Given the present state of theoretical confusion and overlap among these concepts, we do not believe it is empirically productive to add to the complexity and length of the OAI by attempting to develop measures that can detect these fine conceptual distinctions. Much more rigorous and parsimonious theory building is required of these concepts before attempts are made to develop instruments that distinguish power, authority, and influence if, indeed, further theoretical work suggests such efforts are worthwhile.

We do, however, believe it is productive to distinguish the way authority (or power or influence) of various groups is officially structured from the way that authority is perceived inside the organization. Formal records and organization charts represent an intentional plan for interpersonal control. In behavioral practice, however, authority does not exist unless it is perceived by organization members. Thus, a comparison of the formal structure with perceptions of authority can reveal the extent to which the planned or intended structure of authority deviates from the behavioral patterns of authority relationships in an organization.

1. Organization Chart Indices of the Distribution of Authority. As discussed earlier, the structural configuration of an organization not only reflects the division of labor in an organization, but also the distribution of power and authority among organizational positions. As a result, researchers have often relied upon the organization chart to obtain indicators of the structure of authority in an organization (Evan, 1963; Pugh et al., 1963; Tannenbaum, 1965). These indicators include the span of control (Blau and Scott, 1962; Whisler et al., 1967), the number of supervisory levels, and supervisor–staff ratio (Melman, 1958). The greater the number of supervisory levels and the wider the spans of control, the greater the distribution of authority in many positions. For example, an organization with two levels has two

formally recognized locations of authority, whereas one with five levels
has five vertical ranks of authority, and each superordinate level is
assumed to have a greater amount of authority than the subordinate
level. The narrower the spans of control at each level, the more
concentrated is the authority in the supervisor. Thus, the organization
chart represents the formally designated structure of power and
authority.

   2. *Perceived Structure of Authority or Influence Index.* In
behavioral terms, authority, power, or influence are defined as any
processes in which individuals in an organization perceive other persons
or groups to control, determine, or intentionally affect their behavior
(Tannenbaum, 1968:5). An adaptation of the "control graph" developed
by Tannenbaum and his colleagues at the University of Michigan was
used to construct an index of the perceived structure of authority or
influence in organizations. The control graph distinguishes two
important aspects of the perceived authority structure in organizations:
(1) the *distribution of authority*, that is, the degree of influence
exercised by people at different hierarchical levels, which are defined on
the horizontal axis of the graph; and (2) the *total amount of authority*,
that is, how much influence is exercised by all organizational levels
along the vertical axis, which is a rating scale of the degree of influence.
This graph visually reflects the distribution of authority by the shape of
the curve, whereas the total amount of authority is shown in the
average height of the curve. The former emphasizes the relative power
of individuals at different levels within the organization, whereas the
latter considers its absolute amount (Tannenbaum, 1968:33).

   Three basic adjustments were made in this control graph to guide
our development of the perceived authority structure index. First,
simple observations of complex organizations indicate that authority is
distributed not only among hierarchical levels, but also horizontally
among different organizational units within each level as well as other
organizations. Therefore, the horizontal axis of the graph was expanded
to designate not only specific hierarchical levels, but also other units
and people in other organizations (see Table 4-4).

   Second, Tannenbaum and his associates initially tended to construct
their control graphs on the basis of one general question. For example,
all members of an organization are asked in questionnaires to indicate
how much influence people in one group have on what other groups do
in the company (e.g., Whisler et al., 1967). However, they subsequently
found that different patterns of influence are observed depending upon
the organizational issues or practices involved (Zupanov and Tannenbaum, 1968). To capture some of these systematic differences in
authority patterns, it was decided to develop separate graphs on three

issues which reflect three different levels of operation in employment security offices: matters related to the internal operations of each organizational subunit, matters of the total office, and matters related to relationships with other organizations in the community.

Third, as our definition suggests, authority or influence is exerted on an individual only to the extent that it is perceived as being exerted by others in the organization. Those other individuals and units who work in relative isolation from an organizational member will likely be seen by the respondent as having relatively little influence because they exist beyond his or her perceptual range. Therefore, measures of the perceived structure of authority in an organization will systematically vary depending upon the location of the respondent in the organization chart. This explains the recurring phenomenon in empirical studies using the "control graph" that the top manager in the organization is perceived as having less influence than his or her subordinates by all organizational members (Whisler et al., 1967). To be able to statistically control or take perceptual ranges into account in subsequent analysis, the response of each organizational member was coded in terms of the number of vertical supervisory levels between the top manager and the position occupied by the respondent, as reflected in the organization chart.

Based upon the preceding considerations, the perceived-structure-of-authority index in the OAI consists of three questions asked of all organizational members on the amount of influence of different individuals and groups on (1) the internal operations of each unit, (2) the total office, and (3) relationships with other organizations in the community. The individuals and groups specified in the OAI included non-supervisory employees (unit members), unit supervisors, other unit supervisors in the local offices, the office manager (district office director), headquarters (administrators in Madison), and people in other organizations and agencies.

How much say or influence do you think *each* of the following has over the *internal operations* of *your work unit* (e.g., setting unit production goals, allocating work among unit members, and reviewing the performance of unit members?)	HOW MUCH SAY OR INFLUENCE I THINK EACH HAS OVER THE INTERNAL OPERATIONS OF MY UNIT				
	NONE	LITTLE	SOME	QUITE A BIT	VERY MUCH
a. The members of your unit?	1	2	3	4	5
b. Your Unit Supervisor?	1	2	3	4	5
c. Other Unit Supervisors in the office?	1	2	3	4	5
d. The District Office Director?	1	2	3	4	5
e. Administrators in Madison?	1	2	3	4	5
f. People in other organizations and agencies?	1	2	3	4	5

How much say or influence do you think each of the following has over the *internal operations* of *this Job Service Office* (such as setting office policies and goals, allocating resources between units and programs)?	HOW MUCH SAY OR INFLUENCE I THINK EACH HAS OVER THE INTERNAL OPERATIONS OF THIS OFFICE				
	NONE	LITTLE	SOME	QUITE A BIT	VERY MUCH
a. The members of your unit?	1	2	3	4	5
b. Your Unit Supervisor?	1	2	3	4	5
c. Other Unit Supervisors in the office?	1	2	3	4	5
d. The District Office Director?	1	2	3	4	5
e. Administrators in Madison?	1	2	3	4	5
f. People in other organizations and agencies?	1	2	3	4	5

How much say or influence do you think each of the following has over the *external community affairs* and *activities* of *this Job Service Office* (such as developing and maintaining joint manpower programs with other agencies, getting funds and CETA grants, establishing and protecting the role of the U.S. office in the community)?	HOW MUCH SAY OR INFLUENCE I THINK EACH HAS OVER EXTERNAL ACTIVITIES OF THIS OFFICE				
	NONE	LITTLE	SOME	QUITE A BIT	VERY MUCH
a. The members of your unit?	1	2	3	4	5
b. Your Unit Supervisor?	1	2	3	4	5
c. Other Unit Supervisors in the office?	1	2	3	4	5
d. The District Office Director?	1	2	3	4	5
e. Administrators in Madison?	1	2	3	4	5
f. People in other organizations and agencies?	1	2	3	4	5

EVALUATION OF OAI STRUCTURAL CONFIGURATION DIMENSIONS

The evaluation of the preceding OAI organization context and structure measures is conducted in four ways in this section. First, the relationships among the OAI structural configuration measures obtained from the organization charts of 29 Wisconsin ES offices are examined and compared with those obtained by Blau and Schoenherr (1971) in their national survey of 1201 local employment security offices. Second, the concurrent validity of the structural configuration measures are assessed by correlating them with the overall efficiency, effectiveness, and average level of job satisfaction of personnel in the 29 Wisconsin ES offices. Third, the organization context dimensions are evaluated and correlated with the structural configuration measures to determine how the context and structural dimensions are interrelated in terms of the theory discussed previously. Finally, we assess the alternative measures of the distribution of power and influence within the ES offices and evaluate how they are correlated with the other organization context and structure dimensions.

Relationships Among Structural Configuration Dimensions

A statistical analysis of the eight organization structural configuration variables is unnecessary to establish their intrinsic validity. The degree of measurement accuracy in these variables is a direct function of the degree of care and precision taken in following the standards for constructing organizational charts and for computing the measures from the charts as described previously. However, for theoretical and practical purposes it is important to know the pattern of relationships among the structural configuration measures as well as their associations with organizational performance.

Table 4-1 presents the means, standard deviations, and simple correlations of the eight structural configuration measures in the Wisconsin OAI Survey and in the Blau and Schoenherr national survey (1966). Data from the Blau and Schoenherr (1971:419) survey are presented because they provide a useful benchmark to assess the OAI data. Although the two surveys were conducted at different points in time, the standards and conventions followed to construct organization charts and to obtain the structural measures from the charts were the same, with one exception. In computing the number of levels Blau and Schoenherr counted the number of supervisory levels in the deepest division (like the OAI measure) and then added one additional level for first-line nonsupervisory personnel. Although this difference of a constant one is reflected in the mean number of levels, it does not affect the correlations with other variables.

Table 4-1 shows there are considerable differences between the OAI and Blau and Schoenherr surveys on the correlations among the structural configuration variables. We interpret the differences in correlations among the structural configuration measures between the two studies to be due to sample. The Blau and Schoenherr survey is far more extensive than the OAI survey; the latter is a small subset of offices of all local United States employment security offices in the Blau and Schoenherr study. Thus, although the OAI correlations are an accurate representation of the pattern of relations among the structural measures for the 29 offices within one state, Table 4-1 suggests that it would be incorrect to draw inferences from this sample to other employment security offices. The national Blau and Schoenherr survey provides more reliable evidence of the relations among the structural measures for employment security offices than does the OAI survey in Wisconsin. However, by the same argument, it would be incorrect to draw inferences from the Blau and Schoenherr study to other kinds of organizations.

A good theoretical explanation for the observed relations among the structural configuration measures has been provided by Blau and Schoenherr (1971, especially Chapter 7). However, evidence of the concurrent validity of the measures was not provided.

Relationships Between Structural Configuration and Organizational Performance

The major indicators of the practical usefulness of the structural measures for assessing organizations is their relationship with overall organization performance. As described in Chapter 3, three criteria are used to measure the overall performance of local ES offices: efficiency, effectiveness, and the average job satisfaction of office personnel.

Table 3-1 in Chapter 3 reported the correlations among the different efficiency, effectiveness, and job satisfaction measures that were aggregated to obtain the composite office performance measures. Overall, the correlation among composite office efficiency and effectiveness is .78; office efficiency and job satisfaction is .22; effectiveness and job satisfaction is .26. Thus, at the overall office level of analysis, enhancing efficiency is not at the expense of either effectiveness or the average job satisfaction of office personnel.

The bottom three rows of Table 4-1 report the correlations between the structural configuration measures and overall office efficiency, effectiveness, and job satisfaction of office personnel. The correlations show that each of the structural configuration dimensions is significantly related to at least one of the office performance criteria. This provides good evidence of the concurrent validity of the structural configuration measures.

From a practical viewpoint, one can infer some relatively clear guidelines from the data for structuring the local ES offices in this sample. The correlations in Table 4-1 suggest that overall performance of ES offices is most strongly associated with: (1) increases in horizontal division of labor (particularly more geographical service sites and locations in the community and more programmatic sections reporting directly to the office director); (2) decreases in administrative intensity

Table 4-1 Relationships among Organizational Structural Configuration Measures for Local Employment Security Offices in OAI Survey of 29 Offices within Wisconsin and Blau and Schoenherr (B&S) Survey of 1201 Local ES Offices in All States

	Mean	S.D.	Size	Spv. Levels	Job Titles	Sections	Sites	Mgr. Span	Spv. Ratio	% Spv. Upper Levels
			OFFICE STRUCTURAL CONFIGURATION							
1. Office Size										
a. OAI Survey	48.7	61.7	—							
b. B&S Survey	26.7	23.5	—							
2. No. Supervisory Levels										
a. OAI Survey	2.3	.9	.74	—						
b. B&S Survey	3.3	.5	.69	—						
3. No. Job Titles										
a. OAI Survey	10.2	4.4	.80	.83	—					
b. B&S Survey	7.1	2.6	.51	.42	—					
4. No. Sections										
a. OAI Survey	1.1	1.6	.78	.79	.73	—				
b. B&S Survey	2.4	1.2	.61	.33	.45	—				
5. No. Geographical Sites										
a. OAI Survey	1.4	1.7	.47	.67	.55	.61	—			
b. B&S Survey	NA	NA	NA	NA	NA	NA	—			

6. Mgr. Span of Control										
a. OAI Survey	6.4	2.4	.47	.21	.15	.31	.22	—		
b. B&S Survey	6.0	3.1	.31	.09	.31	.27	NA	—		
7. Supervisor–Staff Ratio										
a. OAI Survey	.19	.07	-.13	-.07	-.20	-.05	-.18	-.28	—	
b. B&S Survey	.21	.08	-.45	-.19	-.37	-.16	NA	-.42	—	
8. % Spvs. above bottom Level Unit Spvs.										
a. OAI Survey	.25	.18	.15	.07	.15	-.13	-.18	-.30		—
b. B&S Survey	NA	NA	NA	NA	NA	NA	NA	NA		—
OFFICE PERFORMANCE CRITERIA [a]										
9. Office Efficiency	Z-scores	Z-scores	.11	.07	.22	.15	.43[c]	.02	.19	-.38[c]
10. Office Effectiveness	Z-scores	Z-scores	.17	.31[b]	.17	.42[c]	.52[c]	-.27	.31[b]	-.42[c]
11. Average Job Satisfaction of Office Personnel	3.45	.30	-.25[b]	-.26[b]	-.24[b]	-.14	.09	.29[c]	-.23[b]	-.51[c]

[a] ES office performance criteria to evaluate the concurrent validity of structural configuration measures are based on the OAI survey and are not available in the Blau and Schoenherr (1971) appendix which is the source of the correlations presented above. The ES office performance criteria are defined in Chapter 2.

[b] $p < .10$.

[c] $p < .05$. Significance levels noted only for performance correlations.

or overhead at the middle and upper levels of the hierarchy, attained by decreasing the percentage of supervisors in positions above bottom-level unit supervisors; and (3) increases in administrative intensity and supervision at the lower technical level of direct operations and services, by way of either increasing the supervisor–staff ratio or decreasing the number of nonsupervisory employees per organizational unit.

The significant positive correlation between the number of supervisory levels and office effectiveness in Table 4-1 appears to go contrary to these inferences. However, this simple correlation is produced by the strong correlation of supervisory levels with the numbers of sections and geographical service sites. The zero-order correlation between supervisory levels and office effectiveness of .31 vanishes to $-.04$ when controlling for the number of sections, and $-.06$ when controlling for operating sites. Moreover, when holding the number of service sites constant, the simple correlations of hierarchical levels with office efficiency of .07 drops to a significant $-.33$ ($p = .09$), and with job satisfaction of $-.26$ to an even more significant $-.43$ ($p = .03$). From this we infer that decreases in the number of hierarchical levels (or vertical differentiation) and increases in horizontal divisions of labor explain increases in the performance of ES local offices in this sample.

Finally, we examine the direct associations of office size with office efficiency, effectiveness, and employee job satisfaction because we have often been asked by managers in the ES agency, "What is the most appropriate size for local ES offices?" The simple correlations in Table 4-1 of office size with efficiency and effectiveness are slightly positive, and they are significantly negative with job satisfaction of office personnel. When controlling for the horizontal division of labor in ES offices (specifically, number of geographical sites), the partial correlations of office size become $-.12$ with efficiency, $-.10$ with effectiveness, and $-.33$ with job satisfaction. These partial correlations do not substantially change what the simple correlations in Table 4-1 already show. As has been observed elsewhere (Shull, Delbecq, and Cummings, 1970; Cummings and Schwab, 1973), increasing organization size is negatively correlated with job satisfaction because more impersonal and standardized methods of administration and coordination are necessary among greater numbers of people whose individual contributions become more anonymous and less visible. However, mixed and insignificant relationships have been found among the few studies that directly related organization size to various measures of organization productivity or goal attainment (see review in Berger and Cummings, 1979).

These findings do not provide support to the generally held theory that there are economies of scale and efficiencies that accrue simply with large size. One explanation is that in labor-intensive technologies, such as in local ES offices, there is a low threshold to the scale benefits of size and hierarchy which are quickly outweighed by the costs of coordination, administrative overhead, and temporary or make-work assignments for dislocated or senior employees in the administrative hierarchy who simply "did not work out" in their former productively assigned positions. All these costs tend to accompany increases in the labor component of organizations. In capital intensive technologies, obsolete and unproductive equipment can be disposed of quite readily, and by definition, labor represents a small fraction of the total operating budget. In contrast, labor-intensive organizations obviously do not have such flexibility to dispose of obsolete and unproductive labor for humane reasons, which are today generally reinforced legally by labor union contracts.

Thus, in terms of office performance, the results suggest there is no particularly appropriate number of employees for local ES offices in this sample. Instead, the data suggest that it is the proportional division of labor and management vertically and horizontally within offices that is importantly related to office performance, irrespective of size (at least within the range of 14 to 92 personnel examined in this sample of offices). Proportional decreases in the number of levels and administrative overhead at middle and upper hierarchical levels and increases in horizontal division of labor into sections and geographical sites in conjunction with greater supervisory intensity at the technical direct-service level are significantly correlated with increases in office efficiency, effectiveness, and employee satisfaction.

Increasing the number of geographical service sites is far less costly for labor- than capital-intensive organizations, and it decreases problems of accessibility and coordination of services with employees, job applicants, and other constituents served in communities by local ES offices. Each geographical service site is necessarily smaller in size and less differentiated internally than the overall ES office. The supervisors of these satellite offices tend to represent quasi-autonomous sections (or divisions) in the organization chart which report directly to the overall office director. This form of decentralization increases supervisory intensity at the direct service-delivery level of the overall ES office and, within each geographical site, promotes greater personal supervision and visibility to the contributions of individual employees among their relevant peers, clients, and supervisors. We extrapolate from the data that such a decentralization in the structural configuration of local ES offices will be positively related to overall efficiency, effectiveness, and employee job satisfaction for the offices in this sample.

EVALUATION OF ORGANIZATIONAL CONTEXT DIMENSIONS

Table 4-2 presents the correlations between organization context dimensions and structural configuration and performance. The measures of office service demand (numbers of new job applicants, initial unemployment compensation claims, and new WIN clients) were each correlated .99 with one another. Therefore, in the analysis following a composite average of the three demand indicators is used since no additional information is gained by examining them separately. However, the correlations among the domain complexity and uncertainty measures are sufficiently mixed so that they are analyzed separately. The major results in Table 4-2 are now discussed.

Environmental Factors

Consistent with the economic production function problem discussed in the theoretical section, the correlation between office service demand and the budgeted number of personnel positions in ES offices is .99, suggesting that organizations attempt to equate product or service demand with the supply of resources and personnel positions necessary for meeting their demand. Further, the relationships of service demand and budgeted number of personnel positions with the structural configuration and performance of ES offices are the same as found previously for office size. This is expected, because the budgeted number of positions from fiscal accounting records of the ES agency is a parallel measure of the number of employees in the organization charts used in Table 4-1, and they correlate .96.

Domain Complexity

In the measurement section preceding, we indicated that domain complexity of ES offices was measured with four items: the number of counties served, the average monthly unemployment rate, the percentage of population poor, and the number of different service programs provided by the ES offices. In Table 4-2 the latter measure was excluded from the analysis because there was very little variation on the number of service programs in the ES offices in this sample. With two exceptions, all the ES offices had Employment Service, Unemployment Compensation, and Work Incentive programs. The other two offices have a WIN program. Thus, the analysis here is limited to three indicators of the demographic complexity of the communities served by the ES offices.

The relationships between the three indicators of domain complexity and the other organization context and structural configuration dimensions are largely as expected. Thompson (1967:70) proposed that organizations facing heterogeneous task environments seek to identify homogeneous segments and establish structural units to deal with each. The significant correlations of the domain complexity indicators with the number of geographical service sites in the community, the number of sections, and the percentage of supervisors above the unit level in Table 4-2 provide good support for this proposition.

In the theoretical section preceding, we also argued that complex domains increase problems of coordination and control among structural divisions, sections, and service sites within the organization, not only because complex domains can seldom be divided into a set of *independent* simple domains, but also because personnel within different subdivisions are likely to develop different norms and goal priorities for the services provided by the organization. Evidence for this argument is shown in Table 4-2 by the negative correlations of domain complexity with the degree of consensus among office supervisors on the goal priorities of local ES offices and by the significant positive relationships with managers' perceived uncertainty in knowing how to deal with internal office issues and events. It is noteworthy that whereas significant positive relationships exist between the number of counties served and uncertainty of the labor market and between the unemployment rate and uncertainty of other organizations, the remaining correlations (between the three indicators of domain complexity with uncertainties of issues and events in the labor market, other organizations, and the headquarters office) are insignificant. Overall, this suggests that the major influence of operating in complex domains for ES office managers is felt in an increased uncertainty in managing internal office affairs, and not in dealing with other domain segments of ES offices.

Quite unexpectedly, the three domain complexity indicators are strongly positively correlated with the efficiency, effectiveness, and job satisfaction of personnel in ES offices. However, these simple correlations decrease by approximately one-half when controlling for the

Table 4-2 Correlations among Organization Context Dimensions and with Structural Configuration and Performance for 29 ES Offices

CONTEXT OF ES OFFICES

	Domain Complexity				Uncertainty of Issues in—				Economic—			
	# Counties	Unemp. Rate	% Pop. Poor	Domain Consensus	Labor Mkt.	Other Orgs.	Head-qtrs.	Within Office	Service Demand	Budget Pos.	Mean	SD
1. Domain Complexity												
a. No. Counties Served	—										3.60	2.14
b. Avg. Unemployment Rate	.30	—									.604	.111
c. % Population Poor	.64[b]	.62[c]	—								.101	.325
2. Consensus on Domain Goals	−.29	−.09	−.58[c]	—							.67	.14
3. Uncertainty of Issues & Events in—												
a. Labor Market	.29[a]	.02	−.24	.19	—						4.21	.44
b. Other Organizations	.22	.48[b]	.23	−.10	.41[b]	—					3.53	1.06
c. Headquarters Office	−.10	−.13	−.20	−.19	.31	−.25	—				3.36	1.05
d. Within Local Office	.48[b]	.41[b]	.68[c]	−.58[c]	.15	.21	.21	—			3.92	.51
4. Service Demand	.10	−.01	−.28	.25	.49[b]	.28	−.25	−.33[a]	—		13560	16062
5. Budgeted No. Positions	.15	−.01	−.23	−.10	.50[c]	.31	−.19	−.29	.99[c]	—	34.8	42.9

STRUCTURAL CONFIGURATION

1. No. Supervisory Levels	.28	.21	-.05	-.28	.31[a]	.32	-.30	-.24	.80[c]	.72[c]
2. No. Job Titles	.15	.07	-.07	-.08	.42[b]	.36[a]	-.30	-.09	.85[c]	.81[c]
3. No. Sections	.41[b]	.12	-.03	-.23	.40[b]	.29	-.42[a]	-.17	.75[c]	.78[c]
4. No. Geographical Sites	.70[c]	.52[c]	.45[b]	-.15	.34[a]	.44[b]	-.17	.22	.47[b]	.40[c]
5. Mgr. Span of Control	.09	-.08	-.29	-.02	.38[b]	.20	.08	-.31[a]	.75[c]	.34[b]
6. Spv.–Staff Ratio	-.27	.21	.13	.11	-.39[b]	-.44[b]	.17	.05	-.11	-.12
7. % Spvs. above Bottom Level	-.55[c]	-.29	-.24	.07	-.32[a]	.07	.08	.47[b]	.07	.07
OFFICE PERFORMANCE										
1. Office Efficiency	.52[c]	.56[c]	.66[c]	-.35	.03	.25	-.34	.43[b]	-.23	-.21
—When controlling for sites	.34	.43	.57							
2. Office Effectiveness	.55[c]	.65[c]	.69[c]	-.38[a]	.02	.28	-.46[a]	.36[a]	-.09	-.07
—When controlling for sites	.31	.52	.60							
3. Personnel Job Satisfaction	.23	.44[b]	.13	.07	.24	.31	.41[a]	.36[a]	-.30[a]	-.30[b]
—When Controlling for sites	.24	.46	.10							

[a] $p < .10$.
[b] $p < .05$.
[c] $p < .01$.

135

number of geographical service sites. These partial correlations (not shown but easily computed from Table 4-2) suggest that about one-half of the total effect of ES office domain complexity on performance is explained by structural subdivision of ES offices to manage increasingly complex domains (as the theory suggests). However, the remaining direct effects of domain complexity on office performance are substantial and have practical implications for the location of ES offices in local communities. The data suggest that the performance of offices is enhanced when they are located in more rural and less urban areas (as indicated by the number of counties served) and in areas that have a high need for the services that public ES offices are best equipped to provide (as indicated by high unemployment rates and low-income communities). In the main, public ES offices have been found in studies by the Department of Labor to be more proficient in providing unemployment compensation and job services for a clerical and blue-collar work force than for a more professional, executive-level, white-collar work force.

Domain Uncertainty

As discussed above, domain uncertainty refers to the extent to which office managers indicate they are able to deal strategically with (1) the labor market, (2) other organizations, (3) ES headquarters, and (4) internal office affairs. The "labor market" and "other organizations" indices (3a and 3b in Table 4-2) are measures of *external* domain uncertainty; "headquarters" and "within office" (3c and 3d in Table 4-2) relate to *internal* domain uncertainty.

The external and internal domain uncertainty items differ systematically in their relationships with the other dimensions of organization context, structural configuration, and performance. The external domain uncertainty items are consistently correlated with increases in office service demand, office size, and structural differentiation (number of supervisory levels, job titles, sections, and sites), and with decreases in administrative intensity (supervisor-staff ratio and percentage of supervisors above bottom level). The opposite correlations are found for the internal domain uncertainty items. These results lend themselves to two alternative explanations that are well ingrained in the organizational literature. (1) Organizations cope with external domain uncertainty by adopting more complex structures, which decreases internal domain uncertainty. (2) Managers seek certainty in the internal operations of their organization by creating clearly differentiated structures, which increases external domain uncertainty. The evidence for these two prevailing explanations (which differ in the way one views the causation among external domain uncertainty, structural configuration, and internal domain uncertainty) will now be discussed. As it turns out, both explanations are suspect because their solutions are negatively related to organization performance.

Based upon the theorizing of Thompson (1967), Lawrence and Lorsch (1967), and Dill (1958), the prevailing explanation for the different correlations of internal and external domain uncertainty items with structure is that organizations cope with increasing external environmental uncertainty by adopting more complex structures, and the major benefit gained from this greater structural complexity is less uncertainty of coordinating and controlling internal operations. Specifically, Thompson (1967:20) proposed that "under norms of rationality, organizations seek to buffer environmental influences by surrounding their technical cores with input and output components." In operational terms, this implies that as the external domain of an organization becomes more uncertain, the internal domain is increasingly differentiated horizontally by adding positions, sections, and operating sites to meet the uncertain environmental fluctuations and convert them into steady operations for the core production or service units. To handle the greater information processing and decision requirements that an uncertain external environment generates, organizations will also become more decentralized by decreasing administrative intensity at middle and upper hierarchical levels and placing greater managerial decision-making responsibility in lower-level unit supervisors who have direct contact with external environmental segments. The correlations in Table 4-2 provide good support for this explanation and for Thompson's proposition on the direct effects of external environmental uncertainty on organization structure and internal domain uncertainty.

An alternative explanation exists for the relationships noted in Table 4-2. It may be that it is the structural configuration of ES offices that influences perceptions of an increasingly uncertain external domain but an increasingly certain internal domain. More specifically, although size and structural differentiation increase certainty of internal organizational operations (by way of clear divisions of responsibilities, predictable reporting relations, and the addition of slack positions and units to buffer core operations), they also have a tendency to insulate a greater proportion of organizational units and positions from the external environment (which necessitates reliance upon the perceptions of a smaller proportion of personnel who span the external boundaries of the organization). As March and Simon (1958:165) stated, by virtue of structural differentiation most information about the external environment enters an organization at highly specific points. Direct perceptions by ES office managers of issues and events in the labor market and in other community organizations are largely limited to the personnel who are in direct contact with these external domain segments by virtue of their specialized positions. Of course, these boundary spanners do not pass on direct observation or evidence to other organization personnel. Rather, they transmit their own inferences and value judgments, so that others have limited access to the original information and must rely on the credibility of the transmitter in order to form opinions. Therefore, with increasing organization size and structural differentiation, a greater percentage of organizational personnel are buffered from the external environment and become increasingly unclear of external domain issues and events, as the correlations in Table 4-2 suggest.

Thus, two interesting and plausible explanations for the data in Table 4-2 are that (1) external domain uncertainty predicts structure and perceptions of internal domain uncertainty, or (2) that structure predicts perceptions of internal and external domain uncertainty. However, the validity of both explanations is called into question as one observes the positive correlations of office performance efficiency, effectiveness, and personnel job satisfaction with uncertainties of the labor market, other organizations in the community, and internal office affairs. Central to both explanations is that a reduction in domain uncertainty should increase organization performance either because a decrease in external domain uncertainty permits an organization to be structured more rationally, or a rationally structured organization will decrease internal domain uncertainty by having key boundary spanning units absorb external uncertainties. An increase in the uncertainty of issues and events at the headquarters level of the ES state agency is the only domain uncertainty dimension negatively correlated with office effectiveness and efficiency. All the other domain uncertainty measures are either unrelated or positively correlated with the three office performance criteria. These data question the basic assumption underlying both explanations as well as the appropriateness of the prevailing statement that "uncertainty reduction is the *raison d'etre* for designing organizations." Unfortunately, with cross-sectional data on the small sample of ES offices here, we cannot investigate these interesting findings further. Clearly, however, they are sufficiently interesting and important to be investigated more directly and over time in future organization assessments.

Domain Consensus

It was argued previously that the degree of consensus among decision makers will largely influence the direction of causation among the other organization context and structural configuration dimensions, as well as the distribution of authority (examined in following text). This hypothesis cannot be evaluated on cross-sectional data. However, even if the data were longitudinal, it is doubtful that a valid test of the hypothesis would be possible, because the average domain consensus, as indicated by Kendall's Coefficient of Concordance among unit supervisors within each office on the rank-order of importance of eight service goals is quite high (.67) and has a relatively small standard deviation (.14). Within this range the relationships of the degree of consensus among supervisors within each office with the other context and structural configuration dimensions are in the predicted direction, although they are not generally significant.

However, it is somewhat surprising to observe that increases in consensus among supervisors within offices are strongly associated with decreases in overall office efficiency and effectiveness. Conventionally, it is believed that domain consensus should be positively related with performance because agreement among supervisors on the operating goals of an organization provides unity of direction and purpose and decreases the likelihood of competition and suboptimization (i.e., when the efforts and performance of one unit are at the expense of or conflict with those of other units or of the total organization). It is important to remember that these negative correlations with office performance exist only at the relatively high and narrow range of domain consensus just discussed and are most likely to change in sign at lower levels of domain consensus.

Consistent with Ashby's law of "requisite variety," one should expect a concave relationship between domain consensus and organization performance. If there is little or no agreement among supervisors on the operating goals of an agency, there is anomie which results in disorganization and very low performance effectiveness and efficiency. At the other extreme, when there is complete agreement among decision makers on the operating goals of an organization, it is unlikely that the appropriateness of fallible service goals and operating procedures will be questioned or that sufficient tension exists to search for more efficient and effective modes of operation (Lewin, 1947). However, the middle ranges of domain consensus are likely to be the more durable and interesting conditions for high-performing organizations, because in this range operating goals and procedures are likely to be questioned, evaluated, and improved; the moderate amount of competition among supervisors can be constructively managed to motivate greater effort among various organizational units.

EVALUATION OF AUTHORITY AND INFLUENCE MEASURES

As described previously, measures of the formal structure of authority in ES offices were obtained from organization charts, and indices of the perceived amounts and distributions of influence among various groups in the ES offices were developed in the OAI questionnaires based upon Tannenbaum's (1968) control graph theory. First we evaluate the measurement properties of the perceived influence indices. Then a comparison is made between the perceived patterns of influence and the formal structure of authority (as reflected in the organization chart) as well as the context and performance dimensions of ES offices.

Measurement Properties of Perceived Influence Indices at Organizational Level

Table 4-3 presents an item analysis of the means, standard deviations, and intragroup correlations obtained on the 18 items in the OAI questionnaires, which asked all ES office personnel to indicate how much influence or say each of six groups had in making decisions in each of three areas: unit operations, internal office operations, and external office affairs. The data reported in Table 4-3 are aggregated to the office level by computing the means and standard deviations of responses of all personnel within each ES office. The top half of the table summarizes the office means obtained for all 29 local offices. It provides indicators of the total or average amounts of perceived influence of the six groups overall and in each of the three decision areas. The bottom half of the table reports the standard deviations among personnel within offices for each of the OAI influence items and indicates the distribution or variance in perceptions among within-office respondents on the influence of the six groups on each of the decision areas.

Table 4-3 shows that the correlations between the three decisions for each group are consistently high, suggesting that if any particular group of people is perceived to exert a high degree of influence on the operations of work units, they also do so on internal office operations and external office affairs. In addition, if there are wide distributions in perceptions among office personnel on how much influence a group has in one decision area, there are also wide variances in the amounts of say of that group on the other two decision areas. These correlations are sufficiently high to justify averaging together scores of the three decision areas for each group to obtain composite indices of the influence of each group. Table 4-3 shows the summary scores obtained on these

Table 4-3   Item Analysis of OAI Perceived Influence Index in 29 ES Offices

OAI Indices of Perceived Influence	Mean[a]	SD	Unit Operations	Office Operations	External Affairs
			Intra-Group Correlations among Decision Areas		
TOTAL AMOUNTS OF INFLUENCE					
1. Average Influence of Unit					
Employees—	2.58	.41	.91	.90	.87
a. on unit operations	2.99	.47	—	.71	.73
b. on office operations	2.46	.51		—	.57
c. on external office affairs	2.31	.39			—
2. Average Influence of Unit					
Supervisors—	3.47	.30	.52	.88	.89
a. on unit operations	4.03	.23	—	.28	.24
b. on office operations	3.46	.41		—	.68
c. on external office affairs	2.91	.46			—
3. Average Influence of Office					
Dir.—	3.83	.32	.80	.91	.91
a. on unit operations	3.61	.38	—	.59	.47
b. on office operations	4.07	.36		—	.76
c. on external office affairs	3.81	.37			—
4. Average Influence of Head-					
quarters—	3.53	.29	.86	.90	.65
a. on unit operations	3.21	.30	—	.65	.66
b. on office operations	3.81	.33		—	.74
c. on external office affairs	3.56	.34			—
5. Average Influence of Other					
Spvs. in Office—	2.90	.27	.60	.91	.74
a. on unit operations	2.63	.37	—	.40	−.01
b. on office operations	3.13	.33		—	.65
c. on external office affairs	2.95	.39			—
6. Average Influence of Other					
Organizations—	2.17	.22	.79	.85	.79
a. on unit operations	1.83	.25	—	.63	.34
b. on office operations	1.96	.25		—	.51
c. on external office affairs	2.71	.30			—

Table 4-3 Continued

DISTRIBUTIONS OF INFLUENCE

	Mean[a]	SD	Unit Operations	Office Operations	External Affairs
1. SD of Unit Employees' Influence—	.82	.15	.50	.82	.49
a. on unit operations	1.00	.19	—	.35	.11
b. on office operations	.99	.18		—	.44
c. on external office affairs	1.09	.14			—
2. SD of Unit Supervisors' Influence—	.80	.15	.62	.75	.71
a. on unit operations	.90	.20	—	.47	.08
b. on office operations	1.01	.17		—	.49
c. on external office affairs	1.09	.23			—
3. SD of Office Director's Influence—	.79	.18	.81	.75	.59
a. on unit operations	1.14	.22	—	.41	.43
b. on office operations	.90	.22		—	.51
c. on external office affairs	.98	.22			—
4. SD of Headquarter's Influence—	.88	.16	.54	.65	.54
a. on unit operations	1.26	.15	—	.46	.15
b. on office operations	1.06	.17		—	.24
c. on external office affairs	1.09	.17			—
5. SD of Other Supervisors' Influence in Office—	.79	.16	.41	.74	.74
a. on unit operations	1.13	.16	—	.12	.44
b. on office operations	.94	.19		—	.43
c. on external office affairs	.98	.20			—
6. SD of Other Organizations' Influence—	.77	.15	.71	.76	.70
a. on unit operations	.92	.21	—	.56	.47
b. on office operations	.88	.20		—	.47
c. on external office affairs	1.10	.16			—

[a] All responses were scored on the following answer scale in the OAI Questionnaires

None	Little	Some	Quite A Bit	Very Much
1	2	3	4	5

composite indices (in bold face) and the correlations with their component decision items.

Although the three decision areas are highly correlated for each group, a comparison of the means in the top half of Table 4-3 shows there are systematic differences between the amounts of influence of different groups on different decision areas, and this provides a good indication of the discriminant validity of the OAI influence items.

However, the average distributions of responses within offices to the amounts of influence of each group (in the bottom half of Table 4-3) are somewhat problematic. Since there are many different groups of unit employees, unit supervisors, and other unit supervisors within local offices but only one office director and one headquarters office in the state agency, one should expect the distributions of influence in the former groups to be significantly larger than in the latter two groups. However, Table 4-3 shows that no discernible differences exist among the groups on their average standard deviations of perceived influence. Ideally, if all respondents in each office had a clear and consistent perception of the amounts of influence exerted by the office director and the headquarters office, then the standard deviations on these items would simply indicate measurement error, and these standard deviations should be smaller than those of the other groups because the latter include not only measurement error but also actual "true" differences in the amounts of influence of various groups of unit employees and supervisors within the office. However, the near-equal standard deviations among all groups in Table 4-3 suggest either that there are substantial differences in perceptions among respondents within offices or that there are other important systematic sources of measurement errors in the influence items.

Measurement Properties of Influence Indices at Individual Level

To directly examine differences in the influence scores due to differing frames of reference or perceptual ranges of respondents, each respondent was coded in terms of the number of vertical supervisory levels between him or her and the office director, as reflected in the organization chart. Table 4-4 shows a control graph and summary table of the differences in perceptions of the 1170 respondents in all local ES offices broken down by the number of hierarchical levels separating them from the top office directors. The graph dramatically illustrates that systematic differences in perceptions exist among respondents located in different levels of the organizational hierarchy. As one moves down the levels in the hierarchy, respondents systematically report lower or deflated amounts of influence which unit employees, supervisors, and the office director have in making decisions on unit and office operations and external affairs. This pattern is reversed on the perceived influence of the headquarters office.

In addition to these differences between respondent levels in amounts of influence, the bottom of Table 4-4 shows that there are systematic increases in the standard deviations or distributions of perceptions the greater the number of levels respondents are removed from

Table 4-4 Influence Perceptions of Respondents by Level in Hierarchy

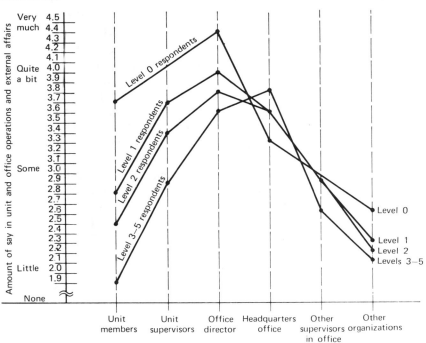

Number of Supervisory Levels Respondents Removed from Office Director		Unit Members		Unit Supervisors		Office Directors		Headquarters		Other Supervisors in Office		Other Organizations	
Levels	Number	$\bar{x}$	σ	$\bar{x}$	σ	$\bar{x}$	σ	$\bar{x}$	σ	$\bar{x}$	σ	$\bar{x}$	σ
0	20	3.7	.65	NA	NA	4.4	.40	3.3	.64	NA	NA	2.6	.58
1	124	2.8	.86	3.7	.78	4.0	.75	3.6	.72	2.9	.70	2.3	.77
2	544	2.5	.88	3.4	.83	3.8	.92	3.6	.98	2.9	.83	2.2	.83
3	360	2.3	.89	3.3	.90	3.8	.94	3.7	.98	3.0	.92	2.2	.88
4	92	2.0	.90	2.9	.91	3.5	.93	3.8	.95	2.6	1.01	2.2	.96
5	30	1.7	.63	2.3	.86	3.5	.93	4.0	1.00	2.5	.98	1.9	.73
Total (Grand Mean)	1170	2.4	.91	3.3	.88	3.8	.90	3.6	.95	2.9	.87	2.2	.84

Differences in Perceptions between Supervisory Levels	Unit Members	Unit Supervisors	Office Directors	Headquarters	Other Supervisors in office	Other Organizations
F-Ratio	23.80	20.63	5.544	4.009	5.83	1.69
Probability Level	0.00	0.00	0.00	.0013	.0001	.1342

144

the office director. However, the F ratios show that the differences between respondents at different supervisory levels are significantly greater on the perceived influence of unit members and supervisors than they are on the amounts of say of the office director and headquarters. These results are more directly consistent with the expectations discussed previously. We interpret the smaller differences between levels on the influence of the single director in each office and headquarters to be due to varying frames of reference of respondents, whereas the larger differences on the influence of unit members and supervisors are due to both varying perceptual ranges of respondents and "true" differences in amounts of influence of various unit employees and supervisors in ES offices.

The findings obtained here are consistent with previous research, which has demonstrated that judgments about individual and group behavior in organizations tend to differ systematically, depending upon the vertical and horizontal position of the respondent in the organization (Porter, 1958; Ghiselli, 1973; Bouchard, 1976; Dearborn and Simon, 1958). As a result, the perceptions of a particular group of informants are not generalizable to the functioning of the entire organization. Unfortunately, too many organizational surveys continue to rely upon the perceptions of a few informants (typically top- or middle-level managers) to measure behavioral characteristics of the total organization. As the data here indicate, if one desires to obtain a complete representation of behavior within organizations, there is a need to sample the perceptions of a cross section of respondents vertically and horizontally in the organizations.

Finally, it is important to note that the slopes of the influence curves in Table 4-4 are generally the same for respondents at all levels in the ES offices. This indicates that whereas there are clear differences in the amounts of influence perceived by respondents at different supervisory levels, respondents are consistent in distinguishing between the relative distributions of influence of the six groups. This suggests that the reliability of a composite index of the amounts of influence of different groups in the organization is enhanced by averaging together the perceptions of all respondents in each ES office, as has been done in Table 4-3. Such a composite index incorporates the differing frames of reference of respondents at all levels in the organization and is believed to provide a nearer approximation to the "true" amounts and distributions of influence of various groups in an organization than would be obtained if the perceptions of respondents from only one or two levels were relied upon. The relationships among these composite influence

Table 4-5 Correlations among Average Amounts and Distributions of OAI Perceived Influence Indices with Context, Structural Configuration, and Performance for 29 ES Offices

	Average Amounts of Influence						Standard Deviations of Influence					
	Unit Empl.	Unit Spvs.	Office Dir.	Hdqtrs. Office	Other Spvs.	Other Orgs.	Unit Empl.	Unit Spvs.	Office Dir.	Hdqtrs. Office	Other Spvs.	Other Orgs.
	AMOUNTS OF INFLUENCE											
Average Perceived Influence—												
1. of Unit Employees	—											
2. of Unit Supervisors	.73	—										
3. of Office Directors	.07	.05	—									
4. of Headquarters Office	-.46	-.33	.31	—								
5. of Other Supervisors in Office	.42	.41	.26	.21	—							
6. of Other Organizations	.02	.28	.43	.17	.18	—						
	DISTRIBUTIONS OF INFLUENCE											
Standard Deviations within Offices on Perceived Influence—												
1. of Unit Employees	-.31	-.20	-.13	.14	-.30	.39	—					
2. of Unit Supervisors	-.31	-.41	-.30	.46	-.12	-.32	.24	—				
3. of Office Directors	-.39	-.24	-.43	.19	.09	.01	.51	.30	—			
4. of Headquarters Office	-.37	-.15	-.06	.24	-.12	.43	.65	.18	.61	—		
5. of Other Supervisors in Office	-.38	-.09	-.29	.26	-.29	.19	.65	.48	.51	.58	—	
6. of Other Organizations	-.46	-.45	.29	.32	-.18	.42	.58	.28	.24	.41	.34	—

146

OFFICE CONTEXT DIMENSIONS

	1	2	3	4	5	6	7	8	9	10	11	12
1. Domain Complexity												
a. No. Counties Served	.11	.12	-.01	.11	.17	-.06	-.12	-.23	.26	.25	-.23	-.26
b. Avg. Unemployment Rate	.48	.39	.23	.23	.07	-.10	-.10	-.03	-.14	-.42	-.04	.02
c. % Population Poor	.04	.08	.01	.29	.04	-.41	-.18	-.08	.08	-.06	-.20	-.34
2. Consensus on Operating Goals	.21	.38	.09	-.24	-.05	.44	.14	-.13	-.02	.42	.29	.15
3. Uncertainty of Domain Segments:												
a. Labor Market	.40	.27	.24	.14	.33	.43	-.26	-.21	-.13	-.40	-.33	.15
b. Other Community Organizations	.30	.45	.07	.69	.28	.13	-.01	-.03	-.02	-.08	-.02	.21
c. Headquarters Office	.14	-.33	.31	-.03	.01	-.51	-.34	.57	-.14	-.30	.07	.25
d. Internal Office Affairs	.48	.31	.28	.22	.31	-.18	-.32	-.25	-.22	-.31	-.41	-.43
4. Service Demand	-.08	-.19	-.22	-.06	-.32	.40	.16	-.09	.03	.15	.16	.40
5. Budgeted No. Positions	-.28	-.40	-.09	.20	-.20	.23	.21	.14	.19	.11	.13	.39

OFFICE STRUCTURAL CONFIGURATION

	1	2	3	4	5	6	7	8	9	10	11	12
1. No. of Supervisory Levels	-.28	-.37	.20	.03	-.06	.34	.40	.17	.32	.31	.17	.51
2. No. Job Titles	-.28	-.41	.14	.01	-.05	.30	.31	.01	.23	.13	.05	.55
3. No. Sections	-.16	-.25	.11	-.07	-.17	.23	.20	-.05	.08	.23	.01	.28
4. No. Geographical Sites	.02	-.02	.19	.00	.02	.19	.14	-.06	.19	.03	.09	.26
5. Manager Span of Control	.15	.09	-.29	-.26	-.17	.05	.19	-.13	.13	.05	.19	-.13
6. Supervisor–Staff Ratio	-.03	.12	.24	-.27	-.27	.12	-.15	-.08	-.45	.19	-.13	-.06
7. % Spvs. above Bottom Level	-.56	-.44	-.15	.38	-.03	-.07	.13	.28	.43	.34	.35	.37

OFFICE PERFORMANCE

	1	2	3	4	5	6	7	8	9	10	11	12
1. Office Efficiency	.46[b]	.28	-.11	-.21	.13	-.07	-.24	-.19	-.05	-.32[a]	.17	-.07
2. Office Effectiveness	.27	.13	.22	.24	-.02	-.07	-.17	-.15	-.22	-.34[a]	.05	-.15
3. Mean Job Satisfaction	.64[b]	.49[b]	.17	-.14	.44[b]	-.08	-.20	-.29	-.08	-.41[a]	-.26	-.28
4. SD Job Satisfaction	-.38[a]	-.38[a]	-.30[a]	.02	-.12	-.04	.32[a]	.28	.28	.11	.26	.26

[a] $p < .10$.
[b] $p < .05$. Significance levels indicated only for performance correlations.

indices of the six groups are now examined, as well as their associations with the other office context, structure, and performance dimensions.

Relations among Influence Measures and Organizational Performance

Table 4-5 presents the correlations among the influence measures of the six groups and with the other macroorganizational dimensions examined thus far. With two exceptions, the table shows quite consistent positive correlations among the average amounts of influence and among the distributions of influence of the six groups. Methodologically, this indicates a substantial convergence among the OAI measures on the amounts and distributions of influence.

Substantively, the results provide support to the argument forcefully presented by Lammers (1968) that decision-making power and influence are not scarce, fixed quantities to be allocated to certain groups at the expense of reducing the influence of other groups in organizations. Instead, the data indicate that the amounts of influence of all groups in ES offices are positively related and tend to either expand or contract for all groups simultaneously. In addition, the consistently negative correlations between the amounts and distributions of influence of unit employees, supervisors, and the director within ES offices indicate that increases in the amounts of influence of all groups in the hierarchy are associated with decreases in the distribution of influence between positions. Thus, not only are increases in the amounts of influence of one group related to increases in the amounts of influence of other groups in ES offices, they also are associated with decreased disparities in power or authority among people within and between these groups. Moreover, Table 4-5 shows that this pattern of increasing the amounts and decreasing the distributions of influence among groups is associated with increases in overall office efficiency, effectiveness, and amount of job satisfaction, and decreases in variations in job satisfaction among personnel in ES offices.

Overall, these results support the theory that greater and more equal amounts of influence among personnel over decisions affecting their work environment increase organizational performance. Explanations for these results are that increases in the perceived power or influence of personnel: (1) open a greater number of egalitarian communication channels among positions and groups in the organization, (2) release more information, both pro and con, relevant to making decisions, (3) increase the probability for conflicts to be solved by confrontation and problem solving among differing groups, rather than by avoiding or smoothing them over, and (4) motivate people to work harder because they have a stake in the operations of their work group and organization. It should be cautioned, however, that the support shown in Table 4-5 for this theory should not be inferred beyond the ES offices in this sample.

Relations of Influence Measures with Other Organizational Characteristics

The positive correlations of the indicators of domain complexity, consensus, and uncertainty with the average amounts of influence of the six groups are largely as expected, but the correlations with the standard deviations of influence are not. One would expect that more diverse communities served by ES offices and greater uncertainties of environmental segments would be associated with greater distributions of influence among decision-making groups. At the present time we are not prepared to explain why the data show these relationships to be negative in the ES offices.

Finally, Table 4-5 indicates a considerable degree of convergence between the influence measures and the indicators of formal authority from organization charts. As found by Melman (1958), Whisler et al. (1967), and Tannenbaum (1968), increases in the number of supervisory levels and administrative intensity at upper hierarchical levels are associated with decreases in the average amounts of influence of all unit employees and unit supervisors in ES offices but positively related to the influence of the office director and headquarters. In addition, increases in vertical and horizontal differentiation tend to be positively correlated with greater distributions or variances in the amounts of influence of all decision-making groups, as expected. Since the correlations between the structural configuration of ES offices and the amounts and distributions of influence of the various groups are moderate to small in size, this suggests that there is not a particularly tight relationship between the formal and informal structures of authority in ES offices.

SUMMARY OF EVALUATION FINDINGS

This section has examined the empirical relationships among the OAI measures of organization context, structure, and performance in our conceptual scheme for assessing macroorganization design. The results presented here are tentative, and caution should be taken in drawing definitive inferences. This is because the conceptual scheme for assessing overall organization design, particularly the part dealing with organization domain, was not developed to the present stage until recently, and instrument construction must necessarily lag theory building. As a result, not all dimensions in our present conceptual scheme were measured in the 1975 OAI, and not all measures of the dimensions that were included in the 1975 OAI turned out to be particularly appropriate for evaluating the new conceptual scheme. Therefore, we have varying degrees of confidence in the measures and the theory proposed for assessing the context, structure, and performance of organizations.

The major results from the evaluation of the OAI macroorganizational measures will now be summarized.

First we focused on the overall structural configuration of an organization and defined and measured it in terms of the organization chart. Although the table of organization is commonly used, relatively little systematic attention has been given to understanding its underlying dimensions and to using it for organization research and analysis. This chapter and Appendix A move in this direction by suggesting specific standards and conventions for constructing organization charts and for using them to obtain eight generally applicable measures of the overall structural configuration of organizations.

Data on 29 and 1201 local ES offices, included in the OAI and Blau and Schoenherr (1971) surveys, respectively, were presented to show the relations among the eight structural configuration measures. Although they were in the same direction, substantial differences in the sizes of the correlations were found to exist between the two surveys. This indicates that the pattern of relations among the structural configuration measures may differ from organization to organization. For the ES offices included in the OAI survey, substantial correlations were found between the structural configuration measures and office effectiveness, efficiency, and personnel job satisfaction. The results suggest good concurrent validity of the measures. The measures were also found to be useful for making strategic decisions on the size and structural configuration of local ES offices in this sample.

It must be underscored that organization charts are a valuable source of data for comparative and longitudinal studies of organizations *if and only if* (a) they are consistently constructed according to a precise set of standards such as suggested in Appendix A, and (b) they have been explained and verified by informants who are familiar with the current operations of the organization being assessed.

Next, we examined the contexts of ES offices in terms of domain complexity, consensus, uncertainty, service demand, and budgeted number of personnel positions. The other contextual factors in our conceptual framework for assessing macroorganization design (organization age, domain type, and domain restrictiveness) were not included in the 1975 OAI because our theory had not developed to the stage to include measures of domain restrictiveness, and there is very little or no variation on the other factors in the sample of ES offices examined here.

Unlike the structural configuration measures from organization charts, which are intended to apply directly to all kinds of organizations, measures of the contextual dimensions are necessarily idiosyncratic to the types of organizations under investigation. This is not to suggest that the contextual factors have different meanings conceptually across organizations—only that they need to be operationalized differently depending upon the type of organization being investigated. Indeed, as argued in the theoretical introduction of this chapter, we believe that at a conceptual level the contextual dimensions have the same definitions and are generalizable across all types of organizations. However, due to the great diversity in types of domains of organizations, we believe that attempts to develop operational indicators which apply to all types of organizations will yield measures that are too general or broad to be sufficiently reliable and valid for assessing organizations.

In general, the dual objectives of developing measures that are specific enough to be useful for assessing a particular organization, yet general enough to permit comparative assessments across organizations represent the traditional constraining forces in constructing any instrument. For the vast majority of dimensions in the OAI, we argue that both objectives can be satisfactorily achieved by developing a single set of measures that are balanced in their degrees of specificity and generalizablility. Indeed, one of the major purposes of this book is to evaluate the extent to which this assumption is valid. However, after several unsuccessful trials, our preliminary conclusion is that a single set of measures of domain complexity, uncertainty, consensus, and restrictiveness for all organizations will yield an unsatisfactory compromise because these domain dimensions exhibit themselves in dissimilar ways across different types of organizations or industries. For example, while unemployment rate, number of counties served, and percentage of population poor are adequate measures of the demographic complexity of communities served by ES offices, they are obviously less appropriate indicators of the domain complexity of a steel corporation. Thus, in the revised OAI presented in Chapter 9 we do not propose to recommend a generalizable set of measures for domain complexity, consensus, uncertainty, and restrictiveness. At this embryonic stage of concept development, we believe that these dimensions are best measured by indicators specific to the type of organization being assessed and that inferences from these studies should be limited to the specific organizations examined.

The correlations between the specific indicators of the context of ES offices and their structure and performance were found to be largely as the theory predicted, although some interesting unexpected relationships were found. These predicted and unexpected findings are as follows.

Consistent with the economic production function problem discussed in the theoretical section, the correlation between office service demand and the budgeted number of personnel positions in ES offices is .99. This supports the hypothesis that organizations attempt to equate product or service demand with the supply of resources and personnel positions necessary for meeting their demand.

In this sample of 29 ES offices, support was found for Thompson's (1967:70) proposition that organizations facing heterogeneous task environments seek to identify homogeneous segments and establish structural units to deal with each. Significant positive correlations were found between the domain complexity indicators and horizontal differentiation within ES offices (i.e., greater number of sections and geographically outstationed service sites in the community) and the placement of a greater proportion of supervisory personnel at the bottom direct service-delivery levels of ES offices. Supporting evidence was also found for the argument that, with increasing domain complexity, ES managers and supervisors perceive less uncertainty of internal office operations and share lower agreement on the operating service goals of the ES office.

Quite unexpectedly, domain complexity was strongly positively correlated with the efficiency, effectiveness, and job satisfaction of personnel in ES offices. Approximately one-half of the total effect of ES office domain complexity on performance was found to be explained by the structural subdivision of ES offices to manage increasingly complex domains (as the theory suggests). The remaining direct effect of domain complexity on office performance was substantial and was discussed in practical terms of guiding location decisions of ES offices in local communities.

Systematic differences were found in the relationships between internal and external domain uncertainty items with the other dimensions of ES office context, structural configuration, and performance.

Uncertainty of the labor market and other organizations had consistent and significant positive correlations with office service demand, size and structural differentiation, and negative relations with administrative intensity. The opposite relations were found for perceived uncertainty of operations within the local offices and at the headquarters office. Two plausible explanations for the data were presented: (a) support exists for Thompson's (1967:20) proposition that "organizations seek to buffer environmental influences by surrounding their technical cores with input and output components," that is, adding more sections and operating sites and proportionately decreasing administrative intensity at middle and upper supervisory levels, or (b) structural configuration influences the perceptions by ES managers of an increasingly unclear external domain but an increasingly certain internal domain as a result of uncertainty absorption processes discussed by March and Simon (1958). However, the utility of both explanations was questioned because the domain uncertainty indicators are positively correlated with the three criteria of ES office performance. Central to both explanations is the expectation that a reduction in domain uncertainty should increase organization performance. The conclusion drawn from this evidence is that uncertainty reduction is not necessarily the *raison d'etre* for designing the ES offices in this sample.

A relatively high and narrow range of consensus on operating goals among supervisors in the ES offices was observed, and within this range the relationships of domain consensus with the other context and structural configuration dimensions were found to be in the predicted direction. However, in this sample of ES offices, domain consensus was strongly negatively correlated to office performance. Consistent with Ashby's law of "requisite variety," the explanation given was that a concave relationship should be expected between domain consensus and organization performance, and the ES office supervisors in this sample were observed at the high end of the consensus continuum. Research in other organizations over a wider range of domain consensus is necessary to substantiate this explanation.

Finally, we examined the measurement properties of the OAI perceived influence indices. Overall, the measures of the amounts of influence of different groups in ES offices on various decisions were found to exhibit satisfactory indications of convergent and discriminant validity. However, significant differences in the frames of reference of respondents at different hierarchical levels in the organization were found. One explanation for this finding is that respondents vary in their familiarity with the activities of other groups. Hence, the perceptions of all personnel—or, at the minimum, a sample of a cross section of all vertical and horizontal positions in the organization—is necessary to obtain a valid composite measure of the perceived structure of authority in organizations (as well as other organizational dimensions that are based on perceptions).

Substantively, it was found that the amounts of influence of unit employees, supervisors, and the director in ES offices are consistently and strongly positively correlated. In addition, increases in the amounts of perceived influence of all groups, and decreases in the distributions or disparities within and between groups on the amount of say they have in making decisions related to the work environment were found to be positively related to the overall efficiency, effectiveness, and personnel job satisfaction of ES offices. Thus, the high-performing ES offices showed greater and more equal amounts of influence by the director and all groups of employees and supervisors.

CHAPTER FIVE

The Context and Design of Organizational Units

Once the overall domain and structural configuration of an organization is assessed, one can begin to examine the design of work units or departments. A focus on organizational units is needed to understand the unique patterns of structure and process that exist within organizations. By definition, a complex organization consists of many subsystems, each making a different contribution to the total system and correspondingly adopting a structure that is appropriate for performing its tasks and functions. Therefore, attempts to compute composite scores on dimensions such as specialization, formalization, and discretion across all organizational units inherently present a distorted, homogenizing view of the organization. As this chapter shows, these dimensions are more appropriately examined at the unit or work group level of analysis.

The organizational unit represents the basic (and smallest) building block for examining collective behavior and is defined as consisting of a supervisor and all personnel reporting directly to that supervisor. Likert's (1967) concept of "linking pins" is used to operationally identify organizational units at all levels of an organization (see Figure 5-1). As early as 1938, Barnard wrote that "all organizations of complex character grow out of small, simple organizations" (Barnard, 1938:104). As a microsocial system, the organizational unit bears many resemblances to large-scale social systems. By studying the unit or work group, we can better understand the interaction between the behavior and decisions of individuals and the structure of the total organization (Shull, Delbecq, and Cummings, 1970:129). Finally, organizational units may obstruct or inhibit the achievement of corporate goals and strategies or, alternatively, support and complement the overall purposes of the larger organization (House, 1963:41).

155

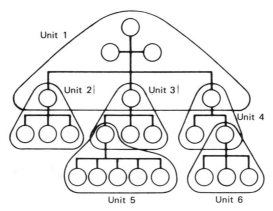

Figure 5-1 Identifying units in an organization chart based on Likert's (1967) linking pin concept.

Figure 5-2 outlines the core dimensions of unit task, structure, and process that are included in the current OAI and are evaluated in this chapter. The theory underlying the development of these dimensions is that the difficulty and variability of the work performed by an organizational unit largely predict how the unit will be organized. *Task variability*, or the number of exceptions encountered in the work, affects the degree to which work processes can be structured in a specialized and standardized way (Perrow, 1967; Hage and Aiken, 1969; Hall, 1962; Litwak, 1961; Woodward, 1965). *Task difficulty*, or the degree to which work can be analyzed and its outcome predicted, directly affects the amount of expertise, discretion, and mutual adjustment required to perform the tasks (Hage, 1965; Bell, 1967; Mohr, 1971; Van de Ven et al., 1976). Furthermore, Van de Ven and Delbecq (1974) found that different structural modes or work programs emerge depending on whether a unit's tasks are low, medium, or high in difficulty and variability.*

The tasks assigned to organizational units represent cycles of activities that are organized into work programs. Programs are the *modus operandi*, or the way repetitive activities are structured (March and Simon, 1958). In varying degrees, a program specifies the following characteristics: (1) *specialization*, the number of different tasks and activities performed by a unit and the interchangeability of tasks among personnel; (2) *standardization*, the procedures and pacing rules that are to be followed in task performance; (3) *discretion*, the decisions and judgments that role occupants (the supervisor and unit employees) are to make during task execution; and (4) *personnel expertise*, the skills

---

* The designs of these different structural modes are discussed in detail in Chapter 9.

required of role occupants to operate the program. Thus, the structural referent of an organizational unit is its work program, and its dimensions are examined in terms of specialization, standardization, discretion, and expertise (Van de Ven, 1976a).

Process is viewed as the patterns of relationships among unit personnel who execute this work program. The *interdependence*, or tightness of couplings among role occupants, is reflected in the flows of work among unit personnel and the extent to which they rely upon each other to receive their work, perform their individual tasks and send their completed work on to others to complete the total job. *Coordination* processes to manage this interdependence are based on the way unit personnel handle their communications and conflict resolution. We hypothesize that interdependence and coordination are positively interrelated and that they co-vary with the task dimensions (difficulty and variability) and structure dimensions (specialization, standardization, discretion, and expertise).

Interdependence is a function of personnel specialization, expertise, and the task dimensions. If personnel within the unit are generalists and are trained sufficiently to perform all the relatively simple tasks encountered by the unit, each role occupant can operate as an inde-

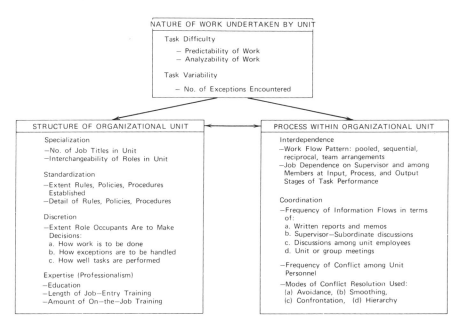

Figure 5-2 Framework for examining unit task, structure, and process in the OAI.

pendent actor. There is little need for mutual adjustments as long as each follows the rules and standard operating procedures established for task performance. However, if each person is trained as a specialist and performs only a small fraction of the unit's work, or if the work is sufficiently difficult to require consultation among members of the group, then interdependence exists, and mutual adjustments (by way of discussions and group meetings) are necessary to coordinate work activities. If these tasks are nonvarying, the necessary adjustments can be programmed through written plans and schedules and standardized operating procedures. However, if these tasks vary greatly, it may not be possible to program mutual adjustments in advance, and the unit may need to pay a higher price for coordination by spending more time in frequent personal and group discussions. Alternatively, an organizational unit may attempt to shift interdependence from between positions to within positions by structurally decreasing personnel specialization and standardization and correspondingly increasing personnel expertise and discretion. This structural change decreases interdependence among unit personnel and, therefore, decreases the need for frequent communications and group meetings to coordinate and control work activities.

Increases in task difficulty and variability are likely to increase the frequency of conflict among unit personnel because a greater number of issues arise on which people may disagree about appropriate strategies for handling them. Conflict may either lead to creative solutions and increased unit performance or result in hurt feelings and decreased unit effectiveness, depending upon how it is managed (Filley et al., 1976; Thomas, 1976; McGrath, 1976). The prevailing research findings are that when disagreements or disputes among personnel are avoided or smoothed over, they become bases for inhibiting communications and relationships among the parties involved, detracting from work performance. On the other hand, when confronted openly, conflict can be the source for creative problem-solving which results in improved performance. Research by Burke (1970) found that forcing a resolution to conflict by resorting to higher authority also tends to be associated with constructive use of differences and disagreements. One explanation for these findings is that avoidance and smoothing-over do not resolve conflicts among contending parties and allow differences of opinion to fester and grow into interpersonal barriers far out of proportion to the initial disagreements. When conflicts are openly confronted among unit personnel or referred to higher levels of supervision, they are resolved, and the parties involved obtain a clearer understanding of the roles and behaviors expected.

More operational definitions and measures of the unit task, structure, and process dimensions are presented and then evaluated in the subsequent section.

DEFINITIONS AND MEASURES OF UNIT DIMENSIONS

1. Task Difficulty. Task difficulty is defined by two conceptually distinct terms, the *analyzability* and *predictability* of the work undertaken by an organizational unit. The construct stems from the work of March and Simon (1958) and was further developed by Perrow (1967), who refers to it as the ability to understand the characteristics of the raw materials or work objects encountered. The construct focuses on the analyzability and predictability of the search process that individuals undertake when they encounter a task, problem, or issue. The analyzability of work is the ease and clarity of knowing the nature and order of tasks to be performed. The predictability of the work is the ease with which one can determine in advance what the outcomes of a particular sequence of task steps will be. At one extreme of task analyzability and predictability, the search process is completely programmed and trivial; at the other extreme, it relies upon chance and guesswork.

Items 1, 4, and 5 following are intended to measure analyzability, whereas items 2 and 3 tap the predictability element in the task difficulty index. All five of these items were included in the OAI unit supervisor and member questionnaires.

1. To what extent is there a *clearly known way* to do the major types of work you *normally encounter*?

NO EXTENT	LITTLE EXTENT	SOME EXTENT	GREAT EXTENT	VERY GREAT EXTENT	
1	2	3	4	5	(Reversed Scale)

2. *How easy* is it for *you* to *know* whether you do your work correctly?

VERY DIFFICULT	QUITE DIFFICULT	SOMEWHAT EASY	QUITE EASY	VERY EASY	
1	2	3	4	5	(Reversed Scale)

3. *What percent of the time* are you *generally sure* of what the outcome of your work efforts will be?

40% OR LESS	41–60%	61–75%	76–90%	91% OR MORE	
1	2	3	4	5	(Reversed Scale)

4. In the past 3 months, *how often* did *difficult problems arise* in your work for which there were no immediate or apparent solutions?

ONCE A WEEK OR LESS	ABOUT 2-4 TIMES A WEEK	ABOUT ONCE A DAY	ABOUT 2-4 TIMES A DAY	5 TIMES OR MORE A DAY
1	2	3	4	5

5. About *how much time* did you spend solving these *work problems?*

LESS THAN 1 HR/WEEK	ABOUT 1-4 HOURS/WEEK	ABOUT 1 HOUR/DAY	ABOUT 2-3 HOURS/DAY	4 HOURS OR MORE PER DAY
1	2	3	4	5

To test the validity of this perceptual measurement index, tasks were also classified according to difficulty in a standardized, nonperceptual way in the 1973 OAI. The procedures for classifying the work of units into levels of difficulty were as follows:

1. In the unit supervisor and member questionnaires all respondents were asked to write the specific tasks they performed in a normal day, as well as the time spent on each task.

2. Working in collaboration with the internal management analysts of the employment security agency, the researchers edited the population of tasks for duplication and classified them into levels of high, medium, and low task difficulty.

3. The task that occupied most of the working time of each respondent was then scored according to its level of task difficulty.

4. Individual scores on task difficulty were then averaged for each unit to obtain the unit task difficulty score.

The correlation between the perceived and classified task difficulty indices in the 1973 OAI was .71, thus establishing the criterion-related validity of the perceived task difficulty index. Since no substantive changes were made in the perceived task difficulty index in the 1975 OAI, the classified task difficulty index was not computed.

2. Task Variability. Task variability is defined as the number of exceptions encountered in the characteristics of the work. For our purposes, task variability focuses only on perceived variations of incoming work materials and objects. In this narrow sense, task variability is similar to materials technology (Hickson et al., 1969:380) and the perceived uniformity and stability of raw materials (Perrow, 1967). Perrow (1967) includes, in his definition of exceptions, the degree to which stimuli are perceived as familiar or unfamiliar. However, we do not include the familiarity of work objects in our definition of task variability because its inclusion would confound our definitions of difficulty and variability.

Task variability was measured as the average response to the following four questions in the unit supervisor and unit member questionnaires.

1. *How much the same* are the day-to-day situations, problems, or issues you encounter in performing your major tasks?

VERY MUCH THE SAME	MOSTLY THE SAME	QUITE A BIT DIFFERENT	VERY MUCH DIFFERENT	COMPLETELY DIFFERENT
1	2	3	4	5

2. How many of these tasks are the same from day-to-day?

ALMOST ALL MY TASKS ARE THE SAME DAY-TO-DAY	MANY OF MY TASKS ARE THE SAME DAY-TO-DAY	ABOUT HALF MY TASKS ARE THE SAME DAY-TO-DAY	SOME OF MY TASKS ARE THE SAME DAY-TO-DAY	ALMOST NO TASKS ARE THE SAME DAY-TO-DAY
1	2	3	4	5

3. During a normal week, *how frequently* do *exceptions arise* in your work which require *substantially different* methods or procedures for doing it?

VERY RARELY	OCCASIONALLY	QUITE OFTEN	VERY OFTEN	CONSTANTLY
1	2	3	4	5

4. *How often* do you *follow* about the *same work methods or steps* for *doing* your major tasks from day to day?

VERY SELDOM	SOMETIMES	ABOUT HALF THE TIME	QUITE OFTEN	VERY OFTEN	
1	2	3	4	5	(Reversed Scale)

To test the validity of these perceptual measures in the 1973 OAI, tasks were classified according to levels of variability in a standardized nonperceptual way. The procedures for classifying the work of unit personnel into levels of variability followed the same four steps outlined previously for task difficulty.

The correlation between the perceived and classified task variability scales in the 1973 OAI was .76, indicating good criterion-related validity. No substantive changes were made in the task variability index in the 1975 OAI, and the classified task variability was not computed for that year.

3. Unit Standardization. Standardization is defined as the degree to which work rules, policies, and procedures are *formalized* and *followed* in an organizational unit. Standards are formalized when they are codified and specified in detail (items 1 and 2 following). Standards are followed when unit personnel perceive they do in fact use formal or informal standard operating practices in their work (items 3 and 4 following). The unit standardization index is based on the following questions answered by all unit personnel.

1. *How many written rules and procedures exist* for doing your major tasks?

VERY FEW IF ANY	A SMALL NUMBER	A MODERATE NUMBER	A LARGE NUMBER	A GREAT NUMBER
1	2	3	4	5

2. *How precisely* do these rules and procedures *specify* how your major tasks are to be done?

VERY GENERAL	MOSTLY GENERAL	SOMEWHAT SPECIFIC	QUITE SPECIFIC	VERY SPECIFIC
1	2	3	4	5

3. To what *extent* did you follow *standard operating procedures* or practices to do your major tasks the past 3 months?

TO NO EXTENT	LITTLE EXTENT	SOME EXTENT	GREAT EXTENT	VERY GREAT EXTENT
1	2	3	4	5

4. When considering the various situations that arise in performing your work, what *percent of the time* do you *have* written or unwritten procedures for dealing with them?

0–20%	21–40%	41–60%	61–80%	81–100%
1	2	3	4	5

As the definitions and measures suggest, there is a fine but important conceptual distinction between task variability and unit standardization. Task variability is concerned with the uniformity of the work, objects, or raw materials encountered by a unit, whereas standardization deals with the uniformity and codification of methods for doing the work. Behaviorally, the difference between the uniformity of the incoming work and the uniformity of methods for doing the work is what distinguishes task variability from standardization. This distinction was not made by Hall (1962) and Hage and Aiken (1969), who refer to both dimensions as task routinization. The reasons it is important to distinguish task variability from standardization are (1) the former is an aspect of technology, the latter of social structure; (2) the former is hypothesized to cause the latter; and (3) separating the dimensions facilitates a more critical analysis of the organization design problem.

4. Personnel Expertise.   Unit personnel expertise refers to the degree of professional skills of people in the unit. People most often obtain job skills from three basic sources: formal school education, job-entry orientation and training, and on-the-job continuing education and reading of materials necessary for maintaining and upgrading job-related skills. Thus, the expertise index consists of three items.

1. *How many hours per week on or off the job* do you spend in some kind of *reading or training* to keep current in the skills needed to do your job?

LESS THAN 1 HR/WK	ABOUT 1–3 HR/WK	ABOUT 4–6 HR/WK	ABOUT 7–9 HR/WK	ABOUT 10 HR/WK OR MORE
1	2	3	4	5

2. When you *began* working in this *unit, how long* a *period* of *orientation and training* did you receive that was *directly related to your tasks* in this unit?

A FEW HOURS OR LESS	ABOUT A DAY	ABOUT A WEEK	ABOUT A MONTH	MORE THAN A MONTH
1	2	3	4	5

3. What is the highest educational level you attained in school?

GRADE SCHOOL DIPLOMA	HIGH SCHOOL DIPLOMA	ATTENDED COLLEGE OR VOCATIONAL SCHOOL AFTER HIGH SCHOOL	COLLEGE BACHELOR'S DEGREE	MASTER'S DEGREE OR HIGHER
1	2	3	4	5

5. Unit Specialization.   Unit specialization is defined as the number of different tasks or jobs delegated to an organizational unit; it refers to the degree of functional differentiation within a unit. The greater the number of different jobs assigned to a unit, the lower the unit specialization and the greater the functional differentiation. This narrow construct was measured by counting the number of different job titles in the unit. Job titles were obtained from a unit personnel roster which each unit supervisor completed by recording the primary function or job title of each employee in the unit. In all cases, the supervisor's job was counted as a unique job title.

To test the validity of this measure, a parallel measure of unit specialization was obtained from the administrative division of the employment security agency. The number of different civil service classifications (excluding grade variations) of personnel within each unit were counted. As discussed in Chapter 4, the number of civil service classifications within a unit is considered a valid measure of functional differentiation because the classification of personnel according to the Civil Service System is highly formalized and routinely monitored. The correlation between the number of job titles and civil service classifications is .77, suggesting good criterion-related validity for job titles as a measure of unit specialization.

6. *Personnel Specialization or Role Interchangeability.* Unit specialization provides an indication of the number of different official job categories and job functions in a unit. In this sense it is simply a measure of the horizontal division of labor within a unit. However, it does not indicate how interchangeable these different jobs are among unit personnel. The latter is the meaning reserved for personnel specialization. In operational terms, interchangeability, or the converse, personnel specialization, means the degree to which A can perform B's job at short notice and B can perform A's, even when A and B have different job titles or different functional assignments (Beer, 1966; Tyler, 1973). In a unit with high personnel specialization, job rotation is very difficult because personnel roles are not interchangeable in the near term. Thus, personnel specialization refers to the bifurcation of skills among unit employees (Blau and Schoenherr, 1971).

It is important to recognize that the level of expertise or professionalism is conceptually independent of personnel specialization. Thus, personnel specialization is different from "role variety" (Tyler, 1973), the number of "specialists" (Hage, 1965; Hage and Aiken, 1967), "functionalization" (Samuel and Mannheim, 1970), and "personal specialization" (V. Thompson, 1961; Blau, 1974; Hall, 1972). Each of these terms has been used to refer to both our personnel specialization and the level of professionalism or expertise of personnel. For purposes of organizational analysis, we find it important to keep unit specialization, personnel specialization, and expertise distinct conceptually and empirically. This permits one to study their interrelations.

Personnel specialization, or role interchangeability, was measured by asking the first three questions following of all unit members and supervisors (with appropriate modification in the referent of the questions), and the last question of only the unit supervisor.

1. During the past 3 months, *how many* of your immediate unit *subordinates* (*members*) *performed the same basic tasks*, or did each perform a different task?

NO ONE PERFORMED SAME TASKS	ONLY A FEW PERFORMED SAME TASKS	ABOUT HALF PERFORMED SAME TASKS	MANY PERFORMED SAME TASKS	ALL PERFORMED THE SAME BASIC TASKS
1	2	3	4	5

2. *How many of your immediate subordinates are qualified* to do one anothers' jobs?

NO ONE	ONLY A FEW	ABOUT HALF	MANY	ALL
1	2	3	4	5

3. *How easy* would it be to rotate the jobs of your *immediate subordinates,* so that each can do a good job performing the others' tasks?

VERY DIFFICULT. MOST MEMBERS WOULD NEED EXTENSIVE RETRAINING.	QUITE DIFFICULT. SOME MEMBERS WOULD NEED EXTENSIVE RETRAINING.	SOMEWHAT DIFFICULT. A FEW MEMBERS WOULD NEED RETRAINING.	QUITE EASY. SOME MEMBERS WOULD NEED MINOR RETRAINING.	VERY EASY. NO MEMBERS WOULD NEED RETRAINING.
1	2	3	4	5

4. During the past 3 months, *how often* did your immediate subordinates *rotate their jobs* by performing one anothers' work?

NOT ONCE	ABOUT EVERY MONTH	ABOUT EVERY WEEK	ABOUT EVERY DAY	ABOUT EVERY HOUR
1	2	3	4	5

7. Employee Discretion. Employee decision making is a relatively narrow construct that refers to the amount of discretion unit members exercise in making work-related decisions. The following questions were answered by unit employees. In the supervisor questionnaire, the referent of the questions focused on unit members.

Listed below are four common decisions about your work.

How much influence do you have in making *each* of the following decisions about your work? (Circle a number on the right for each decision.)	AMOUNT OF INFLUENCE I HAVE IN EACH DECISION				
	NONE	LITTLE	SOME	QUITE A BIT	VERY MUCH
a. Determining what tasks I will perform from day to day?	1	2	3	4	5
b. *Setting quotas* on how much work I have to complete?	1	2	3	4	5
c. *Establishing rules and procedures* about *how* my work is to be done?	1	2	3	4	5
d. Determining *how work exceptions* are to be handled?	1	2	3	4	5

8. Supervisory Discretion. Supervisory decision making refers to the amount of discretion the unit supervisor exercises in making

work-related decisions. The only difference in the meaning of employee
and supervisory decision making is the source of discretion. The latter
was measured with the following items.

Listed below are the same work decisions. This time indicate how *much influence* your immediate supervisor has in making each decision about your work.	AMOUNT OF INFLUENCE MY IMMEDIATE SUPERVISOR HAS IN FINAL DECISION				
	NONE	LITTLE	SOME	QUITE A BIT	VERY MUCH
a. Determining *what* tasks I will perform from day to day?	1	2	3	4	5
b. *Setting quotas* on how much work I have to complete?	1	2	3	4	5
c. *Establishing rules and procedures about how* my work is to be done?	1	2	3	4	5
d. Determining *how work exceptions* are to be handled?	1	2	3	4	5

9. Work Flow Interdependence.   *Work flows* are the materials,
objects, or clients that are sent or transported between people within
organizational units. Two dimensions of work flows are examined:
direction and *amount*. The *direction* of work flow is the order in which
work moves from person to person within a unit. The *amount* of work
flow is the relative quantity of work that is transferred between unit
members during a normal month.

The direction of work flow within a unit identifies the task–instrumental linkage between unit personnel. The amount of work flow in this
linkage indicates the degree of *task interdependence* between people in
a unit. Task interdependence is the work connectedness of unit personnel, or the extent to which people in a unit are dependent upon one
another to perform their individual jobs. Task interdependence is
reflected in the flow of work between unit personnel. A hierarchy of
increasing levels of task interdependence between unit personnel can be
determined by observing whether the work flow is in (1) independent,
(2) sequential, (3) reciprocal, or (4) team arrangements.

On the assumption that these types of work flows exhibit the characteristics of a Guttman scale (as Thompson, 1967, argued), answers to
the following questions were weighted by multiplying the supervisor's
response to independent flow by zero, sequential flow by .33, reciprocal
flow by .66 and team flow by one, and then adding the products to
obtain the overall work flow interdependence score.

THE NEXT FOUR QUESTIONS ARE ABOUT THE INTERNAL FLOW OF WORK BETWEEN YOUR IMMEDIATE SUBORDINATES. LISTED AND DIAGRAMMED BELOW ARE FOUR COMMON WAYS THAT THE WORK PERFORMED IN YOUR UNIT CAN FLOW BETWEEN YOUR IMMEDIATE SUBORDINATES. (YOU, AS THE UNIT SUPERVISOR, SHOULD CONSIDER YOURSELF OUTSIDE THE BOXES BELOW.)

1. Please indicate *how much* of the *normal work* in your unit *flows between your immediate subordinates* in a manner as described by *each* of the following cases:

HOW MUCH WORK NORMALLY FLOWS BETWEEN MY IMMEDIATE SUBORDINATES IN THIS MANNER

	ALMOST NONE OF THE WORK	LITTLE	ABOUT 50% OF ALL THE WORK	A LOT	ALMOST ALL OF THE WORK
a. *Independent Work Flow Case*, where work and activities are performed by your immediate subordinates separately and do not flow between them?	1	2	3	4	5
b. *Sequential Work Flow Case*, where work and activities flow between your immediate subordinates, but mostly in only one direction?	1	2	3	4	5
c. *Reciprocal Work Flow Case*, where work and activities flow between your immediate subordinates in a back-and-forth manner *over a period of time*?	1	2	3	4	5

Work Enters Unit

Work Leaves Unit

Work Enters

Work Leaves

Work Enters

Work Leaves

HOW MUCH WORK NORMALLY FLOWS BETWEEN MY
IMMEDIATE SUBORDINATES IN THIS MANNER

	ALMOST NONE OF THE WORK	LITTLE	ABOUT 50% OF ALL THE WORK	A LOT	ALMOST ALL OF THE WORK
d. *Team Work Flow Case*, where work and activities come into your unit and your immediate subordinates diagnose, problem solve, and collaborate as a group *at the same time* in meetings to deal with the work. Work Enters 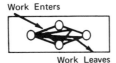 Work Leaves	1	2	3	4	5

To test the validity of this work flow interdependence index, two questions based on Mohr's (1971) index were included in the 1972 OAI questionnaires and were asked of all unit personnel to measure task interdependence in a different way:

1. To what extent do the people in this unit have one-person jobs; that is, to get the work out, to what extent do unit members independently accomplish their own assigned tasks?

2. To what extent do all the unit members meet together to discuss how each task, case, or claim should be performed or treated to do the work in this unit?

These two questions were answered on a 1–10 scale.

Upon examining the empirical characteristics of the 1972 work flow and Mohr interdependence indices, it was found that:

1. The correlation between the two items in the Mohr index is .72.

2. The correlation between the work flow and Mohr interdependence indices is .59.

3. To get some insight into the Guttman-like characteristics of the work flow index, listed in the following table are the means and standard deviations of the Mohr index on the four work flow cases.

Mohr Interdependence Scale	OAI Workflow Interdependence Scale			
	Independent 1	Sequential 3	Reciprocal 5	Team 9
Means	2.8	2.5	4.4	7.1
SD	1.6	1.5	2.7	2.3

If the two indices sample the same domain, then the .59 correlation between the work flow and Mohr indices is an appropriate indicator of construct validity of task interdependence. Further, if the two indices measure the same construct, then the table preceding suggests that the work flow index violates the properties of a Guttman scale for independent and sequential work flow cases. A reverse of the two work flow cases would result in a systematic increase in the means of the Mohr index from 2.5 (sequential), 2.8 (independent), 4.4 (reciprocal), to 7.1 (team work flow). This, however, is not an adequate test of the Guttman-like characteristics of the work flow index. Further psychometric evaluation of the work flow interdependence scale is needed on data from other organizations.

10. Job Dependence on Unit Supervisor and among Unit Members. The work flow index provides only an indication of the work flow interconnectedness of unit personnel. It does not provide an indication of the intensity of dependence between the unit supervisor and subordinates and among unit employees to do their respective jobs. Work flows may be reciprocal among personnel, and yet each person may perform his or her job as though it were self-contained because of buffering, stockpiling, and other slack-creating mechanisms, or due to the standardized nature of the work flowing among role occupants (Thompson, 1967; Galbraith, 1977). Therefore, there is a need to examine also the tightness of coupling among roles within the unit. This is the definition of job dependence. It refers to how much each role occupant's job performance depends upon the activities performed by the supervisor and other personnel in the unit.

Job dependence among unit personnel was measured in the OAI supervisor and employee questionnaires by asking how much the respondent depended upon the supervisor (or subordinates) and other unit members in order to perform his or her job at the input, process, and output stages of task performance.

How much do you have to *depend* on each of the *following people* to *obtain the materials, clients, or information* needed to do your work?

HOW MUCH DEPEND ON OTHER PEOPLE TO GET MATERIALS, CLIENTS, OR INFORMATION NEEDED TO DO MY MAJOR TASKS				
NOT AT ALL	A LITTLE	SOME	QUITE A BIT	VERY MUCH
a. Your unit supervisor? 1	2	3	4	5
b. Other people in your unit? 1	2	3	4	5

How often does your job *require* that you *check* with the following people *while doing your major tasks*?

HOW OFTEN JOB REQUIRES CHECKING WITH OTHERS WHILE DOING MY TASKS				
NO CHECKING REQUIRED	MONTHLY OR LESS OFTEN	ABOUT ONCE A WEEK	ABOUT ONCE A DAY	EVERY HOUR OR MORE
a. Your unit supervisor? 1	2	3	4	5
b. Other people in your unit? 1	2	3	4	5

After you finish your part of the job *how much do you have to rely* on *each* of the following people *to perform the next steps* in the process before the total task or service is completed?

HOW MUCH RELY ON OTHER PEOPLE TO DO NEXT WORK STEPS AFTER I COMPLETE MY PART				
NOT AT ALL	A LITTLE	SOME	QUITE A BIT	VERY MUCH
a. Your unit supervisor? 1	2	3	4	5
b. Other people in your unit? 1	2	3	4	5

Job dependence on the unit supervisor was computed as the mean response to the three questions for the supervisor, whereas job dependence among unit members was the average response to the three questions about other people in the unit.

11. Information Flows. Information flows are work-related messages sent among unit personnel through three different modes of communication: *written* memos, reports and letters; *personal* one-to-one discussions; and *group* or staff meetings among three or more unit personnel. The *direction* and *frequency* of information flows are measured in the OAI information flow index by asking the following questions of the unit supervisor and members (with the referent of the questions changed to reflect the respondents' positions).

During the past 3 months, *how often* did you receive or send *written reports* or *memos* related to your work from or to each of the following:	How Often Received or Sent Written Reports or Memos in Past 3 Months				
	NOT ONCE	ABOUT 1–3 TIMES A MONTH	ABOUT 1–3 TIMES A WEEK	ABOUT 1–3 TIMES A DAY	ABOUT EVERY HOUR
a. Your unit supervisor?	1—	2	3	4	5
b. Other people in your unit?	1	2	3	4	5

During the past 3 months, *how often* did you have *work-related discussions*, (*face-to-face or by telephone*), with each of the following on a one-to-one basis:	How Often had Work Discussions in Past 3 Months				
	NOT ONCE	ABOUT 1–3 TIMES A MONTH	ABOUT 1–3 TIMES A WEEK	ABOUT 1–3 TIMES A DAY	ABOUT EVERY HOUR
a. Your unit supervisor?	1	2	3	4	5
b. Other individuals in your unit?	1	2	3	4	5

During the past 3 months, *how often were you involved in work-related problem solving meetings* with two or more other people in your immediate unit?	How Often Involved in Problem Solving Meeting in Past 3 Months				
	NOT ONCE	ABOUT ONCE A MONTH	ABOUT EVERY 2 WEEKS	ABOUT ONCE A WEEK	SEVERAL TIMES A WEEK

12. Frequency of Conflict among Unit Personnel. The frequency of intraunit conflict refers to how often there are disagreements and disputes among unit personnel. Conflict frequency is measured with a single item in the OAI unit supervisor and employee questionnaires:

How frequently are there *disagreements or disputes* among unit members?

ALMOST NEVER	SELDOM	SOMETIMES	OFTEN	VERY OFTEN
1	2	3	4	5

13. Modes of Conflict Resolution. The modes of conflict resolution refer to the methods by which disagreements and disputes are handled in the organizational unit. Based upon the previous work of Blake and Mouton (1964), Lawrence and Lorsch (1967), Burke (1970), and Filley et al. (1976), four basic methods of conflict resolution were examined in the OAI. (The anecdotes below are based upon Burke's (1970:394) description of the conflict resolution methods.) (1) *Ignoring or avoiding the issues*—easier to refrain than to retreat from an argument; silence is golden. See no evil, hear no evil, speak no evil. (2) *Smoothing over the issues*—play down the differences and emphasize common interests; issues that might cause divisions or hurt feelings are not discussed. (3) *Openly confronting the issues*—open exchange of information about the conflict or problem and a working through of differences to reach a mutually agreeable solution. (4) *Resorting to hierarchy*—having the unit supervisor or other person with power or authority over the contesting parties resolve the matter.

The four modes of conflict resolution were measured with the following questions in the OAI supervisor and employee questionnaires.

When disagreements or disputes occur among members, *how frequently* are they resolved in each of the following ways:	How Often Disputes Resolved This Way				
	ALMOST NEVER	SELDOM	ABOUT HALF THE TIME	OFTEN	VERY OFTEN
a. By ignoring or avoiding the issues?	1	2	3	4	5
b. By smoothing over the issues?	1	2	3	4	5
c. By bringing the issues out in the open & working them out among the parties involved?	1	2	3	4	5
d. By having the unit supervisor resolve the issues between unit members?	1	2	3	4	5

Data Collection and Aggregation

Data on which the above unit task, structure, and process indices are evaluated were collected in the summer of 1975, on 334 work units located in all local and administrative offices of a state employment security agency. Two different questionnaires (one for unit supervisors and one for unit members) were personally administered to all unit personnel present at the time of a scheduled visit to each office by the research team. In all cases, the unit supervisors completed the questionnaire. Approximately 1400 respondents filled out the questionnaires, after a member of the research team explained the research study, described the meaning and intent of the questionnaire items, and answered all questions respondents might have. A standardized format was used by the researchers to make the verbal introductions of the questionnaires to all work units. An available conference room was used so that respondents could leave their work stations and not be interrupted while completing the questionnaires.

The unit of analysis of all the dimensions examined in this chapter is the work unit or department—not the individual or the overall organization. Work unit scores were obtained by assigning equal weights to questionnaire responses from the unit supervisor (½) and unit members (½) as discussed by Hage and Aiken (1967:76–77). This aggregation procedure is justified theoretically because a work unit is defined as consisting of two hierarchically related positions, a supervisor and all employees reporting directly to that supervisor. Because unit supervisors and employees occupy different social positions, as informants they are likely to hold quite different perspectives of the organization of their unit. Therefore, a balanced perspective of work unit design from the two different positions is obtained by weighting equally the responses of the unit supervisor and employees. This balanced perspective is believed to yield an aggregated score that more nearly approximates the definition of a work unit than a simple average of all respondents. The latter overweights the response of employee informants, and underweights those from the supervisory position. Furthermore, the computation of unit scores on the basis of hierarchical position is consistent with classical theory that views organizations as consisting of a series of hierarchically related social positions and not as a simple aggregation of individuals.

Spitalieri, Genet, and Van de Ven (1978) examined the empirical implications of aggregating responses of individuals to the work group level on the basis of hierarchical positions (i.e., weighting the scores of the unit supervisor by one-half to obtain unit scores) versus a simple average of scores of all unit personnel. The analysis was performed on 1975 OAI questionnaire responses of individuals to items measuring task difficulty, task variability, unit standardization, personnel specialization and expertise. When comparing the mean scores obtained on these dimensions with the two aggregation procedures, no statistically significant differences were obtained. In addition, no significant differences were found in the correlations among these unit dimensions between the two aggregation procedures. However, it was found that the correlations among the unit dimensions with the hierarchical aggregation procedure were consistently, although not significantly, smaller than those obtained with the simple average aggregation procedure. The correlations among the unit dimensions obtained with the two aggregation procedures were also compared with those obtained when not aggregating the data. The hierarchical aggregation procedure produced correlations among the dimensions that were closer to the non-aggregated correlations than those produced by the simple average aggregation procedure. Thus, while no statistically significant differences were found between the two aggregation procedures, it appears that the hierarchical aggregation procedure produces correlation coefficients among the unit dimensions that are more conservative and closer to non-aggregated scores than those obtained with the simple average aggregation procedure.

PSYCHOMETRIC PROPERTIES OF UNIT TASK, STRUCTURE, AND PROCESS INDICES

Factor Analysis

A principal components factor analysis was performed on all items in the unit task, structure, and process indices for which it was appropriate. Principal factors were extracted from the correlation matrix with unities as diagonal elements. The procedure was truncated at twelve factors (one for each hypothesized construct), and obliquely rotated with an oblimin procedure to final solution. Oblique rotation was used because the constructs are hypothesized to be interrelated as discussed in the introduction.

Table 5-1 presents the factor analysis of 39 items in the OAI designed to measure each of the constructs except unit specialization, work flow interdependence, conflict frequency, and modes of resolution. Except for interdependence, these constructs were measured by single items rather than multiple measures. The items in the work flow index were designed to form a single Guttman scale; they are not multiple measures of a single construct. Therefore, it is not appropriate to include these items in the factor analysis.

Principle components analysis found that the 39 items break out into ten factors with characteristic roots greater than one, and two additional "factors" with eigenvalues near one (.98 and .94). Eigenvalues equal to or larger than one is a convention established by Kaiser for identifying the number of factors that are "necessary, reliable and meaningful for the explanation of the correlations among variables" (Harman, 1967:198). Table 5-1 presents the primary pattern obtained from the oblimin factor rotation. The 12 factors account for 71 percent of the total common variance among the 39 items, and each of the factors is considered to make a meaningful contribution to this common variance. Most of the item communalities in the far right column (h^2) are in a moderate range, as expected, due to the diversity of constructs intended to be measured and included in this analysis. From a practical viewpoint, all 12 factors are easy to interpret.

As expected, most of the items within each index are represented by a single factor. Using the conventional .40 criterion for a significant loading of an item on a factor, Table 5-1 shows that task variability (factor 1), supervisory discretion (factor 2), employee discretion (factor 3), and unit standardization (factor 8) are distinct and unconfounded indices. No items from these indices load significantly on any factor other than their own. However, two types of departure from the hypothesized structure can be seen in Table 5-1.

One type of departure is the collapse or break out of items in an index into fewer or more factors than expected, with items in each factor not confounded in other factors. The three modes of information flows (written, personal, and group communications) were theoretically defined as a very broad construct and were expected to break out as three factors. However, Table 5-1 shows that the items measuring information flows break out as two unambiguous factors, written (factor 7) and oral (factor 9) communications. One possible reason for this result is that group communications were measured with only one item, and for that reason, should not be expected to break out as a separate factor. Hence, fewer factors than hypothesized actually occurred.

The other example of this type of departure shown by Table 5-1 is found in the personnel expertise index. The three items in this index were expected to load as a single factor. However, educational level and on-the-job training load as one factor, whereas job-entry training is clearly a separate factor, loading by itself in factor 12. Additional items may be needed in the OAI to increase the common factor variance which job-entry training represents.

Since all items in the information flow and expertise indices were measured in behavioral terms, the validity of the items is not being questioned here. Instead, the factor analysis indicates a need to reexamine the manner in which the items are grouped together. For purposes of subsequent analysis here, we evaluate each item separately and defer grouping of the items to future OAI development efforts.

A second type of departure from the hypothesized structure is the loading of items on factors representing indices other than those for which they were developed. Table 5-1 shows this to be the case for one of the items in the task difficulty, personnel specialization, and job dependence on supervisor and member indices. The task difficulty

Table 5-1 Factor Analysis for 39 Items in OAI Designed to Measure Unit Task, Offices (Principal Components: Oblique Rotation)

Items in OAI	I Task Variability	II Supervisory Discretion	III Employee Discretion	IV Personnel Specialization	V Job Dependence Among Members
Task Difficulty Index					
1. Lack Task Clarity	.50[a]	−.04	−.15	−.11	.09
2. Frequency Task Problems	.13	.02	.05	−.05	−.07
3. Time Spent Solving Task Problems	.17	−.03	.16	.08	.03
4. Difficulty Knowing Work Correct	.36	−.01	−.05	.04	−.13
5. Uncertainty of Work Outcomes	−.04	.10	−.02	.13	−.04
Task Variability Index					
6. Encounter Different Tasks	.79[a]	−.02	.14	−.08	.01
7. Number of Daily Tasks Different	.83[a]	.00	.00	−.06	.03
8. Frequency of Exceptions	.57[a]	−.05	.06	.03	−.14
9. Frequency Follow Different Steps	.49[a]	−.07	.03	−.04	.02
Personnel Specialization Index					
10. Perform Same Tasks	.02	.00	−.03	.82[a]	.05
11. Qualified to Perform Same Tasks	−.04	−.02	−.04	.89[a]	.02
12. Job Rotation Ease	−.17	−.03	−.06	.81[a]	−.00
13. Frequency of Job Rotation	.14	.11	.08	.41[a]	−.00
Personnel Expertise Index					
14. Educational Level	.10	−.06	−.10	.26	−.07
15. On-the-Job Training	.20	.11	.04	−.01	.07
16. Job-Entry Training	−.06	.04	.01	.03	−.08
Unit Standardization Index					
17. Number of Written Rules	.03	−.03	−.03	.05	−.01
18. Specificity of Rules	.11	.07	−.02	.09	−.09
19. Percent Time Have SOPs	−.09	.03	−.03	−.04	.06
20. Extent Follow SOPs	.25	.13	.03	.02	−.09
Supervisory Work Discretion Index					
21. SWD—What Tasks to Perform	−.01	.75[a]	−.17	−.09	.00
22. SWD—Setting Work Quotas	−.06	.78[a]	.04	.08	−.01
23. SWD—Setting Work Rules	.02	.84[a]	.02	−.00	−.03
24. SWD—Handling Exceptions	.02	.75[a]	−.01	−.05	.02
Employee Work Discretion Index					
25. EWD—What Tasks to Perform	.04	−.09	.83[a]	−.01	.12
26. EWD—Setting Work Quotas	.01	−.01	.85[a]	−.03	.05
27. EWD—Setting Work Rules	.01	.04	.79[a]	−.06	.02
28. EWD—Handling Exceptions	.08	−.09	.74[a]	−.01	−.17
Job Dependence on Supervisor Index					
29. Input Depends on Supervisor	.14	.01	−.02	.06	−.02
30. Check with Supervisor during Transformation	−.14	.00	−.02	−.12	.04
31. Output Depends on Supervisor	.05	.08	.00	.13	−.10
Job Dependence Among Unit Members Index					
32. Input Depends on Unit Members	.01	.02	.02	.04	−.82[a]
33. Check with Unit Members during Transformation	−.10	.02	−.02	−.02	−.66[a]
34. Output Depends on Unit Members	.02	.01	−.05	−.09	−.80[a]
Intraunit Information Flow Index					
35. Frequency spv.–sub. Written Reports	−.04	.06	−.03	−.03	.15
36. Frequency Written Reports among Members	.04	−.05	−.01	−.16	−.19
37. Frequency spv.–sub. 1–1 Talks	.13	.03	.02	.03	.19
38. Frequency 1–1 Talks among Members	.01	−.00	.03	.05	−.37
39. Frequency Group Meetings	.12	−.00	.05	.14	−.15
Eigenvalues	6.71	4.18	2.96	2.60	2.01
Cumulative Percentage of Common Variance	17	28	36	42	47

176

Structure and Process Constructs on 334 Units in Local Employment Security

VI Job Dependence on Supervisor	VII Written Communication	VIII Unit Standardization	IX Oral Communication	X Education and OJT	XI Task Difficulty	XII Job-Entry Training	h² Item Communalities
.11	.02	.34	−.09	.13	−.17	.00	.61
−.02	−.06	.03	.02	−.13	−.70[a]	−.15	.70
−.08	−.09	.12	−.03	−.31	−.50[a]	−.20	.71
.13	.07	.15	−.06	.01	−.52[a]	.12	.65
.12	−.21	.20	−.13	.04	−.62[a]	.21	.65
−.11	−.01	−.03	−.06	−.10	.06	.13	.73
−.05	−.09	−.11	.02	−.02	.01	−.04	.70
−.11	.09	.05	.02	−.13	−.25	−.14	.63
.03	−.12	.33	−.17	−.07	−.05	−.02	.64
−.04	.14	−.15	.02	−.06	−.13	−.06	.76
−.05	.08	−.04	−.05	−.00	−.09	.02	.83
−.12	−.03	.07	.01	.02	.15	.02	.75
.15	−.12	.07	−.08	.55[a]	.38	−.10	.68
.13	−.19	.12	−.08	−.57[a]	−.08	−.05	.64
.11	−.10	.01	−.12	−.66[a]	.05	−.03	.61
.04	.01	.04	.00	−.03	.05	−.93[a]	.87
.09	−.06	−.89[a]	−.01	−.01	−.06	−.01	.76
.07	−.00	−.83[a]	−.01	.18	.01	.02	.76
−.06	.02	−.63[a]	−.14	−.16	.17	−.03	.55
−.18	.09	−.48[a]	.05	−.00	.22	.06	.63
−.12	.04	.12	−.04	−.05	.16	−.02	.70
.00	−.14	.03	.03	−.16	.01	.13	.68
.04	.07	−.07	−.03	.01	−.06	−.03	.71
−.01	.02	−.10	.01	.16	−.15	−.14	.67
.04	−.10	−.11	−.07	.12	−.16	−.04	.79
−.07	.06	−.08	.01	.14	−.13	−.05	.77
.10	−.02	.23	.03	−.07	.16	−.05	.73
−.05	.10	.06	.00	−.17	.12	.14	.70
−.80[a]	−.07	−.07	−.05	.09	.01	−.03	.70
−.58[a]	.06	.04	−.58[a]	.08	−.11	−.11	.77
−.79[a]	−.09	.14	.05	−.04	.05	.05	.68
−.05	−.08	−.10	.11	−.03	−.08	.01	.71
.03	.01	.04	−.46[a]	.02	.03	.00	.74
−.08	.04	.01	.02	.06	−.02	−.11	.67
−.05	−.86[a]	−.09	.02	−.06	−.14	−.00	.80
−.11	−.81[a]	.02	−.02	.03	.09	.00	.76
−.21	−.05	−.04	−.76[a]	−.03	−.02	−.01	.73
.20	−.04	−.12	−.64[a]	−.03	.03	.05	.70
.11	−.09	−.06	−.54[a]	−.27	−.06	−.06	.62
1.86	1.56	1.42	1.18	1.08	.99	.94	
52	56	60	63	66	68	71	

177

Table 5-1   Continued

Items in OAI	I Task Variability	II Supervisory Discretion	III Employee Discretion	IV Personnel Specialization	V Job Dependence Among Members
FACTOR CORRELATION MATRIX					
I Task Variability	1.00				
II Supervisory Discretion	−.10	1.00			
III Employee Discretion	.17	−.23	1.00		
IV Personnel Specialization	−.07	.07	−.11	1.00	
V Job Dependence among Members	−.04	−.04	.01	−.04	1.00
VI Job Dependence on Supervisor	.04	−.12	.02	.06	.01
VII Written Communication	−.21	−.12	−.01	−.02	.08
VIII Unit Standardization	.28	−.14	.01	−.10	.03
IX Oral Communication	−.18	−.05	−.03	−.10	.19
X Education and OJT	−.20	.04	−.05	.02	.09
XI Task Difficulty	−.33	.05	.00	.01	.05
XII Job-Entry Training	−.08	−.09	−.06	−.02	.06

[a] Significant loading of items on factor equal to or greater than .40.

index, consisting of items 1 through 5 in Table 5-1, was hypothesized to load as a single factor. However, the first item, lack task clarity, loads higher on factors 1 and 8 than it does on the task difficulty factor 11. Because this item does not load significantly on factor 11, it does not converge or measure the same sampling domain as the other four task difficulty items. The personnel specialization index was designed to consist of four items, 10 through 13 in Table 5-1. However, item 13, frequency of job rotation, loads more highly on the expertise factor (10) than on the personnel specialization factor (4). Empirically, this item confounds the personnel specialization and expertise indices.

The job dependence items, process checks with supervisor (item 30) and unit members (item 33), load significantly on their respective factors (6 and 5); however, they also load at .40 or greater on the oral communication factor (9). This confounding is not surprising because the content of these two items implies personal communication during task execution.

As in previous evaluations of the 1972 and 1973 OAI, these departures in the 1975 OAI become one source of information for identifying where further improvements in the OAI are necessary. The data suggest the need to revise or eliminate item 1 in the task difficulty index, and item 13 in the personnel specializaton index. To proceed with the present evaluation of the OAI, these items have been eliminated. However, revision of these items may be more prudent than elimination in future applications of the OAI. Thus, the subsequent analyses of task

VI Job Dependence on Supervisors	VII Written Communication	VIII Unit Standardization	IX Oral Communication	X Education and OJT	XI Task Difficulty	XII Job-Entry Training
1.00						
.01	1.00					
.06	−.11	1.00				
.10	.17	.01	1.00			
−.02	.17	−.09	.12	1.00		
−.06	.11	−.20	.10	.19	1.00	
.11	−.05	.06	.07	−.02	.05	1.00

difficulty and personnel specialization are based on the remaining items in the respective indices. In the case of the job dependence items (30 and 33), subsequent analysis will include them in their respective indices. They are integral to those indices, and Table 5-1 indicates that they do load more strongly with the other items in the job dependence indices (factors 6 and 5) than with the oral communications items (factor 9). Revision of these items (30 and 33) and the communications items (33 through 39) in a future OAI should decrease the confounding effects seen here.

Other Criteria of Intrinsic Validity of Unit OAI Indices

The factor analytic results were examined with three further procedures to evaluate other criteria of the intrinsic validity of the OAI indices: (1) coefficient alpha to estimate the internal consistency of each index, (2) median correlations of items within indices with all other items to determine how well each index discriminates from others, and (3) correlations with parallel measures as described previously to review the criterion-related validity for some of the indices.

Table 5-2 shows the reliabilities of the OAI indices in terms of expected and observed coefficient alpha, median correlations with other indices, and correlations with parallel measures. With three exceptions, the internal consistency reliabilities of all indices lie well within the

Table 5-2 Reliabilities of the OAI Unit Task, Structure, and Process Dimensions

	Number of Items in Index	Average Correlation in Index	Coefficient Alpha Expected	Coefficient Alpha Observed	Median Correlation with All Other Items	Correlation with Parallel Measure (1973 OAI)
1. **Task Difficulty**	4	.46	.55–.70	.72	.11	.71 (with classified task difficulty)
2. **Task Variability**	4	.51	.70–.90	.81	.13	.76 (with classified task variability)
3. **Personnel Expertise**	3	.17	.55–.70	.38	—	—
a. Educational Level	1	—	—	—	.12	—
b. On-the-Job Training	1	—	—	—	.11	—
c. Job-Entry Training	1	—	—	—	.06	—
4. **Unit Standardization**	4	.50	.70–.90	.80	.09	—
5. **Unit Specialization**	1	—	—	—	.08	.77 (with number of civil service classes)
6. **Personnel Specialization**	3	.65	.70–.90	.85	.09	—
7. **Employee Work Discretion**	4	.57	.70–.90	.84	.07	—
8. **Supervisory Work Discretion**	4	.51	.70–.90	.81	.07	—
9. **Work Flow Interdependence**	1 Guttman Scale	—	—	—	.06	.59 (with Mohr (1971) index of task interdependence)
10. **Job Dependence on Supervisor**	3	.46	.70–.90	.72	.07	—
11. **Job Dependence among Unit Members**	3	.49	.70–.90	.74	.07	—
12. **Unit Information Flows**	5	.30	.35–.55	.68	—	—
a. Written Communication	2	—	—	—	.11	—
b. Personal 1–1 Discussion	2	—	—	—	.11	—
c. Group or Staff Meetings	1	—	—	—	.14	—
13. **Conflict Frequency**	1	—	—	—	.06	—
14. **Conflict Resolution Modes**						
a. Avoidance	1	—	—	—	.07	—
b. Smoothing	1	—	—	—	.04	—
c. Confrontation	1	—	—	—	.09	—
d. Authority	1	—	—	—	.06	—

expected ranges for coefficient alpha. The exceptions are minor for task difficulty but considerable for the expertise and information flow indices. They provide corroborating evidence for the problems identified and discussed in the factor analysis results. The median correlations of an index with all other unit items range from .04 (smoothing conflict) to .14 (staff or group meetings) and are far smaller than the observed coefficient alphas for their respective indices. Overall, these results suggest that both the internal consistency reliabilities of the OAI indices and the discriminant validity of the items are good.

The correlations with parallel measures for the task difficulty (.71), task variability (.76), unit specialization (.77), and work flow interdependence (.59) are also good. They suggest that the criterion-related validities of these indices are satisfactory. No indications of criterion-related validity are available for the other indices.

The preceding results provide an indication of the intrinsic validity of the OAI unit task, structure, and process indices. Equally important is the practical usefulness of these measures for research and organizational analysis. The next section evaluates the extrinsic validity of the OAI indices (1) by partially testing a task-contingent model of work unit design upon which the OAI unit dimensions are based, and (2) by assessing the design and performance of different types of work units in local ES offices.

PARTIAL TEST OF THEORY ON WORK UNIT DESIGN

Table 5-3 shows the correlations among the OAI unit dimensions and a number of contextual (or situational) factors at the work unit and overall organizational levels of analysis. The correlations are based on all 334 organizational units in the local and headquarters offices of the state employment security agency. This section focuses on these correlations to evaluate: (1) the task contingent model of work unit design, (2) the linkage between macroorganizational characteristics and work unit design, and (3) the relationships among the unit structure and process dimensions.

1. Test of Task Contingent Model of Work Unit Design. As implied by its name, the task-contingent model hypothesizes that the difficulty and variability of a unit's work are the most important predictors for explaining the design of an organizational unit. Table 5-3 shows substantial support for this hypothesis. The task dimensions are

Table 5-3 Correlations among Unit Structure and Process Dimensions Employment Security Offices

		1	2	3	4	5
		OAI	**UNIT**	**STRUCTURE**		
1.	Number Job Titles in Unit	—				
2.	Role Interchangeability	$-.24^b$	—			
3.	Unit Standardization	$-.17^a$	$.20^b$	—		
4.	Average Educational Level	$-.20^b$	$.16^b$	$-.20^b$	—	
5.	Time in On-the-Job Training	$.21^b$	$-.05$	$-.14^a$	$.41^b$	—
6.	Length of Job-Entry Training	$-.05$	$.17^a$	$.07$	$.16^a$	$.10$
7.	Supervisory Work Discretion	$.01$	$.17^a$	$.26^b$	$-.12$	$-.03$
8.	Employee Work Discretion	$.10$	$-.35^b$	$-.10$	$.01$	$.07$
9.	Work Flow Interdependence	$.20^b$	$.07$	$.06$	$.06$	$.14^a$
10.	Job Dependence on Supervisor	$-.17^a$	$.19^a$	$.13$	$-.05$	$.03$
11.	Job Dependence among Members	$.21^b$	$.08$	$.22^b$	$.11$	$.05$
12.	Freq. Written Reports & Memos	$.14^a$	$-.17^a$	$-.13$	$.37^b$	$.25^b$
13.	Freq. of 1–1 Discussions within Unit	$.09$	$.19^a$	$.07$	$.32^b$	$.23^b$
14.	Freq. of Group Meetings within Unit	$.15^a$	$.13^a$	$-.01$	$.45^b$	$.36^b$
15.	Freq. of Conflict within Unit	$.25^b$	$-.06$	$-.12$	$-.03$	$.02$
	Methods Used to Resolve Conflicts					
16.	By Avoiding or Ignoring Conflicts	$.06$	$-.05$	$.04$	$-.05$	$-.12$
17.	By Smoothing over Conflict	$.01$	$-.04$	$.05$	$-.01$	$-.11$
18.	By Confronting Conflict	$-.23^b$	$.15^a$	$-.07$	$.05$	$.12$
19.	By Resorting to Higher Authority	$-.07$	$.01$	$.03$	$-.10$	$-.02$
		CONTEXTUAL	**FACTORS**			
20.	Task Difficulty	$.10$	$-.06$	$-.48^b$	$.45^b$	$.37^b$
21.	Task Variability	$.10$	$-.19^b$	$-.41^b$	$.34^b$	$.37^b$
22.	Unit Size	$.43^b$	$.07$	$.07$	$-.25^b$	$-.13$
23.	#Levels Unit from Top Manager	$-.23^a$	$.25^b$	$.14^a$	$-.06$	$-.21^a$
		CONTEXTUAL	**FACTORS**			
24.	Organization Size (#Employees)	$-.02$	$.09$	$-.11$	$.01$	$-.02$
25.	Number Supervisory Levels in Office	$-.12$	$-.04$	$-.23^b$	$.01$	$-.11$
26.	Number of Sections	$-.21^b$	$.04$	$-.26^b$	$.02$	$-.14^a$
27.	Manager's Span of Control	$-.07$	$.04$	$-.04$	$-.03$	$.01$
28.	Organization Domain Uncertainty	$.08$	$-.03$	$-.31^a$	$.10$	$.08$
29.	Number of Counties Served by Office	$-.06$	$.07$	$.04$	$.02$	$.00$
30.	Monthly Unemployment Rate	$-.17$	$.01$	$-.26$	$.04$	$-.06$

$^a p < .01.$
$^b p < .001.$

6	7	8	9	10	11	12	13	14	15	16	17	18	19

& PROCESS DIMENSIONS

6	7	8	9	10	11	12	13	14	15	16	17	18	19
$.20^b$	—												
$-.13$	$-.45^b$	—											
$.28^b$	$.05$	$.12$	—										
$.17^a$	$.51^b$	$-.09$	$.08$	—									
$.24^a$	$.16^a$	$-.07$	$.10$	$.21^b$	—								
$.07$	$.05$	$.19^b$	$.15$	$.19^b$	$.17^a$	—							
$.15^a$	$.25^b$	$.06$	$.22^b$	$.45^b$	$.57^b$	$.24^b$	—						
$.15^a$	$.03$	$.07$	$.20^b$	$.11$	$.35^b$	$.21^b$	$.56^b$	—					
$.06$	$.00$	$.05$	$.07$	$-.15^a$	$.09$	$.01$	$-.04$	$.02$	—				
$-.08$	$-.05$	$-.25^b$	$-.08$	$-.15^a$	$.09$	$-.09$	$-.15$	$-.18$	$.54^b$	—			
$-.09$	$.05$	$-.24^b$	$.02$	$-.02$	$-.02$	$-.08$	$-.04$	$.01$	$.34^b$	$.51^b$	—		
$.13$	$.07$	$.18^b$	$.05$	$.26^b$	$-.12$	$.11$	$.20^b$	$.23^b$	$-.46^b$	$-.46^b$	$-.28^b$	—	
$.03$	$.12$	$.12$	$-.14^a$	$.33^b$	$-.20^b$	$.04$	$.05$	$.07$	$-.18^a$	$-.20^b$	$-.14^a$	$.33^b$	—

AT UNIT LEVEL

6	7	8	9	10	11	12	13	14	15	16	17	18	19
$.25^b$	$.20^b$	$.21^b$	$.13$	$.23^b$	$.27^b$	$.25^b$	$.20^b$	$.36^b$	$.07$	$.03$	$-.05$	$-.02$	$-.14$
$.13$	$.15^a$	$.35^b$	$.24^b$	$.08$	$.25^b$	$.28^b$	$.27^b$	$.35^b$	$.10$	$-.08$	$-.13$	$.13$	$.03$
$.01$	$.18^b$	$-.19^a$	$.06$	$.12$	$.09$	$.12$	$-.06$	$-.08$	$.24^b$	$.11$	$.06$	$-.17^a$	$.05$
$.06$	$.02$	$-.20^b$	$-.20^b$	$.08$	$-.18^a$	$-.07$	$-.25^b$	$-.22^b$	$-.20^b$	$-.02$	$.07$	$-.09$	$.05$

AT ORGANIZATION LEVEL

6	7	8	9	10	11	12	13	14	15	16	17	18	19
$-.03$	$-.10$	$-.01$	$.06$	$-.13$	$-.07$	$.08$	$-.05$	$-.07$	$.00$	$.00$	$.06$	$.02$	$-.04$
$.14^a$	$-.09$	$.00$	$-.07$	$-.06$	$.00$	$.05$	$-.09$	$-.07$	$.04$	$.03$	$.12$	$.02$	$-.01$
$.12$	$-.09$	$.00$	$-.14^a$	$-.09$	$-.06$	$-.02$	$-.12$	$-.11$	$-.06$	$-.03$	$.03$	$.01$	$.06$
$.03$	$.02$	$.05$	$.02$	$-.15^a$	$-.08$	$-.04$	$.07$	$-.06$	$-.03$	$-.05$	$-.03$	$.09$	$.04$
$-.04$	$-.07$	$.00$	$-.02$	$.14$	$.08$	$.06$	$.12$	$.05$	$-.13$	$-.20^a$	$-.22^b$	$.06$	$.03$
$.17$	$-.04$	$.02$	$-.03$	$.11$	$.16$	$.07$	$.11$	$.12$	$.21^a$	$.22^a$	$-.12$	$.13$	$.18$
$-.01$	$-.02$	$-.15^a$	$-.17$	$.10$	$-.09$	$.01$	$-.15$	$-.11$	$-.08$	$-.05$	$-.03$	$-.04$	$.03$

183

more strongly correlated than contextual factors on 12 of the 19 unit structure and process dimensions. As the work of organizational units increases in difficulty and variability, there are significant decreases in the standardization of work procedures and significant increases in (1) the expertise of unit personnel, in terms of formal education, job-entry and on-the-job training, (2) the amounts of work discretion exercised by both unit members and the supervisor, (3) the degrees of work and job interdependence among members and the unit supervisor, and (4) the frequency of information flows of all kinds: among unit personnel written reports and memos, one-to-one discussions, and group meetings. These observed relationships in the employment security units are highly consistent with the theory discussed in the introduction of this chapter.

The correlations in Table 5-3 indicate that the size of an organizational unit and the number of hierarchical levels that it is removed from the top manager are also significantly related to various characteristics of its structure and process. Increases in the size of work units are strongly associated with (1) greater internal differentiation in terms of job titles (as observed at the macroorganizational level in Chapter 4), (2) more frequent conflicts among unit personnel, presumably because with greater differentiation, group cohesiveness decreases and subgroup formation increases (Jennings, 1960; Miller, 1952), and (3) increased demand on the supervisor to coordinate work and make decisions while demand on the group members decreases, as has been observed often in small group laboratory studies (e.g., Hemphill, 1950; Maas, 1950; and Van de Ven, 1974).

When examining the vertical position of work groups in the organization hierarchy, Table 5-3 shows that the greater the number of hierarchical levels a unit is removed from the top manager: (1) the more homogeneous or specialized it tends to become, and the easier it is to interchange jobs among unit personnel; (2) the lower the amount of on-the-job training and work discretion exercised by unit members; (3) the lower the interdependence and the less frequent the communications among unit members; and (4) the fewer the conflicts among unit personnel. These findings in ES offices correspond quite well with other studies that relate organizational levels of individuals with job behaviors and attitudes, as reviewed by Porter and Lawler (1965) and Berger and Cummings (1979).

2. Linkage Between Macroorganization and Unit Design Characteristics. Table 5-3 shows that most correlations of overall domain and structure of the organization (items 24–30) with unit structure and process dimensions are near zero. This finding brings out an important point. The data do not support the view, widely held by both analysts and practitioners, that inferences can be drawn about the design of work units from the design of the organization as a whole, and vice versa.

Organizations, by virtue of their complexity, contain units of widely differing designs. Thus, for example, we cannot conclude that organizational units have an organic or mechanistic structure simply because they exist in organizations that are small or large, simple or complex, or facing uncertain or certain environments. The data suggest there is no necessary relationship between these macroorganizational factors and the designs of work units.

Thompson's (1967) explanation for the diversity of organizational unit designs is that under norms of rationality, organizations facing uncertain and complex environments will assign the function of responding to the environment to a few selected units. Hence, the majority of units are buffered from the environment and can adopt structures "fitted" to their particular tasks.

3. Relationships Among Unit Structure and Process Dimensions. The hypothesized pattern of relationships among the unit structure and process dimensions hinges on the dual benefits of unit specialization, as Blau (1974) has discussed in greater detail. First, increasing the specialization of a unit can promote output efficiency and economies of scale by reducing a complex task into simple nonvarying tasks, by standardizing and automating procedures, and by creating specialized jobs to perform each procedure. The greater efficiency that can be derived from specialization is the most well-known and traditional justification for the division of labor (Adam Smith, 1937). A second important benefit from specialization is that it promotes quality and success in the performance of highly difficult and varying tasks by assigning them to experts (who by definition and necessity tend to be trained in depth in narrow areas or disciplines that are difficult to interchange) and by allowing these experts to exercise high degrees of flexibility and discretion in task performance (since rules and standards cannot be specified in advance of task execution).

Because of these alternative benefits of specialization, we should expect the correlations among the unit design characteristics to differ—depending upon the nature of the task and the form of specialization adopted. Within the ranges of low to medium task difficulty and variability, an increase in unit specialization (for the purpose of enhancing efficiency) is hypothesized to be positively correlated with role interchangeability, unit standardization, and supervisory discretion and negatively correlated with personnel expertise, employee discretion, job dependence among unit members, and the frequency of discussions and group meetings among unit members. The opposite pattern of correlations with the unit design factors would be expected with unit specialization when its purpose is to promote successful performance of highly difficult and variable tasks.

The directions of the correlations in Table 5-3 plus the fact that task difficulty and variability are in the low to medium range (with means of about 2.15 and standard deviations of .75 on a 1 to 5 point scale) suggest that specialization is primarily used to enhance efficiency in this sample of ES units. Unit specialization (that is, decreases in the number of job titles in a unit) is positively related to standardization because narrowing the range of unit functions simplifies the job to a smaller set of more frequent operations. Standardizing this narrower range of tasks and functions: (1) makes job interchangeability easier; (2) decreases the education and training requirements; (3) limits the amount of work discretion by unit members and permits exceptions to be referred to the unit supervisor; and (4) permits interdependence to exist among unit personnel without a large amount of mutual adjustment (discussions and group meetings) or conflict, because most work interdependencies are standardized and routinized.

The correlations among the other unit structure and process dimensions in Table 5-3 are largely as expected. Work and job interdependencies among unit personnel (items 9 and 11) are high when there are many job titles in a unit (meaning low unit specialization but high individual specialization); these interdependencies are also high when job-entry training is extensive and when task difficulty and variability are high. Further, the frequencies of all forms of communication (written reports, discussions, and group meetings) are strongly correlated with increases in work and job interdependencies among unit personnel. In addition, as one might expect, the more the unit supervisor makes decisions on what work is to be done and who is to do it (item 7), the more unit members are dependent upon the supervisor for performing their jobs (item 10).

Finally, the frequency of conflict among unit personnel is significantly correlated with only two of the unit structure and process dimensions: increases in the number of different job titles (or functional differentiation) within the unit, and decreases in the extent to which unit members depend upon the supervisor. As is seen in the next section, the simple frequency of conflict itself does not appear to signficantly affect the performance of ES units. Instead, it is the manner in which conflict is resolved. As shown in Table 5-5 the less conflicts are avoided or smoothed over and the more they are confronted or resolved by resorting to higher levels of authority, the greater the efficiency, effectiveness, and job satisfaction of ES unit personnel. The reason these findings are stated here prematurely is because they indicate that the findings on conflict, as for the other OAI task structure and process dimensions, are highly consistent with the theories on which they are based.

These results provide one important test of the extrinsic validity of the OAI unit task, structure, and process indices. A second important test of extrinsic validity is their usefulness in diagnosing organizations, to which we now turn.

AN ASSESSMENT OF UNITS IN LOCAL EMPLOYMENT SECURITY OFFICES

If the OAI unit indices are to be useful for diagnosing organizational units, they should be able to detect systematic variations in the designs of different types of work units and explain variations in their performance. A one-way analysis of variance was computed for each task, structure, and process dimension across five basic types of units commonly found in local ES offices: intake, adjudication, placement, counseling, and work incentive units (see Table 5-4). For each of these units the OAI indices were correlated with a unique measure of unit efficiency, effectiveness, and job satisfaction to evaluate how well the OAI dimensions predict and explain unit performance (see Table 5-5). Different measures of efficiency and effectiveness are used to evaluate the performance of the ES units because each is assigned and held accountable for performing different functions in an ES office. These different unit performance criteria were described in Chapter 3.

Table 3-1 in Chapter 3 reported the correlations among the different unit efficiency, effectiveness, and job satisfaction measures. It is important to restate the finding that the various efficiency, effectiveness, and job satisfaction measures of ES units are either unrelated or positively correlated. This suggests that enhancing efficiency is not at the expense of either effectiveness or job satisfaction for a given unit and that increasing the efficiency, effectiveness, and job satisfaction of personnel in a particular unit does not occur at the expense of decreasing the performance of other units or the overall performance of the ES office. Thus, the problem of suboptimization (in other words, the optimal performance of a given unit being at the expense of other units' or overall organization performance), often found in other studies, does not exist here.

Table 5-5 presents the simple correlations between the OAI unit task, structure, and process indices and the different measures of effi-

Table 5-4 Comparison of Five Basic Types of Units in Local Employment Security Offices on Unit Task, Structure, and Process Dimensions

Unit Task, Structure, Process Dimensions	Intake & Claims Processing Units N = 20		Adjudication Units N = 22		Placement & Employer Relations N = 53		Employment Counseling Units N = 15		Work Incentive Program Units N = 42		F-test for Statistical Significance
	$\bar{x}$	σ	$\bar{x}$	σ	$\bar{x}$	σ	$\bar{x}$	σ	$\bar{x}$	σ	
1. Task Difficulty	1.79	.40	2.08	.45	2.25	.42	2.51	.52	2.35	.47	7.92 $p < .001$
2. Task Variability	2.19	.43	2.44	.44	2.37	.39	2.65	.54	2.52	.45	3.30 $p < .013$
3. # Job Titles in Unit	4.15	1.57	2.86	.77	4.06	1.89	3.71	1.20	3.56	1.07	3.18 $p < .016$
4. Job Interchangeability	3.21	.73	3.43	.66	3.37	.67	2.89	.76	3.15	.77	1.96 $p < .105$
5. Unit Standardization	3.82	.42	3.60	.44	3.33	.51	2.93	.68	3.47	.50	7.86 $p < .001$
6. Personnel Expertise											
a. Educational Level	2.45	.32	3.34	.45	3.74	.57	4.03	.48	3.76	.55	30.67 $p < .001$
b. On-the-Job Training	1.55	.48	2.30	.72	2.38	.60	2.40	.76	2.44	.61	7.97 $p < .001$
c. Job-Entry Training	2.55	.92	3.32	.89	2.99	.85	2.30	.73	2.65	.74	4.99 $p < .001$
7. Supervisory Work Discretion	2.93	.56	2.73	.36	3.08	.59	3.09	.59	2.86	.54	2.09 $p < .085$
8. Employee Work Discretion	3.76	.32	3.65	.45	3.51	.57	3.90	.46	3.65	.65	1.91 $p = .112$
9. Work Flow Interdependence	4.52	1.80	3.95	1.62	5.11	1.63	4.85	1.41	5.14	1.72	2.42 $p = .05$
10. Job Dependence on Supervisor	2.54	.50	2.77	.44	2.33	.53	2.19	.35	2.60	.48	5.19 $p < .001$
11. Job Dependence among Unit Members	2.65	.39	2.93	.50	2.66	.64	2.69	.55	2.80	.74	.94 $p = .445$
12. Information Flows											
a. Written Communications	1.38	.23	1.52	.46	1.74	.51	1.95	.40	1.95	.50	6.60 $p < .001$
b. Personal 1–1 Discussions	2.94	.40	3.29	.54	3.16	.60	3.10	.76	3.23	.60	1.02 $p = .399$
c. Group or Staff Meetings	2.06	.42	2.68	1.21	2.76	.97	2.86	1.03	3.15	1.01	3.95 $p < .005$
13. Conflict Frequency	2.61	.61	1.86	.77	2.20	.87	2.07	.83	2.26	.88	2.15 $p < .079$
14. Conflict Resolution Modes											
a. Avoidance	2.39	.78	1.77	.92	2.35	.98	2.00	.88	2.10	.82	2.07 $p < .089$
b. Smoothing	2.61	.50	2.05	.72	2.80	.85	2.00	.78	2.62	.81	5.48 $p < .001$
c. Confrontation	3.06	.64	4.00	.93	3.16	.97	3.43	1.02	3.28	.83	4.06 $p < .004$
d. Authority	2.67	.59	2.86	.56	2.63	.82	2.36	.93	2.54	.91	1.00 $p < .410$

188

ciency, effectiveness, and job satisfaction for each of the ES unit types. Because of small sample size, no evidence of concurrent validity of the OAI indices is presented for counseling units. The far right column of Table 5-5 shows the correlations between the OAI dimensions and the efficiency, effectiveness, and job satisfaction of all units combined in ES offices.

To reduce the complexity of the analysis and to determine the proportions of variance in unit performance explained by the fewest and most important OAI dimensions, multiple stepwise regressions on each performance criterion were computed for each unit. Table 5-6 shows the beta coefficients of those OAI dimensions that entered significantly into each stepwise regression (i.e., those beta coefficients that were at least twice as large as their standard errors). Once the OAI factors which entered the regression equations were taken into account, the other OAI dimensions were found to explain little additional variance in either unit efficiency, effectiveness, or job satisfaction. The bottom rows of Table 5-6 show the overall F-ratios for each regression and the overall percentages of variance explained (R^2) in each performance criterion by the key OAI factors that entered the regression equations.

Results

The ability of the OAI indices to detect variations in organizational design and performance for each kind of unit in ES offices are discussed in this section.

1. Intake units are responsible for the reception, registration, and processing of all job seekers and claimants for Unemployment Compensation (UC). In the case of a job application, intake personnel provide instructions to applicants for filling out a registration card and refer them to other units in the office that can provide the needed services. Initial and continued UC claims received from claimants are also taken and routinely processed by this unit. "In today, out today" is the basic motto that all intake units strive to achieve in processing UC claim cards and sending them to the state administrative office for further computer processing and payment. In most offices, the intake units also perform the clerical functions of the office, such as typing, filing, and completing performance reports.

The intake units were created in most local ES offices in 1974 as a result of a merger of UC claims processing units and employment service clerical units (originally mutually independent). By law, individuals receiving unemployment compensation must indicate a willing-

Table 5-5 Correlations of OAI Unit Task, Structure, and Process Each Type of Unit in Local ES Offices

Performance Criteria Used to Assess Work Units in Local Employment Security Offices	Intake & Claims Units ($n = 19$)			Adjudication Units ($n = 22$)		
	Unit Efficiency —# Claims & Applicants Processed per Position	Unit Effectiveness —No Measure Available	Job Satisfaction of Unit Personnel	Unit Efficiency —# Disputed Claims Determined per Position	Unit Effectiveness —% Claim Determinations Not Appealed	Job Satisfaction of Unit Personnel
1. Task Difficulty	.00	—	-.13	-.01	-.19	-.30[a]
2. Task Variability	.10	—	-.03	-.03	-.03	.13
3. No. Job Titles in Unit	-.51[b]	—	-.26	.42[b]	.22	-.32[a]
4. Role Interchangeability	-.38[a]	—	.14	-.31[a]	-.31[a]	.09
5. Unit Standardization	.15	—	.24	.02	-.03	.07
6. Personnel Expertise:						
a. Educational level	.19	—	.22	-.08	-.05	.05
b. Time in on-the-job training	-.06	—	.13	.28[a]	.04	.19
c. Length of job-entry training	.06	—	.01	-.39[b]	-.41[b]	.06
7. Supervisory Work Discretion	.03	—	.09	.15	-.08	.06
8. Employee Work Discretion	.00	—	.17	.09	.30[a]	.07
9. Work Flow Interdependence	-.10	—	.24	.21	.18	-.06
10. Job Dependence on Supervisor	.22	—	.28	.33[a]	.12	.03
11. Job Dependence among Unit Members	-.54[b]	—	-.02	.08	-.11	.11
12. Information Flows within Unit:						
a. Freq. written reports & memos	-.40[a]	—	-.21	-.49[c]	-.54[c]	.35[a]
b. Freq. of 1-1 discussions	.11	—	.15	.00	.04	.26
c. Freq. of group meetings	-.04	—	-.01	.30[a]	.27	.23
13. Freq. of Conflict within Unit	.03	—	-.41[b]	-.06	-.23	-.54[c]
14. Methods Used to Resolve Conflicts:						
a. By avoiding or ignoring conflict	.15	—	-.17	-.06	-.05	-.54[c]
b. By smoothing over conflict	-.09	—	-.24	-.25	-.36[b]	-.58[c]
c. By confronting conflict	.20	—	.37[a]	.11	.36[b]	.73[c]
d. By resorting to higher authority	.14	—	.48[b]	.22	.38[b]	.25

[a] $p < .10$.
[b] $p < .05$.
[c] $p < .01$.

ness to seek employment by making an application for a job with the employment service. The merger decreased the need for clients to stand in two waiting lines to apply for unemployment compensation and employment services.

Table 5-4 shows the organization design of the intake units in terms of the OAI dimensions. Consistent with the preceding description, relative to other units in ES offices the intake units were found during the summer of 1975:

Indices with Efficiency, Effectiveness, and Job Satisfaction for

Placement & Employer Relations Units (n = 42)			Work Incentive Program Units (n = 34)			All Local Office Units Combined (n = 163)		
Unit Efficiency —# Job Placements per Position	Unit Effectiveness —% Job Openings Filled	Job Satisfaction of Unit Personnel	Unit Efficiency —# WIN Clients Placed in Jobs per Position	Unit Effectiveness —% WIN Clients De-registered from Welfare after Placed in Jobs	Job Satisfaction of Unit Personnel	Office Efficiency —Mean of Unit Efficiency Measures	Office Effectiveness —Mean of Unit Effectiveness Measures	Job Satisfaction of all Unit Personnel in Office
$-.20$	$-.06$	$.01$	$.32^b$	$.39^c$	$.02$	$.02$	$.05$	$.09$
$.06$	$.10$	$.26^b$	$.45^c$	$.23^a$	$-.03$	$.16^b$	$.06$	$.06$
$.16$	$.02$	$-.12$	$.25^a$	$.09$	$.12$	$.08$	$-.13$	$-.10$
$.04$	$.15$	$-.23^a$	$-.40^c$	$-.19$	$.05$	$-.10$	$.10$	$-.01$
$.23^a$	$.13$	$-.02$	$-.26^a$	$-.13$	$.14$	$-.05$	$.00$	$.22^c$
$.03$	$.12$	$-.41^c$	$.25^a$	$-.02$	$.13$	$.06$	$.11$	$-.20^c$
$.16$	$.07$	$.24$	$.06$	$-.01$	$-.03$	$.08$	$-.09$	$.07$
$.42^c$	$.47^c$	$.16$	$.27^a$	$.56^c$	$.18$	$.13^a$	$.17^b$	$.18^c$
$.16$	$-.04$	$-.08$	$.07$	$.41^c$	$.23^a$	$.04$	$-.06$	$.19^c$
$.44^c$	$.41^c$	$.65^c$	$.21$	$.20$	$.26^a$	$.15^b$	$.10$	$.22^c$
$.14$	$.23^a$	$-.08$	$.13$	$.32^b$	$.23^a$	$.10$	$-.10$	$.00$
$.15$	$.42^c$	$.28^b$	$.10$	$.25^a$	$.23^a$	$.09$	$.21^c$	$.20^c$
$.28^b$	$.13$	$.12$	$.32^b$	$.08$	$.18$	$.17^b$	$.09$	$.07$
$.30^b$	$.11$	$.24^a$	$.29^b$	$.03$	$.01$	$.10$	$.04$	$-.18^c$
$.24^a$	$.05$	$.04$	$.30^b$	$.26^a$	$.40^c$	$.13^a$	$.04$	$.10$
$.17$	$.23^a$	$.10$	$.30^b$	$.39^c$	$.62^c$	$.14^b$	$.08$	$.10$
$.44^c$	$-.36^c$	$-.56^c$	$.18$	$.01$	$-.38^b$	$-.10$	$-.18^c$	$-.29^c$
$.52^c$	$-.50^c$	$-.54^c$	$.06$	$-.31^b$	$-.34^b$	$-.15^b$	$-.12^a$	$-.38^c$
$-.34^b$	$-.27^b$	$-.39^c$	$.24^a$	$.21$	$-.09$	$-.10$	$-.05$	$-.21^c$
$.36^c$	$.28^b$	$.75^c$	$.06$	$.24^a$	$.29^b$	$.13^a$	$.02$	$.37^c$
$.11$	$.36^b$	$.50^c$	$.16$	$.05$	$.44^c$	$.14^a$	$.21^c$	$.45^c$

a. To undertake the least difficult and variable work;

b. To be the most differentiated internally in terms of the number of different job titles;

c. To have personnel with the least formal education and who spent the least time in on-the-job-training, but who went through a moderately long job-entry training and orientation program to become familiar with detailed work procedures;

d. To have the least frequent internal unit communications, in terms of written reports and memos, discussions, and group meetings; and

Table 5-6 Multiple Stepwise Regressions of Unit Efficiency, Effectiveness, Unit in Local ES Offices

Performance Criteria Used to Assess Extrinsic Validity of OAI Unit Task, Structure, and Process Dimensions	Intake & Claims Units (n = 20)			Adjudication Units (n = 22)		
	Unit Efficiency—# Claims & Applicants Processed per Position	Unit Effectiveness—No Measure Available	Job Satisfaction of Unit Personnel	Unit Efficiency—# Disputed Claims Determined per Position	Unit Effectiveness—% Claim Determinations Not Appealed	Job Satisfaction of Unit Personnel
1. Task Difficulty						
2. Task Variability						
3. No. Job Titles in Unit				.24		−.30
4. Role Interchangeability	−.60					
5. Unit Standardization						
6. Personnel Expertise:						
a. Educational level						
b. Time in on-the-job training				.30		
c. Length of job-entry training				−.30	−.34	
7. Supervisory Work Discretion						
8. Employee Work Discretion					.32	
9. Work Flow Interdependence						
10. Job Dependence on Supervisor						
11. Job Dependence among Unit Member	−.67					
12. Information Flows within Unit:						
a. Freq. written reports & memos				−.45	−.43	
b. Freq. of 1–1 discussions	.48					
c. Freq. of group meetings						
13. Freq. of Conflict within Unit						
14. Methods Used to Resolve Conflicts:						
a. By avoiding or ignoring conflict						
b. By smoothing over conflict						−.29
c. By confronting conflict						.54
d. By resorting to higher authority			.48		.21	
F-Ratio for the Regression	6.49	NA	4.37	4.04	4.57	11.14
Level of Statistical Significance for Regression	$p < .001$	NA	$p < .05$	$p < .01$	$p < .01$	$p < .001$
R^2, or % of Variance in Performance Explained	64%	NA	25%	52%	55%	66%

  e. To report the greatest frequency of conflict among unit personnel and a high tendency to resolve conflicts by avoidance or smoothing over (relative to other ES units).

Within the ranges of scores obtained on the OAI dimensions in Table 5-4, Table 5-5 shows that the performance efficiency of intake units and Job Satisfaction on Significant OAI Dimensions for Each Type of

Placement & Employer Relations Units (n = 50)			Work Incentive Program Units (n = 41)			All Local Office Units Combined (n = 149)		
Unit Efficiency —# Job Placements per Position	Unit Effectiveness —% Job Openings Filled	Job Satisfaction of Unit Personnel	Unit Efficiency —# WIN Clients Placed in Jobs per Position	Unit Effectiveness —% WIN Clients De-registered from Welfare after Placed in Jobs	Job Satisfaction of Unit Personnel	Office Efficiency —Mean of Unit Efficiency Measures	Office Effectiveness —Mean of Unit Effectiveness Measures	Job Satisfaction of all Unit Personnel in Office
		.42		.41				.14
		.34						
.27								.25
		−.14					.13	.14
.28	.34			.40				
							−.19	
.22		.44	.31			.17		
	.25				.14			.25
					.19	.21		
								−.22
		.18			.61			
−.36	−.33							−.20
			.20	.39	−.40			
		.51		.50				.17
					.45	.14	.18	.33
7.41	3.68	31.81	4.12	11.84	10.25	3.54	3.01	11.63
p < .001	p < .001	p < .001	p < .01	p < .001	p < .001	p < .05	p < .05	p < .001
47%	43%	73%	45%	65%	67%	8%	11%	41%

during fiscal year 1975 was significantly associated with greater unit and personnel specialization (fewer job titles and less role interchangeability or job rotation), lower job dependence among unit members (but slightly more dependence on the unit supervisor) and less frequent written reports and memos among intake unit personnel to coordinate work activities. These results go somewhat contrary to the merger that was undertaken in 1974 of the UC claims processing and employment service clerical units into combined intake units to form. Under the 1974 unit merger, the units were required to perform a greater variety of functions, and intake unit supervisors were encouraged to expand the jobs of unit members by cross-training them in the ES and UC functions formerly performed independently by their predecessor units. However, Table 5-4 shows that in fact very little time was being spent by intake unit personnel in on-the-job training (on the average less than two hours per week) during the summer of 1975. Other than placing the claims processing and clerical unit personnel under a common supervisor, the researchers observed that little of the merger had actually taken place. Under these conditions, one should expect, as the regression analysis in Table 5-6 shows, that the highly efficient intake units were those where there was little job rotation and where unit personnel continued to perform their jobs autonomously as they did before the reorganization.

The stepwise regression also indicates that once the interchangeability of roles, job dependence, and communications among unit personnel are taken into account, the specialization of intake units (as reflected in the number of job titles) becomes an insignificant factor in explaining the efficiency of intake units. These results suggest that the operating efficiency of intake units can be significantly enhanced by spending more time in cross-training unit personnel, increasing the frequency of discussions among unit personnel, and structuring jobs so that individuals can function somewhat autonomously of one another. Since the tasks encountered by intake units are quite simple and nonvarying, a moderately high level of job specialization can be tolerated and may indeed increase efficiency.

In terms of job satisfaction of intake unit personnel, Tables 5-5 and 5-6 show that the frequency of conflict and methods of conflict resolution are the critical OAI factors. Presumably as a result of the many different job titles and functional differentiation within intake units (see Table 5-4), personnel within intake units reported the greatest frequency of conflicts. A decrease in the frequency of conflicts and resolution of these conflicts by confrontation and higher authority significantly explain variations in job satisfaction of intake unit personnel.

2. Adjudication units are responsible for investigating, documenting, and resolving all UC contested claims. Adjudication personnel are paraprofessionals; they are not lawyers. They obtain the views of both claimants and employers about disputes over whether a claimant is eligible for receiving compensation and make determinations on the basis of a highly codified UC law. In fact, in the site visits to the ES offices, several adjudication personnel stated they used a check list of legal requirements that must be met to resolve most claim disputes.

While the 1975 OAI survey was being conducted in the ES local offices, a decentralization of decision-making on disputed claims was being implemented. Previous to the decentralization, adjudication units submitted written recommendations on contested claims to an administrative office bureau which made the final decisions. However, a large backlog of unresolved disputed claims chronically existed at the headquarters level, and claimants were telephoning their state legislators with increasing frequency to have the ES agency take action on their behalf. Therefore, to expedite resolutions of contested unemployment compensation claims, local office adjudication unit personnel were being trained during the summer of 1975 to make the final determinations on disputed claims.

Table 5-4 shows that the adjudication units exhibit a profile on the OAI dimensions that largely reflects the codified and standardized procedures followed in making determinations on contested claims in accordance with the UC law. Relative to other units, the adjudication units are the most specialized, with the longest period of job-entry training and orientation (to become familiar with UC law) and the least work flow interdependence among unit personnel (because of the fact each employee handles his or her own disputed claims, although their roles are the most interchangeable). Next to the intake units, they perform the least difficult tasks, follow the most standardized work procedures, spend the least amount of time in continuing on-the-job training, and have the least frequent group or staff meetings to coordinate their work. Finally, the adjudication units reported the least frequent conflict among unit personnel; the most frequent method of resolving these conflicts was by openly confronting the disagreements and problem solving.

During this transition period in 1975, Table 5-5 shows that the efficiency, effectiveness, and job satisfaction of adjudication units were significantly associated with 14 of the OAI unit task, structure, and process dimensions. A considerable reduction in the complexity of explaining the performance of these units is provided by the stepwise regressions in Table 5-6. Specifically, 52 percent of the variation in efficiency of adjudication units is explained by decreases in the frequency of written memos and reports for coordinating work activities and in the length of job-entry training and orientation, and by increases in the amount of time spent in continuing on-the-job training and decreases in the specialization of adjudication units; 55 percent of the variation in effectiveness of these units is similarly explained by decreasing the frequency of written communications and the length of job-entry training, and increasing the amount of work discretion exercised by adjudication unit personnel and relying upon hierarchy to resolve conflicts. Finally, 66 percent of the variation in job satisfaction of adjudication unit personnel is accounted for by increasingly relying upon confrontation and less upon smoothing-over approaches to conflict resolution and by increasing unit specialization. Although it is dangerous to draw dynamic conclusions from these cross-sectional data, the results are supportive of the overall decentralization effort within the ES agency, and provide a strong indication of the concurrent validity of selected OAI dimensions for explaining the performance of adjudication units.

3. Placement units are responsible for (1) interviewing and assessing the occupational skills of job seekers and referring them to appropriate job openings, and (2) obtaining job orders from employers. Placement unit personnel are the "salesmen" of an ES office. They represent the office to employers in the community by telling them of the services it offers and the need to find jobs for the unemployed in the community and requesting that they place their orders for job openings with the ES office. The working time of placement unit personnel is normally divided, two-thirds of the time in the office interviewing and referring applicants to jobs and one-third of working time out of the office calling on employers to obtain job orders.

Table 5-4 shows that an intermediate degree of structuring was found in the placement units, as would be expected when units perform moderately difficult and variable tasks. Relative to other ES units, the placement units are moderately specialized and have intermediate scores on the other structure and process dimensions.

When considering the ranges in Table 5-4 over which the relations hold, Table 5-5 shows that the performance of placement units was significantly correlated with 17 of the 21 OAI unit task, structure, and process dimensions. However, Table 5-6 shows that when controlling for the common variance among these OAI dimensions, the two most important predictors of placement unit efficiency and effectiveness are decreases in the relatively high frequency of avoiding or ignoring conflict and an increase in the length of the job-entry/orientation program. In addition, efficiency is significantly explained by somewhat greater standardization of work procedures and the exercise of more work discretion by unit employees, whereas somewhat greater dependence on the unit supervisor for work direction and coordination is the third factor that significantly accounts for the effectiveness of placement units. These OAI dimensions accounted for 47 and 43 percent of the variances in placement unit efficiency and effectiveness, respectively, during 1975.

Finally, Table 5-6 shows that 73 percent of the variance in job satisfaction of placement unit personnel is significantly explained by increased confrontation of conflicts when they occur, increased employee work discretion, and slightly decreased levels of formal education of unit personnel. Overall, then, the findings suggest that the performance of placement units is basically a function of (1) confronting rather than avoiding conflicts when they occur; (2) increasing the length of job-entry training and orientation so that new employees become adequately skilled and socialized in the alternative services provided to a variety of job seekers and employers by placement units; and (3) once properly trained, delegating greater amounts of decision making responsibilities to employees to handle the varying tasks and clients they encounter. These are findings one would expect of units organized according to a discretionary mode of structure (Van de Ven and Delbecq, 1974).

4. Counseling unit personnel are expected to obtain a master's degree in counseling or a related discipline to ascend in their careers. This unit is responsible for providing services to applicants who need special help to become ready for available job openings. Such help may include in-depth assessing and counseling of applicants, developing a particular job training program for unemployed individuals, and following up to coordinate client referrals with other helping organizations.

Table 5-4 shows that counseling units undertake the most difficult and variable tasks of the units in the ES office. Correspondingly, they have the highest level of education, exercise the greatest amount of employee work discretion, and have the least standardized work procedures. In addition, there is a moderate level of interdependence among unit counselors, which is coordinated by moderately frequent work-related discussions and group meetings.

Performance data were available for only 8 counseling units in 1975. Since correlations on only 8 observations are highly unstable, no indications of the concurrent validity of the OAI dimensions are provided for counseling units.

5. The WIN units administer the Work Incentive program in local ES offices. The WIN program provides intensive job assessment, development, and placement services for people on welfare (AFDC recipients). Since the people served by WIN units are generally referred to ES offices from county welfare departments and other rehabilitative agencies, WIN unit personnel coordinate more with other organizations than do other units in the ES offices. Beyond the fact that WIN units serve different clients, they were found in 1975 to be performing tasks similar to those performed by placement and counseling units combined. In effect, federal legislation (The Talmadge Amendments of 1973) reorganized WIN units to provide a job service delivery system for AFDC recipients which duplicates that provided by placement and counseling units for the general public. in the 1972 and 1973 OAI surveys, the WIN units were found to be serving more severely disadvantaged clients, and they reflected a developmental mode structure (see Van de Ven and Delbecq, 1974; Van de Ven, 1976b). It follows that the 1975 scores on the task, structure, and process dimensions for the WIN units in Table 5-3 are largely intermediate to those of the placement and counseling units.

Table 5-5 shows that the performance of WIN units is significantly correlated with 20 of the 21 OAI unit task, structure, and process dimensions. Table 5-6 substantially reduces the complexity of the analysis by identifying the OAI factors that significantly entered the stepwise regressions and explained 45, 65, and 67 percent of the variances, respectively, in the efficiency, effectiveness, and job satisfaction of WIN units. These results again provide strong support for the concurrent validity of the OAI unit indices.

Substantively, the data in Tables 5-5 and 5-6 indicate that the high-performing WIN units undertake more difficult and varying tasks, are less specialized and standardized, and their personnel spend more time in job-entry training and exercise more discretion on work-related matters than low-performing WIN units. Further, there are greater work and job interdependencies and more frequent communications of all kinds among high- than low-performing WIN units. In short, the high-performing WIN units are designed more in a developmental mode (Van de Ven and Delbecq, 1974), and personnel are more tightly coupled than those in low-performing WIN units.

In terms of conflict resolution methods, greater reliance on confrontation and authority are positively related to effectiveness and job satisfaction, as expected. However, contrary to expectations and to observations of all other ES units, the data show that tendencies to smooth over conflicts when they occurred in WIN units was a significant positive predictor of efficiency and effectiveness rather than a negative predictor as observed for job satisfaction. The absolute frequency of smoothing over conflicts is intermediate to that observed in other ES units (see Table 5-4), and therefore the WIN units examined here do not represent a skewed sample of units on this dimension. At the present time we are at a loss to explain this unexpected finding.

6. All Units Combined in Local ES Offices. The far right-hand column of Table 5-5 shows the relationships obtained when the OAI dimensions for all units are correlated with their respective measures of efficiency, effectiveness, and job satisfaction without breaking out the units by the type of task or function they contribute to the organization. The sizes of the correlations in this column are much smaller than those obtained for each type of unit individually in columns 1 to 4. Many of the correlations between the OAI dimensions and performance are near zero and indicate a "wash-out" effect when examining the correlations for all units combined. Further, Table 5-6 shows the results of the stepwise regressions of the OAI dimensions on the three performance criteria for all units combined. The overall results are that only 8, 11, and 41 percent of the variances in unit efficiency, effectiveness, and job satisfaction, respectively, are explained. In contrast, when each type of ES unit is examined separately, the OAI dimensions explain averages of 52, 55, and 57 percent of the variances in unit efficiency, effectiveness, and job satisfaction, respectively. Clearly, this evidence underscores the need to carefully identify and discriminate between the different types of units within organizations if one desires to meaningfully understand how the designs of organizational units are related to their performance.

CONCLUDING DISCUSSION

This chapter has described and evaluated the initial phases in the development of 21 unit task, structure, and process indices in the Organization Assessment Instruments (OAI). Factor analysis revealed the existence of several strong indices: task variability, supervisory discretion, employee discretion, and unit standardization. It also identified specific items that require revision in the task difficulty, personnel specialization, job dependence on supervisor, and job dependence among unit members indices. In addition, the factor analysis raised a question about the particular grouping of items in the information flow and personnel expertise constructs. These findings become a basis for the refinements made in the revised OAI presented in Appendix A.

Tests of the intrinsic validity of the OAI indices were also made with coefficient alpha, median correlations with other indices, and correlations with parallel measures. With minor exceptions, the internal reliability of the indices lie well within the expected ranges for coefficient alpha, and the median correlations with other OAI unit indices were found to be far smaller than the observed coefficient alphas for each index. Thus, the data suggest that both the internal consistency reliabilities and discriminant validities of the OAI indices are quite good. In addition, the criterion-related validities for task difficulty, task variability, unit specialization, and work flow interdependence were satisfactory.

To test the extrinsic validity of the OAI dimensions, a partial test of the task-contingent model of work unit design (Van de Ven, 1976a) was first conducted. A comparison of the magnitude of correlations between various contextual factors at the overall organization and work unit levels indicated that task difficulty and task variability were the strongest predictors of the structures and processes of the organizational units in the ES administrative and local offices. The correlations between macroorganizational factors and unit design were found to be near zero. From this we concluded that it is not correct to draw inferences about the designs of work units from the structure and context of the overall organization, and vice versa. Finally, the correlations in Table 5-3 among the unit task, structure, and process dimensions were found to be in the hypothesized directions.

Next, the assessment of different units within local ES offices provided impressive evidence of the extrinsic validity of the OAI indices in detecting systematic variations in the designs and performance of different types of organizational units. Consistent with on-site observations on the functioning of local ES offices over the years, the OAI unit task, structure, and process dimensions detected systematic and significant differences between five different types of units commonly found in local ES offices.

In addition, scores on the OAI dimensions for each type of unit were correlated and regressed on key performance measures that were selected and used by ES managers for evaluating the efficiency and effectiveness, as well as job satisfaction, of each type of unit. It was found that not all the OAI indices were equally important in explaining the performance of each unit. However, Table 5-5 shows that each OAI factor is significantly associated with the efficiency, effectiveness, and job satisfaction of at least one of the four types of ES units. Stepwise regression analyses for each type of ES unit (Table 5-6) found that three to five key OAI unit dimensions on the average explained 52, 55, and 57 percent of the variances in unit efficiency, effectiveness, and job satisfaction, respectively. In contrast, when the regressions were conducted on all ES units combined, only 8, 11, and 41 percent of the variances in unit efficiency, effectiveness, and job satisfaction, respectively, were explained. Thus, the OAI indices represent a compromise between being (1) general enough to apply to a wide variety of work units, and

(2) specific enough to be highly related to efficiency, effectiveness, and job satisfaction for each type of unit. The results also underscore the need to carefully identify and discriminate between the different types of units within complex organizations if one desires to predict and explain their performance.

The data in Tables 5-5 and 5-6 bring out several complexities in explaining organization–performance relationships. The direction of relationships between most of the OAI factors and productivity change in sign from plus to minus across the unit types. Part of the flip-flopping correlations may be due to the fact that a different efficiency and effectiveness measure is used as the criterion for evaluating the performance of each type of unit. Since different organizations and units within them strive to attain different measures of performance, organization–performance relationships may not be generalizable.

Another possible explanation is that the designs of organizational units are seldom in equilibrium as the static analysis implicitly assumes. Therefore, the relationships may only hold over a very narrow range (as indicated in Table 5-4) and over a short period of time. Personnel turnovers, cyclical workload fluctuations, and constantly changing directives and policies from higher administrative levels have significant impact in maintaining a constant state of disequilibrium in the design of organizational units. As a result, an understanding of organization–performance relationships for a given unit may require time-series analysis.

A third plausible explanation is to accept the correlations between the OAI dimensions and productivity for each type of unit and then to confront the complexity of designing and managing complex organizations. Since the data clearly show (see Table 5-5 and 5-6) that a design dimension may be positively correlated with performance in one unit type and negatively correlated with performance in another, no uniform strategy will serve to increase efficiency and effectiveness in all units. A uniform organizational intervention will, in effect, increase performance in some units and decrease performance in others—hence, a stalemate. These results suggest that contingency theorists need to develop more operational frameworks and that practitioners should become more selective in managing and organizing different types of organizational units.

In only three areas do the data in Table 5-5 show consistent directions in the correlations between the OAI dimensions and the efficiency, effectiveness, and job satisfaction of all types of ES units. Although varying in magnitude, employee work discretion and job dependence on the unit supervisor are consistently positively correlated with the performance criteria of each ES unit. The existence of a positive relationship between employee work decision-making discretion and performance, regardless of the type or context of organizational units examined, has been observed elsewhere (Lammers, 1968; Trist, 1970; Pennings, 1973; Mohr, 1971) and is consistent with the findings in Chapter 4 of positive relations between the amounts of perceived influence of different organizational groups and overall performance of ES offices.

The resolution of conflicts by confronting them or resorting to higher authority is consistently positively correlated with the efficiency, effectiveness, and job satisfaction of all ES units, whereas the correlations are generally negative when conflicts tend to be avoided, ignored, or smoothed over. These results provide substantial support for the hypotheses and literature on conflict management reviewed previously.

It is noteworthy that although the frequency of conflict is shown in Table 5-5 to be negatively correlated with the performance of each unit, it is not a significant predictor of the performance of any of the ES units when the other OAI factors (particularly the methods of conflict resolution) are taken into account (see Table 5-6). Practically, this suggests that it is not the simple frequency of conflicts, disagreements, or disputes among unit personnel that affects the performance of organizational units; rather, it is the methods by which these conflicts are resolved that make a difference in terms of performance efficiency, effectiveness, and job satisfaction.

Finally, throughout our discussion of the five types of ES units, we addressed some practical reorganization questions that were being raised by the ES managers while the OAI survey was being conducted. The purpose here was to exemplify how results from an OA survey can be used for practical problem solving and managerial decision making. However, it is important to point out that our assessments were based not only on the numerical OAI data but also upon the qualitative understanding of the day-to-day functioning of ES offices obtained as a result of on-site observations and discussions with ES personnel. Clearly, the individual character of the organization must be incorporated into any overall assessment. In the hands of a competent analyst or manager who is intimately familiar with the organization, the OAI provide valuable quantitative data for assessing the correctness of qualitative observations, problems, and intuitions.

CHAPTER SIX

The Context and Design of Jobs

At the micro level of analysis, the job or position that individuals occupy is the core focus of any in-depth assessment of organizations. As Figure 6-1 illustrates, complex organizations consist of numerous units, and a unit, in turn, is composed of identifiable jobs or positions.

In developing the 1975 OAI, we included some measures of jobs and certain background characteristics of individuals (e.g., age, sex, seniority and position in the organization, job pressures, and job incentives). The major focus of the 1975 OAI, however, centered on the larger organizational and unit levels of analyses. In our subsequent review of theories on job design, we have concluded that the OAI would be considerably enhanced by extending its measurement of job dimensions and by reappraising some dimensions used in the 1975 OAI.

CONCEPTUAL PERSPECTIVE ON JOB DESIGN

Since the advent of scientific management (Taylor, 1911), administrative management theory (Fayol, 1949), and bureaucratic theory (Weber, 1947), the design of jobs or positions has become a central concern of management practitioners and researchers. This is because the way a job is structured: (1) is a basic criterion for personnel selection, training, promotion, and pay (e.g., Ghiselli and Brown, 1955; Guion, 1965); (2) largely defines and controls the roles and behavior of individuals who occupy the jobs or positions (Weber, 1947; Argyris, 1962; Emery and Trist, 1960), and (3) influences productivity, effectiveness, job satisfaction, and the general quality of working life (Trist, 1970; Hulin and Blood, 1968; Hackman and Lawler, 1971).

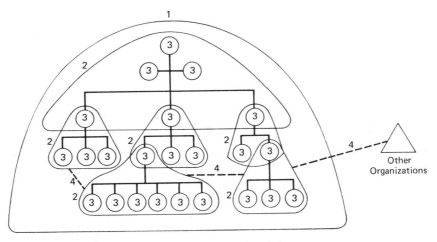

Key to Numbers: 1 = Overall Organization Focus of Analysis
2 = Organizational Unit Focus of Analysis
3 = Individual Job or Position Focus of Analysis
4 = Relations within and between Units Focus of Analysis

Figure 6-1   Illustration of levels of analyses involved in conducting an in-depth organization assessment.

The initial expectation of classical management theories and industrial engineering was that by simplifying, specializing, and standardizing jobs, work could be carried out more efficiently, less skilled employees would be required, management control over production would be increased, and ultimately organizational work performance would be enhanced. Subsequent research by numerous scholars showed that simple, routine, nonchallenging jobs often led to employee dissatisfaction, increased absenteeism and turnover, and substantial difficulties in effectively managing employees who work on simplified jobs (see review in Hulin and Blood, 1968). As a result many organizational psychologists began to argue for job expansion or enlargement (Trist, 1970; Argyris, 1957; Herzberg, Mausner and Snyderman, 1959). However, the theories that advocate job enrichment or enlargement can be criticized for two basic limitations that are also present in the classical prescriptions for job simplification.

First, the theories assume that a "normal person" exists. They do not admit to the fact that individuals vary in the degrees to which they desire challenging, risky, responsible, and accountable work settings (Porter et al., 1975). More recently, the work by Turner and Lawrence

(1965), Blood and Hulin (1967), Hackman and Lawler (1971), Hackman and Oldham (1975), and Oldham et al. (1976) has begun to reconcile much of the conflict over job simplification versus enlargement by developing a theory and obtaining preliminary research evidence indicating that certain characteristics of individuals themselves must be taken into account along with job characteristics to generate valid predictions about the behavior and outcomes of employees at work. These individual differences may include items such as a person's age, sex, organizational tenure, level in the hierarchy, and growth need strength (i.e., the degree to which a person values personal growth, challenge, and accomplishment in the work setting).

Second, with the early notable exception of Trist and his colleagues at the Tavistock Institute in England in the 1940s and 1950s, the literature has tended to design jobs in an organizational and work group vacuum (Steers and Mowday, 1977). As Pierce (1978) points out, only very recently have attempts been made to integrate and examine the connections between the designs of jobs, of work groups, and of the overall organization, and how they interact to explain variations in the performance of individuals, groups, or the total organization. Morse and Lorsch (1970) argued that employee motivation and unit performance should be highest when there is a congruency between the structure of the organization and the structure of the employee's job. Porter et al. (1975), Nemiroff and Ford (1976), and Hackman (1976) suggested that a three-way fit between the organization or work group, job design, and an individual's background is necessary for achieving high levels of job satisfaction and performance. Finally, Pierce (1978) and Hall et al. (1978) point out that the job is "closer" to the worker and is experienced on a more regular and direct personal basis than properties of organization design. As a consequence, they argue that employee responses (e.g., job satisfaction and work motivation) should be more strongly associated with job design than with the structure of the organization or work unit. Turner and Lawrence (1965), on the other hand, focused on the technology employed in the organization as an important predictor of how tasks are designed and how employees respond to their jobs. Along this line, Pierce (1978) suggests that job design intervenes in the relationships among characteristics of unit task, structure and process (examined in Chapter 5), and employee job satisfaction. From our perspective this suggests that the difficulty and variability of the work performed by employees should be directly related to the design of their jobs and indirectly related to employee job satisfaction and work motivation.

This literature is important because it suggests that individual background characteristics and the design of organizational units represent more than just the context for job design. Instead a more overall perspective is implied in which one examines simultaneously the designs of jobs and organizational units. Such a perspective suggests that there may be a large set of options and tradeoffs to blend the organizational unit, the job, and the individual. By investigating these alternatives, we may come to appreciate that a far broader and richer repertoire of alternative options exists for designing jobs, organizational units, and personnel recruitment programs than is presently envisioned or used by organizational managers and analysts.

Proposed OA Dimensions of Job Design

As a starting point in considering and developing this repertoire of unit and job designs, Figure 6-2 proposes five core dimensions for assessing job design and sets forth a revision in the dimensions of unit structure that were examined in Chapter 5. Two basic considerations lead to the selection of the five job design dimensions and the revised unit structure dimensions. First, an expansion of the OA framework and instruments to include jobs or positions as a separate level of analysis requires that a clear distinction be made between the characteristics of jobs (examined at the individual level) and the properties of organizational units (which are appropriately examined at the aggregated work group level). The work of Lazarsfeld and Menzel (1969) is particularly useful for making clear conceptual distinctions between global properties of work groups and analytical properties of individuals' jobs or positions. The job design dimensions proposed in Figure 6-2 are *analytical* properties or characteristics of members which are defined and measured without reference to characteristics of the group or collective to which they belong. The organizational unit dimensions are *global* properties or macrocharacteristics of the group collective itself which have no meaning in terms of the members or jobs individually.

Certain reclassifications are useful in building two distinct indices for job design versus unit design. Some dimensions included as aspects of unit design in the 1975 OAI (described in Chapter 5)—such as employee discretion, standardization, and expertise—fall clearly into the domain of job measurement. Other dimensions, however—such as unit specialization, role interchangeability, and supervisor discretion (better labeled unit centralization)—are clearly global properties of organizational units.

The logical conclusion we draw from following the guidelines of Lazarsfeld and Menzel (1969) is to propose five core dimensions of jobs which represent member-level counterparts to the five global unit design dimensions. Specifically, as the operational indicators in Figure 6-2 show, unit and job specialization, unit personnel composition and job expertise, unit and job standardization, unit centralization and job discretion, and unit and job incentives, respectively, tap similar constructs from different levels of analyses.

Although the revised job and unit dimensions measure different domains (and are not simply an average of the jobs of unit personnel), their parallel referents are important for identifying what options or tradeoffs may exist between the design of jobs and units. For example, Hackman (1976) indicates that one important option in the design of autonomous work groups is to determine under what conditions heterogeneous skills should be structured within a job (by decreasing job specialization) or between jobs in a unit (by staffing a unit with experts from different disciplines; i.e., increasing skill heterogenity).

The second basic consideration in selecting the five OA job dimensions is that they are very similar to the five core job dimensions in the Job Diagnostic Survey (JDS) developed by Hackman and Oldham (1975). The OA and JDS job constructs differ in the way they are operationalized. We concur with Pierce and Dunham (1976) and Steers and Mowday (1977) that the JDS represents a major conceptual and empirical contribution to the study of job design because the theory builds upon and integrates much of the earlier work on job design. The JDS model specifies what job characteristics lead to critical psychological states for job incumbents with certain individual background characteristics, resulting in either positive or negative outcomes in the work place. In addition, for the practitioner the JDS provides a detailed procedure for conducting a diagnosis of the work place to determine whether or not job enrichment is a useful organizational change strategy.

Whereas the Hackman and Oldham job dimensions focus more heavily on the attitudinal aspects of jobs, the five proposed OA job factors emphasize their behavioral aspects more. The reason we lean toward a behavioral description of jobs is because behaviors are more objective and are easier for analysts and practitioners to observe, control, and change than the more subjective attitudes of people regarding their jobs. Further, in their test of the measurement properties of the

JOB CONTEXT FACTORS	JOB DESIGN FACTORS	AFFECTIVE RESPONSES TO JOB
1. Task Difficulty & Variability	1. Job Specialization	1. Satisfaction with:
2. Level of Job in Hierarchy	—# Different Tasks Performed	—Job
3. Person's Prior Work Experiences or Job Career History	2. Job Expertise	—Supervisor
4. Growth Need Strength of Job Incumbent*	—Educational Level	—Co-workers
	—Length of Job-Entry Training	—Pay
	—Time in On-The-Job Training	—Past Career Progress
	3. Job Standardization	—Career Potential
	—Detail of Job Description*	2. Work Motivation
	—# and Detail of Job Rules & Procedures	—Effort in Job
	4. Job Discretion	—Attempts to Improve Work Performance
	—Authority to Make Work Decisions	
	—Accountability for Decisions & Behaviors*	
	—Work Load Pressure or Slack	
	5. Job Incentives	
	—Feedback from Work and Others	
	—Job Contingent Rewards & Sanctions	

STRUCTURE OF ORGANIZATIONAL UNITS
(Counterpart Dimensions of Job Design)
(Revised from Chapter 5)

1. Unit Specialization
   —# Different Job Titles in Unit

2. Unit Personnel Composition
   —Heterogeneity of Personnel Skills*
   —Interchangeability of Roles or Jobs

3. Unit Standardization
   —Automation of Work Methods*
   —# & Detail of Unit Rules & Procedures*

4. Unit Centralization of Decision Making
   —Degree to which Unit Supervisor Decides:
   a. What tasks employees perform
   b. Work quotas & rules to be followed
   c. How exceptions are to be handled

5. Unit Performance Norms & Incentives
   —Quality/Quantity Control Emphasis*
   —Group/Individual-Based Incentives*
   —Group Pressures to Conform (Soldiering)*

Items marked with an asterisk (*) are new dimensions not measured in the 1975 OAI.

Figure 6-2 Factors included in OA framework on job design and corresponding revision of unit structure dimensions.

JDS, Dunham, Aldag, and Brief (1976) found considerable instability in the factor structure of the JDS indices. These operational distinctions are clarified in the following section by defining and describing the measurement procedures of each OA job dimension in relation to the JDS job characteristics.

Definitions and Measures of OA Job Dimensions

1. Job Specialization—refers to the number of different tasks performed in a job and the scope or breadth of these tasks. Individuals are generalists when their jobs involve a large number of broadly defined tasks, problems, or issues, whereas they are specialists when a small number of rather narrow tasks and problems occupy most of their working time. In comparison with the JDS, job specialization is the same as the variety component of the skill variety factor (i.e., the degree to which a job requires performing a variety of different activities) and task identity (or job scope) (Hackman and Oldham, 1975). However, whereas the JDS asks respondents to indicate how much variety they perceive they have in their jobs and the extent to which their jobs involve doing a whole and identifiable piece of work, the OA job specialization dimension is measured in the more traditional industrial psychology approach by determining the time spent performing different tasks in each job and by classifying the breadth of these tasks according to some external standard (e.g., a dictionary of occupational tasks and job titles).

Job specialization was measured in the 1975 OAI by first asking respondents to record the number of hours per week they normally spent performing different types of tasks. Figure 6-3 illustrates the list of tasks actually used in the OAI questionnaires to measure job specialization in ES offices. From the responses obtained, job specialization was computed as the number of different tasks that the respondent worked at for five or more hours per week. Thus, an adjudicator would indicate the majority of his/her time spent on adjudication and investigations (item 5 in Figure 6-3), whereas a placement person might spend five hours or more per week on job development (item 8), order taking (item 9), and file search and job matching (item 10). The adjudicator would have a job specialization score of 1 and the placement person a score of 3. The adjudicator has a more specialized job than the placement person.

Obviously, this measure of job specialization is limited to the various kinds of local ES offices. A measurement of job specialization in other

WE WOULD LIKE TO KNOW THE SPECIFIC TYPES OF TASKS YOU PERFORMED IN THE PAST 3 MONTHS IN YOUR JOB. LISTED BELOW ARE CATEGORIES OF TASKS COMMONLY PERFORMED IN DISTRICT JOB SERVICE OFFICES. YOU NEED NOT DO ALL THE TASKS IN A CATEGORY.

PLEASE INDICATE THE NUMBER OF HOURS PER WEEK YOU NORMALLY SPENT PERFORMING EACH TYPE OF TASK DURING THE PAST 3 MONTHS. (IF YOU DID NOT PERFORM A TASK, WRITE "00" HOURS.)

Types of Tasks	My Average Hours per Week Spent Doing This Task
1. Intake and reception tasks (including CETA Certifications, WIN Registrations & De-Registrations)	(1) ☐☐ hr/wk
2. Clerical filing, typing or steno tasks	(2) ☐☐ hr/wk
3. ESARS, CETA, UC, or other program reporting tasks	(3) ☐☐ hr/wk
4. Taking and processing program allowances, claims, etc.	(4) ☐☐ hr/wk
5. Adjudications and investigations	(5) ☐☐ hr/wk
6. Self-Service Assistance	(6) ☐☐ hr/wk
7. Assessments and screening (includes testing, group orientations, and WIN Appraisals)	(7) ☐☐ hr/wk
8. Job development, placement interviewing, referrals, and intensive manpower services	(8) ☐☐ hr/wk
9. Order taking	(9) ☐☐ hr/wk
10. File search and job matching	(10) ☐☐ hr/wk
11. Selection and referral to classroom training and follow-up contracts	(11) ☐☐ hr/wk
12. Employer relations	(12) ☐☐ hr/wk
13. Employment contracting (negotiation, followthrough and invoicing)	(13) ☐☐ hr/wk
14. Community services	(14) ☐☐ hr/wk
15. Employment counseling	(15) ☐☐ hr/wk
16. Obtaining and processing labor market information	(16) ☐☐ hr/wk
17. Working with other agencies	(17) ☐☐ hr/wk
18. Management and supervision	(18) ☐☐ hr/wk

Figure 6-3 Types of tasks in an employment security office.

organizations requires the researcher to develop a list of the different kinds of tasks performed by individuals in the organization under investigation and then ask respondents how much working time they spend on each task.

2. Job Expertise—is the level of skills of job incumbents in terms of formal education, length of job-entry orientation and training, and the amount of time spent in on-the-job reading and in-service training. Thus, expertise refers to the level of professionalism of the job incumbent. Job expertise is not examined directly in the JDS, and only the skill component of the skill variety factor roughly approximates it but confounds with specialization (i.e., the degree to which a job requires use of a number of different skills and talents of the employee) (Hackman and Oldham, 1975).

The measures that were used in Chapter 5 (page 163) to measure unit personnel expertise are more appropriately examined at the individual level as the index of job expertise. The reason is because the level of education, amount of time spent in on-the-job training, and length of job-entry orientation and training are analytical properties of members in an organizational unit and do not refer to any global characteristics of the work unit. Further, the nature and demands of the individual job (rather than characteristics of the organizational unit in which the job is housed) generally dictate the amount of education and the kinds of job-entry and on-the-job training required for successful job performance.

3. Job Standardization—is the dimension that many practitioners consider primary in job analysis or job design. Job standardization is twofold, measuring the degree to which roles and tasks are spelled out in a job description and the degree to which rules and procedures are defined. In other words, job standardization focuses on the clarity and detail of guidelines regarding the duties and responsibilities of the position and methods for performing these duties. These guidelines or job standards can vary from having very clear and very detailed written job descriptions, to relatively clear and terse job descriptions, to verbally clear but unwritten job descriptions, to implicit, nonverbalized and unwritten job norms. The JDS does not measure job standardization as defined here; instead, many of its items tap employee reactions to the standardization of their jobs.

A reexamination of the 1975 OAI unit standardization index described in Chapter 5 (page 161) suggests that it is more appropriately used to measure job standardization since the four questions in the standardization index all pertain to the individual work and not that of the unit. For this reason, we have averaged the four standardization items (aggregated and used in Chapter 5 to measure *unit* standardization) and applied the result (unaggregated) to our analysis of *job* standardization in this chapter. For future assessments, the revised OAI (presented in Appendix A) distinguishes rules and procedures pertaining to the individual job from those pertaining to the larger unit.

4. Job Discretion—is the degree of latitude that a job incumbent exercises in making job-related decisions, the amount of work load pressure involved in the job, and the degree to which the job incumbent is held accountable for his or her work behavior and decisions. Job discretion, then, is a very broad construct with three elements (job authority, pressure, and accountability), and three different indices are used to measure it. Overall, much of the meaning of the proposed OA job discretion construct is captured in the JDS job autonomy factor, defined as the degree to which the job provides substantial freedom, independence, and discretion to the employee in scheduling his work and determining work procedures (Hackman and Oldham, 1975).

Job discretion increases with the amount of *job authority* the incumbent has in making job-related decisions regarding: (a) what tasks, projects, and assignments to perform, (b) how the work is to be done in terms of what procedures and rules to follow, (c) how work exceptions and problems are to be handled, and (d) what performance criteria should be met.

Our analysis of the 1975 OAI again shows that the employee discretion index (Chapter 5, page 165) should be reclassified as a job measure rather than a unit measure. However, the unit supervisory discretion index (in Chapter 5 page 166) remains an appropriate indicator of the degree of centralization of decision making in the organizational unit, which is a global property of the group.

The second element of job discretion is *work load pressure*, defined as (1) the individual's control over job deadlines, (2) the degree to which the individual is constained by preset quality standards, and (3) the amount of lead time or prior notification normally given on incoming work. The more job pressure experienced by an individual, the lower the job discretion because deadlines, exacting standards, and workload crunches usually represent externally determined mandates or demands over which the job incumbent can exercise little discretion once they appear.

In the 1975 OAI employee and supervisory questionnaires, the following items were included to capture some of the operational indicators of job pressure in ES offices.

How heavy was your work load during the past 3 months?

OFTEN NOT ENOUGH TO KEEP ME BUSY	SOMETIMES NOT ENOUGH TO KEEP ME BUSY	JUST ABOUT THE RIGHT AMOUNT	HARD TO KEEP UP WITH	ENTIRELY TOO MUCH FOR ME TO HANDLE
1	2	3	4	5

During the past 3 months, how much *control* did you have in setting the pace of your work?

NONE	VERY LITTLE	SOME	QUITE A BIT	VERY MUCH
1	2	3	4	5

How far in advance do you generally know how much work will be asked of you?

ABOUT AN HOUR OR LESS IN ADVANCE	ABOUT A DAY IN ADVANCE	ABOUT A WEEK IN ADVANCE	ABOUT A MONTH IN ADVANCE	ABOUT 6 MONTHS OR MORE IN ADVANCE
1	2	3	4	5

The scaled responses to the second and third questions were reversed and then averaged with the first to compute the job pressure index for each respondent.

The third element of job discretion is *job accountability*, defined as the extent to which the job incumbent answers for or holds him/herself responsible for work decisions and job behavior. An individual may be authorized to exercise much authority in making work-related decisions but may, in fact, exercise little job discretion by refusing to make decisions or by refusing to accept responsibility for decisions made. Job accountability was not measured in the 1975 OAI. A proposed index is included in the revised OAI in Appendix A.

5. *Job Incentives*—refer to the amount of feedback on work performance that the job incumbent receives from simple observation of his/her own work and from other agents (the supervisor and peers), and the extent to which the job incumbent perceives that doing a good job will be rewarded (with informal recognition or formal promotion) and doing a poor job will be punished (with informal reprimands or formal demotions). Feedback from the job and other agents comes directly from the JDS and is used as an indicator of job incentives because feedback provides the job incumbent the positive and negative external cues necessary for error detection, learning, and conformance to expected job performance standards and procedures. The extent to which rewards and sanctions are contingent upon job performance is not included in the JDS, but is highly consistent with expectancy theories of motivation upon which Hackman and Oldham's (1975) model is largely based.

Job feedback is the degree to which the respondent knows the results of his/her task efforts. There are two parts to this construct, feedback from others and feedback from the job itself. Only feedback from others was measured by the 1975 OAI questionnaires with the following items:

To what *extent* do you *depend on others* to know whether you do your work correctly?

TO NO EXTENT	LITTLE EXTENT	SOME EXTENT	GREAT EXTENT	VERY GREAT EXTENT
1	2	3	4	5

During the past year how often did your unit supervisor discuss your work performance with you?

NOT ONCE	ABOUT 1–4 TIMES A YR	ABOUT ONCE A MONTH	ABOUT ONCE A WEEK	ABOUT EVERY DAY OR SO
1	2	3	4	5

When your work performance was discussed with you, how often did you receive practical suggestions for improving your work?

NEVER	SELDOM	ABOUT HALF THE TIME	OFTEN	EVERY TIME
1	2	3	4	5

The *expectation of rewards* is the degree to which the respondent anticipates that good performance will result in some reward, be it formal promotion or informal recognition. It was measured by two questions in the 1975 OAI employee and supervisory questionnaires.

If you attain the performance level that is expected of you, how likely is it that each of the following will happen:

	NO CHANCE	SMALL CHANCE	50% CHANCE	QUITE LIKELY	ALMOST A CERTAINTY
a. You will be *recognized for your good work* (e.g., given a special word of appreciation or a pat-on-the-back)?	1	2	3	4	5
b. You will be *promoted* in this organization?	1	2	3	4	5

The *expectation of sanctions* is the degree to which the respondent anticipates that poor performance will result in some punishment, either informal reprimand or formal demotion. It was also measured by two questions in the 1975 OAI questionnaires.

If you do not attain the performance level that is expected of you, how likely is it that each of the following will happen?

		NO CHANCE	SMALL CHANCE	50% CHANCE	QUITE LIKELY	ALMOST A CERTAINTY
a.	You will be *reprimanded* or told to improve your work.	1	2	3	4	5
b.	You will be demoted in this organization.	1	2	3	4	5

Definitions and Measures of Job Context and Outcome Factors

In addition to the job design dimensions, the other job context and outcome factors listed in Figure 6-2 were defined and measured in the following ways in the 1975 OAI.

1. Task Difficulty and Task Variability—which were described and examined in Chapter 5, are examined here at the individual level to determine how the job design factors are associated with the technical requirements of assigned work.

2. Level in the Hierarchy—is defined and measured from organization charts as the number of supervisory levels between the job incumbent and the top manager in an ES office. This measure is included here as an indicator of the location of a job in the organization's hierarchy. Consistent with Parsons' (1960) description of the qualitatively different functions performed at technical, managerial, and institutional levels in an organization, one should expect to find systematic differences in the designs of jobs or positions at different hierarchical levels in the organization, just as was observed for work units in Chapter 5 and by Hall (1962).

3. Tenure in the Organization—is defined as the number of years that the job incumbent has worked in the organization. Tenure provides an indication of the previous work experiences and the amount of socialization in the organization by the job incumbent. As the research by Morgan (1977) suggests, it would also be useful to examine the job career histories of job incumbents prior to working in the organization. However, no measure of work experiences of respondents prior to their being hired by the ES agency was obtained in the 1975 OAI.

Tenure in the organization was measured with the following item in the OAI supervisory and employee questionnaires:

How long have you worked in this organization?

LESS THAN 6 MONTHS	6 MONTHS– 2 YEARS	3–5 YEARS	6–10 YEARS	MORE THAN 10 YEARS
1	2	3	4	5

4. Growth Need Strength—is defined by Hackman and Oldham (1975) as the degree to which a job incumbent has a strong versus weak desire to obtain "growth" satisfaction from his or her work. Individuals with high growth needs have been shown by Oldham et al. (1976) to respond positively (i.e., with high satisfaction and internal work motivation) to complex, challenging, and "enriched" jobs, whereas individuals with low growth needs tend *not* to find such jobs satisfying or motivating. Growth need strength was not measured in the 1975 OAI but will be in the revised OAI (see Appendix A).

5. Job Satisfaction—is an affective reaction or feeling by an employee on how happy or satisfied he or she is with his/her job, supervisor, co-workers, pay, and current and future career progress and potential. The construct was measured by asking the following questions, which represent a modified version of the job satisfaction index in the Survey of Organizations (Taylor and Bowers, 1972).

	VERY UNSATIS- FIED	QUITE UNSATIS- FIED	SOME- WHAT SATIS- FIED	QUITE SATIS- FIED	VERY SATIS- FIED
All in all, *how satisfied* are you with your job?	1	2	3	4	5
How *satisfied* are you with your supervisor?	1	2	3	4	5
How *satisfied* are you with your pay?	1	2	3	4	5
How *satisfied* are you with the friendliness and cooperativeness of your *coworkers*?	1	2	3	4	5
How *satisfied* do you feel with the *career progress* you have made in this organization *up to now*?	1	2	3	4	5
How *satisfied* do you feel with your *chances for career advancement* in this organization *in the future*?	1	2	3	4	5

6. Work Motivation—is the amount of effort an employee puts into his/her job and task performance. Only two items were used in the 1975 OAI questionnaires to measure work motivation.

	NONE	A LITTLE	SOME	QUITE A BIT	VERY MUCH
How much effort do you put into your work?	1	2	3	4	5
How much did you try *to improve* your performance the past 3 months?	1	2	3	4	5

7. Salary—is the amount of pay a job incumbent receives from the organization. It was measured in the 1975 OAI questionnaires with the following item:

What was your net salary the past two weeks (i.e., how big would your last 2-week take-home pay check have been had you not had optional deductions)?

LESS THAN $100	$100– $199	$200– $299	$300– $399	$400– $499	$500– $599	$600 OR MORE
1	2	3	4	5	6	7

Hypotheses on Job Context and Design Dimensions

Figure 6-4 presents the patterns of relationships expected among the job context and design dimensions for highly effective jobs (i.e., jobs that produce high job satisfaction, work motivation, and productivity). The hypothesized relationships are based on three key propositions.

First, highly effective job outcomes occur when the design of the job closely matches the background skills and interests of the job incumbent. This proposition is not intended at Taylor's (1911) extreme prescription of "one best man for one best job." It is simply a reflection of the prevailing job design theory and research of today, which show that the skills obtained in previous job experiences and growth need strength of job incumbents moderate the relationship between the design of a job and employee reactions to it. Specifically, in highly effective jobs, the skills a person obtains through previous education, job career experiences, and job promotion sequences closely match the skill requirements of the job (Morgan, 1977). Further, in highly effective jobs, there is a close match between an individual's desires for personal growth development and challenge, and the extent to which the design of the job offers these opportunities (Brief and Aldag, 1975; Hackman and Oldham, 1975; Oldham et al., 1976; Wanous, 1974). In terms of the five OA job design factors, an enriched or enlarged job would consist of

	Task Difficulty & Variability of Unit	Levels From Top Manager	Person's Prior Work Experience	Growth Need Strength	Job Specialization	Job Expertise	Job Standardization	Job Discretion	Job Feedback
Levels From Top Manager	−								
Prior Work Experience and Job Career History of Person	+	−							
Growth Need Strength of Person	+	0	0						
Job Specialization	∪	+	0	∪					
Job Expertise	+	−	+	+	∪				
Job Standardization	−	+	0	−	∩	−			
Job Discretion	+	−	+	+	∪	+	−		
Job Feedback	+	0	0	+	−	+	+	+	
Job-Contingent Rewards & Sanctions	0	0	0	+	?	?	?	?	+

Figure 6-4 Relationships among job context and design dimensions expected for highly effective jobs (i.e., jobs that produce high job satisfaction, work motivation, and productivity).

low to high (but challenging) job specialization, moderate to high job expertise and discretion, low to moderate job standardization, high amounts of feedback from the work itself and from others, and high expectancies of rewards for doing a good job and sanctions for doing a poor job.

Second, highly effective job outcomes occur when the design of the job closely matches the technical and functional work requirements of the organization. This proposition assumes sufficient flexibility on the technological side of almost any organization to suit social requirements of individuals for a high quality working life, a proposition central to sociotechnical theory and convincingly argued by Trist (1970). Within the limits of this assumption, Figure 6-4 operationally reflects this proposition in terms of the influences of task difficulty and variability and the location of the job in the organization's hierarchy upon job design characteristics. The explanations given in Chapter 5 on the relationships between unit task and structure dimensions are analogous at the job design level.

Third, highly effective job outcomes occur when there is an internal consistency in the pattern of relationships among the job design dimensions. Specifically, we hypothesize that the more the job design dimensions interrelate in the directions shown in Figure 6-4, the higher the job satisfaction, work motivation and productivity of job incumbents. As argued at the unit level in Chapter 5, the concave and convex relations of job specialization with the other job dimensions reflect the dual nature of specialization: job designs may either promote efficient performance of simple and nonvarying tasks (within the limits of proposition 1) or may promote quality performance of very difficult and novel tasks (within the limits of proposition 2).

At the present time, we are not prepared to address a fourth crucial proposition but simply state it to indicate our future directions: *Highly effective organizational units and jobs occur when they reflect logical and internally consistent counterpart patterns in the unit and job design dimensions* in Figure 6-2. Clearly, much further theory building and research work lies ahead to develop and test these four major propositions.

PSYCHOMETRIC PROPERTIES OF JOB DESIGN INDICES

As described previously, the job design characteristics were measured in the 1975 OAI supervisory and employee questionnaires which were completed by 1670 respondents in all headquarters and local offices of the state employment security agency. Based on this survey, we now evaluate the measurement properties of the job design indices. Throughout the analysis following, the data are examined at the individual respondent level of analysis; the data are *not* aggregated.

Factor Analysis

Table 6-1 shows the results of a factor analysis after varimax rotation on 27 items that were included in the indices of job design and employee affective responses to their jobs. Job specialization, level in hierarchy, and work experience are excluded from the analysis because they were measured with single items. The indicators of job expertise, task difficulty, and variability were also excluded from the factor analysis because their measurement properties were already evaluated in Chapter 5. However, the measures of job satisfaction and work motivation are included in the factor analysis to test how well they discriminate from the structural characteristics of jobs.

The results of the factor analysis shown in Table 6-1 are quite encouraging for this initial attempt at developing the job design indices. The results identify five unique factors of job design: job authority (factor I), job standardization (factor III), job feedback (factor IV), expectation of sanctions (factor VII), and work load pressure (factor VIII). In addition, the two items that were intended to measure work motivation load together highly on factor V. However, the two items measuring expectation of rewards confound with the job satisfaction items in factor II. We believe this confounding is the result of the strong empirical relationships between two conceptually distinct indices. When pilot interviews were conducted to evaluate the content validity of the measures, respondents had no difficulty in correctly distinguishing between the items intended to measure job satisfaction from the expectation of rewards. Therefore, in this preliminary analysis we continue to treat these two indices as conceptually distinct in content and defer making any revisions until the next evaluation of the OAI.

Specific items in the job satisfaction (factor II), job feedback (factor IV) and work load pressure (factor VIII) indices have substantial loadings (near .40 or higher) on other factors. In the case of work load pressure, item 11 (lack of work advance time) loads more highly on the job authority factor than it does with the other two items in its index in factor VIII. Item 22, satisfaction with job, also loads quite strongly on the work motivation factor (V). In addition, item 16, dependence on others' feedback, confounds with factor VI (set work quotas). In all these cases, however, the confounding items have a higher loading on their hypothesized factors than on the other factors, which indicates that they are most closely related to the other items in the indices for which they were intended. Attempts are made to modify or restate these questions in the revised OAI (Appendix A) to reduce their tendency to confound with other factors.

Factor VI is the only one that is not interpretable. Although five items load quite highly on this factor, no theoretical explanation is available for the combination of these five items. Hopefully, a revision of the items confounding with this and other factors will eliminate this meaningless factor in future evaluations of the OAI.

Table 6-1 Factor Analysis of 27 Items in OAI Designed to Measure Job Design Constructs of 1670 People in Employment Security Offices

Hypothesized Factors	I Job Authority	II Satisfaction and Expec. Reward	III Job Standardization	IV Feedback from Others	V Work Motivation	VI ?	VII Expectation of Sanctions	VIII Work Load Pressure	Communalities (h^2)
Job Standardization									
1. Number Written Rules	.03	.04	.80[a]	.04	.05	-.04	.06	.10	.66
2. Specificity of Rules	-.02	.05	.81[a]	.04	.09	.08	.06	.01	.68
3. Percent Time have SOPs	-.00	.06	.71[a]	.08	-.07	.04	.00	-.02	.51
4. Extent Follow SOPs	-.20	-.02	.61[a]	-.05	.17	.18	.01	-.23	.52
Job Authority									
5. Decide What Tasks to Perform	.83[a]	.06	.01	-.01	.05	.03	-.06	.00	.70
6. Set Work Quotas	.80[a]	.06	.01	-.03	.09	.08	-.04	-.17	.71
7. Set Work Rules	.81[a]	.06	-.15	-.02	.04	.12	-.04	.02	.69
8. Handle Exceptions	.79[a]	.02	-.08	.04	-.00	.14	-.11	.10	.70
Work Load Pressure									
9. Heaviness of Work Load	.08	-.03	.00	.03	.25	-.05	-.07	.79[a]	.70
10. Lack of Control of Work Pace	-.48[a]	-.06	-.08	.01	-.11	-.00	-.05	.58[a]	.59
11. Lack of Work Advance Time	-.38	-.12	-.21	-.22	.11	.31	.03	-.15	.38
Expectation of Rewards									
12. Chance of Recognition	.22	.42[a]	.10	.35	.03	.43[a]	.04	.04	.55
13. Chance of Promotion	.11	.62[a]	.05	.20	-.02	.11	.19	.05	.48

	1	2	3	4	5	6	7	8
Expectation of Sanctions								
14. Chance of Reprimand	−.09	.01	.10	.16	.05	.02	.78[a]	.65
15. Chance of Demotion	−.12	.09	.01	.05	.12	−.05	.80[a]	.68
Feedback from Others								
16. Depend on Others' Feedback	−.21	.13	−.00	.51[a]	.15	−.43[a]	−.15	.62
17. Frequency of Performance Review	.01	.03	.04	.74[a]	.05	.15	.16	.60
18. Frequency get Suggestions for Improvement	.01	.14	.08	.75[a]	−.03	.15	.11	.62
19. Clarity of Expected Performance Standards	.21	.09	.27	.06	.08	.62[a]	.11	.53
Work Motivation								
20. Effort in Job	.11	.10	.09	−.07	.79[a]	.16	.08	.72
21. Try to Improve	.02	.08	.08	.12	.83[a]	.04	.11	.73
Job Satisfaction								
22. Satisfaction with Job	.17	.56[a]	.05	.03	.41[a]	.31	−.07	.61
23. Satisfaction with Supervisor	.07	.39	.08	.28	.13	.60[a]	−.10	.63
24. Satisfaction with Pay	−.08	.69[a]	.02	−.09	−.09	.08	−.01	.51
25. Satisfaction with Co-workers	.04	.21	−.03	.18	.17	.43[a]	−.16	.34
26. Satisfaction with Past Career	.10	.82[a]	.02	.07	.16	.03	−.03	.71
27. Satisfaction with Career Potential	.04	.84[a]	.06	.11	.10	.03	.04	.73
Eigenvalue	4.79	3.16	2.11	1.59	1.50	1.26	1.13	1.03
Cumulative Percentage of Variance Accounted for	17.7	29.5	37.3	43.1	48.7	53.4	57.5	61.3

[a] Significant loading of item on factor equal to or greater than .40.

Results such as those shown in Table 6-1 are not atypical for preliminary efforts in index construction. Several factors (I, III, V, and VII) are good (that is, none of their items load significantly on any other factor); several factors (II, IV, and VIII) do have items that confound with other factors; and one factor (VI) has no discernible meaning. To continue the analysis here, composite indices were computed on the basis of the items originally hypothesized to be a part of each index. The one exception to this is job feedback. Item 19 in Table 6-1 (clarity of expected performance standards) does not tap the same dimension that the other items in that index do. Therefore, it will be eliminated from the composite job feedback index. In each case, the composite indices were computed as the simple average of the items making up the index.

Other Criteria of Intrinsic Validity

Table 6-2 presents other indicators of the intrinsic validity of the job indices in terms of coefficient alpha and median correlations with items in other indices. For those indices measured by two or more items, both an expected and an observed coefficient alpha are shown. Each job design index was narrowly defined as consisting of only one conceptual element; hence a coefficient alpha of .7 to .9 is expected (see Chapter 3). The observed coefficient alphas for job standardization, job authority, work motivation, and job satisfaction all fall within this expected range. The observed coefficient alphas for expectation of rewards and expectation of sanctions are lower than expected; however, at .66 and .62, respectively, they do not indicate any serious problem with the items in the index. Additional items in these indices would probably increase the observed coefficient alphas. Job feedback and workload pressure, in particular, fall short of .7 on observed coefficient alpha. The items in these indices apparently do not measure the same domain. Therefore, revisions are necessary to improve their internal consistencies (see Appendix A).

The median correlations with all other items are quite satisfactory for all the dimensions shown in Table 6-2. These median correlations range from .04 for job specialization to .13 for expectation of rewards. For those indices with both an observed coefficient alpha and a median correlation with all other items, the median correlation is significantly lower than the coefficient alpha, indicating that the indices do discriminate well.

The coefficient alphas and median correlations shown in Table 6-2 corroborate the results shown in Table 6-1. Some of the indices are more

Table 6-2 Reliabilities of the OAI Individual Job Design Dimensions

	Number of Items in Index	Average Correlation in Index	Coefficient Alpha		Median Correlation with All Other Items
			Expected	Observed	
Job Design Factors					
1. Job Standardization	4	.42	.70–.90	.75	.07
2. Job Authority	4	.62	.70–.90	.87	.11
3. Work Load Pressure	3	.10	.70–.90	.24	.05
4. Expectation of Rewards	2	.46	.70–.90	.66	.13
5. Expectation of Sanctions	2	.42	.70–.90	.62	.07
6. Feedback from Others	3	.26	.70–.90	.51	.07
7. Job Specialization	1	—	—	—	.04
8. Education Level	1	—	—	—	.10
9. On-the-Job Training	1	—	—	—	.08
10. Job-Entry Training	1	—	—	—	.06
Job Context Factors					
11. Length of Service with Organization	1	—	—	—	.12
12. Level in Hierarchy	1	—	—	—	.11
Individual Outcomes					
13. Work Motivation	2	.53	.70–.90	.74	.11
14. Job Satisfaction	6	.38	.70–.90	.78	.09

225

reliable and valid than others. In particular, job standardization, specialization, authority, work motivation, and job satisfaction show good indications of convergent and discriminant validity. However, work load pressure and job feedback require modifications to improve their measurement qualities.

EXTRINSIC VALIDITY OF THE INDIVIDUAL JOB DESIGN DIMENSIONS

Just as important as the preceding indicators of intrinsic validity of the OAI indices is their extrinsic validity, or practical usefulness for organizational research and diagnosis. As in previous chapters, the extrinsic validity of these measures is evaluated (1) by determining how well they discriminate among different job categories found in employment security (ES) units; (2) by assessing their concurrent validity with employee affective responses to their jobs; and (3) by examining the correlations among the OAI indices in terms of the theory.

Ability of the OAI Indices to Discriminate among Job Categories

Table 6-3 shows the results of one-way analyses of variance for each of the individual job design dimensions across five basic functions performed by ES personnel. These functions include (1) claims taking, processing, and clerical functions; (2) adjudication, a specialized function with highly codified guidelines; (3) job development, part of the placement function; (4) employment counseling; and (5) management and supervision, including supervisors at all levels in ES offices. Measures of respondents' age, sex, and number of dependents (spouse and children) are included in Table 6-3 to provide additional normative data on the job incumbents in different functions.

As one might expect, supervisors and managers are older than those in other job categories. They also tend to be men (mean 1.8; female designated by 1 and male designated by 2). Employment counseling personnel are the most educated, and people performing clerical claims processing activities are the least educated. Most counselors have a master's degree, whereas most claims processors are high school graduates. One might also expect, as the analyses show, that supervisors and managers would have the longest tenure in the organization, and by definition they should be fewer hierarchical levels from the top manager as well as have greater job authority.

Table 6-3 Comparison of Different Types of Jobs in Local ES Offices on Job Context, Design, and Outcome Dimensions

	Clerical Claims Processing n = 254		UC Claims Adjudication n = 128		Job Placement n = 254		Employment Counseling n = 75		Management & Supervision n = 173		Test for Differences	
	$\bar{X}$	σ	$\bar{X}$	σ	$\bar{X}$	σ	$\bar{X}$	σ	$\bar{X}$	σ	F-Ratio	Probability
Job Context Factors												
1. Task Difficulty	1.98	.69	2.03	.71	2.24	.65	2.78	.71	2.36	.71	18.81	.0001
2. Task Variability	2.04	.63	2.26	.69	2.27	.69	2.75	.74	2.71	.69	21.36	.0001
3. Levels from Top Manager	4.61	.84	4.49	.89	4.66	.96	4.21	.64	3.31	1.13	43.41	.0001
4. Years Worked in Organization	2.56	1.28	3.18	1.43	2.96	1.08	3.75	.93	4.51	.77	62.55	.0001
5. Age of Person	33.9	13.5	38.1	12.4	34.3	10.1	36.3	9.3	45.2	10.8	19.77	.0001
6. Sex (1 = Female, 2 = Male)	1.11	.31	1.63	.48	1.55	.50	1.79	.41	1.80	.40	103.8	.0001
7. Number of Dependents	1.70	1.51	2.06	1.57	2.33	1.61	2.67	1.81	3.03	1.92	12.84	.0001
Job Design Factors												
1. Number of Tasks Performed (Reverse of Job Specialization)	2.09	1.03	1.80	1.01	3.20	1.59	2.50	1.16	2.81	1.57	25.67	.0001
2. Educational Level	2.75	.77	3.91	.91	3.67	.75	4.84	.44	3.68	.88	121.68	.0001
3. Length of Job-Entry Training	2.85	1.37	3.61	1.42	2.93	1.16	2.87	1.28	2.77	1.50	7.95	.0001
4. Time in On-the-Job Training	1.49	.83	2.09	1.09	2.16	1.07	2.47	1.13	2.64	1.11	36.70	.0001
5. Job Standardization	3.39	.88	3.51	.85	3.35	.81	2.91	.92	3.02	.86	8.46	.0001
6. Job Authority	2.77	1.21	3.02	1.10	3.21	1.04	3.63	.91	4.08	.75	27.28	.0001
7. Job Work Load Pressure	3.36	.64	3.52	.67	3.44	.75	3.21	.57	3.19	.56	4.97	.0001
8. Job Feedback	2.30	.74	2.56	.76	2.47	.63	2.39	.62	2.44	.65	4.58	.0001
9. Expectation of Rewards	2.38	.96	2.63	.99	2.69	1.10	2.29	.89	2.64	.83	3.85	.0004
10. Expectation of Sanctions	2.98	.93	2.76	.89	2.90	.90	2.86	.82	2.84	.78	1.41	.2000
Job Outcome Factors												
11. Work Motivation	4.40	.63	4.53	.60	4.38	.60	4.25	.65	4.39	.57	2.13	.0400
12. Job Satisfaction	3.40	.80	3.41	.81	3.29	.81	3.31	.71	3.53	.66	1.88	.0700
13. Salary	3.25	.85	3.88	1.09	3.86	.96	4.69	1.02	5.18	1.12	61.03	.0001

Employment counseling positions are the least standardized jobs, whereas adjudicators have the most standardized jobs. Adjudicators use highly codified guidelines in their work to investigate and determine how to settle claims disputes. Adjudication is also the most specialized job category included in Table 6-3. Job placement personnel, on the other hand, have the broadest, most general tasks to perform. These differences are consistent with our observations of these functions over the years.

There are no discernible differences among the five types of job functions on three dimensions: expectation of rewards, expectation of sanctions, and job feedback. Although the F-ratios (based on 884 observations) may be statistically significant in these cases, there is little difference in the means for these dimensions across the different job categories. There are virtually no differences between the job categories on employee affective responses to their jobs. ES personnel seem to be equally satisfied and motivated regardless of their tasks or positions. This supports the idea that people self-select the types of jobs that they like; people find their niche in an organization. This observation was repeatedly brought out in the interviews with all ES unit supervisors in 1972.

Concurrent Validity of the OAI Job Design Indices

The far right-hand columns of Table 6-4 shows the correlations of the job context and design factors with work motivation, job satisfaction, and salary for all 1670 employees in the ES state agency. Overall, although work motivation is significantly correlated with eight of the ten job design indices, the magnitude of these correlations ranges from only .11 to .20. Nine of the ten job design factors are significantly associated with job satisfaction, and the correlations are somewhat larger, ranging from .10 to .56. In terms of potentially meaningful relationships, the expectation of rewards from doing good work is clearly the most important predictor of work motivation ($r = .20$) and job satisfaction ($r = .56$). In addition, practically important relationships with job satisfaction exist for job feedback, .26; job authority, .19; and also the level of job occupant in the organizational hierarchy, $-.21$. The magnitude and directions of these correlations between the OA job design factors and employee affective responses are quite similar to those obtained by Hackman and Oldham (1975) and Oldham et al. (1976) on the JDS job characteristics. The findings are also consistent with other research reviewed by Hackman and Lawler (1971) and Berger and Cummings

Table 6-4 Correlations of Job Context and Design with Work Motivation and Job Satisfaction for Different Types of ES Jobs

	Clerical Claims Processing n = 254		UC Claims Adjudication n = 128		Job Placement n = 254		Employment Counseling n = 75		Management & Supervision n = 173		All Respondents n = 1670		
	Mot.	Sat.	Mot.	Sat.	Mot.	Sat.	Mot.	Sat.	Mot.	Sat.	Mot.	Sat.	Salary
Job Context Factors													
1. Task Difficulty	-.24[a]	-.26[a]	-.18	-.25	-.13	-.13	-.14	-.06	.00	.11	-.10[a]	-.09[a]	.30[a]
2. Task Variability	-.03	-.15	.00	-.01	.13	.11	.15	.09	.10	.17	.06	.07[a]	.38[a]
3. Levels From Top Manager	-.25[a]	-.28[a]	-.06	-.28[a]	.01	-.20[a]	-.18	-.09	.00	-.28[a]	-.07	-.21[a]	-.31[a]
4. Years Worked	.14	-.03	.07	.09	-.12	-.11	-.19	-.09	-.01	.18	.01	.03	.59[a]
5. Age of Person	.29[a]	.26[a]	.10	.21	.03	.04	.05	.00	.02	.15	.14[a]	.18[a]	.41[a]
6. Sex (1 = Female, 2 = Male)	.02	-.04	-.27[a]	-.38[a]	-.10	-.08	.17	.16	-.15	.09	-.09[a]	-.07[a]	.46[a]
7. Number of Dependents	.14	.16	-.02	-.10	.09	.04	.01	.09	-.02	.13	.05	.05	.22[a]
Job Design Factors													
1. Job Specialization (Scale of # of Tasks Revised)	-.07	.01	.01	-.08	-.07	-.07	-.06	.09	.05	-.10	-.01	.01	-.16[a]
2. Educational Level	-.10	-.13	-.13	-.33[a]	-.12	-.21	.14	.19	-.07	-.05	-.12[a]	-.15[a]	.39[a]
3. Time in On-the-Job Training	.13	.14	.00	-.17	-.02	.11	.07	.23	.16	.08	.07[a]	.10[a]	.29[a]
4. Length of Job-Entry Training	.19	.08	.03	-.05	.25[a]	.18	.09	-.12	.24[a]	.13	.11[a]	.08[a]	.02
5. Job Standardization	.13	.17	.07	.10	.11	.18	.23	.18	.11	.01	.16[a]	.14[a]	-.16[a]
6. Job Authority	.20	.18	.22	.15	.09	.38[a]	-.01	.22	.14	.16	.11[a]	.19[a]	.31[a]
7. Job Work Load Pressure	.05	-.02	-.15	-.25	.02	-.18	.07	-.12	-.03	-.16	.04	-.12[a]	-.05
8. Job Feedback	.13	.28[a]	-.01	.20	.13	.32[a]	.06	.46[a]	.09	.30[a]	.11[a]	.26[a]	.00
9. Expectation of Rewards	.18	.53[a]	.19	.57[a]	.17	.60[a]	.21	.68[a]	.22	.45[a]	.20[a]	.56[a]	-.01
10. Expectation of Sanctions	.09	.03	.11	.00	.19[a]	.08	.09	.08	.07	.11	.15[a]	.05	-.08[a]

[a] $p < .001$.

229

(1979). Hackman and Lawler found significant positive relationships between work motivation and promotions and between general job satisfaction and (1) prestige of job inside company, (2) participation in work-related decisions, and (3) job promotions.

Employee salary, on the other hand, is most strongly associated with the job context factors as well as the expertise and job authority of the employee, but not with job incentives. As might be expected in an organization with a uniform and highly regulated Civil Service employee pay and compensation system, the most observable characteristics of employees are used to establish pay scales. In the ES agency, employee seniority and age (which correlate .61), sex, education, level in the hierarchy, and task variability and difficulty, in that order, are the strongest predictors of employee salaries. The positive association between sex (1 = female, 2 = male) and salary indicates that men rather than women employed by the ES agency have greater education (r = .57), seniority (r = .29), a greater number of dependents (r = .28), and hold positions higher in the organizational hierarchy (r = .22). The less observable and more intrinsic job incentives (i.e., job feedback, and expectations or rewards and sanctions for doing good or poor work) are unrelated to employee pay, whereas they were found to be the strongest predictors of work motivation and job satisfaction. These data suggest that employee salaries are generally unrelated to job performance, as has been observed in many other organizations (e.g., Berger and Cummings, 1979). Indeed, salary correlates .00 with work motivation and .05 with job satisfaction for employees in the ES agency.

To examine these relationships more specifically, the first ten columns in Table 6-4 show the correlations of job context and design with work motivation and job satisfaction for each of the five functional areas. These five different types of jobs show a relatively consistent pattern in the direction and magnitude of the correlations between each job design factor and work motivation and job satisfaction. In Chapter 5 significant differences across different types of ES units were observed in the relationships of unit design with unit efficiency, effectiveness, and the average level of job satisfaction of personnel within organizational units. At the individual job design level, this flip-flopping of the correlations does not exist nearly as much as was observed at the work unit level.

The overall implication of this consistency in correlations between job design and employee affective responses across different types of ES functional areas is that the relationships tend to hold irrespective of the types of jobs employees hold. This result makes an assessment of the design of jobs far less complex than assessing the design of organizational units. This is not to suggest that an assessment of jobs is a simple task—only that the differences between types of jobs should not intervene in our examination of relationships among job context and design dimensions.

Relationships among Job Context and Design Factors

Table 6-5 shows the correlations among the job context and design dimensions that were obtained for ES employees who reported low and high levels of job satisfaction. The data on all 1670 respondents in the ES agency were classified and subsetted into low, medium, and high levels of job satisfaction to determine if the correlations among the job context and design dimensions would differ between employees who report high versus low job satisfaction.

Employees with medium levels of job satisfaction (i.e., with scores ranging from 3.2 to 3.7 on a five-point scale) represent 32 percent of the total sample and were excluded from the sample to minimize classification error. A total of 574 employees reported low levels of job satisfaction (i.e., with scores ranging from 1.0 to 3.1 on the five-point scale), and their correlations among the job context and design dimensions are presented in the top row of each cell in the matrix of Table 6-5. The same correlations for 679 highly satisfied employees (with scores ranging from 3.7 to 5.0 on the five-point scale) are presented in the lower row of each cell in the matrix.

When examining the different types of ES jobs in Table 6-3, it was found that ES employees seem equally satisfied regardless of their tasks or positions. However, a comparison of the means and standard deviations in Table 6-5 between highly satisfied and unsatisfied employees shows that there are measurable and systematic differences in the contexts and designs of their jobs. In comparison with the unsatisfied employees, the highly satisfied personnel have slightly less difficult tasks but more variety in their work, are fewer hierarchical levels removed from the top office manager (i.e., have jobs in offices with flatter structural configurations), and have worked longer in the ES agency.

In terms of job design, highly satisfied employees have slightly less formal education but spend more time in job-entry and on-the-job training, have somewhat more standardized or clearly defined jobs, exercise more work decision-making authority, experience slightly less work pressure, get considerably more feedback from others, have significantly greater expectations of being rewarded for doing good work, and expect to be sanctioned slightly more for doing poor work. Finally, the

Table 6-5 Correlations among Job Context and Design Dimensions for ES Employees Low and High in Job Satisfaction.

Correlations for employees with low job satisfaction ($n = 574$) are placed above and for those with high job satisfaction ($n = 679$) are below each cell in matrix

	Mean	SD	1	2	3	4	5	6	7	8	9	10	11	12	13
Job Context Factors															
1. Task Difficulty	2.15	.76	—												
	2.00	.72	—												
2. Task Variability	2.16	.75	.52[a]	—											
	2.27	.75	.57[a]	—											
3. Levels from Top Manager	4.75	1.06	−.18[a]	−.27[a]	—										
	4.26	1.07	−.31[a]	−.32[a]	—										
4. Years in Organization	3.00	1.25	.15[a]	.30[a]	−.33[a]	—									
	4.26	1.37	.22[a]	.25[a]	−.37[a]	—									
Job Design Factors															
5. Job Specialization (Scale of # Tasks Reversed)	2.46	1.30	−.17[a]	−.19[a]	.15[a]	−.14[a]	—								
	2.53	1.41	−.16[a]	−.16[a]	.17[a]	−.14[a]	—								
6. Educational Level	3.46	.96	.33[a]	.22[a]	−.08	.11	−.17[a]	—							
	3.15	.99	.36[a]	.38[a]	−.14[a]	.15[a]	−.09	—							

	Mean	SD	1	2	3	4	5	6	7	8	9	10	11	12	13
7. Length of Job-Entry Training	1.85	1.08	$.21^a$	$.31^a$	$-.15^a$	$.15^a$	$-.14^a$	$.24^a$	—						
	2.01	1.08	$.30^a$	$.33^a$	$-.25^a$	.11	$-.20^a$	$.33^a$	—						
8. Time in On-the-Job Training	2.70	1.37	.06	.09	$-.05$	.02	.03	.05	.12	—					
	2.97	1.31	$-.08$	$-.04$	.09	$-.03$	.03	.06	.01	—					
9. Job Standardization	3.10	.94	$-.26^a$	$-.27^a$	.05	$-.06$	.03	.11	$-.01$	.06	—				
	3.40	.87	$-.42^a$	$-.37^a$	$.18^a$	$-.11$	.14	$-.20^a$	$-.05$	$.17^a$	—				
10. Job Authority	3.01	1.21	.01	$.25^a$	$-.27^a$	$.31^a$	$-.12$	.07	.06	.09	$-.09$	—			
	3.47	1.07	$.15^a$	$.32^a$	$-.30^a$	$.34^a$	$-.22^a$	$.13^a$	$.21^a$	.00	$-.23^a$	—			
11. Work Load Pressure	3.40	.73	.12	.04	$-.05$	.05	$-.03$	.05	$-.02$	.00	$-.05$	$-.32^a$	—		
	3.21	.62	.04	$-.02$	.04	$-.04$	$-.02$	$-.10^a$	$-.13^a$	$-.08$	$-.07$	$-.29^a$	—		
12. Feedback from Others	2.14	.63	$.14^a$	.04	.02	$-.11$	$-.05$	.09	.10	.09	.11	$-.08$	$-.01$	—	
	2.51	.70	$.16^a$	.06	.05	$-.13$	$-.07$	$.19^a$	$.22^a$	$.16^a$	.10	$.15^a$	$-.05$	—	
13. Expectation of Rewards	1.93	.79	$-.10$	.05	$-.06$	$-.04$	$-.05$	.00	.05	.16	.10	.09	$-.14^a$	$.19^a$	—
	3.13	.94	$-.08$	.02	$-.01$	$-.12^a$	$-.06$	$-.07$	$.12^a$	.05	.10	$.24^a$	$-.05$	$.27^a$	—
14. Expectation of Sanctions	2.86	.97	$-.02$	$-.04$	$.14^a$	$-.09$	.03	$-.07$	$-.03$	$-.01$	$.13^a$	$-.20^a$	.04	$.22^a$	.00
	2.97	.88	$-.05$	$-.06$	.07	$-.17^a$	.05	.00	.09	$-.01$	$.13^a$	$-.16^a$	$-.01$	$.22^a$	$.18^a$

[a] $p < .001$.

highly satisfied employees receive slightly more pay and perceive they exert significantly more effort in their jobs. Although these differences between satisfied and unsatisfied employees are not large, they present an overall impression that the highly satisfied ES employees have somewhat more "enriched" jobs than the unsatisfied personnel.

Test of Propositions on Job Design

In presenting the hypotheses on the job context and design dimensions previously, we propositioned that highly effective job outcomes occur when the design of the job closely matches the background skills and interests of the job incumbent on the one hand, and the work requirements of the organization on the other hand. In terms of the data available in Table 6-5 this proposition translates into expecting the correlations of seniority (one indicator of a person's background experience) and task difficulty, variability, and level in the hierarchy (indicators of work and position requirements of the organization) with the job design dimensions to be larger for the highly satisfied employees than those perceiving low job satisfaction. The correlations in Table 6-5 show some support for the proposition in terms of job expertise (i.e., the job incumbent's formal education and length of job-entry training), job standardization, and job authority. Although the differences are not large, the correlations between these dimensions and the job context factors are systematically larger and more in the expected directions for satisfied than for unsatisfied employees. The other job design dimensions show no systematic differences between satisfied and unsatisfied employees.

It is noteworthy that job expertise, standardization, and authority represent the more formal aspects of job design, and they are most strongly related to the indicators of an organization's work requirements (task difficulty, task variability, level in hierarchy). Workload pressure, job feedback, and expectations of rewards and sanctions represent less formal aspects of a job and are not strongly correlated with these factors. However, the research by Hackman and Oldham (1975) and Oldham et al. (1976) suggests that these less formal aspects of a job may be more strongly predicted from the growth need strength of a job incumbent (which was not measured in the 1975 OAI). Future research, of course, is necessary to examine these propositions adequately, as well as to explore if individual background and job requirements significantly predict different job design characteristics.

We also proposed that highly effective job outcomes occur when there is an internal consistency in the pattern of relationships among the job design dimensions as hypothesized in Figure 6-4. Table 6-5 shows considerable support for the proposition. The correlations among the more formal characteristics of job design (i.e., among job specialization, educational level, length of job-entry training, job standardization, and job authority) are consistently larger and more in the expected directions for highly satisfied employees than they are for those who perceive low job satisfaction. In addition, educational level, job-entry training, and job authority correlate somewhat more strongly with job feedback and expectations of reward in those jobs whose incumbents perceive high versus low job satisfaction. No consistent differences between satisfied and unsatisfied employees are evident in the correlations among the time spent in on-the-job training, work load pressure, and expectations of sanctions. In fact, most of the correlations among these three factors and with the other job design characteristics for both satisfied and unsatisfied employees are near zero. Thus, the data show there is a consistently stronger pattern of interrelationships on seven of the ten dimensions of job design which distinguishes ES employees with high versus low job satisfaction. Although these differences are not large, they certainly warrant further theoretical and empirical examination.

In Figure 6-4 it was hypothesized that job specialization would have nonlinear associations with the task and other job design characteristics because specialization has two alternative purposes: (1) efficient performance of simple, nonvarying, and standardized tasks, or (2) quality performance of difficult and varying tasks that require high amounts of expertise and discretion.

Only a partial test of this hypothesis is possible here because of the relatively narrow ranges of scores obtained on task difficulty, variability, and job specialization in this sample of ES jobs. The tasks performed by most ES employees range from low to medium in difficulty and variability (i.e., with means of about 2.15 and standard deviations of .75 on a 1- to 5-point scale). In addition, the jobs of most ES employees are moderately to highly specialized (i.e., on the average, ES employees spend most of their work time performing 2.5 different types of tasks, with a standard deviation of 1.35). Within these ranges, an examination of the scatter-plots (not shown here) indicates that the associations of job specialization with the task and other job design dimensions are mostly linear.

This evidence suggests that we can only examine one tail of the hypothesized curvilinear relationships between specialization and job design—and that job specialization is used in this sample of ES jobs primarily for achieving the benefits of increased efficiencies by reducing complex tasks into simple, nonvarying, specialized, and standardized jobs that require little decision-making discretion and less costly (unskilled) employees. This pattern of relationships among the task and job design characteristics is consistent with the correlations in Table 6-5, particularly for employees with highly satisfying jobs. Decreases in task difficulty and variability from medium to low levels are positively related to job specialization, decreases in the educational level of employees and in the time spent in on-the-job training, and also decreases in the amount of authority exercised in making work-related decisions.

The opposite pattern of correlations would be expected if the purpose of job specialization were to increase the probability of achieving quality performance of highly difficult and varying tasks. Specifically, in this case, increases in task difficulty and variability from medium to high levels would be positively correlated with increases in job specialization, which permits one to hire highly trained and educated employees, to delegate high amounts of job discretion to them, and to decrease the standardization of work procedures and rules. Research on a greater range of different types of tasks and jobs than those observed in this sample of ES organizations is necessary for testing this interesting hypothesis on the dual benefits of job specialization.

CONCLUDING SUMMARY

This chapter has taken the initial step in expanding the Organization Assessment framework and instruments to examine the context and design of jobs. The job design dimensions included in the OA framework focus more heavily on the behavioral aspects of jobs than do those used by Hackman and Oldham (1975) in the Job Diagnostic Survey. The reason we lean toward a behavioral description of jobs is because behaviors are more objective and easier for analysts and practitioners to observe, control, and change than the more subjective attitudes of people regarding their jobs.

The expansion of the OA framework to include job design required certain revisions. Structural dimensions formerly analyzed with reference to work units (specifically, unit expertise and employee discretion) confounded conceptually with properties of jobs—and were therefore reanalyzed at the individual job level of analysis. The work of Lazarsfeld and Menzel (1969) was particularly useful for making clear the distinctions between global properties of work groups and member properties of individual jobs or positions. This resulted in developing five core unit structural dimensions and five job design counterparts which tap similar conceptual domains but from different levels of analysis. Although the counterpart dimensions of units and jobs have clearly different reference points and require different measurement procedures, it was suggested that their parallel communalities permit one to conceptualize and observe the options and tradeoffs that exist between the design of individual jobs and organizational units.

Our theory-building efforts have not yet progressed to a stage to examine the relationships between global properties of organizational units and the member characteristics of jobs nested within them. In addition, much additional work is necessary to develop and evaluate measures of individual and job characteristics not included in the 1975 OAI, as well as the new dimensions of work unit structure (unit skill heterogeneity, standardization, and incentives) which were added to the OA framework. Indices to measure these new dimensions are presented in Appendix A.

The results of an evaluation of the job design indices that were included in the 1975 OAI are quite encouraging for this initial attempt at developing measures of job design. Overall, the factor analysis identified five basic factors of job design: job authority, standardization, feedback from others, expectation of sanctions, and work load pressure. It was found that revisions are necessary in some specific items within these indices because they confounded with other factors. In addition, the two items measuring expectation of rewards loaded highly with the job satisfaction items. However, in our pilot study of the content validity of these measures, respondents correctly distinguished between measures expectation of rewards and measures of job satisfaction. In the revised OAI presented in Appendix A, attempts are made to modify or restate these items to reduce their tendency to confound with other indices of job design and satisfaction.

A further evaluation of the intrinsic validity of the job design indices in terms of coefficient alpha and median correlations with other indices essentially corroborated the results of the factor analysis. Some of the indices are more reliable and valid than others. In particular, job standardization, specialization, authority, expectation of sanctions, work motivation, and job satisfaction show satisfactory indications of convergent and discriminant validity, whereas work load pressure, expectation of rewards, and feedback from others require some modifications to improve their measurement qualities.

The extrinsic validity of these measures was evaluated by: (1) determining how well they discriminate between different job categories found in ES offices, (2) assessing their concurrent validity with employee affective responses to their jobs, and (3) examining the correlations among the job context and design characteristics in terms of the theory.

When comparing five different types of jobs commonly found in ES offices, it was found that significant and meaningful differences were detected by 14 of the 17 job context and design factors (see Table 6-3). These differences are consistent with our personal observations over the years of the behavior of ES employees in these different jobs, and provide a preliminary indication that the discriminant validities of the OAI job context and design indices are quite good. This is true particularly in light of the fact that virtually no differences were found between the ES jobs on employee work motivation and job satisfaction. Thus, one cannot attribute the significant differences in job contexts and designs among the ES job categories to the possibility that they simply reflect variations in employee affective responses to their jobs. ES employees seem to have found their niche in the organization by self-selecting the types of jobs that they like; they claim to be equally satisfied and motivated despite job differences.

In terms of concurrent validity, it was found that although eight or nine of the ten job design indices were significantly correlated with work motivation and job satisfaction in a statistical sense, only three or four of the correlations were large enough to be potentially meaningful for predicting or explaining employee affective responses to their jobs (see Table 6-4). However, the sizes and directions of the correlations obtained are quite similar to those on similar dimensions in other studies. For example, as found elsewhere, job satisfaction of ES employees is most importantly associated with: (1) an employee's expectations of being rewarded for doing good work, (2) feedback from others on work performance, (3) the amount of authority exercised in making work decisions, and (4) the number of supervisory levels the employee is removed from the top manager (in that order).

The salary of ES employees, on the other hand, is most strongly associated with the characteristics of individuals and their positions in the organization (i.e., employee seniority, age, sex, education, level in the hierarchy, and task variability and difficulty, in that order, are the strongest predictors of salary). The explanation given is that in an organization with a uniform and highly regulated Civil Service compensation system, the most observable characteristics of employees are used to establish pay scales, even though they are unrelated to work motivation and job satisfaction.

Next, we conducted a partial test of the proposition that employees will be highly satisfied with their jobs when the design of their jobs closely matches their background skills and interests and the technical and functional work requirements of the organization. When comparing the correlations among job context and design for satisfied and unsatisfied employees in Table 6-5, support was found for the proposition on the more formal characteristics of jobs (i.e., job expertise, standardization, and authority) but not for the less formal aspects of jobs (work load pressure, job feedback, and expectations of rewards and sanctions).

When combining these results with those of Hackman and Oldham (1975) and Oldham et al. (1976), we speculated that these less formal aspects of jobs may be more strongly predicted by individual difference characteristics, particularly growth need strength (which was not measured in the 1975 OAI). The more formal properties of jobs, on the other hand, may largely reflect the task and position requirements of a job by the organization. An interesting direction for future research to explore is if and how different background characteristics of individuals and organizational task and position requirements explain and predict different job design characteristics.

Finally, considerable support was obtained for the proposition that employees will be highly satisfied with their jobs when there is an internal consistency in the pattern of relationships among the dimensions of job design themselves. A consistently stronger pattern of interrelationships among seven of the ten dimensions of job design was found for ES employees with high versus low job satisfaction. Of course these findings are preliminary because they are only based on one sample of jobs in ES organizations, and a relatively narrow range of scores on some job context and design dimensions was noted. However, the findings indicate to us that a potentially fruitful and interesting direction for futher research is to examine the proposition that affective responses of employees to their jobs (examined here in terms of job satisfaction) are a function not only of (1) the fit between job design, individual background, and organization context but also (2) the congruence and possible tradeoffs among the design characteristics of jobs themselves.

Methodologically, we conclude that promising results have been obtained from tests conducted in this chapter to evaluate the potential usefulness of the OAI job indices for organizational diagnoses and research purposes. This conclusion is warranted in light of the fact that the indices represent only an initial attempt to develop measures of job design in the OAI. Appendix A describes the changes that have been made in the revised OAI to correct specific limitations that were identified in the 1975 OAI job indices. In addition, the appendix proposes a new set of indices to measure the dimensions of job context and design that are included in the revised OA framework but not measured in previous versions of the OAI. Obviously, only future evaluations of the measurement properties of these new and revised indices will tell if they are satisfactory for research and practice.

CHAPTER SEVEN

External Unit Relationships

This chapter focuses on how organizational units relate to their unique environments. The relationships are examined in terms of the flows of work and information between units and supervisory levels within the organization and with units in other organizations as well. Most of the early studies on the influence of environmental characteristics on organizations were conducted at the macroorganizational level of analysis and treated the environment broadly as a set of constraining social and economic phenomena external to the organization (see review in Van de Ven, Emmett, and Koenig, 1974). Conceptualizing environment in this gross sense limits the potential for systematic research because different units within complex organizations deal with different relevant environments. In addition, relevant environments for various units exist just as much inside the organization as outside (Starbuck, 1976). By definition, complex organizations have multiple domains, purposes, and tasks which are assigned to various organizational units. As seen in Chapter 5, each unit, in turn, adopts a different structural design and necessarily deals with a different relevant environment.

Recognition that different units have different relevant environments and that relevant environments exist just as much inside the organization as outside is implicit in Lawrence and Lorsch (1967). They distinguished the relevant environments for various organizational divisions. In addition, they examined differentiation not only in terms of structural attributes but also in terms of individuals' cognitive and emotional orientations. Although Thompson (1967) recognized that different organizational units have different relevant environments, he viewed the environment as existing only outside the organization. Thus, he proposed that under norms of rationality, organizations facing heterogeneous environments will segment the environment and adopt

241

unique proactive or reactive strategies to cope with each subenvironment. Some units perform boundary-spanning functions to buffer and protect the core technology from the environment. A logical conclusion is that the relevant environments for the buffered units within the technical core must be located within the organization. The purpose of the boundary-spanning units is to establish a more stable environment for the technical core. The characteristics of the environments of units within the technical core, then, hinge on how well the various boundary-spanning units perform their buffering functions.

Thus, the location and salience of the environment varies for different organizational units and depends upon the nature of the tasks assigned to the unit and its relative position in the organizational hierarchy. Attempts to define the environment as completely outside the organization—or to aggregate across the relevant environments of different organizational units—result in a distorted, homogenized image of the environment. A more complete understanding of the pluralistic and multidimensional nature of environments is obtained by (1) focusing on the unit or departmental (rather than the organizational) level of analysis, (2) identifying relevant environments both inside and outside the organization, and (3) measuring the same dimensions in each of the relevant environments. By taking this approach, the characteristics of different relevant environments may be compared to one another and examined in relation to the characteristics of their respective units.

This chapter reports the interim results of our efforts to follow these guidelines in conceptualizing and measuring unit environmental relationships. Figure 7-1 lists the dimensions that were identified and measured in the OAI to examine the relationships of each organizational unit with its environment. As Figure 7-1 suggests, a process orientation is taken to the study of these relationships. The dimensions are conceptualized in terms of the flow of work and information of a unit with other units, levels, and organizations. This chapter argues that work and information flows are the two basic links between organizational units and their environments. Then operational definitions and measures of each dimension of work and information flow are presented and evaluated.

WORK AND INFORMATION FLOWS

Conceptual Basis of Work and Information Flows

Work flow* refers to the materials, objects, or clients and customers that are transacted between units, hierarchical levels, and organizations. The major dimensions used for measuring the external work flows

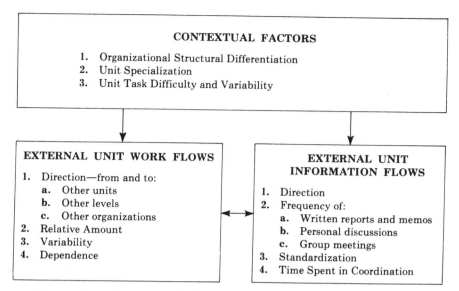

Figure 7-1   Framework for examining external unit relations with other units, levels, and organizations in the OAI.

of an organizational unit in the OAI are:

1. *Direction:* the names of specific organizational units, supervisory levels, and other organizations that a unit receives its incoming work from and sends its completed work to;

2. *Relative Amount:* The percentage of a unit's total incoming work that is received from each source and sent to each destination upon completion;

3. *Variability:* the degrees of interruptions and problems encountered in the flows of a unit's work from each source and to each destination; and

4. *Dependence:* the extent to which unit personnel perceive that the input, process, and output of their work depend upon the activities performed in the other units, levels, and organizations.

---

* Because the OAI focus primarily upon the work of an organization, the discussion singles out work flow. However, work flow is a subconcept of *resource flow*, which includes money, physical equipment, staff, support services, and work. If a comprehensive assessment of processes within an organization is desired, then an extension of the OAI is required to examine all forms of resource flows. For example, in Chapter 8, where interorganizational relationships are examined in greater detail, all these different forms of resource flows between organizations are defined, measured, and evaluated.

The concept *information flow* refers to messages or communications about the materials or work objects that are transmitted between people through a variety of media (e.g., signs, rules, reports, personal discussions, and group or committee meetings). Corresponding to work flows, the OAI measure the following dimensions of information flows:

1. *Direction:* the names of specific units, levels, and organizations to or from which unit personnel send or receive work-related messages;

2. *Frequency:* the number of times per day, week, or month that unit personnel communicate with the other units, levels, and organizations through (a) written reports and memos, (b) one-to-one personal discussions, and (c) group meetings;

3. *Standardization:* the degree to which the content of communications ranges from novel to routine work-related matters and the extent to which rules, policies, and procedures are established to coordinate work activities with the other units, levels, and organizations;

4. *Time:* the average number of hours per day that unit personnel spend in coordinating work activities with the other units, levels, and organizations.

An assessment of external unit relations focuses upon these dimensions of work and information flows because they indicate—in a concrete, behavioral sense—four important facts about intra- and inter-organizational activity.

First, work and information flows are the basic elements of process in organizations. They are the living function of an organization; whatever remains are relics of past behavior.

Second, all social systems, if they are to survive, must perform the parallel functions of task-instrumental goal attainment and pattern maintenance or integration (Parsons, 1960; Katz and Kahn, 1966; von Bertalanffy, 1972). Task-instrumental functions are manifest in work flows, whereas maintenance functions are manifest in information flows. Disequilibriums or disruptions within and between subsystems occur when there is a change in the direction, amount, or stability of either work or information flows. The complex process of adaptation that takes place will be toward the establishment of an equilibrium in the patterns of work and information flows (that is, a congruence or balance between the performance of instrumental and maintenance functions). Thus, work and information flows when measured over time are hypothesized to be reciprocally interdependent and dynamic indicators of system growth, adaptation, and survival. From longitudinal measurements of the dimensions of work and information flows one can develop and analyze dynamic or time-lagged models of organizational movements at different stages of equilibrium and disequilibrium and relate these movements to variations in organizational effectiveness.

Third, information and work flows provide a way to operationalize sociotechnical theory (Emery and Trist, 1960), which is concerned with the problem of organizing the interface between technology and people so that the best match can be obtained (Trist, 1970; Davis and Trist, 1972). For example, the degree of technological integration, intensity of couplings, and programming of the technical system are directly observable with work flow direction and amount, dependence, and variability, respectively. The centrality of communication channels, intensity of connections, and programming of relationships in the social system are exhibited in information flow direction, frequency and time investment, and standardization, respectively. Most important, the problems of interfacing the sociotechnical system can be dealt with by examining the interrelations among these counterpart dimensions of work and information flows. The increasingly sophisticated social and technical systems within complex organizations today and the severity of problems created by inappropriate interfaces (e.g., Davis and Trist, 1972) heighten the need for an operational way to incorporate sociotechnical theory into any framework for organization assessment.

Finally, the dimensions of work and information flows are important process indicators for linking the overall organization (Chapter 4) and work unit (Chapter 5) levels of analysis. These macro–micro linkages are first explored from the perspective of an organizational unit and then with a focus on the total organization.

Work and Information Flows from the Perspective of an Organizational Unit

For a given organizational unit, the *sources* and *destinations* of work and information flows largely define the unit's functional position and boundary-spanning role relative to its environment inside and outside the organization. The greater the *amounts* of work and information received and sent by a unit from and to other components, the greater the centrality or strategic position of that unit within the organization. Conversely, the smaller the amounts of work and information flows with other components, behaviorally speaking, the more autonomous is the unit.

Variations in the amounts of these external work and information flows for a unit are hypothesized to be a function of unit specialization and the difficulty and variability of unit tasks. Increasing unit specialization means that a unit is delegated smaller and smaller pieces of an overall job or task, and this increases the amount of external unit work flows for the job to be completed. However, as March and Simon (1958:159) suggest, an increase in the amount of external unit work flow by itself does not increase problems of coordination or perceptions of dependence as long as the patterns of work flows are stable or nonvarying. In this case, coordination of work flows can be programmed by standardizing language; establishing coordination rules, policies, and procedures; and monitoring through periodic memos, reports and, ultimately, computerized information systems.

The common element of these mechanisms for coordination by programming is that a codified blueprint of action is impersonally specified in advance of its execution. Departures from the blueprint are immediately obvious, and human discretion does not enter into the determination of what, where, when, and how activities among units and levels are to be articulated to coordinate interdepartmental work flows (Van de Ven, Delbecq, and Koenig, 1976:323). To the extent that these mechanisms of coordination by programming are impersonally prescribed and repetitively followed, over time they become a normal repetitive way for transferring work flows among units, and the parties involved largely become unconscious of their work flow interdependencies.

Recognition of dependence increases when the tasks of a unit become more difficult and variable. In these instances, unit personnel either need the assistance of other units to perform their tasks, or they encounter problems and variations in the unit's external work flows which cannot be predicted and programmed in advance. In either case, personal and group modes of coordination are required to make mutual adjustments. It is in this sense that March and Simon (1958:159) proposed that "the more repetitive and predictable the situation, the greater the tolerance for interdependence. Conversely, the greater the elements of variability and contingency, the greater is the burden of coordinating activities that are specialized by process."

Thus, when focusing on organizational units, we hypothesize that the greater the unit specialization, the greater the amount of external unit work flows. When controlling for the variability of work flows, an increase in the amount of external unit work flows is associated with increases in the standardization of information flows and the frequency of written reports and memos but is unassociated with perceptions of external unit dependence. Increases in task difficulty and variability increase problems in managing external unit work flows and also increase a unit's perception of dependence on its environment. Increases in external unit dependence and work flow variability will increase the frequency of personal discussions and group meetings as well as the amount of time unit personnel spend making mutual adjustments with other units. However, those aspects of unit relationships that remain stable and predictable will continue to be coordinated by programming. Hence, personal discussions and group meetings will become more frequent when external unit dependence increases, but these will not replace written reports and memos.

Work and Information Flows from an Overall Organizational Perspective

For the organization as a whole, the *direction* of work and information flows between organizational units and levels identifies the network or cluster of relationships within a complex organization. The *amounts* of work and information flows indicate the *intensity* of the intraorganizational network, that is, the strength of task-instrumental and maintenance activities in the network. The *variability* or *standardization* of work and information flows indicates the *routinization* of network relationships.

Moreover, from these dimensions one can empirically determine the various clusters of organizational units that differ in degrees of linkage along the range from tightly to loosely joined networks. The manner in which such intraorganizational networks develop and are connected can be examined in terms of the theory of loosely joined hierarchical systems, as Aldrich (1979) has proposed. As described further in Chapter 8, this model posits that organizational units are linked into richly joined subsystems that are further linked into the organizational network as a whole by a relatively small number of dominant units.

A comparison of the sociometric flows of work and information between units and levels with reference to the table of organization may reveal significant deviations between the formal organization hierarchy (as described in Chapter 4) and behavioral patterns. The major reason for expecting departures from the formal organization is that hierarchy is but one mechanism of coordinating interdependence which quickly becomes overloaded when frequent problems and exceptions are encountered in work flows between units. As a result, when interdependence among units and levels increases and the corresponding amounts of information needed to coordinate these activities expand, organizations will increasingly rely upon other nonhierarchical methods of processing information.

Figure 7-2 illustrates three basic coordination modes (impersonal, personal, and group) which are used frequently in organizations for managing different degrees of interunit interdependence. Within each mode is listed a set of specific mechanisms that differ in their capacities to process impersonal, personal, and group forms of information. Van de Ven, Delbecq, and Koenig (1976) argue that the distinction between impersonal, personal, and group modes of coordination is one of kind, whereas that between mechanisms within each mode is one of degree.

The simplest and least costly method of coordinating independent work activities among organizational units is to specify impersonally the behaviors to be followed in advance of their execution (March and Simon, 1958). However, Galbraith (1977) suggests that rules, policies and procedures have limited information-processing capacities. As interdependence or variations in work flows among units increase to a moderate amount, a greater need arises for hierarchy in addition to impersonal coordination. In this case predictable variations are programmed through plans, schedules, and forecasts, whereas excep-

Amount of communication		IMPERSONAL	PERSONAL	GROUP
	High	Computerized information systems	Coordination departments	Task forces Standing committees
	Medium	Manual reports of plans, schedules, and forecasts	Assistant managers and staff coordinators	Ad hoc group meetings
	Low	Rules Policies Procedures	Simple line hierarchy	Simple direct contact
		Low	Medium	High

Amount of interdependence

Figure 7-2 Alternative coordination modes within organizations.

tions are referred to higher levels of authority. This combination of coordination mechanisms is functional within the limited capacities of the mechanisms process information.

As interdependence and the number of mutual adjustments increase, still more elaborate coordination mechanisms are required. Simple direct horizontal contacts between units and group meetings (when a number of units and levels need simultaneous feedback to make adjustments) will be added, whereas the capacity and sophistication of impersonal and personal coordination modes will be expanded. Thus, manualized reports, schedules, and forecasts may be replaced with computerized information systems to process greater amounts of impersonal information more expeditiously and among a larger number of actors. Two ways to "extend the arms of a manager" are by appointing assistant managers and adding support staff to handle technical and administrative matters. Ultimately, the personal mode of coordination between organizational units and levels may expand to the point where coordination departments are established—as frequently observed in matrix or program management organizations (Galbraith, 1971; Delbecq and Filley, 1974). Finally, temporary group meetings to handle recurring unstructured problems among highly interdependent units can be expanded by establishing standing committees and task forces representing individuals from the affected units.

The key ideas suggested here are that (1) these methods of coordination are *additive rather than substitutive* linkage mechanisms that an organization will use to deal with increases in work flow interdependence (amount and variability) and (2) hierarchy is but one of a number of mechanisms of coordination available to an organization to manage interdependence. Therefore, one should not expect any particularly close relationship between work and information flow patterns in an organization and its formal hierarchy as represented by the organization chart. High amounts of nonvarying work flows (e.g., purchase orders) can often be performed most efficiently with a capital intensive machine (e.g., a computer) which is centralized because it is too costly to purchase for each unit. These work flows—like plans, schedules, and MIS information required for coordination—are not usually transmitted through hierarchical channels. Hierarchy may be important in establishing and legitimizing these programs, but the communication and work involved in executing these highly programmed activities do not generally follow the "lines of command" (Bakke, 1950).

March and Simon (1958) point out that the patterns of work and information flows in any particular organization may be as much a function of social conditioning as they are of specialization and technology. Channels of work and information flows tend to be self-reinforcing—in the same way that activities, interactions, and sentiments among members in a group develop and reinforce each other over time (Homans, 1950). If a given work or information channel is initially used for one purpose, over time it tends to become used for other unrelated purposes whenever no special-purpose or informal channel exists or is known to the sender.

> Thus, in part, the communication network is planned; in part it grows up in response to the need for specific kinds of communication; in part it develops in response to the social functions of communications. At any given stage in its development, its gradual change is much influenced by the pattern that has already become established. Hence, although the structure of the network will be considerably influenced by the structure of the organization's task, it will not be completely determined by the latter. (March and Simon, 1958:168)

Conclusion

This section has described the conceptual basis for examining the direction, amount, variability, and dependence of work flows and the direction, frequency, standardization, and time requirements of information flows among organizational components in the OAI. The discussion suggested some ways in which these dimensions can be used to behaviorally describe important patterns of activities for individual units and the organization as a whole. Before going on to describe and evaluate our operational definitions and measures of work and information flows, it is important to point out that some relatively obvious dimensions of work and information flows are not included in the OAI. In their review of the literature, Roberts and O'Reilly (1974) state that among the information flow facets most frequently discussed and investigated are the accuracy and distortion of information (Read, 1962; Wilensky, 1967), gatekeeping of information (Davis, 1968; Rosen and Tesser, 1970; O'Reilly and Roberts, 1975), information overload (Porat and Haas, 1969), and desire to interact with others (Rogers and Bhowmik, 1970). Although no studies (to the authors' knowledge) have examined work flows in terms of these dimensions, case descriptions by Dalton (1959) and Trist and Bamforth (1951) suggest they may shed important insights on the functioning of the technical system and its relationship with the social system. While we have sidestepped some of these issues here, current research on communications in organizations (summarized by Porter and Roberts, 1976) promises to provide useful material for future constructive expansion and revision of the OAI.

DEFINITIONS AND MEASURES OF EXTERNAL UNIT RELATIONS

1. Direction and Relative Amount of External Unit Work Flows. The *relative amount* of work flow is defined as the proportion of a unit's work that is received from and sent to the following *directions*: other units and levels within the organization and other organizations. The directions and amounts of external unit work flows were measured in the OAI supervisory questionnaire as follows.

WORK FLOW is defined as receiving and sending work materials or clients into and out of your unit. By *WORK* we mean task assignments, referring applicants or claimants to certain places, sending claims cards, job orders, and applicant records for computer input, sending training contracts and written determinations for further processing, etc.

Please keep this definition in mind as you answer the next set of questions about the flow of work INTO and OUT OF your immediate unit.

During the past 3 months, *from where did your unit obtain its work?* Please indicate two things:

1. *HOW MUCH* of the *total work* that flows INTO your unit came from *each* of the following places?

2. Where asked, WRITE the NAME of the specific units from which your unit received its work.

	AMOUNT OF TOTAL WORK RECEIVED BY MY UNIT FROM THIS PLACE DURING PAST 3 MONTHS				
	NONE OR VERY LITTLE	SOME	ABOUT 50% OF ALL UNIT'S WORK	A LOT	MOST OF UNIT'S WORK
a. Amount of work or clients received from or initially screened by *other units in this office* and then sent to your unit? —Name specific units _____	1	2	3	4	5
b. Amount of work received from the *Administrative Office*? —Name specific units in Administrative Office. _____	1	2	3	4	5
c. Amount of work or client referrals received directly from *other organizations or agencies?* —Name specific organizations and agencies _____	1	2	3	4	5

During the past 3 months, *where* did
your unit *SEND* its *completed work*?
Please indicate two things:

1. HOW MUCH of the *total work* that
   was completed by your unit was
   sent to *each* of the following places?
2. Where asked, WRITE the NAME
   of the specific units to which your
   unit sent its completed work.

AMOUNT OF TOTAL WORK COMPLETED BY MY UNIT
THAT WAS SENT TO THIS PLACE DURING THE PAST 3
MONTHS

	NONE OR VERY LITTLE	SOME	ABOUT 50% OF ALL UNIT'S WORK	A LOT	MOST OF UNIT'S WORK
a. Amount of work or clients sent to *other units* in this *office*? —Name specific units _____	1	2	3	4	5
b. Amount of work sent to the *Administrative Office in Madison*? —Name specific units in the Administrative Office ____	1	2	3	4	5
c. Amount of work or client referrals sent to *other organizations or agencies*? —Name specific organizations and agencies ____	1	2	3	4	5

The names of the specific units, levels, and outside agencies listed by
the supervisor provide important information for qualitatively coding
the web of work flow connections for each unit as it relates to other
units in an organization. Furthermore, the distinction between work
flows into and out of each unit allows the researcher to identify the position
of organizational units in the long-linked series of connected units
in an organization.

   2. Work Dependence on Other Units, Levels, and Agencies.
The work flow index only provides an indication of the proportional
amount of work a unit transacts with other units, levels, and organizations.
It does not provide an indicator of the degree to which unit
personnel perceive they are dependent on other units, levels, and
agencies to do their jobs. A unit may receive and send all its work from
and to one other organizational unit and yet may operate as though it
were self-contained because of buffering, stockpiling, or the standardized
nature of the work flowing among units (Thompson, 1967).
Therefore, there is a need to examine how tightly coupled a unit is with
other units, levels, and agencies. Work dependence refers to how much
unit personnel perceive their work performance depends upon the
activities performed in other units, levels, or organizations.

Work dependence was measured in terms of input, transformation, and output, using the following questions in the OAI supervisor and member questionnaires:

How much do you have to depend on each of the *following people to obtain the materials, clients, or information* needed to do your work?	HOW MUCH DEPEND ON OTHER PEOPLE TO GET MATERIALS, CLIENTS, OR INFORMATION NEEDED TO DO MY TASKS				
	NOT AT ALL	A LITTLE	SOME	QUITE A BIT	VERY MUCH
1. People in other units of this office?	1	2	3	4	5
b. The Administrative Office?	1	2	3	4	5
c. People in other organizations outside Job Service Division?	1	2	3	4	5

After you finish your part of the job *how much do you have to rely* on *each* of the following people *to perform the next steps* in the process before the total task or service is completed?	HOW MUCH RELY ON OTHER PEOPLE TO DO NEXT WORK STEPS AFTER I COMPLETE MY PART				
	NOT AT ALL	A LITTLE	SOME	QUITE A BIT	VERY MUCH
a. People in other units of this office?	1	2	3	4	5
b. People in the Administrative office?	1	2	3	4	5
c. People in other organizations or agencies?	1	2	3	4	5

How often does your job *require* that you *check* with the following people *while doing your major tasks*?	HOW OFTEN JOB REQUIRES CHECKING WITH OTHERS WHILE DOING MY TASKS				
	NO CHECKING REQUIRED	MONTHLY OR LESS OFTEN	ABOUT ONCE A WEEK	ABOUT ONCE A DAY	EVERY HOUR OR MORE
a. People in other units in this office?	1	2	3	4	5
b. People in the Administrative Office?	1	2	3	4	5
c. People in other organizations or agencies?	1	2	3	4	5

Under the three questions, parallel items (a-a-a, b-b-b, c-c-c) were averaged to obtain composite indices of work dependence on other units, levels, and organizations, respectively.

3. Variability of Work Flows. Variability refers to the number of exceptions encountered in the flow of work into and out of an organizational unit. The construct differs from task variability in that the latter focuses on exceptions in the characteristics of the work (see Chapter 5), whereas the former focuses on exceptions in the flows or means of transporting work. Work flow variability is operationalized in terms of the interruptions and problems encountered by a unit in transacting its work with other units, levels, and organizations. It is measured with the following questions in the OAI supervisor and member questionnaires.

During the past 3 months to what *extent* did your unit *encounter interruptions, delays* to the *normal flow* of *work* from or to *each* of the following:	EXTENT INTERRUPTIONS OCCURRED IN PAST 3 MONTHS				
	TO NO EXTENT	LITTLE EXTENT	SOME EXTENT	GREAT EXTENT	VERY GREAT EXTENT
a. Other units in this office?	1	2	3	4	5
b. The Administrative Office?	1	2	3	4	5
c. Other organizations or agencies?	1	2	3	4	5

During the past 3 months, to what *extent* did you *encounter problems in coordinating your work* with *each* of the following:	EXTENT ENCOUNTERED PROBLEMS IN COORDINATING MY WORK WITH OTHERS					
	N/A	TO NO EXTENT	LITTLE EXTENT	SOME EXTENT	GREAT EXTENT	VERY GREAT EXTENT
a. People in other units in this office?	0	1	2	3	4	5
b. People in the Administrative Office?	0	1	2	3	4	5
c. People in other organizations and agencies?	0	1	2	3	4	5

Under the two questions, items a, b, and c, respectively, were averaged to obtain composite indices of work flow variability with other units, levels, and organizations.

4. Direction and Frequency of Information Flows. Information flows refer to work-related messages sent between people through one-to-one contacts, in group meetings, and through reports and memos. The **frequency** of information flows refers to how often messages are sent through each of these modalities. The **direction** of information flows refers to messages sent or received by unit personnel with other units, levels, and organizations. Thus, except for the difference in the source and destination of information flows, the construct is the same as intraunit communications (Chapter 5).

The following questions were used in the OAI unit supervisor and member questionnaires to measure communications with other units, levels, and organizations.

1. During the past 3 months, *how often* did you receive or send *written reports or memos* from or to each of the following to coordinate the work of your unit:	HOW OFTEN RECEIVED OR SENT WRITTEN REPORTS OR MEMOS IN PAST 3 MONTHS				
	NOT ONCE	ABOUT 1–3 TIMES A MONTH	ABOUT 1–3 TIMES A WEEK	ABOUT 1–3 TIMES A DAY	ABOUT EVERY HOUR
a. People in other units of this office?	1	2	3	4	5
b. People in the Administrative Office?	1	2	3	4	5
c. People in other organizations or agencies?	1	2	3	4	5

2. During the past 3 months, *how often* did you have *work-related discussions*, (face-to-face or by telephone) with each of the following on a one-to-one basis:	HOW OFTEN HAD WORK DISCUSSIONS IN PAST 3 MONTHS				
	NOT ONCE	ABOUT 1–3 TIMES A MONTH	ABOUT 1–3 TIMES A WEEK	ABOUT 1–3 TIMES A DAY	ABOUT EVERY HOUR
a. Individuals in other units of this office?	1	2	3	4	5
b. Individuals in the Administrative Office?	1	2	3	4	5
c. Individuals in other organizations?	1	2	3	4	5

3. During the past 3 months, *how often* were you involved in *work-related problem-solving meetings* with the following:	HOW OFTEN INVOLVED IN PROBLEM SOLVING MEETINGS IN PAST 3 MONTHS					
	NOT ONCE	ABOUT ONCE A MONTH	ABOUT EVERY 2 WEEKS	ABOUT ONCE A WEEK	ABOUT 2–4 TIMES A WEEK	ONCE A DAY OR MORE
a. Two or more people from other units in this district office?	1	2	3	4	5	6
b. Two or more people from the Administrative Office?	1	2	3	4	5	6
c. Two or more people from other organizations or agencies?	1	2	3	4	5	6

5. Standardization of Coordination. Coordination means linking or integrating different parts of an organization to accomplish a collective set of tasks. Information flows are process mechanisms for coordination. However, under norms of rationality, organizations will attempt to minimize coordination costs by standardizing the issues or content of information that is sent between organizational components (March and Simon, 1958) and by establishing a structure of rules, policies, and procedures to guide coordination among units (Thompson, 1967). Then personal and group forms of communication can be limited to dealing only with exceptions. Thus, the standardization of coordination refers to the degree to which the content of communications ranges from novel to routine work-related matters and the extent to which rules, policies, and procedures are established to coordinate activities with other units, levels, and organizations. It is measured in the OAI supervisor and member questionnaires with the following questions.

1. To what extent are written or unwritten *rules and procedures established* to *coordinate* your work with each of the following?		EXTENT RULES & PROCEDURES ESTABLISHED TO COORDINATE MY WORK WITH OTHERS				
	N/A	TO NO EXTENT	LITTLE EXTENT	SOME EXTENT	GREAT EXTENT	VERY GREAT EXTENT
a. People in other units in this office?	0	1	2	3	4	5
b. People in the Administrative Office?	0	1	2	3	4	5
c. People in other organizations and agencies?	0	1	2	3	4	5

2. When you check with each of these people while doing your work, *what kinds of issues* are you mainly communicating about:	MAIN KINDS OF ISSUES COMMUNICATED ABOUT			
	NO CHECKING REQUIRED	MOSTLY STANDARD INFORMATION MATTERS	MOSTLY OLD RECURRING PROBLEMS OR MISTAKES	MOSTLY NEW PROBLEMS REQUIRING NOVEL SOLUTIONS
a. People in other units in this office?	1	2	3	4
b. People in the Administrative Office?	1	2	3	4
c. People in other organizations?	1	2	3	4

The scales for the second question were reversed, and then items a, b, and c, respectively, were averaged to obtain composite indices of unit coordination standardization with other units, levels, and organizations.

6. *Time Spent in Coordination.* Time spent in coordination is the average number of working hours per day that unit personnel report coordinating work activities with other units, levels, and organizations. The construct is an indicator of the *cost of coordination* in terms of the investment of time unit personnel allocate to maintaining external unit relationships rather than performing their work and assigned tasks. Coordination time was measured with the following questions in the OAI supervisor and member questionnaires.

We realize that your activities may vary a great deal from day to day. However, during the past month, *on the average how many hours per day* did you *normally spend* in *each* of the following activities? (Your answers do not need to add up to eight hours.)	HOURS PER DAY I NORMALLY SPENT DOING THIS IN THE PAST MONTH
a. *Keeping track* of my work activities and *recording* them on Time Distribution Reports and on performance records.	**a.** _____ HR/DAY
b. Talking informally to people, taking coffee breaks, and taking care of personal matters (exclude lunch hour).	**b.** _____ HR/DAY
c. *Coordinating* work *with other units in this office*, discussing and solving work problems encountered with other units, performing office-wide projects and activities.	**c.** _____ HR/DAY
d. *Coordinating* work activities *with* people from the *Administrative Office*, issuing requests, responding to directives, and working out issues with the Administrative Office.	**d.** _____ HR/DAY
e. *Coordinating* activities *with other organizations* outside the Job Service Division, developing and maintaining manpower services and programs with other agencies, obtaining resources (e.g., CETA grants), and doing community service projects.	**e.** _____ HR/DAY
f. Providing *direct* services to applicants, claimants, or employers.	**f.** _____ HR/DAY

Items c, d, and e from the preceding index are used as the measures of time spent in coordinating with other units, levels, and organizations, respectively.

Data Collection and Aggregation

Data on the preceding dimensions of external unit work and information flows were collected in the summer of 1975, on 334 work units in the employment security agency, as described in Chapter 5. The procedures for aggregating the data are also the same as those described in Chapter 5. The constructs examined here focus on linkages between organizational units, and the level at which the data are examined is the work unit. The scores could be aggregated to the organizational level (as Hage et al., 1971, and others have done). However, it is believed that too much information is lost by averaging the data to the organizational level. At the work unit level one can examine the external linkages of each unit individually as well as the different patterns of linkages among different types of organizational units. Empirical justification for analyzing external relationships at the work unit level is shown in the subsequent section on the extrinsic validity of these OAI indices.

PSYCHOMETRIC PROPERTIES OF EXTERNAL UNIT RELATIONS INDICES

Factor Analysis

A preliminary principal-components factor analysis was performed on all 36 items in the OAI external unit linkage indices. Principal factors were extracted from the correlation matrix with unities as diagonal elements. The results (not shown here) found that 41 percent of the variance among the 36 items was explained by the first three factors, which represented the external relationships of a unit with other units, levels, and organizations. Six additional factors with eigenvalues larger than one were obtained, but they were difficult to interpret. Therefore, it was decided to first run a principal components analysis truncated at three factors on all 36 items and then to run three separate factor analyses on just the items measuring unit relations with other units, levels, and organizations, respectively. These procedures enable us to determine how well the 36 items converge and discriminate among the three major sources of external unit relationships and between the different constructs within each of these three sources.

Table 7-1 shows the varimax rotated results of the principal components analysis truncated at three factors. The table indicates quite clearly that the 36 items load on factors representing a unit's external relationships with other units, levels, and organizations. Using .40 as a rough rule of thumb for a significant loading of an item on a factor, Table 7-1 shows that factor 1 includes those items pertaining to the linkages of a unit with other organizations. Factor 2 represents linkages with other supervisory levels, and factor 3 includes the items of a unit's relations with other organizational units. Factors 2 and 3 are somewhat weaker than factor 1 in the sense that loadings of some items on their factors are smaller and fall below .40, but these items have larger loadings on their designated factors than on the other two factors. Finally, the item communalities in the right column of the table are very low in most cases, and only 40 percent of common variance is accounted for by the three factors. This indicates that there is much heterogeneity among the items and that the three factors do not adequately summarize the diversity of sampling domains of the 36 items.

To examine more specifically how the indices load within each of these three factors, separate factor analyses were performed on the items dealing with external unit relationships with other units, other levels, and other organizations. Tables 7-2 through 7-4 show the results of these principal components analyses after varimax rotation. Our overall interpretation of these tables is that the factor analyses provide indications of good convergent and discriminant validity for three of the five indices in the OAI. The items in the work dependence, work flow amount, and communication frequency indices with other units, levels, and organizations clearly load together as unique factors in each of the three factor analyses. The only exception here is that in Table 7-2 written communication breaks out as a specific factor (V) from the common oral communications factor (III).

The work flow variability and standardization of coordination indices require substantial revision. The items in these two indices are highly unstable across the three factor analyses, and Tables 7-2 to 7-4 show considerable confounding of these items with the work dependence and communication factors. Although we argued previously that work flow variability and standardization of coordination are distinct concepts, these factor analyses suggest that respondents had difficulty distinguishing between the items intended to measure these different constructs. Therefore, the work flow variability and coordination standardization indices are not adequate for testing the theory described previously for assessing external unit relations. Since complete revisions of these two indices are required, these two indices are dropped below because there is little point in evaluating their measurement properties further at this point.

Other Criteria of Internal Validity

Table 7-5 presents the means, standard deviations, expected and observed coefficient alphas, and median correlations with other items for each composite index of external unit relations. The time unit personnel spend per day in coordinating with other units, levels, and

Table 7-1 Factor Analysis of 36 Items in OAI Designed to Measure External Unit Relations with Other Units, Levels, and Organizations

(n = 334 units, Principal Components, Truncated at 3 Factors, Varimax Rotation)

	Factor 1 Relations with Other Organizations	Factor 2 Relations with Other Levels	Factor 3 Relations with Other Units	Item Communalities (h^2)
UNIT RELATIONS WITH OTHER UNITS				
Work Flows with Other Units				
1. % Work Received—Other Units	-.27	-.07	.27	.14
2. % Work Sent to Other Units	-.09	-.31	.35	.22
Variability of Work Flows—Other Units				
3. Work Flow Interruptions	.04	-.05	.23	.06
4. Work Flow Problems Encountered	-.07	-.05	.42*	.19
Work Dependence on Other Units				
5. Work Input Dependence	-.02	.05	.56*	.32
6. Work Process Dependence	.15	.12	.61*	.40
7. Work Output Dependence	-.03	-.12	.63*	.40
Communications with Other Units				
8. Freq. Written Reports and Memos	.18	.07	.31	.15
9. Freq. 1–1 Discussions	-.01	.26	.52*	.36
10. Freq. Group Meetings	.25	.31	.27	.30
Standardization of Coord.—Other Units				
11. Extent Coord. Rules Exist	.06	-.01	.56*	.33
12. Routineness of Communications	-.04	.11	.63*	.41
UNIT RELATIONS WITH OTHER LEVELS				
Work Flows with Other Levels				
13. % Work Received—Other Levels	.04	.62*	-.26	.43
14. % Work Sent to Other Levels	-.16	.44*	-.25	.25
Variability of Work Flows—Other Levels				
15. Work Flow Interruptions	.19	.29	-.03	.14
16. Work Flow Problems Encountered	-.05	-.36	-.29	.24

Work Dependence on Other Levels

17. Work Input Dependence	−.01	.64*	.12	.44
18. Work Process Dependence	−.05	.78*	.15	.63
19. Work Output Dependence	−.27	.70*	.21	.54
Communications with Other Levels				
20. Freq. Written Reports and Memos	.03	.75*	−.07	.57
21. Freq. 1-1 Discussions	.07	.84*	−.04	.73
22. Freq. of Group Meetings	.33	.55*	−.10	.48
Standardization of Coord.—Other Levels				
23. Extent Coordination Rules Exist	.15	.56*	.16	.42
24. Routineness of Communications	−.05	.68*	.14	.48

UNIT RELATIONS WITH OTHER ORGANIZATIONS

Work Flows with Other Organizations

25. % Work Received—Other Orgs.	.69*	−.11	−.19	.46
26. % Work Sent to Other Organizations	.54*	−.05	−.22	.31
Variability of Work Flows—Other Orgs.				
27. Work Flow Interruptions	.56*	.05	−.18	.33
28. Work Flow Problems Encountered	.44*	.04	−.29	.32
Work Dependence on Other Organizations				
29. Work Input Dependence	.72*	−.06	.22	.59
30. Work Process Dependence	.69*	.03	.30	.64
31. Work Output Dependence	.71*	−.09	.20	.56
Communications with Other Organizations				
32. Freq. Written Reports and Memos	.69*	.11	.01	.52
33. Freq. 1-1 Discussions	.81*	.09	.05	.72
34. Freq. of Group Meetings	.76*	.14	−.08	.63
Standardization of Coord.—Other Orgs.				
35. Extent Coordination Rules Exist	.64*	−.06	.24	.49
36. Routineness of Communications	.60*	.02	.32	.51
Eigenvalue	7.59	4.02	3.11	
Percent of Variance	21.1%	11.2%	8.6%	

Table 7-2 Factor Analysis of 12 Items in OAI Designed to Measure Unit Relationships with Other Organizational Units

(n = 334 units, Principal Components, Oblimin Rotation)

	Factor I Dependence & Standardization	Factor II Work Flow Amount	Factor III Oral Communication	Factor IV Work Flow Variability	Factor V Written Communication	Item Communalities (h^2)
Work Flows with Other Units						
1. % of Work Received—Other Units	.02	.75*	-.05	.35	.09	.65
2. % of Work Sent to Other Units	.12	.66*	.29	-.34	.22	.71
Variability of Work Flows—Other Units						
3. Work Flow Interruptions	-.06	.10	-.52*	.56*	-.39	.74
4. Work Flow Problems Encountered	-.03	.11	.12	.85*	-.09	.77
Work Dependence on Other Units						
5. Work Input Dependence	.80*	.05	.05	.07	-.19	.62
6. Work Process Dependence	.50*	-.08	-.36	.06	.21	.55
7. Work Output Dependence	.70*	.06	.00	-.29	.20	.64
Communication with Other Units						
8. Freq. Written Reports & Memos	-.07	.17	-.20	-.11	.81*	.78
9. Freq. 1-1 Discussions	.23	.12	-.68*	.03	.16	.69
10. Freq. Group Meetings	-.02	-.12	-.74*	-.10	.08	.59
Standardization of Coord.—Other Units						
11. Extent Coordination Rules Exist	.68*	-.13	-.06	.20	.21	.60
12. Routineness of Communications	.60*	.09	-.03	-.15	.12	.47
Eigenvalues	3.22	1.35	1.23	1.08	.91	
FACTOR CORRELATION MATRIX	I	II	III	IV	V	65% variance explained
I. Dependence & Standardization	1.00					
II. Work Flow Amount	.10	1.00				
III. Oral Communications	-.24	-.08	1.00			
IV. Work Flow Variability	-.12	-.09	.05	1.00		
V. Written Communications	.16	.00	-.14	-.02	1.00	

262

Table 7-3 Factor Analysis of 12 Items in OAI Designed to Measure Unit Relations with Other Organizational Levels

(n = 334 Units, Principal Components, Oblimin Rotation)

	Factor I Dependence & Standardization	Factor II Communications	Factor III Work Flow Amount	Factor IV Work Flow Interruptions	Factor V Work Flow Problems	Item Communalities (h^2)
Work Flows with Other Levels						
1. % Work Received—Other Levels	-.19	.17	.86*	-.16	-.21	.80
2. % Work Sent to Other Levels	.07	.12	.94*	-.05	.06	.94
Variability of Work Flows—Other Levels						
3. Work Flow Interruptions	-.07	.12	.04	.91*	-.07	.86
4. Work Flow Problems Encountered	-.01	-.01	.09	-.04	.93*	.89
Work Dependence on Other Levels						
5. Work Input Dependence	.63*	.35	-.21	-.28	-.04	.72
6. Work Process Dependence	.71*	.28	-.09	-.06	-.06	.75
7. Work Output Dependence	.88*	-.12	.12	.02	.04	.74
Communications with Other Levels						
8. Freq. Written Reports & Memos	.23	.61*	.13	.23	.07	.67
9. Freq. 1-1 Discussion	.34	.62*	.05	.18	-.02	.78
10. Freq. of Group Meetings	.07	.67*	-.06	.23	.07	.56
Standardization of Coord.—Other Levels						
11. Extent Coordination Rules Exist	.47*	-.01	.14	.13	-.39	.55
12. Routineness of Communications	.78*	-.05	.07	.04	-.08	.66
Eigenvalues	4.84	1.41	1.05	.86	.78	74.5% variance explained
FACTOR CORRELATION MATRIX	I	II	III	IV	V	
I Dependence & Standardization	1.00					
II Communications	.38	1.00				
III Work Flow Amount	.13	.14	1.00			
IV Work Flow Interruptions	.12	.18	.11	1.00		
V Work Flow Problems	-.28	-.23	-.03	-.07	1.00	

Table 7-4 Factor Analysis of 12 Items in OAI Designed to Measure Unit Relationships with Other Organizations

(n = 334 Units, Principal Components, Oblimin Rotation)

	Factor I Dependence & Coord. Rules	Factor II Communi- cations & Interruptions	Factor III Work Flow Amount	Factor IV Work Flow Problems	Factor V Coord. Routineness	Item Commu- nalities (h^2)
Work Flows with Other Organizations						
1. % Work Received—Other Orgs.	.34	.19	.47*	.13	.32	.76
2. % Work Sent to Other Orgs.	-.06	-.01	.96*	-.02	-.11	.90
Variability of Work Flows—Other Orgs.						
3. Work Flow Interruptions	-.18	.84*	.12	-.11	.18	.75
4. Work Flow Problems Encountered	-.06	-.06	.00	.94*	-.04	.94
Work Dependence on Other Orgs.						
5. Work Input Dependence	.74*	.04	.01	-.16	-.10	.75
6. Work Process Dependence	.68*	.17	-.10	-.03	-.27	.78
7. Work Output Dependence	.69*	-.06	.06	-.32	-.05	.75
Communications with Other Orgs.						
8. Freq. Written Reports & Memos	.19	.80*	.14	.00	.01	.72
9. Freq. 1-1 Discussions	.31	.59*	.08	.02	-.23	.77
10. Freq. of Group Meetings	-.03	.65*	.17	-.05	-.39	.76
Standardization of Coord.—Other Orgs.						
11. Extent Coordination Rules Exist	.83*	.00	-.02	.03	-.01	.68
12. Routineness of Communications	.31	.01	.16	-.06	.69*	.82
Eigenvalues	5.64	1.54	.93	.67	.60	78% variance explained

FACTOR CORRELATION MATRIX

	I	II	III	IV	V
I Dependence & Coord. Rules	1.00				
II Communications & Interruptions	.39	1.00			
III Work Flow Amount	.24	.39	1.00		
IV Work Flow Problems	-.31	-.25	-.04	1.00	
V Coord. Routineness	-.34	-.15	-.02	.23	1.00

Table 7-5 Analysis of External Unit Relationships Indices and Items in OAI

External Unit Relations Indices	Mean	Standard Deviation	Coefficient Alpha		Median Correlations with Other Items
			Expected	Observed	
Relations with Other Units					
1. % Work Flows with Other Units	2.50	1.10	.55–.70	.35	.08
2. Work Dependence on Other Units	2.40	.58	.70–.90	.61	.09
3. Mean Communications—Other Units	2.21	.57	.35–.55	.60	.13
a. Freq. written reports & memos	1.75	.62	—	—	.17
b. Freq. 1–1 discussions	2.71	.76	—	—	.14
c. Freq. group meetings	2.17	.92	—	—	.20
4. Hr/day Coord. Time—Other Units	1.08	.88	—	—	.06
Relations with Other Levels					
1. % Work Flows with Other Levels	2.29	.96	.55–.70	.45	.09
2. Work Dependence on Other Levels	1.96	.68	.70–.90	.81	.13
3. Mean Communications—Other Levels	1.90	.65	.35–.55	.80	.16
a. Freq. written reports & memos	2.07	.78	—	—	.18
b. Freq. 1–1 discussions	2.09	.80	—	—	.28
c. Freq. group meetings	1.54	.73	—	—	.27
4. Hr/day Coord. Time—Other Levels	.46	.44	—	—	.20
Relations with Other Organizations					
1. % Work Flows with Other Orgs.	2.02	1.04	.55–.70	.62	.08
2. Work Dependence on Other Orgs.	2.00	.73	.70–.90	.87	.13
3. Mean Communications—Other Orgs.	1.87	.67	.35–.55	.83	.14
a. Freq. Written Reports & Memos	1.70	.60	—	—	.28
b. Freq. 1–1 Discussions	2.16	.80	—	—	.22
c. Freq. Group Meetings	1.76	.84	—	—	.22
4. Hr/day Coord. Time—Other Orgs.	.44	.49	—	—	.24

organizations is included in Table 7-5. These indices were excluded from the factor analyses because they are measured with single items.

By definition, each work dependence index is a narrow construct. According to the standards established in Chapter 3, work dependence was expected to obtain a coefficient alpha between .70 to .90. With the exception of work dependence on other units, which has an internal consistency reliability of .61, the work dependence indices fall well within the hypothesized range for coefficient alpha. The work flow amount indices are moderately broad constructs for which coefficient alpha should range between .55 and .70. Only unit work flows with other organizations fall within this range. The internal consistency reliabilities of work flows with other units and supervisory levels are somewhat lower than anticipated. This indicates a not particularly close association between the input sources and output destinations of unit work flows in employment security offices. The communication indices are defined as broad constructs and were expected to obtain coefficient alphas ranging from .35 to .55. As suggested by the factor analyses results, Table 7-5 shows that the internal consistencies of the communication items with other units, levels, and organizations sample a narrower domain of information flows than anticipated. The same results were obtained in Chapter 5, where it was found that the three modes of information flows also had higher correlations than expected. Thus, depending upon the degree of specificity and concreteness desired, one could assess external unit communications generally in terms of an overall composite or specifically in terms of the frequency of each mode of communication.

The median correlations of all items in each index with all other external unit relations items range from .08 for work flows with other units to .16 for communications with other levels. Table 7-5 shows that these median correlations of each index with other items are far smaller than their respective coefficient alphas, and this suggests that the discriminant validity of each index relative to its internal consistency is quite good.

Table 7-6 presents the simple correlations among the 18 OAI indices for all 334 units in the state employment security agency. The table shows that the correlations among work flows, work dependence, communications, and time spent in coordination within each task environment (i.e., with other units, levels, and organizations) are smaller than their respective coefficient alphas and much larger than their correlations with other task environments. This again indicates good convergent and discriminant validity for the OAI external unit relations indices.

EXTRINSIC VALIDITY OF THE EXTERNAL UNIT RELATIONS INDICES

Just as important as the preceding indications of intrinsic validity of the OAI indices is their extrinsic validity or practical usefulness for organizational research and diagnosis. As in previous chapters, the extrinsic validity of these measures is evaluated in three ways: (1) by examining the correlations among the OAI indices in terms of the theory, (2) by determining how well they discriminate between the external relationships of different types of local employment security (ES) units, and (3) by assessing their concurrent validity with criteria used to evaluate the performance of local ES office units. This section evaluates the extrinsic validity of the OAI external unit relations indices in each of these three ways.

Test of Theory on OAI External Unit Relations Indices

Overall, the correlations among the OAI dimensions in Table 7-6 are largely as expected by the theory. The table shows that increases in work flows and dependence are significantly associated with increases in the frequencies of written reports, discussions, and group meetings, which in turn are positively related to the amounts of time spent by unit personnel in coordinating with each of their task environments (i.e., with other units, levels, and organizations). The correlations in Table 7-6 show that these overall hypotheses are supported much more strongly on unit relations with other levels and organizations than with other units within the office.

In the introduction, a specific path model was developed for the associations among the external unit dimensions and three situational factors: office structural differentiation (the number of levels and units in an office—see Chapter 4), unit specialization (the number of job titles in a unit), and task difficulty and variability (the analyzability, predictability, and number of exceptions encountered in the work—see Chapter 5). Only a partial test of the model is possible here because the measures of variability of work flows and standardization of coordination indices were found to be inadequate.

The parts of the model that can be tested here consist of the following basic propositions: (1) Although the amount of external unit work flow is primarily a function of overall structural differentiation and unit specialization, increases in actual perception of dependence on external

Table 7-6 Correlations among External Unit Relations Dimensions for All Units in Employment Security Offices
(n = 334 units)

	Relations with Other Units						Relations with Other Levels						Relations with Other Organizations						Task Difficulty & Variability	Office Structural Complexity
	Work Flows	Dependence	Reports	Discussions	Meetings	Time	Work Flows	Dependence	Reports	Discussions	Meetings	Time	Work Flows	Dependence	Reports	Discussions	Meetings	Time		
Relations with Other Units																				
1. % Work Flows with Other Units	—																			
2. Work Dependence on Other Units	.13	—																		
3. Freq. Written Reports—Other Units	.16	.17	—																	
4. Freq. 1-1 Discussions—Other Units	.15	.45	.34	—																
5. Freq. Group Meetings—Other Units	.02	.22	.20	.42	—															
6. Hr/day Coord. Time—Other Units	-.03	-.01	.16	.01	.05	—														

Relations with Other Levels

	1	2	3	4	5	6	7	8	9	10	11	12	13	14	15	16	17	18	19	20	21
7. % Work Flows with Other Levels	-.16	-.13	.00	.10	.09	.11	—														
8. Work Dependence on Other Levels	-.17	.15	.08	.17	.17	.17	.37	—													
9. Freq. Written Reports—Other Levels	-.16	.03	.18	.26	.30	.06	.47	.50	—												
10. Freq. 1-1 Discussions—Other Levels	-.20	.05	.14	.29	.32	.05	.48	.63	.69	—											
11. Freq. Group Meetings—Other Levels	-.18	.03	.10	.18	.47	.05	.35	.33	.44	.58	—										
12. Hr/day Coord. Time—Other Levels	-.16	-.01	.20	.14	.24	.30	.36	.31	.42	.54	.46	—									

Relations with Other Organizations

	1	2	3	4	5	6	7	8	9	10	11	12	13	14	15	16	17	18	19	20	21
13. % Work Flows with Other Orgs.	-.13	-.03	.08	-.01	.07	.06	.11	-.06	.07	.05	.18	.03	—								
14. Work Dependence on Other Orgs.	-.12	.22	.16	.10	.25	.03	-.11	.17	.07	.12	.20	.04	.40	—							
15. Freq. Written Reports—Other Orgs.	-.21	.07	.39	.17	.30	.05	.06	.06	.31	.28	.32	.18	.39	.47	—						
16. Freq. 1-1 Discussions—Other Orgs.	-.19	.14	.21	.25	.30	.02	.04	.07	.22	.34	.39	.16	.51	.65	.57	—					
17. Freq. Group Meetings—Other Orgs.	-.22	.07	.13	.14	.45	.02	.09	.04	.18	.33	.58	.21	.49	.50	.57	.68	—				
18. Hr/day Coord. time—Other Orgs.	-.26	-.04	.22	.04	.15	.12	.11	.05	.10	.14	.27	.24	.36	.31	.27	.39	.41	—			

Situational Factors

	1	2	3	4	5	6	7	8	9	10	11	12	13	14	15	16	17	18	19	20	21
19. Unit Task Difficulty & Variability	-.11	.14	.12	.16	.42	.06	.06	.21	.17	.30	.39	.27	.24	.39	.35	.48	.49	.32	—		
20. Office Structural Complexity —# Vertical Levels & Horizontal Units	.19	.11	.14	.05	-.02	-.01	-.22	-.08	-.07	-.10	-.05	-.10	.04	.01	.06	-.04	-.02	-.07	-.02	—	
21. Unit Specialization (# Job Titles in Unit)	-.06	.07	-.02	.02	.06	.15	.09	-.04	-.06	.01	.03	-.01	.08	.21	.03	.10	.12	.17	.12	-.22	

groups are primarily a function of unit task difficulty and variability. (2) An increase in the amount of external work flow, by itself, should not substantially increase perceptions of work dependence since stable patterns of work flows can be coordinated by programming. Therefore, when controlling for task difficulty and variability, the associations between external unit work flows and perceived work dependencies should diminish. (3) External unit work flows will be most strongly related to the frequency of written reports to coordinate by programming. However, increases in task difficulty, variability and external work dependence will largely predict the frequency of discussions and group meetings to make the mutual adjustments necessary for coordination. (4) Those aspects of unit relationships that remain stable and predictable will continue to be coordinated by programming. Hence, an increase in external unit dependence and the difficulty and variability of the work will not be associated with a decrease in written reports and memos. (5) The time spent in coordinating external unit relationships will be an increasing function of the frequency of written reports, personal discussions, and group meetings, respectively, since they are increasingly more time-consuming methods of coordination.

Figures 7-3 to 7-5 show the path analyses results of three tests of this overall model for 334 units in the ES agency in terms of unit relationships with: other units within ES offices (Figure 7-3), other levels between the headquarters and field office units (Figure 7-4), and other organizations (Figure 7-5). The six equations in the structural system for each test are clearly underidentified, and standard multiple regression analyses found that the F-ratios for each equation in each test were significant beyond the .01 level. Figures 7-3 to 7-5 show the path coefficients (or standardized regression coefficients) on the arrows to each endogenous variable from the predictor (independent) variables included in each equation. The predictor variables that were significant in each equation are asterisked and are those path coefficients which were at least twice as large as their standard errors. Finally, the residual path coefficients (U_i) indicate the proportions of variance in the endogenous variables that were not accounted for by their predictor variables. These residual coefficients were computed as $\sqrt{1 - R^2}$, where R^2 is the percentage of variance explained.

Overall, the three tests of the model on the OAI external unit dimensions are quite stable and consistent with the theory, particularly the parts of the model that predict variations in the frequencies of reports, discussions, and meetings and the time spent in coordination with other units, levels, and organizations. A decomposition of the direct and indirect effects of task difficulty and variability, external unit work

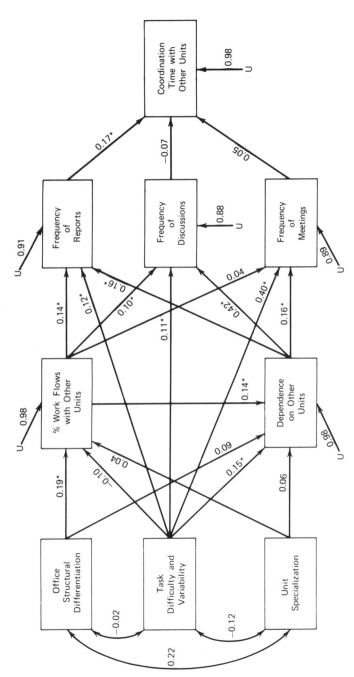

Figure 7-3 Path model of unit relationships with other units in the office.

271

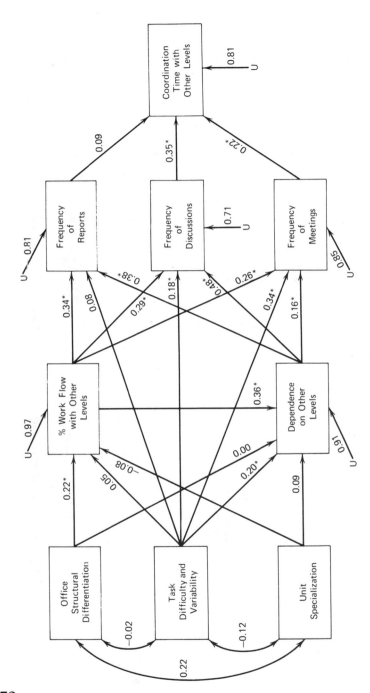

Figure 7-4 Path model of unit relations between headquarters and field office levels.

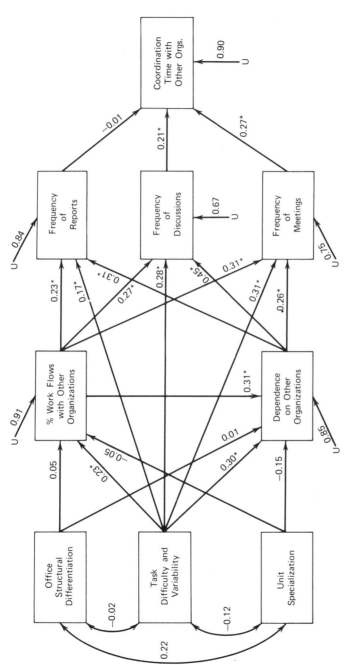

Figure 7-5 Path model of unit relationships with other organizations.

flows, and dependence with the time spent in coordination with other units, levels, and organizations (see the correlation matrix in Table 7-6) will show that the frequency of reports, discussions, and meetings moderate these relationships. Information flows account for most of the variations in time spent in coordination. The interested reader can compute these direct and indirect effects from Table 7-6 and Figures 7-3 to 7-5 and will find there is little to be gained from including direct paths to coordination time from external unit work flows, dependence, and the exogenous variables in the model.

The figures also show that perceived work dependence on other units, levels and organizations is consistently explained by two significant factors: the difficulty and variability of a unit's work and the percentage of external work flows. However, contrary to the theory, the direct relationships between external unit work flows and dependence, when controlling for task difficulty and variability, did not diminish as much as expected. The data indicate that perceptions of external unit dependence are not only a function of the degree of problems and exceptions encountered in performing the work, but are also due to the sheer quantity of work a unit transacts with its task environments.

The major differences between the three tests of the model are in the effects of office structural differentiation and unit task difficulty and variability on the percentages of unit work flows with other units, levels, and organizations. As hypothesized, increases in office structural differentiation significantly explain increases in interunit work flows within ES offices. This result was expected because increasingly dividing the work among units and levels within an organization means that each unit is delegated a smaller fraction of the total job, and this increases the amount of work flow among units needed to complete the total job. However, contrary to our initial hypothesis, increasing office structural differentiation decreases the amount of work flows between headquarters and field office levels of the complex state ES agency. A rather simple explanation for this finding is that increasing structural differentiation (which comes with greater size—see Chapter 4) permits an office to build its own functional support staff and technical equipment to operate more autonomously than smaller, less differentiated offices. Figures 7-3 and 7-4 show that once overall office structural differentiation has been taken into account, unit specialization and the difficulty and variability of the work have an insignificant effect on unit work flows with other organizational units and levels. This suggests that vertical and horizontal work flows within organizations are primarily the result of overall organization structure and not work unit design.

Unit relationships with other organizations, however, are another matter. Figure 7-5 shows that unit work flows with other organizations are significantly explained by increases in unit task difficulty and variability and are basically unrelated to office structural differentiation and unit specialization. There are two possible explanations for this finding. Either (1) units facing difficult and variable tasks find it necessary to seek assistance outside the organization, or conversely, (2) units that interact intensely with other organizations, by virtue of the complexity of their boundary-spanning, uncertainty-absorbing function, find that their tasks have become more difficult and variable. As March and Simon (1958) and Thompson (1967) discuss, the two explanations are highly complementary. By virtue of specialization, most work and information enter and leave an organization through a few boundary-spanning units. To achieve efficiency and rationality, the vast majority of tasks can be simplified and made highly predictable by delegating them to specialized units within the technical core and buffering them from outside organizational uncertainties. Buffering is achieved by designating a few other units to deal exclusively with external agents at the input and output sides of organizational operations. As a result, overall structural differentiation and unit specialization should not be expected to be highly related to the amount of work flows with other organizations for all units. Instead, it is just the boundary-spanning units (which, by virtue of their buffering function, encounter more difficult and varying tasks) that should explain variations in work flows across organizational boundaries.

Differences in Explanatory Power of Model

Finally, Figures 7-3 to 7-5 show that the residual path coefficients in the three tests of the model are somewhat smaller for unit relationships with other levels and organizations than they are for other units in ES offices. In other words, the model has more explanatory power for unit relationships with other levels and organizations than for interunit relationships within ES offices. This is a reflection of the fact that in Table 7-6 the correlations among the OAI indices pertaining to interlevel and interorganizational relationships are somewhat larger than those dealing with interunit relations.

A substantive explanation for the smaller correlations and lower explanatory power of interunit dimensions may be that social conditioning influences the patterns of work and information flows among units within an office more than relationships between administrative and field offices of an organization or with other organizations. As discussed previously, when a given work or information channel is initially used for one purpose, it tends to become used for other unrelated purposes. As a result, correlations among the dimensions of work and information flows should diminish, because whereas the patterns of communications will be considerably influenced by work flow patterns, this influence will not be absolute. Table 7-5 shows that the average amounts of work flows, perceived dependence, and frequencies of communications among units in the same office are considerably higher than those for unit relations with other levels or organizations. This suggests that social conditioning should be more prevalent in unit relations with other units than with other levels or organizations.

A methodological explanation may be that respondents' frames of reference in answers to OAI measures about relations with other units are less clear than for measures pertaining to other levels or organizations. The OAI questionnaires asked respondents in local ES offices to answer in terms of relations with individuals "in other units of this office" or "in the administrative office" ("in district offices" for administrative office respondents) or "in other organizations and agencies." Only in the supervisory questionnaire did respondents write the names of the specific other units, levels, or organizations with which their units deal. As discussed in the next section, it turns out that work and information flow relationships between the administrative headquarters and local office units and between ES units and other organizations are quite well defined and limited to a few specific relationships for each type of ES unit. Relationships among units within offices are more diffuse. As a result, although respondents may have had clear frames of reference in mind while answering questions pertaining to other levels and organizations, respondents may have been thinking of different units in responding to the OAI measures on relations with other units in the office.

Whether it is social conditioning or frame of reference that accounts for different correlations in relationships with other units versus other levels and organizations can only be determined by first clarifying the frame of reference in the measurement instrument. Revisions have been made in the new version of the OAI (see Appendix A) by asking respondents to answer the external unit relations questions in terms of specifically named other units, levels, and organizations.

The Ability of the OAI Indices to Discriminate the Task Environments of ES Units

Table 7-7 shows the results of one-way analyses of variance for each of the external unit relations indices on the five different kinds of units commonly found in local ES offices. As described in Chapter 5, each of these units deals with different tasks and functions and correspondingly deals with a different task environment. Overall, the similarities and differences in external relationships of the five ES units are highly consistent with what we have come to understand in on-site observations of the functioning of units within ES offices over the years.

As expected, the five units are most similar in their reported relationships with each other. Although some differences obviously exist in the degree and content of relationships among the units, the lack of statistically significant differences on five of the six OAI interunit dimensions indicate there is considerable convergence among the units on how they view their relationships with each other.

A more specific indication of convergence among pairs of units on their coordination patterns would be desirable not only for evaluating the extrinsic validity of the OAI indices but also for diagnosing relationships between specific pairs of units when conducting an organization assessment. However, this cannot be provided here, since the OAI measures asked about each unit's relationships with other units in general and not specifically named other units. To obtain a more specific and concrete diagnosis of the external relationships of an organizational unit, there is a need to make the OAI questions more specific by asking respondents to specify the names of the other units and organizations with which they deal.

Table 7-7 shows that the differences in task environments of the five ES units are clearly evident on the OAI indices pertaining to relations with other levels of organizations. In administering the local functions of the standardized and centralized unemployment compensation program in the state, the UC units (claims processing and adjudication) are tightly coupled vertically with the administrative headquarters level and have minimal horizontal contact with other organizations in their local communities. In contrast, the employment service units (placement and counseling) have minimal and only functional contact with the headquarters level, and their relevant task environment is dealing with other organizations in the community (to obtain job orders from employers, to refer job applicants to employers for job placements, and to refer clients to other social service organizations for employment development and training services). Finally, the Work Incentive program is a separately funded and administered federal program for socially and economically disadvantaged AFDC recipients. As Table 7-7 shows, the local office WIN units are tightly coupled both vertically with the state WIN bureau for direct line supervision and funding, and horizontally with departments of public welfare to receive WIN client referrals and community employers and social service agencies for job placements and rehabilitation services. The scores in Table 7-7 of the ES

Table 7-7 Comparison of Five Basic Types of Employment Security Local Office Units on External Unit Relations Dimensions

External Unit Relationships Indices & Items in OAI	Intake & Claims Units (n = 20)		Adjudication Units (n = 22)		Placement & Employer Relations Units (n = 50)		Employment Counseling Units (n = 13)		Work Incentive Program Units (n = 41)		Differences Among ES Units	
	Mean	SD	Mean	SD	Mean	SD	Mean	SD	Mean	SD	F-Ratios	p-levels
Relations with Other Units												
1. % Work Flows with Other Units	2.33	1.09	2.66	.94	2.53	1.00	2.30	.72	2.34	1.30	.51	.73
2. Work Dependence on Other Units	2.50	.36	2.44	.32	2.41	.47	2.41	.52	2.29	.53	.80	.53
3. Mean Communications—Other Units												
a. Freq. written reports & memos	1.43	.29	1.39	.51	1.71	.50	1.83	.52	1.72	.48	3.76	.006
b. Freq. 1-1 discussions	2.60	.66	3.05	.51	2.84	.63	2.73	.46	2.74	.63	1.68	.16
c. Freq. groups meetings	1.93	.73	2.11	.74	2.36	.70	2.13	.61	2.35	.87	1.64	.17
4. Hr/day Coord. Time—Other Units	.82	.43	.88	.34	.80	.42	.84	.47	.98	.44	1.11	.36
Relations with Other Levels												
1. % Work Flows with Other Levels	2.85	.91	2.41	.84	1.91	.75	1.60	.47	2.37	.93	7.72	.000
2. Work Dependence on Other Levels	1.88	.30	2.47	.39	1.66	.37	1.48	.35	1.82	.40	22.61	.000

3. Mean Communications—Other Levels												
a. Freq. written reports & memos	2.10	.82	2.54	.38	1.89	.57	1.83	.45	2.09	.62	5.49	.000
b. Freq. 1-1 discussions	2.00	.64	2.48	.45	1.89	.53	1.90	.47	2.03	.58	4.83	.001
c. Freq. group meetings	1.40	.60	1.50	.56	1.40	.45	1.47	.48	1.71	.47	2.65	.035
4. Hr/day Coord. with Other Levels	.51	.44	.44	.34	.32	.36	.32	.33	.50	.52	1.51	.202
Relations with Other Organizations												
1. % Work Flows with Other Organizations	1.47	.51	1.08	.19	1.95	.76	2.38	.58	3.00	1.20	22.35	.000
2. Work Dependence on Other Organizations	1.43	.24	1.52	.33	2.14	.56	2.64	.48	2.43	.67	21.21	.000
3. Mean Communications—Other Organizations												
a. Freq. written reports & memos	1.25	.38	1.27	.37	1.73	.51	1.80	.56	2.17	.53	18.09	.000
b. Freq. 1-1 discussions	1.50	.49	1.86	.49	2.28	.52	2.67	.59	2.76	.72	20.64	.000
c. Freq. group meetings	1.20	.47	1.18	.37	1.86	.70	2.30	.73	2.46	.95	17.59	.000
4. Hr/day Coord. Time—Other Organizations	.08	.11	.13	.16	.54	.41	.86	.65	.70	.50	14.62	.000

units on the OAI indices are highly consistent with this brief description and provide a good indication of the ability of the OAI dimensions to detect these systematic differences in unit task environments.

Concurrent Validity of the OAI External Unit Relations Indices

To evaluate how well the OAI external unit relations indices predict and explain unit performance, they were correlated with three kinds of performance criteria for each of the ES units: efficiency, effectiveness, and the average level of job satisfaction of unit personnel. These performance measures are the same as those used in Chapter 5.

Table 7-8 presents the simple correlations between the 18 OAI external unit relations indices and the different measures of efficiency, effectiveness, and job satisfaction for each of the types of units commonly found in local ES offices. Because of small sample size, no evidence of concurrent validity of the OAI indices is presented for counseling units. The far right column of Table 7-8 shows the correlations between the external relations indices and the overall average efficiency, effectiveness, and job satisfaction of all units in the ES offices. To ensure equal weighting of the unit efficiency measures in the overall average, they were standardized to their z-scores before averaging.

Within the ranges specified in Table 7-8, Table 7-9 shows that not all of the OAI external unit relations indices correlate significantly with the efficiency, effectiveness, and job satisfaction of personnel in all types of ES units. However, all the OAI dimensions correlate significantly with the three performance criteria for at least one of the four kinds of ES units. Hence, these OAI indices represent a compromise between being (1) general enough to apply to a wide variety of task environments of work units, and (2) specific enough to significantly explain the performance of each type of unit in terms of the different external relationships they maintain with other units, supervisory levels, and outside organizations.

A more direct indication of this compromise in the concurrent validity of the OAI indices is obtained by regressing efficiency, effectiveness, and job satisfaction of each ES unit on the 18 OAI external relations indices. However, sample sizes are too small to include all 18 OAI indices as independent variables in multiple regressions of performance for each type of ES unit. To minimize spurious results from statistical analysis on a relatively small number of ES units, multiple stepwise regressions were performed by including only the OAI dimensions that correlated significantly with the dependent measure of unit performance.

Table 7-9 presents the results of these stepwise regression analyses. Standardized beta coefficients are shown for only those OAI dimensions that entered significantly into each stepwise regression equation. The other OAI dimensions in Table 7-8 that are significantly correlated with a measure of performance for a given unit, but did not enter the regression equations, did not make a significant contribution to explaining unit performance after the other OAI factors were taken into account. This does not mean that these other significant OAI dimensions are not importantly associated with unit performance, only that they are also highly correlated (as Table 7-6 shows) with the OAI dimensions that did enter the regression equations. Once the common variance among these OAI dimensions was taken into account by the factors that did enter into the regression equations, the additional unique variance in unit performance contributed by the other significantly correlated OAI dimensions was minimal. Thus, the multiple stepwise regressions are used here to reduce the complexity of the analyses by identifying the fewest possible OAI dimensions which explain the greatest proportions of variance in efficiency, effectiveness, and job satisfaction for each type of ES unit.

The bottom rows of Table 7-8 show the overall F-ratios for each regression and the overall percentage of variance explained (R^2) in each unit performance measure by the OAI factors which entered the regression equations.

The major findings shown in Table 7-9 are the following:

1. Three to six of the OAI dimensions significantly explain from 29 to 71 percent of the performance efficiency of the four types of ES units. However, when including all 157 local office units in the regression analysis, the right column of Table 7-9 shows that two significant OAI indices explain only 7 percent of the variation in overall office efficiency.

2. In terms of goal attainment, 33 to 68 percent of the effectiveness of the different types of ES units are significantly explained by 3 to 6 of the OAI external unit relations dimensions. When all local office units are combined, only 4 percent of the variation in overall office effectiveness is explained by 2 significant OAI dimensions.

3. In terms of job satisfaction, an average of 3 OAI factors significantly explain 23 to 69 percent of the variance in job satisfaction of personnel in the different ES units. However, only 18 percent

Table 7-8 Correlations between External Unit Relations Dimensions and Performance Criteria for Types of Employment Security Units

External Unit Relationships Indices in OAI / Employment Security Local Office Performance Criteria Used to Assess Extrinsic Validity of OAI External Unit Relations Dimensions	Intake & Claims Units (n = 20)			Adjudication Units (n = 22)			Placement & Employer Relations Units (n = 50)			Work Incentive Program Units (n = 41)			All Local Office Units Combined (n = 149)		
	Unit Efficiency—# Claims & Applicants Processed per Position	Unit Effectiveness—No Measure Available	Job Satisfaction of Unit Personnel	Unit Efficiency—# Disputed Claims Determined per Position	Unit Effectiveness—% Claim Determinations Not Appealed	Job Satisfaction of Unit Personnel	Unit Efficiency—# Job Placements per Position	Unit Effectiveness—% Job Openings Filled	Job Satisfaction of Unit Personnel	Unit Efficiency—# WIN Clients Placed in Jobs per Position	Unit Effectiveness—% WIN Clients Deregistered from Welfare after Placed in Jobs	Job Satisfaction of Unit Personnel	Office Efficiency—Mean of Unit Efficiency Measures	Office Effectiveness—Mean of Unit Effectiveness Measures	Job Satisfaction of All Unit Personnel in Office
Relations with Other Units															
1. % Work Flows with Other Units	−.28[a]		.00	.22	−.05	−.43[b]	.14	.07	−.25[b]	−.33[a]	−.43[c]	−.23[a]	−.08	−.02	−.21[c]
2. Work Dependence on Other Units	−.42[b]		−.26	−.38[b]	−.40[b]	−.34[b]	.24	.22	.04	.12	.09	.34[c]	.13[a]	.16[b]	.12[a]
3. Freq. Written Reports—Other Units	−.29[a]		−.55[c]	−.32[a]	−.64[c]	−.50[c]	.34[c]	.23	.24[a]	.02	.05	.06	.22[c]	.21[c]	−.14[b]
4. Freq. 1-1 Discussions—Other Units	−.11		−.51[c]	−.13	−.31[a]	−.31[a]	.32[c]	.07	−.19[a]	.06	.02	−.00	.11[a]	.06	−.12[a]

5. Freq. Group Meetings—Other Units	-.08	—	-.14	.36[b]	.05	-.03	.39[c]	.35[c]	.07	.24[a]	.00	.26[b]	.13[a]	.03	.10[a]
6. Hr/day Coord. Time—Other Units	-.02	—	-.23	.10	.06	-.20	.41[c]	.23	.06	.24[a]	-.27[b]	.32[b]	-.10	-.08	-.06
Relations with Other Levels															
7. % Work Flows with Other Levels	-.20	—	.26	-.05	.39[b]	.24	.37[c]	.10	.20[a]	.00	.25[a]	.01	.08	.03	.13[a]
8. Work Dependence on Other Levels	.05	—	.10	.19	.30[a]	.20	.14	.16	.12	.28[b]	.52[c]	.18	.07	.00	.14[b]
9. Freq. Written Reports—Other Levels	.14	—	.29[a]	.34[b]	.28	.46[b]	.27[b]	.12	-.02	.48[c]	.31[b]	.28[b]	.08	.03	.01
10. Freq. 1-1 Discussions—Other Levels	.00	—	.20	-.44[b]	-.19	.18	.29[b]	.17	.04	.39[c]	.32[b]	.28[b]	.04	.03	.02
11. Freq. Group Meetings—Other Levels	.01	—	.14	.23	.14	-.08	-.05	-.21[a]	-.10	.38[c]	.47[c]	.42[c]	.07	-.03	-.02
12. Hr/day Coord. Time—Other Levels	.26	—	.19	-.14	-.14	-.18	.16	.17	.07	.28[b]	-.06	.20	-.01	.01	.02
Relations with Other Organizations															
13. % Work Flows with Other Orgs.	-.19	—	.20	-.11	-.02	-.08	.25[c]	.18	.25[b]	.42[c]	.39[c]	.15	.10	.03	-.06
14. Work Dependence on Other Orgs.	-.31[a]	—	-.04	.50[c]	.19	-.10	.11	.07	.06	.52[c]	.42[c]	.43[c]	-.01	-.06	-.10[a]
15. Freq. Written Reports—Other Orgs.	.09	—	-.11	-.06	-.04	.31[a]	-.17	-.29[b]	.18[a]	.57[c]	.41[c]	.20[a]	.18[b]	.06	-.09
16. Freq. 1-1 Discussions—Other Orgs.	.20	—	-.18	-.01	-.26	.10	.18	-.06	.15	.55[c]	.43[c]	.31[b]	.02	-.06	-.17[c]
17. Freq. Group Meetings—Other Orgs.	.23	—	.21	.15	.20	-.10	.07	-.18	.18[a]	.46[c]	.37[c]	.37[c]	.01	-.07	-.02
18. Hr/day Coord. Time—Other Orgs.	.13	—	-.02	.54[c]	.47[b]	.00	.30[b]	.07	.29[c]	.49[c]	.16	.07	.17[b]	.06	-.02

[a] $p < .10$.
[b] $p < .05$.
[c] $p < .01$.

283

Table 7-9 Multiple Stepwise Regressions of Efficiency, Effectiveness, and Job Satisfaction on Significant OAI Dimensions for Each Type of Unit in ES Offices

External Unit relationships Indices & Items in OAI / Employment Security Local Office Performance Criteria Used To Assess Concurrent Validity of OAI External Unit Relations Dimensions	Intake & Claims Units (n = 20)			Adjudication Units (n = 22)			Placement & Employer Relations Units (n = 50)			Work Incentive Program Units (n = 41)			All Local Office Units Combined (n = 149)		
	Unit Efficiency—# Claims & Applicants per Position	Unit Effectiveness—No Measure Available	Job Satisfaction of Unit Personnel	Unit Efficiency—# Disputed Claims Determined per Position	Unit Effectiveness—% Claim Determinations Not Appealed	Job Satisfaction of Unit Personnel	Unit Efficiency—# Job Placements per Position	Unit Effectiveness—% Job Openings Filled	Job Satisfaction of Unit Personnel	Unit Efficiency—# WIN Job Placements per Position	Unit Effectiveness—% WIN Clients Taken Off Welfare after Job Placement	Job Satisfaction of Unit Personnel	Office Efficiency—Mean of Unit Efficiency Measures	Office Effectiveness—Mean of Unit Effectiveness Measures	Job Satisfaction of All Unit Personnel in Office
	betas	betas	betas	betas	betas	betas	betas	betas	betas	betas	betas	betas	betas	betas	betas
Relations with Other Units															
1. % Work Flows with Other Units	-.43					.66									-.21
2. Work Dependence on Other Units														.12	.21
3. Freq. Written Reports—Other Units	-.34		-.50	-.43	-.59	-.73			.22				.19	.18	-.10
4. Freq. 1-1 Discussions—Other Units			-.24		-.18				-.41						-.18

284

#	Variable	3.23	4.99	9.86	12.13	13.48	4.89	6.34	3.28	6.90	7.17	5.85	3.95	3.35	4.63
5.	Freq. Group Meetings—Other Units		.21												.22
6.	Hr/day Coord. Time—Other Units						.25	.52		.29	-.30	.34			.12
Relations with Other Levels															
7.	% Work Flows with Other Levels					.20	.28			.14	.51				
8.	Work Dependence on Other Levels	.39		.23			.22			.21					
9.	Freq. Written Reports—Other Levels										.26				
10.	Freq. 1-1 Discussions—Other Levels		-.48					-.16			.37	.38			
11.	Freq. Group Meetings—Other Levels														
12.	Hr/day Coord. Time—Levels														
Relations with Other Organizations															
13.	% Work Flows with Other Orgs.	-.32				.21				.22	.19	.18			
14.	Work Dependence on Other Orgs.									.21	.19				
15.	Freq. Written Reports—Other Orgs.							-.40							
16.	Freq. 1-1 Discussions—Other Orgs.														-.21
17.	Freq. Group Meetings—Other Orgs.														
18.	Hr/day Coord. Time—Other Orgs.			.53	.52				.21	.27				.13	
	F-Ratio for the Regression	3.23	4.99	9.86	12.13	13.48	4.89	6.34	3.28	6.90	7.17	5.85	3.95	3.35	4.63
	Level of Significance	$p < .10$	$p < .05$	$p < .001$	$p < .001$	$p < .001$	$p < .01$	$p < .01$	$p < .02$	$p < .01$	$p < .01$	$p < .01$	$p < .05$	$p < .05$	$p < .01$
	R^2 or % Variance in Performance Explained	38%	52%	71%	68%	69%	29%	33%	23%	58%	59%	34%	7%	4%	18%

of the variation in job satisfaction is accounted for by 7 OAI dimensions when all local office units are included in the analysis.

The results in Tables 7-8 and 7-9 bring out several complexities in organization–performance relationships. The direction of relationships between many of the OAI external relations dimensions and unit performance criteria change in sign from plus to minus across the different types of ES units. Part of the flip-flopping correlations and beta coefficients may be due to the fact that different efficiency and effectiveness measures are used as criteria for evaluating the performance of each kind of ES unit. Since different organizations and units within them strive to attain different performance criteria, organization–performance relationships may not be generalizable. However, this explanation is largely refuted by the fact that the correlations and regression weights between the OAI indices and job satisfaction, which were measured in the same way across all units, also change in sign and flip-flop across the different types of ES units.

A second explanation, which we cannot evaluate here, is that the external relationships of organizational units are seldom in equilibrium, as this static analysis implicitly assumes. Therefore, the relationships may hold only over a relatively narrow range (as indicated in Table 7-7) and over a specific period of time. Cyclical work load fluctuations, constantly changing directives from higher administrative levels, and changing social and economic conditions in the community have significant impact in maintaining a constant state of disequilibrium in the external relationships of organizational units. As a result, an understanding of organization–performance relationships for a given unit may require time-series analysis, which can only be obtained with longitudinal research.

A third plausible explanation, which we tentatively adopt here, is to accept the correlations between the OAI dimensions of performance criteria for each type of unit as stable and replicable relationships and confront the unique requirements of designing the external unit relationships in complex organizations. General principles and uniform strategies for different types of units will not increase or necessarily decrease the efficiency, effectiveness, and job satisfaction of personnel in all units of a complex organization. A uniform change in the design of external unit relations may contribute positively to performance in one type of unit and detract from performance in another; hence, a stalemate. For example, Table 7-8 suggests that attempts to increase communications and coordination among units within ES offices may significantly increase the efficiency and effectiveness of placement and employer relations units but will be detrimental to the performance of claims processing and adjudication units. Similar results were found in Chapter 5 on the OAI unit task, structure, and process dimensions. This evidence underscores the need to be selective in assessing and managing the external relationships of different types of organizational units. It also points up the need for contingency theorists to become more operational in specifying under what conditions their theories of organization–performance relationships are likely to apply and not apply.

The far right-hand columns of Tables 7-8 and 7-9 show the small correlations and regression weights that are obtained on the OAI dimensions with overall office efficiency, effectiveness, and job satisfaction for all local office units combined. The size of these relationships and the percentages of explained variance in performance are much smaller than those obtained for each type of unit individually. This "wash-out" effect, which occurs when all units are combined, brings out the importance of breaking out the different kinds of units in complex organizations and assessing them separately if one desires to understand how their external affairs are associated with performance. Attempts to relate the combined scores of different types of organizational units to performance inherently creates a distorted and homogenized view of no associations between unit external relationships and the efficiency, effectiveness, and job satisfaction of unit personnel. Tables 7-8 and 7-9 show that large and important relationships exist between the OAI dimensions and performance when examined for each type of unit individually.

Practical Applications of OAI Data

The preceding quantitative results present impressive evidence to support the concurrent validity of the OAI external unit relations indices. However, the OAI dimensions do not provide information on the qualitative nature of these external unit relationships. Nor do they clearly suggest how the results could be used for practical decision making and managerial action. As is shown in following text, practical use of the quantitative data obtained with the OAI is greatly enhanced when combined with other qualitative information available to one well acquainted with the organization being assessed. For the manager or analyst well informed of organizational day-to-day operations and strategic decisions being contemplated, the OAI data provide a powerful analytical framework for addressing practical organizational problems. This is particularly true when OAI surveys are conducted repetitively over time in an organization. Thus, *it is important to recognize that the OAI does not, nor is it intended to, supplant the need for understanding the qualitative nature and functioning of an organization.*

While the 1975 OAI survey was being conducted in the state ES agency, its administrators and managers were contemplating or had made three strategic decisions to reorganize local ES offices on which the OAI external unit relations data are particularly relevant. These decisions were:

1. To make the intake units the centralized point of coordinating clients and paper work among units in local ES offices;

2. To decentralize decisions on resolving disputed unemployment compensation claims from the administrative headquarters level to local office adjudication units; and

3. To integrate WIN unit operations more closely with the ES placement and counseling units in local ES offices.

Based upon the OAI evidence, we draw some practical inferences to briefly assess these three decisions.

1. Should intake units become the centralized point for coordinating the reception, referral, and processing of clients and paper work among local ES units? In varying stages this decision was already in effect in local ES offices when the 1975 OAI survey was conducted. The correlations and regressions in Tables 7-8 and 7-9 indicate that what significantly distinguishes the high from the low performing intake units (in terms of efficiency and job satisfaction) is that the former operate as more autonomous units and have less work interdependence and coordination with other units in their local ES offices than the low performers.

The assumption made by ES managers was that if intake units perform the major share of interunit coordination, then other units in the local ES offices could perform their functions more efficiently and effectively, and the intake units would thereby contribute to the overall performance of local offices. Since the efficiency of intake units is strongly correlated with the overall efficiency of ES offices ($r = .72, p < .001$), the OAI data question the validity of this assumption. The significant correlations in Table 7-8 indicate that greater buffering of the standardized functions of the intake units from other units within ES offices and from other organizations increases their efficiency. Indeed, Table 7-9 shows that 38 percent of the variation in performance efficiency of intake units is explained by these factors. In addition, the strong negative correlations between the frequency of written reports and discussions with other units and job satisfaction of intake unit personnel indicate that the content or procedures of communications between intake unit personnel and other units require improvements.

In open-ended responses to the question in the OAI questionnaires, "What problems does your unit encounter in coordinating your work with other units in this office?", one of the issues most frequently mentioned by intake unit personnel was that individuals in other units often made requests or orders that intake unit members considered "unfair," "inappropriate," or constantly interruptive to their work procedures. Thus, the OAI results suggest that the ES managers should reexamine their assumption, decision, and/or specific procedures used to structure the intake units as the centralized point of client and paper work coordination among units in the local ES offices.

2. *Should decisions on disputed unemployment compensation claims be decentralized from the administrative headquarters level to local office adjudication units?* While the 1975 OAI survey was being conducted, the decentralization was taking place. Indeed, adjustments in the schedules for conducting the OAI survey in local offices were necessary because a team from the administrative office was simultaneously visiting local offices to train adjudication unit personnel in making final adjudication decisions. Previous to the decentralization, adjudication units submitted written recommendations on contested claims to an administrative office bureau which made the final decisions. However, a large backlog of disputed claims chronically existed at the headquarters level and forced the decentralization of decision making to local offices.

The decentralization implies greater responsibility and accountability on the part of local office adjudication unit personnel to correctly and promptly resolve disputes between community employers and laid-off workers on whether the latter are eligible for receiving unemployment compensation pay according to the terms in the state UC law. This greater responsibility and accountability should increase the responsiveness of adjudication unit personnel to local community employers and claimants on the status of their disputes and bring them into closer contact with the local community (Table 7-7 shows that next to intake units, adjudication units have the lowest scores on relations with other organizations).

During interviews with all adjudication unit supervisors in the 1972 OAI survey, many of them reported that "aloofness" was important for remaining impartial in resolving disputed claims. However, the data in Tables 7-8 and 7-9 do not support this operating assumption. The single best predictor of the promptness and accuracy of adjudication units in determining disputed claims is an increase in the amount of time they spend in coordinating with other organizations in the community. The regression analyses also show that, although adjudication unit personnel derive satisfaction from continued dependence on the administrative office to do their work, a decrease in the frequency of written reports (most of which are claim determinations) is the second most important factor in increasing the efficiency of resolving disputed claims. Therefore, we infer from the OAI data that the decentralization will achieve its stated objectives of increasing efficiency and effectiveness (at some cost of job satisfaction).

Two further issues have been a chronic source of conflict between adjudication and ES (placement and counseling) units in local offices: (1) the aloofness of adjudicators toward community employers versus the attempts of placement and counseling units to obtain a positive image with employers in the community of the ES office, and (2) the question of priorities on whether a person laid off from work should be paid a UC check or put back into a job. We attribute the strong negative correlations between adjudication unit performance and their relationships with other local office units to these problems. These two sources of conflict were among the larger issues which stimulated the overall reorganization of the ES state and local offices. The reorganization plan responded to these two sources of conflict by attempting to (1) increase the responsiveness of local offices to their local communities, and (2) assign equal priorities to the prompt payment of UC checks and job placements for laid-off workers in the community. We infer from the OAI data that increasing adjudication unit interaction with community employers and other organizations and increasing the frequency of group meetings (while decreasing impersonal written communications with other units) may go a long way to confront these issues and attain the goals of the reorganization plan.

3. *Should WIN units be integrated more closely with employment service placement and counseling units in local ES offices?* This question was being contemplated as part of the overall reorganization of local ES offices, but had not been implemented when the 1975 OAI survey was conducted. Although the WIN units are located within ES offices, they are separately funded to administer the national Work Incentive program by providing intensive job assessment, development and placement services for people on welfare (AFDC recipients). As Table 7-7 shows, WIN units maintain a close functional reporting relationship with the state WIN bureau in the headquarters office. Clients served by WIN units are referred by the Department of Public Welfare in the community, which keeps a record of all welfare recipients who enroll and are eligible for the WIN program. In terms of their relationship with other units in local ES offices, WIN units are closely connected with counseling and placement units because they often work with the same community agencies to send their clients for job training programs and with the same employers to find different kinds of job openings for their clients. Competition and conflict between placement and WIN units over obtaining job orders and referring clients to employers for job placements was frequently observed. Placement unit personnel often claimed that WIN units would "cream" or "pirate" the "best" job openings in the commonly shared job bank for their clients. WIN unit personnel countered by indicating that they were just as instrumental as the placement units in obtaining the job orders from community employers and that their disadvantaged clients required special considerations and negotiations with employers if they were to be successfully placed in the jobs available.

Table 7-8 shows that the efficiency, effectiveness, and job satisfaction of WIN unit personnel is strongly positively correlated with increased work interdependence, communications, and time spent in coordinating vertically with the state WIN bureau and horizontally with other community organizations. In terms of relationships with other units in local ES offices, the correlations of WIN unit performance are strongly negative with work flows, positive with group meetings, and mixed for time spent in coordination with other units. However, after the relations with the state WIN bureau and other organizations are taken into account, the regression results in Table 7-9 show that only the time spent in coordinating with other ES units significantly explains increases in efficiency and job satisfaction of WIN units and decreases in effectiveness.

We infer from this evidence that the overall performance of WIN units can be enhanced by concentrating on tightening relationships with the state WIN bureau and with other local community organizations. The former is necessary for clarifying WIN program direction, providing technical assistance, and maintaining accountability of WIN unit performance. These have been the traditional functions of the state WIN bureau, and it has been performing quite well, as Tables 7-8 and 7-9 show. Closer relationships with the community are necessary for local WIN units to obtain cooperation of employers and social service organizations in creating training programs and jobs that match the skill levels of severely disadvantaged WIN clients.

However, the empirical evidence does not support the strategy of structurally integrating WIN operations with other ES units by, for example, having the counseling units assess and counsel WIN clients and the placement units interview and refer WIN clients to available job openings. Although there are some duplicate functions performed by WIN units and ES placement and counseling units, their major differences lie with the different and more problematic clients served by WIN units. The conflict between placement and WIN units over their common dependence on the same community employers might be worked out simply by spending more time in coordinating contacts with employers through more frequent discussions and group meetings among personnel in these units. Attempts to structurally integrate the ES and WIN programs may jeopardize the integrity of both programs. Indeed, Table 3-1 shows that the correlations among performance efficiency and effectiveness of WIN, placement, and counseling units are strongly positive, and suggest that allowing each unit to pursue its unique program objectives under the current structural arrangement contributes positively to the overall performance efficiency and effectiveness of local ES offices.

CONCLUSION

Of course, the results and implications of the OAI external unit relations indices reported in this chapter are limited to the ES offices in which this study was conducted. Very different profiles of external unit relations—their intercorrelations and abilities to explain variations in performance—may be obtained in other organizations. Therefore, caution must be used in drawing conclusions on the intrinsic and extrinsic validity of the OAI and on the practical inferences drawn for administrative action. Yet, in the sample of ES offices and units examined here, the evaluation of the OAI external unit relations indices has produced the following major findings.

The factor analysis of the OAI dimensions found that three of the five indices pertaining to unit relations with other units, levels, and organizations had satisfactory properties of convergent and discriminant validity by breaking out as unique unconfounded factors. They are work flows, work dependence, and communications with other units, levels, and organizations. The written and oral communications items tended to break out as separate factors in the analysis. Hence, we decided to treat the different modes of communication separately in subsequent evaluation of the instrument and theory. However, the items in the work flow variability and standardization of coordination indices require substantia' revision because they were found to be highly unstable across the factor analyses on relations with other units, levels, and organizations (see Tables 7-2 to 7-4). Since these two indices are important to the theory, they have been revised and are presented in Appendix A.

Supporting evidence of the intrinsic validity of the three strong indices from the factor analyses—plus three other indices: amounts of time spent coordinating with other units, levels, and organizations—was provided in terms of coefficient alphas and median correlations with other items (see Table 7-5). Overall, the results indicate that the discriminant validity of each index relative to its internal consistency is quite good.

An evaluation of the OAI indices in terms of the theory found that the correlations and path coefficients among the dimensions are largely as expected, particularly those pertaining to relationships with other levels and organizations (see Table 7-6). The associations among OAI indices on relations with other units were somewhat smaller. Two explanations were given: (a) The influences of social conditioning are greater in relations among units than in relations with headquarters or field office levels or in relations with outside organizations and (b) respondents' frames of reference were less clear on questions pertaining to relations with other units than they were with other levels or organizations. Determination of which explanation is most plausible requires structuring the frames of references in the OAI more clearly by asking respondents to answer the external unit relations questions in terms of specifically named units, levels, and organizations. These modifications have been made in the revised OAI presented in Appendix A.

Next, we evaluated the ability of the OAI indices to discriminate empirically the different task environments of ES local office units. Similarities and differences between five types of ES units on the OAI external unit relations dimensions in Table 7-7 were found to be highly consistent with knowledge gained from on-site observations.

To evaluate concurrent validity, the OAI dimensions were correlated and regressed on three different performance criteria—efficiency, effectiveness, and job satisfaction—for each type of unit in local ES offices. The correlations in Table 7-8 and stepwise regressions in Table 7-9 indicate that the OAI dimensions represent a compromise between being (a) general enough to apply to a wide variety of task environments of work units, and (b) specific enough to significantly explain the performance of each type of unit in terms of the different external relationships they maintain with other units, supervisory levels, and other organizations. Specifically, when regressing the OAI dimensions that were significantly correlated with a measure of performance for intake, adjudication, placement, and WIN units individually:

a. 29 to 71 percent of the variation in unit efficiency (i.e., units of output per position),

b. 33 to 68 percent of the variation in unit effectiveness (or degree of goal attainment), and

c. 23 to 69 percent of the variation in the average level of job satisfaction of unit personnel

were significantly explained by the OAI external unit relations dimensions. However, when combining all types of local office units in the regression analyses, only 7, 4, and 18 percent of the variations were explained, respectively, in overall office efficiency, effectiveness, and job satisfaction.

Although these results provide impressive evidence to substantiate the concurrent validity of the OAI external unit relations indices, they also bring out several complexities in assessing organization–performance relationships.

The direction of relationships between many of the OAI dimensions and performance criteria was found to change in sign from plus to minus across the different types of ES units (as was found on the OAI unit task, structure, and process dimensions in Chapter 5). After exploring several possible explanations, it was concluded that there is a need to apply unique guidelines for external relationships to each individual type of unit. General principles and uniform strategies for organizing the external task environments of different types of units will neither increase nor necessarily decrease the overall performance of a complex organization. Unknowingly some units will increase whereas others will decrease in performance from a uniform organizational intervention.

The correlations and regression weights of the OAI indices on overall office performance for all types of units combined were found to be much smaller than those obtained when each type of unit was examined separately. This "wash-out" effect, which occurs when all units are combined, brings out the importance of breaking apart the different kinds of units in complex organizations and assessing them separately if one desires to understand how their external affairs are associated with performance.

Finally, three reorganization decisions contemplated by administrators and managers of the ES agency were assessed to exemplify how OAI data can be used for practical decision making and managerial action. It should be underscored that this assessment was possible only because we have become quite well acquainted with day-to-day operations and strategic managerial concerns of the ES state agency over the years. Thus, it is important to recognize that the OAI do not, nor are they intended to, supplant the need for understanding the qualitative nature and functioning of an organization.

CHAPTER EIGHT

The Interorganizational Field

How can one assess patterns of coordination among organizations* that are linked together to solve complex problems or attain joint goals? How and why do interorganizational relationships emerge? What factors are important for maintaining them successfully over time? These questions become increasingly important when assessing organizations because many social and economic problems and opportunities are beyond the capabilities of any one organization to handle by itself. Witness, for example, the construction of the Alaska pipeline, industry cooperation in dealing with shared external threats or regulations, and the growing intervention of government in organizational practices. Many complex social and economic problems require joint interorganizational planning and programming because the requisite resources, expertise, and motivation are contained within autonomous organizations and vested interest groups. Thus, organizations must increasingly establish coordinated relationships with other agencies, creating, in effect, organizations of organizations.

This chapter expands the OA perspective to deal with the interorganizational field to address these questions and issues. Little is objectively known about these questions and issues. Knowledge of the interorganizational field is still at a primitive stage (Warren et al., 1974). No generally accepted framework, theory, or methods have emerged from research or practice as yet. Therefore, the first part of this chapter will attempt to build a partial foundation for assessing interorganizational relationships (IRs). Section I suggests a framework for viewing an IR as a social action system and operationally defines its

* Throughout this chapter, the terms organization, agency, and firm are used synonymously.

characteristics in terms of structure, process, and ends. Section II presents a theory to explain how and why IRs develop and are maintained over time. Definitions and measures for each of the factors included in the theory are presented in Section III and evaluated in Section IV. The OAI measures are evaluated on the first wave of data collected in a longitudinal study of interagency relationships among Texas child care organizations, which the authors now have in progress.

SECTION I: A FRAMEWORK FOR ASSESSING INTERORGANIZATIONAL RELATIONSHIPS (IRs)*

An interorganizational relationship (IR) occurs when two or more organizations transact resources of any kind (money, physical facilities and materials, customer or client referrals, technical staff services). An IR can be very temporary with a one-time resource transaction, or long-lasting with ongoing exchanges over time. The nature of this relationship and the behavior of organizations within it can be examined from a *pairwise, set,* or *network* perspective. Although these three different levels of focus are highly related in theory and method (described as follows), it is useful to first illustrate their differences.

The simplest form of IR is the *pairwise relationship* between two organizations, which is illustrated in Figure 8-1a. The dyad is the basic building block for studying IRs and is concerned with understanding the relational properties between organizations, or the characteristics of the line connecting Agencies 1 and 2. The dyad has been the focus of most research on IRs to date (e.g., Litwak and Hylton, 1962; Reid, 1964; Klonglan et al., 1973; Hall and Clark, 1974; Aldrich, 1974). These studies generally focus on various characteristics of the line connecting A1 and A2 in terms of direction (the arrows on the A1–A2 line) and degree of intensity (n). For example, the study of dyadic relations between child care organizations reported in Section IV attempts to explain the amount of resources transacted between two organizations on the bases of the perceived dependency, communication frequency, awareness, and consensus among the parties involved. Later sections of this chapter extend this focus upon the A1–A2 line in Figure 8-1a by defining and quantifying some of its properties.

---

* This section is a revised statement of the framework for assessing IRs presented previously in Van de Ven, Emmett, and Koenig (1974) and Van de Ven (1976c).

a. Pairwise or Dyadic Interorganizational Relationship

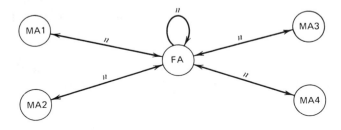

b. Interorganizational Set

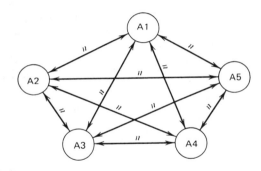

c. Interorganizational Network

Figure 8-1   Levels of interorganizational relationships.

Figures 8-1*b* and *c* show that the interagency set and network can be viewed as nothing more than a series of pairwise relations. However, in addition to dyadic relations, the interagency set and network can provide increasingly more information on IR.

An *interorganizational set* focuses upon the cluster of dyadic IRs of one focal agency (FA) with other member agencies (MA) in its environment (Evan, 1966; Caplow, 1964). Since the primary focus is upon the dyadic relations of a focal agency, the study of interagency sets is generally limited to assessing a series of FA–MA relationships. No attempt is made to measure and compare relations among member agencies. The interagency set can provide an understanding of how a focal agency affects or is affected by its member agencies. Moreover, the interagency set perspective allows one to examine how a change in one dyadic relationship affects other pairwise interagency relations of the focal agency.

The *interorganizational network* is defined as the total pattern of interrelationships among a cluster of organizations that are meshed together as a social system to attain collective and self-interest goals or to resolve specific problems for a target population. The primary focus of analysis shifts from the relationships *between* agencies to patterns of relationships *among* an identifiable cluster of organizations bound together by allied domains, geography, target client populations, or problems (Levine and White, 1961:379).

Although the interorganizational network is theoretically and empirically far more complex than a series of interagency dyads or sets, it is important to recognize that an interagency network can be analyzed from a pairwise or set perspective. A complete network will contain $n(n - 1)/2$ pairwise relationships (where n is the number of agencies in the network). If each focal agency maintains relations with other agencies that are not in the network, a complete network will contain as many partial interagency sets as there are agencies in the network. Thus, interagency sets and networks are created by aggregating dyadic relationships, and the network incorporates interagency dyads and sets. In this sense, the network provides an overall framework for studying IR. Each level of analysis is appropriate for answering different kinds of questions about interorganizational behavior.

The IR as a Social Action System

Interorganizational dyads, sets, and networks are defined as social action systems on the premise that the following elements of collective behavior are present in all IRs.

1. Behavior among members is aimed at attaining collective and self-interest goals.

2. Interdependent processes emerge through the division of tasks and functions among members.

3. An IR can act as a unit and has a unique identity that is separate from its members.

When two or more organizations become involved in a relationship, they create a social system. As a social system, the actions of the organizational parties are interdependent, and over time member organizations or their representatives take on specialized roles and develop behavioral expectations of each other regarding the rights and obligations of membership in the IR (Homans, 1950). In this sense, Clark (1965: 234) suggests that two or more interdependent organizations bind themselves together by performing specialized activities to attain an objective for a limited period of time, often by the terms of a contract.

The social structure among organizations in an IR is such that it can *act as a unit* and make decisions to attain the joint self-interests of the organizations involved in the relationship. This implies that the IR can perform actions (i.e., pursue goals) similar to an autonomous organization and that it can participate in, and adapt to, other social systems more encompassing than itself, just as an individual organization does by being a member of an IR (Lessnoff, 1968:186). Generally, decisions are allowed to emerge out of the interaction among various organizational participants. Modifications and changes that are necessary in making a joint decision "occur incrementally through the waxing and waning of the resource allocation mechanism, and through changes in legitimation of shifting domains"—and changes in roles of members within the IR (Warren, 1967:413).

An examination of IRs as social action systems requires a very focused perspective. The analyst must identify within the interorganizational field specific clusters of organizations that are linked together and that act as units for some special purpose. Membership in these IRs may overlap, just as membership of personnel in different organizations may overlap. However, IRs, like organizations, are not identified by membership but by their functional goals, role structure, and behavior as a social action system. Further, since the IR can act as a unit, this suggests, as Durkheim (1947) does with his concept of "collective consciousness," that many behavioral acts and events of the IR cannot be explained simply in terms of analyzing the behavior of individual organizations that are members of the IR. Rather, these observable *social facts* are collective events that arise out of the actions of the social system and are formally a property of the IR itself (Timasheff, 1967:108). Warren et al. (1971:54–55) observe that "one can describe and analyze as a single system of interaction any group of oganizations whose properties may differ from those of the interacting organizations and cannot be reduced to the properties of these individual organizations." The appropriate unit of analysis for examining an IR, therefore, is the social system itself.

The objective of organizations involved in an IR is the attainment of goals that are unachievable by organizations independently. For example, Litwak and Hylton (1962) and Levine et al. (1963) suggest a number of ends for human service organizations to join together: (1) to establish a clearing house for client referrals, (2) to promote areas of common interest, (3) to jointly obtain and allocate a greater amount of resources than would be possible by each agency independently, and (4) to adjudicate areas of dispute or competition. Furthermore, Warren et al. (1974) describe the even more frequent occurrence of a single organization that sets out to pursue some objective that it cannot achieve by itself. As a result, it initiates contacts with other organizations to secure help, which, if successful, result in the formation of a pairwise relationship usually short term and ad hoc in nature. Because organizations participate in IRs to pursue their individual and collective interests, one can measure the ends or effectiveness of interagency coordination in a manner similar to that described in Chapter 2 (i.e., as the extent to which the parties perceive they attain their self-interests and the extent to which they believe their involvement in the IR is worthwhile, equitable, productive, and satisfying).

To attain its goals as a unit, a social action system adopts a structure and process for organizing the activities of its members. *Structure* refers to the administrative arrangements that are established to define the role relationships among members. *Process* is conceptualized as a flow of activities and refers to the direction and frequency of resources and information that actually flow between members. Thus, the structure and process of an IR is the "organizational form" for interorganizational collaboration. Furthermore, since an IR has been argued to exhibit the basic elements common to any organized form of collective behavior, the analytic dimensions commonly used to measure social structure and process should also apply to an IR.

The operational dimensions for assessing IRs at the pairwise, set, and network levels are developed only in terms of networks because a network incorporates dyads and sets. Because structure is a concept that derives from the processes in a social system (Bakke, 1959), we first define the basic processes in an IR and then indicate how four major characteristics of network structure (formalization, complexity, centralization, and intensity) are associated with these processes.

Process Dimensions of an IR Network

As in Chapter 7, the major processes in an IR are argued to be resource and information flows. *Resource flows* are the units of value that are transacted between organizations (such as money, physical space and equipment, staff, customer or client referrals, and other materials and services). The major dimensions used for measuring resource flows between organizations are their *direction* (Thompson and McEwen, 1958; Johns and Demarche, 1957; Reid, 1964), *amount* (Evan, 1966; Marrett, 1971; Aldrich, 1974), and *variability* (Hall and Clark, 1968; Klonglan, et al., 1973). *Information flows* are messages or communications (about the units of exchange or the nature of the relationships) that are transmitted between organizational parties through a variety of media (e.g., written reports and letters, phone calls, face-to-face discussions, and group or committee meetings). Corresponding to resource flows, the major dimensions often used for measuring information flows between organizations are the *direction* (Marrett, 1971; Aldrich, 1974), *frequency* (Levine and White, 1961; Warren et al., 1971; Klonglan et al., 1973), and *quality* or *conflict* (Litwak and Hylton, 1962; Litwak and Rothman, 1970).

In practice, the distinction between resource and information flows can admittedly become blurred. For example, in certain instances, information may be considered either a valued resource that is exchanged between organizations or communication about the units of exchange. However, for conceptual clarity we find it useful to maintain a distinction between resource and information flows. The reason that it is analytically useful to distinguish between resource and information flows in studying an IR is that they differentiate between task instrumental and pattern maintenance concerns of any social system.

As discussed in Chapter 7, task-instrumental functions are manifest in resource flows. Without some ongoing transaction of resources it is highly probable that one or more agencies will terminate their membership in an IR. The comment, "We coordinated but nothing happened," exemplifies this lack of task-instrumental concern. Maintenance functions are manifest in information flows between organizational parties in a relationship. In the absence of information flows necessary for the maintenance and integration of activities in an IR, it is highly probable that one or more organizations will lose sight of their purpose for being in the IR. As a result, means and ends become inverted, and members soon perceive the IR to be an aimless series of threatening and chaotic resource transactions.

Disequilibriums or disruptions within an IR occur when there is a change in either resource or information flows. The process of adaptation that takes place will be toward the establishment of a consonance or balance in the pattern of resources and information flows. In this sense, resource and information flows are reciprocally interdependent and are good indicators of growth, adaptation, and survival of IRs over time.

Structural Dimensions of an IR Network

The predominant approach to examining the structure of IRs has been to identify nominal classifications of alternative types of structures, such as mediated (where an intermediary handles the relationship between parties) versus ad hoc or unmediated arrangements (e.g., Reid, 1964), federated versus corporate structures (Clark, 1965), or unitary, federative, coalitional, and social choice interagency networks (Warren, 1967).

Although these clusters or types of interagency structures may well be the most frequently observed by researchers, the dimensional method of defining and studying structure has the major advantages of inclusiveness and generality. With dimensions (such as the degrees of formalization, centralization, and complexity), the analyst can incorporate the complete array of alternative profiles of interorganizational structure, and this provides greater potential for drawing inferences from one study to the next. This is particularly needed to overcome the lack of synthesis and noncumulative nature of interorganizational research observed by Hall et al. (1977) and Rieker et al. (1974).

Four dimensions appear to capture the structural essence of an interorganizational network: formalization, complexity, centralization, and intensity. The first three dimensions come from the intraorganizational literature, where they have been extensively used in theory and research (e.g., Pugh et al., 1963; Hage, 1965; Hall, 1972). The particular contribution here is to apply these three dimensions to interorganizational studies. Intensity has been offered by Marrett (1971) as an indicator of the degree of activity in the network.

1. *Formalization* is the degree to which rules, policies, and procedures govern the role behavior and activities of organizations in networks. Two aspects of the formalization of agency roles are examined: the extent to which rules, policies, and procedures govern the interagency *agreement* and *contacts*. An interagency agreement exists once any form of expression has been made between the parties regarding the terms of their relationship. Its formalization increases the more the agreement is verbalized, written down, contractual, and mandatory. Two indicators of the formalization of interagency contacts are (1) the extent to which rules and policies are established to transact activities between parties and (2) the number of procedures (e.g., agendas, minutes, schedules, etc.) followed by a committee or group that governs the network.

2. The *structural complexity* of a network refers to the number of different elements that must be integrated for an IR to act as a unit.

Within organizations, complexity is generally defined as the number of different work groups (departments or sections) and the number of different task specialties (e.g., see Hage, 1965; Hall, 1972). The counterpart definition of complexity at the interorganizational level appears to be (1) the number of different cliques, clusters, or subsystems (they are used synonymously) in the interorganizational network and (2) the number of different kinds of resources that are transacted between agencies in the network. The former is an indicator of social differentiation, whereas the latter indicates the degree of instrumental differentiation in the network. The greater the number of different kinds of resources transacted between organizations, the more complex the relationship (Levine et al., 1963; Reid, 1964; Guetzkow, 1966; Aiken and Hage, 1968).

The number of different communication cliques or subsystems in a network comes from the sociometric literature on group structure and behavior (see Glanzer and Glaser, 1959; 1961 for reviews). Doreian (1969) has developed a mathematical procedure for detecting cliques within cliques (or subsystems within systems) in a network (see Appendix F). The procedure reveals clearly the different clusters or organizations within a network. It is also possible to detect peripheral agencies of each cluster or subsystem. Furthermore it is possible to look for spaces where a simple link could bind separate cliques together or could join isolated agencies to a subsystem.

3. *Centralization* refers to two aspects of centrality in an IR: centrality of decision making and centrality of information and resource flows. The two concepts are highly related and will now be discussed.

Decision-making centralization refers to the locus of authority in the network. The degree of hierarchy of authority is the conventional measure of centralization within organizations (e.g., Hall, 1963; Blau, 1974; Hage, 1965). However, Litwak and Hylton (1962:396) point out that interorganization analysis (as opposed to intraorganization analysis) stresses the study of social behavior among autonomous agencies under conditions of nonhierarchical authority.

Warren et al.'s (1974:148-167) conceptualization of "concerted decision-making" over time appears useful for examining the locus of decision-making in an IR. Warren begins with the observation that individual organizations in a network will continue to maximize their self-interests, but certain aspects of decision-making are pooled. What earlier were individual organization decisions now become inclusive decisions, characterizing an enterprise with its own system of differentiated roles, tasks, and maintenance functions. The structure of inclusive decision-making is initially very weak, with a minimum of

authority, a high degree of self-orientation among parties, and a con-
sequent difficulty in making concerted decisions that are not in accord
with the self-interests of all the parties. "As the inclusive organization
grows in strength in relation to its members, it begins to take on the
characteristics of a formal organization." To the extent that it does so,
the organizational model for concerted decision-making, as developed
in administrative theory, becomes increasingly relevant (Warren et al.,
1974:166).

The locus of decision-making in an IR is in the network itself; to suggest that it resides within a member agency shifts the analysis to the
intraorganizational level. The degree of centralization of decision-making, then, is defined as the degree of inclusive or concerted decision-
making by the aggregate of organizations that are members of the IR.
Concerted decisions are normally made by a board, committee, or group
of individuals representing the member agencies of the network.
Centralization can be measured as the mean perception of these organizational representatives concerning the extent to which decisions made
by the interagency committee are binding upon member organizations.

The centrality of the network refers to the pattern of connections
between agencies in terms of information and resource flows. Figure 8-2
shows the structural patterns of very centralized and very decentralized
networks of five agencies each. Centrality is the degree to which
information and resource flows in a network are centered on one or a
few agencies. In a totally decentralized network all agencies participate
equally, and there is perfect symmetry or reciprocity in the in-flow and
out-flow of information and resources for each organization.

When data are properly collected on the incidence of information
and resource flows between agencies, directional arrows and frequency
values can be added to the networks illustrated in Figure 8-2. Then it
becomes apparent that the notion of centrality is not a limited set of
possibilities. Instead of asserting whether a network is or is not

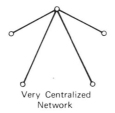

Very Centralized
Network

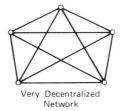

Very Decentralized
Network

Figure 8-2   Network centrality.

centralized, one can compute an index to quantify the degree to which a network is centralized.

Since the pioneering work of Bavelas (1948) many refinements and more generally applicable indices of centrality have been developed by small group researchers (Glanzer and Glaser, 1961). Mackenzie (1966) has developed a network centrality index that appears most useful for our purpose. As described in Appendix F, Mackenzie's centrality index can be computed from an incidence matrix of actual communications or resource flows between agencies in a network. The index can be computed for the network as a whole, as well as for individual agencies, to obtain a ranking of the agencies as to their communication or resource dominance.

4. *Intensity* is the strength of the network and has been offered by Marrett (1971) as an indicator of the investment agencies make in an interorganizational relationship. At the individual agency level, intensity is computed as the sum frequency of information out-flows and amount of resource out-flows to other agencies in a network. This represents the contribution of an organization to the IR. At the network level, intensity is the total sum frequency of information flows and amount of resource flows in the network divided by the number of agencies in the network.

Summary

The framework presented here for assessing relationships among two or more organizations as a social action system is based on the premise that an interorganizational relationship exhibits the basic common properties of any form of organized collective behavior: Behavior is aimed at a goal, interdependence exists between members, the IR can act as a unit with an identity separate from its members. Operating from this premise, an IR can be studied by defining and quantifying its dimensions in terms of process (resource and information flows), structure (formalization, complexity, centralization, and intensity), and ends (perceived effectiveness of interagency relationships).

SECTION II: A THEORY ON HOW AND WHY IRs DEVELOP AND ARE MAINTAINED

Now we return to the original questions which motivate our interests in studying IRs. How and why do they develop? How do they function, grow, adapt, and dissolve over time? What factors are important for planning and managing collective action so that desired results of various interest groups are attained? This section proposes answers to these questions by developing an operational theory on the formation and functioning of IRs. Again, the argument focuses upon the interorganizational network because it encompasses interagency dyads and sets.

Figure 8-3 summarizes the variables in the model which are used in the argument. Overall, six situational factors are used to explain why and how interagency networks develop. The model hypothesizes that variations in the structural dimensions of an IR can be largely explained by the six situational factors. It is also hypothesized that the effectiveness of an interagency network can be predicted from the four structural dimensions and six situational factors. Figure 8-4 presents the basic assumptions and hypotheses that are used to explain how and why IRs emerge and function.

Why and How Do IRs Emerge?

Organizations do not coordinate for coordination's sake. Instead, organizations strain to maintain their autonomy (Gouldner, 1959). This is the first assumption. Autonomy means that organizations are capable of choosing the course of action they desire to pursue (Levine and White, 1961; Clark and Wilson, 1961). From an organization's point of view, to become involved in an IR implies (1) that it loses some of its freedom to act independently when it prefers to maintain control over its domain and affairs, and (2) that it must invest some of its scarce resources and energy to develop and maintain relationships with other organizations when the potential returns on this investment are often unclear or intangible. For these reasons, organizational decision makers prefer not to become involved in relationships with other organizations unless they are compelled to do so.

Two reasons appear sufficiently compelling for interagency activity to emerge: (1) an internal need for resources or (2) a willingness to respond to an external problem, opportunity, or mandate. Generally, the first reason is generated within organizations to achieve their self-interests, whereas the latter is stimulated by information about problems, opportunities, or mandates in the overlapping domains of organizations. The former is often a product of internal organizational planning and change, and the latter emanates from planning and change in the interorganizational field. In addition, whereas the former is more tangible and project oriented (Warren et al., 1974:67), the latter is more diffuse and emerges out of an awareness of changing need priorities,

SITUATIONAL FACTORS

1. **Resource Dependence**
   —Agency's need for external resources
   —Agency's need for other agencies in network

2. **Response to Problem, Opportunity, or Mandate**
   —Perceived willingness to respond to external problem, opportunity, or mandate

3. **Awareness**
   —Knowledge of system needs, problems, or opportunities
   —Knowledge of other agency's services and goals
   —Personal acquaintance of agency representatives

4. **Consensus**
   —Agreement among agencies on solutions to needs or problems
   —Agreement on services and goals of agencies in network
   —Conflict on means and ends of network

5. **Domain Similarity**
   —Sameness of agency goals, services, staff skills, and clients with other agencies in network

6. **Size**
   —Number of agencies in network

STRUCTURAL DIMENSIONS

1. **Intensity**
   —Amount of resource flows among agencies in network
   —Frequency of information flows among agencies in network

2. **Formalization (Standardization)**
   —Codification of interagency agreements and contacts
   —Standardization of resource flows in the network

3. **Complexity (Differentiation)**
   —Number of different resources transacted in network
   —Number of cliques and subgroups in communication network

4. **Centralization**
   —Extent IR Committee decisions are binding upon members
   —Centrality of resource and communication flows in network

EFFECTIVENESS

Perceived Effectiveness
—Extent agencies carry out commitments and believe relationships are worthwhile, productive, and satisfying

Figure 8-3   Dimensions in model on interagency networks.

Assumptions

A. Organizations strain to maintain their autonomy.

B. Organizations maximize gains and minimize losses in becoming involved in relationships with other agencies.

C. Organizations attempt to protect and enhance their domains.

D. Increases in the size of the interagency network and in the amount of resource flows between agencies increase problems of integration and pattern maintenance of the interagency network.

E. Interagency networks emerge incrementally and grow with successful previous encounters at coordination.

Hypotheses in Resource Dependence Model

1. The greater the resource dependence, the greater the frequency of interagency communications.

2. The greater the frequency of interagency communications, the greater the awareness of other agencies and the greater the consensus among parties.

Hypotheses in System Change Model

3. The greater the frequency of interagency communications, the greater the awareness and willingness to respond to system problems, opportunities, or mandates.

4. The greater the willingness to respond to system problems, opportunities, or mandates, the greater the consensus among agencies.

Hypotheses on Emergence and Structure of Interagency Network

5. The intensity of an interagency network is a function of resource dependence, awareness, willingness to respond to external issues, and consensus.

6. There is a concave ($\cap$-shaped) relationship between domain similarity and the intensity of an interagency network.

7. The greater the number of agencies in a network, the greater the formalization, centralization, and complexity of the network.

8. The greater the intensity of an interagency network, the greater the formalization, centralization and complexity of the network.

9. The greater the perceived effectiveness of an interagency network at time 0, the greater the interdependence and issue commitment among the agencies at $t + 1$, over time periods $0, 1, 2, \ldots, n$.

Figure 8-4 Assumptions and hypotheses about the emergence and functioning of interagency networks

resource distribution channels, or power relationships in the environment (Emery and Trist, 1965).

Thus, while resource dependence identifies the intraorganizational reason for an IR, responsiveness to problems, opportunities, or mandates emphasizes the larger interorganizational field or system as a reason for an IR (Terreberry, 1968). The relative importance of these reasons for becoming involved in relations with other organizations, of course, will differ by agency. IRs are usually a product of diverse individual motivations. However, to argue that either resource dependence or responsiveness to external issues is the compelling reason for an IR to emerge, it is useful to treat each reason separately and to examine the different processes each entails. The processes set in motion by an organization's need for resources will be called the *resource dependence model*, whereas the activities associated with an organization's motivation to respond to external issues will be called the *system change model*. Although the two models initially require different hypotheses, Figure 8-5 shows how they become fused when predicting the overall emergence of interorganizational networks.

Resource Dependence Model

In varying degrees all organizations depend upon their environments (or other organizations) for personnel, information, monetary and physical resources, and clients, customers, or markets to attain their self-interest

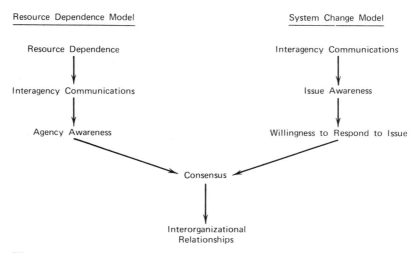

Figure 8-5 Branch diagram in resource dependence and system change models leading to interagency relationships.

objectives (Levine, White, and Paul, 1963; Aiken and Hage, 1968; Aldrich, 1972; Clark and Wilson, 1961). In this sense, Guetzkow (1966) notes that the roots of interagency activity are internal to each organization, whereas Aiken and Hage (1968:914-915) state that organizations are "pushed into such interdependencies because of their need for resources—not only money, but also resources such as specialized skills, access to particular kinds of markets, and the like." If organizations were self-sustaining entities, there would be little need for interorganization analysis (Clark, 1965; O'Toole et al., 1972; Perlman and Gurin, 1972:161).

The first reason why interorganizational activity emerges, therefore, is the rational response to a lack of resources for attaining self-interest goals. In assessing IRs, dependence indicates the extent to which agencies rely upon one another's resources for attaining their individual goals. The greater the resource dependence, the more agencies will engage in communications with others which may lead to establishing a relationship (hypothesis 1). However, dependence is a necessary but not sufficient condition for interagency relationships to emerge; also required are *awareness* and *consensus*.

Awareness.   An organization must also be aware of some possible sources in other organizations where its needed resources can be obtained. Otherwise the agency's boundary spanner is likely to reach the conclusion that the goal that motivates the search for resources cannot be attained. Alternatively, the agency may try to minimally commit itself to achieving its goal within the limitations of its own resources. Therefore awareness is a second necessary condition for IRs to emerge in the resource dependence model (Litwak and Hylton, 1962; White et al., 1971). Two levels of awareness appear particularly important in predicting interorganizational activity.

At a general level is the extent to which boundary spanners of an organization are informed about the specific goals, services, and resources that exist in other agencies. This level of awareness identifies the perceived number of potential alternative sources for obtaining needed resources (Turk, 1973). Since organizations attempt to minimize losses and maximize gains (assumption B), and because they strive to maintain their autonomy (assumption A), they attempt to develop relationships with a number of organizations to obtain a given set of resources. This strategy reduces an organization's degree of dependence on a given source (Levine and White, 1961; Aiken and Hage, 1968; Turk, 1973), and provides the organization the opportunity to select the type of environment in which it will operate (Child, 1972). This also permits the organization to segment its market and to use unique strategies for coping with each market (Thompson, 1967).

A more specific level of awareness is the degree of personal acquaintance between the organization's boundary spanner and key decision makers in other organizations. Although personal acquaintance as a variable has been largely ignored in survey research studies on IR, case studies by Burke (1965), Gilbert (1969), and O'Toole et al. (1972) emphasize its importance, particularly in mobilizing ad hoc interagency activity. Personal and business acquaintances between organizational boundary spanners become fused in the context of mobilizing interagency coordination (Warren et al., 1974). Boundary-spanning activity is often acted out during coffee breaks and luncheons, at night clubs, and during other social, political, and recreational engagements. The greater the length of time and degree of intimacy in the personal relationships between organizational boundary spanners, the more similar their attitudes, values, and goals, and the greater their mutual trust of one another. As a result, the greater the personal acquaintance of boundary spanners, the greater their predisposition to help one another out by committing their organizations to an interagency relationship.

Consensus. This refers to the degree to which an organization's specific goals and services are agreed upon by the parties (Levine et al., 1963; Evan, 1966) or, conversely, disputed (Levine and White, 1961; Aldrich, 1972; Miller, 1958). Domain consensus by organizations in a system is prerequisite to exchange, and achieving it may involve orientation, negotiation, and legitimation (Levine and White, 1961: 599). When the functions of the interacting agencies are diffuse, achieving domain consensus is a complex process of constant readjustment and compromise—a process that entails negotiating and bargaining. However, the more specific the functions and objectives of each organization, the more domain concensus is attained merely by orientation. A more formalized but less frequent process for attaining domain consensus is the licensing or "legitimating" of one organization by another to operate in a particular community, industry or area of service (Levine and White, 1961).

Thus, in the resource dependence model it is argued that through informal communications and personal acquaintances with people in the environment, organizations become aware of the services, goals, and resources of other agencies, with each setting out to sell the importance of its needs. Out of these interactions arise areas of common interest and *quid pro quo* compromises. The more successful each agency is in establishing awareness and consensus on the part of other agencies on joint and self-interest objectives, the greater the potential for an IR to emerge. However, if agreement is not established or if severe conflict is encountered between the parties involved, it is likely that negotiations will be terminated at this point and that agency boundary spanners will look elsewhere to obtain needed resources.

The System Change Model

The system change model is well known to community organizers and planners. It is the normative externally induced model for community change—change often caused by the infusion of money from a resource-granting agency or by the redistribution of resources (e.g., revenue sharing). This type of disruption, opportunity, or mandate in the environment is argued to be the stimulating factor that sets the system change model in action. External intervention stimulates interagency communications, which in turn increase an organization's awareness of needs, problems, or opportunities in its environment. This awareness motivates organizational involvement and commitment because the environmental problems or opportunities exist in the legitimate but overlapping domains of member agencies and because each agency will attempt to protect or enhance its domain (Warren, 1974:44).

Although the causation is reversed, the logic in the arguments for the resource dependence and system change models is basically the same. The interagency communications set in motion by resource dependence are *externally* directed from the organization to the environment, and the causation among variables moves from dependence to communications to awareness and to consensus. In the system change model the interagency communications are *internally* directed from the environment into the organization, and the causation among variables moves from communication to awareness of environmental issues, to willingness to respond to the issue, and to consensus.

At the point where consensus is formed, the resource dependence and system change models become fused as one to explain how and why an IR develops. The divergent motivations and objectives of organizations become fused through negotiations, bargaining, and compromise. Through such processes, consensus emerges on specific means and ends for joint collaboration. From the preceding discussion it follows that the formation of an IR is a function of resource dependence and/or commitment, awareness, and consensus.

What Kind of Organizations Will Be Joined in an IR?

Domain similarity refers to the extent to which organizations obtain their money from the same sources, have the same goals, have staff with the same professional skills, and provide the same kind of services to the same clients or customers. It is a qualitative indicator of the kinds of organizations that are likely to become involved in IRs.

The evidence is conflicting on whether domain similarity helps or hinders the establishment of an IR. When organizations have similar domains, it is more likely than not that they are aware of one another and that they have complementary resources needed to help each other achieve their individual goals. The more complementary the resources of organizations, the greater the potential for establishing *quid pro quo* arrangements to transact resources that are mutually beneficial to the parties involved. In this sense, domain similarity facilitates the formation of an IR. However, similar domains also increase the potential for territorial disputes and competition between the organizations involved. If organizations have highly similar domains, they are also likely to have and need the same kinds of resources, which reduces the potential benefits of making exchanges. Therefore, highly similar domains hinder the potential for an IR to emerge. Maximum inducement to form an IR would, by this logic, occur when the organizations have some degree of complementarity, not identity, in the nature of resources available for exchange. Therefore, it is hypothesized that there is a concave (⌒shaped) relationship between domain similarity and the amount of resource flow between organizations in an IR.

At the low extremes of domain similarity, organizations have nothing in common and are unlikely to be aware of one another or to need the same resources. As a result, it is unlikely that an IR will emerge. At the high extreme of domain similarity, the organizations are almost identical and may either continue to coexist in cutthroat competition (which permits no transaction of resources between the agencies) or may merge as a single organization (in which case the intraorganization level of analysis applies). Thus, the polar ends of domain similarity are unlikely and unstable conditions for an IR. The intermediate ranges of domain similarity appear the most interesting and stable conditions because in that range organizations have complementary resources, are likely to be aware of one another's interdependence, and are also likely to be involved in some competition and territorial disputes. Furthermore, Reid (1964) suggests that tension and crisis can promote a convergence of objectives among different organizations and a greater willingness to risk exchanges. However, crisis-provoked relationships tend to diminish as the crisis recedes unless specific steps are taken to formalize the new patterns of collaboration (Morris, 1963).

This explanation relies solely upon the resource dependence model discussed previously, where organizations form a relationship to optimize joint resource usage. However, domain similarity is also a critical factor in the system change model. Here, organizations with similar domains can increase their power and influence by joining together to deal with a shared external threat or opportunity. For example, cutthroat competitors in the stock brokerage business do not exchange resources much (at least not willingly) but form a healthy IR with respect to dealing with the Securities and Exchange Commission. Similarly, within a small community, the retail business organizations, by nature of their highly similar trades and limited common sales market, may coexist in cutthroat competition and at the same time join together in a cooperative chamber of commerce to enhance the well-being of the community.

Size of network is the number of organizations belonging to an IR. The influence of size upon intraorganizational structure has been extensively researched (see Hall, 1972; Child, 1973; and Blau, 1974, for reviews). As discussed in Chapter 4, increasing organization size provides the sheer quantity or mass necessary to permit economies of scale and specialization through the division of labor. However, increases in size also increase structural complexity and the corresponding administrative burdens of coordination and control of the organization.

The analogous effects of size on the structure of interorganizational networks are expected. Litwak and Hylton (1962) and Evan (1966) have indicated that size is an important predictor of the complexity of IRs in terms of coalition formation and specialization of boundary-spanning roles. In addition, as the number of organizations in an IR increases, formalization and centralization of the network should expand for coordination and control (hypothesis 7, see Figure 8-4).

In summary, resource dependence (and/or willingness to respond to external issues), awareness, and consensus have been argued as the necessary and sufficient conditions for IRs to emerge. Domain similarity is a qualitative factor for explaining what kind of organizations are likely to choose one another in a relationship. Finally, since interagency networks generally consist of many more than two organizations, it is important to evaluate the influence of size upon the structure of an IR.

The Functioning of IRs

Given the existence of an IR, what remains to be explained is how it functions, grows, adapts, or dissolves over time. The last two assumptions in Figure 8-4 are the basis for dealing with this problem.

It is important to recognize that the defining criterion of an interorganizational network used in the argument thus far has been the intensity of the network. Intensity is the strength of the network in terms of the amount of resource flow and the frequency of information flows between network parties. Growth, adaptation, or dissolution of an IR can be monitored directly by observing variations in network intensity over time.

Integration and pattern maintenance become critical issues when resource flows increase (assumption D). An immediate response to variations in resource flows is to increase the frequency of communications through personal contacts and committee meetings. However, personal contacts and committee meetings absorb much time and effort and are inefficient mechanisms for coordinating activities that can be standardized. Therefore, under norms of rationality the IR coordinating committee will increase formalization by developing a set of policies and standardized reporting procedures for integrating and maintaining the higher level of resource flow. Through the consent of the organizational representatives on the committee, this decision binds the behavior of the network members.

Agreements reached in this way usually specify mechanisms to maintain reciprocity among members, thus increasing network complexity. The latter statement is based on assumptions B and C that an organization is reluctant to increase commitments of resources to other agencies without formal arrangements made for reciprocal flows of a desired (usually different) resource back to the organization. Thus, the greater the intensity of resource flows in an interagency network, the greater its formalization, centralization, and complexity (hypothesis 8).

As the hypotheses in Figure 8-4 imply, the *timing* of activities and events is a key factor in understanding the emergence, adaptation, and growth of an IR. We do not assume that these processes occur in one fell swoop. Instead, IRs are more likely to emerge incrementally and grow with small, successful encounters at coordination (assumption E). The case study by O'Toole and his associates of the Cleveland Rehabilitation Complex gives a particularly good description of how an IR emerges through a slow, flexible, developmental process, with many small thrusts of exchanges around specific problems, followed by periods to congeal new developments. O'Toole et al. (1972) emphasize that interagency relationships grow and build upon previous small but successful exchanges between agencies. By moving gradually toward coordination, each organization sees the positive aspects and learns to deal with the negative implications of coordination. Further, commitments and formalized arrangements are not developed prematurely, when the nature of commitment or involvement is still unclear and provides no tangible indication of direct benefits available to the parties (O'Toole et al., 1972).

The emergence and functioning of IRs, therefore, are viewed as a result of (1) a need for resources or a response to external issues, (2) interorganizational communications to spread awareness and consensus, (3) resource transactions, and (4) structural adaptation and pattern maintenance over time. What may start as an interim solution to a problem or as an attempt to obtain a specific resource may eventually become a long-term, interorganizational commitment of resources *if* previous cycles in the process are perceived by the parties to have been successful or effective encounters. It follows that the greater the perceived effectiveness of a relationship among organizations at time t, the greater the dependence, awareness, and consensus among the agencies at $t + 1$, over time period 0, 1, 2, . . . , n (hypothesis 9).

An IR may also dissolve or terminate when the organizations have achieved their self-interest objectives and no longer depend upon the IR even though previous encounters were perceived as highly effective. We therefore do not expect that all of the variations in resource flows at later time periods are explained by the perceived effectiveness of a network in prior time periods. However, there is a tendency within organizations to adopt new goals, solve new problems, and market new products when previous goals have been attained, old problems solved, and old product lines terminated (e.g., witness the March of Dimes, long-lasting industrial enterprises, and specially commissioned governmental agencies). Like Terreberry (1968), we would expect the analogous tendency in an IR. In the long run, historically successful interagency relationships become netted together in a web of interdependencies.

Summary and Research Directions

From the five assumptions in Figure 8-4 we have derived nine testable hypotheses for explaining why and how interorganizational networks emerge and how they adapt, grow, and dissolve. As presented, the theory is not complete. No attempt has been made to relate the situational and structural factors to ultimate effectiveness outcomes. As argued in Chapter 2, the selection of appropriate and relevant effectiveness goals and criteria for an interorganizational network is a value judgment to be made by the principal users in the setting where a study of IRs actually takes place. Once goals are determined, the theory may be expanded to include hypotheses to predict and explain the effectiveness of interorganizational coordination. The relevant question here is not whether coordination is good or bad. The key question is a pragmatic one: "What alternative structures are effective in different situations?"

If one adopts the perspective taken here, the following steps appear necessary for collecting data on interorganizational relations in general and networks in particular.

A.   Identify the relevant organizations that constitute the core system of IRs under investigation.

B.   Identify the boundary spanners in each organization who are the most knowledgeable about their agencies' relations with other organizations in the system.

C.   Collect data by having each boundary spanner respond to questions about each of the other agencies in the IR.

A.   Selection of Organizations.   In most interorganizational networks or service delivery systems the total number of agencies and actors belonging to the system is so large that it seems wise not to study them all. Limited resources and manpower generally forbid it. Therefore, decision rules are needed to determine what agencies to define as the core system in a study of large IRs. A useful appendix in Warren et al. (1974) provides a starting point to identify criteria for a purposive sampling scheme. The objective is to select a broad variety of agencies and actors to represent the total population in the social action system. To the extent that appropriate selection criteria have been developed, one can draw inferences from the sample of core agencies to the population of organizations in the action system.

B.   Identify Agency Informants.   The second step is to identify the boundary spanners in each organization who are most knowledgeable about their respective agencies' relations with other organizations in the system. In complex organizations, boundary-spanning roles are differentiated, and seldom is one boundary spanner knowledgeable about all the different functions or activities inherent in one pairwise interagency relationship, let alone the total cluster of relations maintained by the organization with all other agencies in the social action system.

For example, a relationship maintained by DPW (Department of Public Welfare) with another agency often includes many functions (e.g., licensing, funding transactions, and technical assistance), and different boundary spanners within DPW are responsible for each function. In addition, boundary-spanning responsibilities with each network agency are assigned to different units within DPW. As a result, the researcher should expect that the more complex the organization, the greater the number of informants required to measure accurately all the roles of the organization with other agencies in the network.

C. Data Collection Process. In general, the third step is to collect data by having informants answer the same set of questions about the relations they maintain with each organization in the core system and about the functioning of the network overall. (Each informant may be asked to provide information for only a limited subset of organizations in the core systems that he or she is knowledgeable.) With this kind of data collection strategy, one can systematically examine a network at different levels of analysis. The smallest unit of analysis is the pairwise relationship, which can be obtained by matching and merging each agency's perceptions of the other. Because the dyad is the simplest form of a social action system, all the dimensions suggested in this chapter apply to the pairwise relationship. Of course, some dimensions manifest in large IRs will be salient or emergent in dyadic relationships. At higher levels of aggregation, Appendix F suggests how dyadic relations can be grouped in certain ways to permit a sociometric evaluation of the total cluster of pairwise relations between organizations in the IR. Finally, many activities in an IR cannot be explained simply by analyzing relationships between pairs or clusters of organizations. Instead, many events are collective social facts which emerge out of the actions of the network as a unit (Durkheim, 1974). Therefore, a study of an IR should also examine the overall structure and functioning of the system itself.

SECTION III: MEASUREMENT OF DYADIC INTERORGANIZATIONAL RELATIONS

The specific data collection procedures and measures to be discussed and evaluated in this section are those used in a study of 133 pairwise relationships between 14 early childhood development (ECD) organizations and 133 other agencies in Texas during the spring of 1974. As described in Liston and Van de Ven (1976), the ECD agencies were formed in 1973 as a response to the service needs of children (ages 0–6) and their families in 14 local Texas communities. By December 1974, the average size of these ECD agencies was 23 employees who provided a variety of child development, day care, health care, and parental education services.

The study focused on the pairwise relationships each ECD agency maintained with other community organizations during spring 1974. The directors of the ECD agencies first completed a "focal agency" (FA) questionnaire which was personally administered by the researchers. The FA questionnaire asked the same questions for each of seven to eleven organizations. All respondents were asked to answer for four organizations which were believed to constitute the core child care network in each county: the departments of public welfare and public health, the independent school district, and the office of childhood development. In addition, the FA respondents selected and answered the questions for three to seven other agencies that they reported as being directly involved with in some way during the past six months. After the FA questionnaires were completed, the respondents were asked about and unanimously consented to the preparation and mailed distribution of a "member agency" (MA) questionnaire to the contact persons of all organizations that the respondents answered for in the FA questionnaire.

The MA questionnaire was an abbreviated version of the FA questionnaire. It included questions that matched those in the FA instrument on only the key attitudinal variables, including the perceived dependence, awareness, consensus, and effectiveness of relationships.

Three weeks after the MA instruments were distributed, a reminder letter was mailed to the nonresponding MAs. After another three-week period, the researchers made telephone calls to all nonresponding MAs. Finally, after another two weeks, a final reminder letter was mailed to the remaining nonrespondents to request return of the completed questionnaires. Following these procedures an 89 percent return rate of the MA questionnaires was obtained.

Operational definitions and measures of the interorganizational dimensions are now presented. It is important to remember that the unit of analysis here is the *pairwise relationship* between an ECD organization (the FA) and one other organization (the MA). Therefore, responses to matching questions in the FA and MA instruments were averaged to obtain composite pairwise perceptions of each dyadic relationship. This aggregation procedure is justified because we believe that the combined perceptions of the two parties to a dyadic relation will approximate a balanced "true" score of interorganizational constructs more than that obtained from only one party or some other weighting scheme. Of course, it is quite appropriate that others (e.g., Schmidt and Kochan, 1977) may desire to examine and compare differences in FA–MA perceptions to answer other questions about the relative status, power, and so on of the parties to a relationship.

To avoid redundancy, unless otherwise indicated all questions in the FA and MA instruments have the following Likert-type response scale:

DON'T KNOW	NO EXTENT	LITTLE EXTENT	SOME EXTENT	MUCH EXTENT	GREAT EXTENT
0	1	2	3	4	5

Resource Dependence

Dependence is defined as the extent to which an organization needs external resources to attain its self-interest goals for a specified period of time. In a pairwise relationship, resource dependence refers to the extent to which the FA needs the MA and the MA needs the FA to achieve their individual goals. These were measured with the following questions asked in both the FA and MA questionnaires.

1. "In order for this *other agency* to attain its goals, to what extent does it need the services, resources, or support from your organization?" (closed-ended response on 0–5 scale)

2. "For *what* specific services, resources, or support does *this other agency need your organization*?" (open-ended response)

3. "In order to attain *your goals*, to what extent does your organization need the services, resources, or support from this agency?" (closed-ended response on 0–5 scale)

4. "For what specific services, resources, or support does *your organization need this other agency*?" (open-ended response)

The perceptions of the FA and MA respondents to questions 1 and 3 were averaged to obtain the overall pairwise resource dependence measure. Answers to the open-ended questions were content analyzed to obtain a qualitative understanding of the nature of dependence between the FA and MA.

Agency and Personal Awareness

As described in Section II, two levels of awareness are of interest in studying interorganizational relations: agency awareness and personal acquaintance. In a dyadic relation, agency awareness is the extent to which the MA respondent is familiar with the services and goals of the FA, and the extent to which the FA respondent is familiar with the services and goals of the MA. Personal acquaintance refers to how long and how well the FA and MA boundary spanners know each other on a personal basis. The first two questions following measure agency awareness whereas the last two tap the personal acquaintance dimension in the FA and MA questionnaires.

1. How well *informed* are *you* about the specific goals and services that are provided by this other agency?

DON'T KNOW	NOT INFORMED	LITTLE INFORMED	SOMEWHAT INFORMED	QUITE INFORMED	VERY WELL INFORMED
0	1	2	3	4	5

2. To what extent did this agency participate in earlier phases of planning your ECD project? (0–5 extent scale responded to only by the FA)

3. How many years and months have you personally known the contact person in this agency? (_____ years and _____ months responded to only by the FA)

4. How well are you personally acquainted with the contact person in this agency?

NO PERSONAL ACQUAINTANCE	NOT VERY WELL	SOMEWHAT WELL	QUITE WELL	VERY WELL
1	2	3	4	5

Responses to questions 1 and 2 were averaged to compute a composite agency awareness index, and question 4 (for the FA and MA) was averaged to obtain a composite measure of personal acquaintance.

Consensus

Consensus is defined as the degree of agreement or disagreement among parties in an IR on (1) the needs and problems of the community service delivery system in general and (2) the specific means (services) and ends (goals) of each agency involved in the network. At the pairwise level, consensus refers to the degree of agreement between the FA and MA boundary spanners on these two central issues.

In the Texas pairwise interagency study the consensus index consisted of the following four questions answered by the FA and the MA respondents.

To what extent do *you* and the contact person in this agency *agree* on:

1. The most important needs of children from ages 0–6 in your community?

2. The way service in general should be provided to young children in your community?

3. The service goals of the ECD Project?

4. The specific way early childhood services are provided b、 che ECD Project?

The response scale for the preceding four questions is:

DON'T KNOW	DISAGREE MUCH	AGREE A LITTLE	AGREE SOMEWHAT	AGREE QUITE A BIT	AGREE VERY MUCH
0	1	2	3	4	5

The perceptions of the FA and MA respondents on all four questions were averaged to obtain the composite consensus measure.

Domain Similarity

Domain similarity refers to the extent to which organizations in a relationship obtain their money from the same sources, have the same goals, have staff with the same professional skills and provide the same kind of services to the same clients or customers. Thus, domain similarity is a very broad construct of the degree of overlap in domains of the organizations in a relationship. It was measured with the following five questions, answered only by the FA respondent.

To what extent does this agency:

1. Obtain its funding from the *same sources* as your organization does?

2. Provide the *same kind* of child care *services* as your organization?

3. Provide services to the *same clients or families* as your organization?

4. Have the *same* kind of *operating program goals* as your organization?

5. Have *staff* with the same kinds of professional skills or training as those required of staff for your organizations?

The preceding questions were answered on the 0–5 extent scale and averaged to obtain the composite domain similarity measure.

Frequency of Communications

Communication frequency is defined as the number of times during the past six months that messages about the nature of the relationships or units of exchange were transmitted between the FA and MA through the following media: written reports and letters, telephone calls, face-to-face discussions, and group or committee meetings. Communication frequency was therefore measured with the following questions asked only of the FA respondent:

1. How frequently were *letters or written reports* of any kind exchanged with this agency during the past six months?

2. How frequently were personal *face-to-face discussions* held with people in this agency during the past six months?

3. How frequently were *telephone calls* made with this agency during the past six months?

The following answer scale was used for the preceding questions:

0 = No or zero times during the past six months
1 = One time during the past six months
2 = Two times, or about every three months
3 = Three times, or about every two months
4 = About every month, or six times
5 = About every two weeks, or twelve times
6 = About every week, or 24 times
7 = About every 2–3 days
8 = About every day

4. Indicate the number of times that the interagency committee or group has met during the past six months. _____# times.

Thus, communication frequency is a broad construct reflecting the incidence of different forms of information flows between the FA and MA.

In the Texas pairwise interagency study, no attempt was made to measure the direction of each mode of communication between the FA and the MA (due to the length of the FA questionnaire). However, the framework presented in Section II and the procedures for developing indices of interorganizational networks require that directional measures of who initiates communications with whom should be included in future studies. This can be accomplished by asking the questions presented previously twice—once for the frequency of contacts initiated by the FA to the MA and second for the frequency of MA-initiated contacts to the FA.

Resource Flows

As described in Section II, the operational criterion of the existence of an interorganizational relationship is a transaction of resources between the agencies involved. A resource is broadly defined to include any valued transaction between agencies, whether tangible or intangible. Tangible resources include money, office space, and physical equipment, client or customer referrals, and also specific joint problem-solving or planning activities among agencies. Intangible resource flows include consultation or technical assistance, public visibility, goodwill, and prestige that an agency either gives or receives in its involvement with other organizations.

In the Texas pairwise interagency study the degrees and directions of these types of resource flows from the FA to the MA and from the MA to the FA were measured with the following questions in the FA questionnaire.

A. *Resource flows from FA to MA*
   To what *extent* did *this agency* (the MA) *receive each* of the following *resources* or rewards for its involvement with your organization during the past six months:
   1. Money?
   2. Use of your organization's staff?
   3. Client referrals?
   4. Consultation or technical assistance?
   5. Public visibility, goodwill, or prestige?
   6. Attainment of its own goals or mandates?

B. *Resource flows from MA to FA*
   To what *extent* did *your organization receive each* of the following *resources* from this agency during the past six months?
   1. Money?
   2. Use of their staff?
   3. Client referrals?

4. Consultation or technical assistance?
5. Public visibility, goodwill, or prestige?
6. Physical equipment or space?

The 0–5 extent response scale was used to answer each of the preceding questions, and pairwise resource flows were computed by adding the responses for each resource flowing to and from the FA and MA. In the initial pilot study of the FA questionnaire, an attempt was made to use ratio response scales for each question, for example, dollars, number of days of consultation, number of clients referred. However, it was found that respondents could not answer the questions. Therefore, the extent scale was used. Although this scale does not provide an absolute indication of resource flows, in the pilot study respondents stated that their responses were a fairly accurate reflection of the amounts of each resource that they transacted with each agency *relative* to other agencies in their set.

Formalization of Interagency Agreement

An interagency agreement refers to the terms that parties to an IR expect of one another. The formalization of an interagency agreement refers to the degree to which the role behavior and activities of each agency are clearly prescribed and codified. An interagency agreement exists once any form of expression has been made between the parties regarding the terms of their relationship. Its formalization increases the more the agreement is verbalized, written down, contractual, and mandatory. Thus, the formalization of interagency agreements was measured in the Texas pairwise study as the mean of the following questions in the FA questionnaire.

Has any form of *agreement been established* to define the relationship between your organization and this agency? Yes or No. (filter question)

—If yes, to *what extent* is/was the agreement with this agency:

1. Explicitly verbalized and discussed?

2. Written down in detail?

3. Legally binding or contractual?

4. Mandatory by law (e.g., licensing requirement)?

The 0–5 extent response scale was used for the four questions.

Formalization of Interagency Committee

Committee, here, refers to the organizational representatives who meet together to make decisions regarding the terms of the IR. The formalization of this "committee" increases the more it acts officially as a standing committee, follows standardized procedures (e.g., has agendas, minutes, rules of order), and makes decisions that are considered to be binding on the agencies involved. The formalization of the interagency committee was measured as the mean response to the following questions in the FA questionnaire.

Has any kind of *interagency committee* or *group been established* to coordinate activities between your organization and this agency? Yes or No. (filter question)

—If yes, please answer the next questions:

1. Is this an *ad hoc* or *standing committee*? (scored 0, 1)

2. To what extent is this committee formalized with agendas, minutes, etc.? (0–5 extent response scale)

3. To what extent are the *decisions* made by this committee *binding* upon your organization and this agency? (0–5 extent response scale)

Perceived Effectiveness of Relationship

The perceived effectiveness of an IR is defined as the extent to which the involved parties perceive each agency to carry out its commitments and judge the relationship to be worthwhile, productive, and satisfying. It was measured as the mean response to the following questions in the FA and MA questionnaires.

1. To what extent does this agency *carry out the commitments* it initially agreed to in regard to your organization? (0–5 extent scale)

2. To what extent do you feel the relationship between your organization and this agency is *productive*? (0–5 extent scale)

3. To what extent is the *time and effort spent* in developing and maintaining the relationship with this agency *worthwhile*? (0–5 extent scale)

4. Overall, to what extent are you *satisfied* with the relationship between your organization and this agency? (0–5 extent scale)

Quality of Communications

Communication quality refers to the clarity and ease of sending and receiving messages between agencies in the relationship. Although the quality of communications was not formally introduced in the theory in Section III, it is considered an important variable to control for when testing relationships between communication frequency and the other dimensions of interagency relations. Communication quality was measured as the mean response by the FA and MA to the following questions:

1. When you wanted to communicate with persons in this agency, *how much difficulty* have you had *getting in touch* with them? (answer scale was reversed)

NO CONTACT	NONE	LITTLE	SOME	MUCH	GREAT
0	1	2	3	4	5

2. Overall, how would you characterize the quality of your communications with persons in this agency during the past six months?

NO CONTACT	POOR	FAIR	GOOD	VERY GOOD	EXCELLENT
0	1	2	3	4	5

3. In your attempts to communicate with persons in this agency during the past six months, *how often did your messages "get lost"* or not get a follow-through response or return call? Answered only by FA on the following response scale, which was reversed.

NO CONTACT	NEVER	VERY SELDOM	OCCASIONALLY	QUITE OFTEN	VERY OFTEN
0	1	2	3	4	5

SECTION IV: PSYCHOMETRIC PROPERTIES OF DYADIC INTERORGANIZATIONAL DIMENSIONS

A principal components factor analysis was performed on 33 of the preceding IR dimensions on 133 pairwise relations among the Texas child care agencies. The measures of resource flows were excluded from the factor analysis because they are single-item indices. The factor analysis procedure was truncated at ten factors (one for each construct). Principal components analysis found that the 33 items broke out into eight factors with characteristic roots greater than one and two additional factors with eigenvalues .88 and .82. The ten factors account for 82 percent of the total common variance among the 33 items. The factors were then rotated with an oblimin procedure to final solution. Table 8-1 presents the primary pattern obtained from the oblimin factor rotation. The table shows that most of the items within each index are represented by a single factor. However, five departures from the hypothesized structure can be seen in Table 8-1.

First, the resource dependence items confound with the consensus and communication frequency factors. The two items making up the resource dependence index load together rather weakly on factor VIII, just above the conventional .40 criterion for a significant item loading on a factor. However, the resource dependence items have about equal loadings on factors I and VII. This indicates that the correlations among the resource dependence items may not be much greater than their correlations with communication frequency and consensus. However, the loadings of the consensus items in factor I and the communication items in factor VII are much greater than those of the resource dependence items on factors I and VII, whereas the consensus and communications items have very small loadings (near zero) on the resource dependence factor VIII.

These results are difficult to interpret because: (1) the theory presented in Section II predicts that resource dependence should largely influence interagency communications and consensus, (2) a pilot study conducted to evaluate the content validity of the measures found that respondents had no problems in correctly interpreting and distinguishing the meanings of the resource dependence, communications, and consensus items, and (3) the differences in the size of the loadings between the consensus items and one dependence item in factor I and between the communication items and the other dependence item in factor VII are sufficiently large to suggest that the dependence items are tapping a sampling domain different from that of the consensus and communications items. Therefore, we suspend judgment on the resource dependence items until further evaluation following.

The second departure from the hypothesized structure in Table 8-1 is the confounding of item 6, extent personally acquainted, of the acquaintance index with consensus. This item loads more highly on the consensus factor I. One should expect the degree of personal

Table 8-1 Factor Analysis of 33 Items Designed to Measure Interorganizational Dimensions on 133 Pairwise Relationships among Texas Child Care Agencies (Principal Components, Oblimin Rotation)

Indices and Items	I Consensus	II Committee Formalization	III Perceived Effectiveness of Relation
Resource Dependence			
1. Extent FA Needs MA	.07	.01	−.13
2. Extent MA Needs FA	.42[a]	.06	−.17
Agency Awareness			
3. Informed of Other Agency Goals	.29	.02	−.07
4. Participate in Other Agency Activities	.07	.03	−.00
Personal Acquaintance			
5. Time Known Contact Person	.11	−.02	−.04
6. Extent Personally Acquainted	.48[a]	−.07	.04
Consensus			
7. Agree on Community Needs	.86[a]	.07	−.06
8. Agree on Service Delivery Methods	.88[a]	.03	−.08
9. Agree on Project Goals	.78[a]	−.01	−.04
10. Agree on Project Methods	.87[a]	.04	−.04
Domain Similarity			
11. Provide Same Services	.11	−.01	−.07
12. Serve Same Clients	.06	.04	.03
13. Have Same Agency Goals	.07	.15	−.03
14. Have Same Staff Skills	−.09	.07	.05
15. Obtain Resources from Same Sources	.07	.02	−.01
Information Flows			
16. Freq. of Written Letters, Reports	.01	.18	−.04
17. Freq. of Face-to-Face Talks	−.06	.07	−.26
18. Freq. of Telephone Calls	−.03	.00	−.08
19. Freq. of Committee Meetings	−.06	.90[a]	−.03
Formalization of Agreement			
20. Extent Agreement Verbalized	−.02	.06	−.16
21. Extent Agreement Written Out	−.03	.10	−.03
22. Extent Agreement Legal	−.03	.07	−.01
23. Extent Agreement Mandatory	.00	.01	−.02
Formalization of Committee			
24. Ad hoc or Standing Committee	.04	.99[a]	−.03
25. Extent Follows Formalized Procedures	.02	.99[a]	.00
26. Extent Decisions Binding on Agencies	.04	.92[a]	.07
Perceived Effectiveness of Relation			
27. Other Agency Carries out Commitments	.08	.05	−.71[a]
28. Extent Relation Productive	.04	.04	−.83[a]
29. Extent Effort Worthwhile	−.02	.03	−.89[a]
30. Satisfaction with Relationship	.04	−.04	−.87[a]
Quality of Communications			
31. Difficulty Making Contacts (Reversed scale)	−.08	−.01	−.26
32. Freq. No Follow Through (Reversed scale)	.00	.07	.13
33. Overall Quality of Communications	.25	−.04	−.58[a]

[a] Significant loading of item on factor equal to or greater than .40.

IV Communication Quality	V Agreement Formalization	VI Personal Acquaintance	VII Communication Frequency	VIII Resource Dependence	IX Agency Awareness	X Domain Similarity	h² Item Communalities
.10	.03	−.14	−.42ᵃ	.43ᵃ	−.15	.00	.58
.02	−.14	−.11	−.07	.45ᵃ	.10	.03	.64
.05	−.06	−.06	−.04	.06	−.72ᵃ	.03	.89
.08	−.16	.02	−.02	−.03	−.84ᵃ	−.02	.89
.06	.06	.62ᵃ	−.01	−.02	−.03	.05	.46
.05	−.13	.41ᵃ	−.20	−.10	−.02	−.05	.55
.03	.06	.00	.04	−.05	−.06	.14	.90
−.00	.04	−.05	−.02	.00	.07	.06	.90
−.05	−.02	.10	.03	.19	−.19	−.06	.91
−.06	.05	.08	.06	.05	−.09	−.02	.91
−.12	−.14	.03	.25	.15	−.03	.48ᵃ	.40
.05	.02	−.03	−.03	−.01	.02	.52ᵃ	.32
.07	−.07	−.01	−.00	.51ᵃ	.10	.17	.53
−.08	.03	.22	.01	.09	−.16	.46ᵃ	.33
−.14	−.06	−.26	−.09	.12	.08	.37	.40
−.01	−.16	.03	−.69ᵃ	−.00	.07	−.13	.69
−.22	.06	.14	−.48ᵃ	−.10	−.16	.31	.71
−.17	−.04	.01	−.77ᵃ	.08	−.12	.05	.71
.07	−.03	.07	−.01	−.04	.05	.13	.91
−.21	−.59ᵃ	.28	.02	.15	−.08	−.20	.71
−.09	−.80ᵃ	−.09	−.03	−.03	−.15	−.13	.88
−.04	−.82ᵃ	−.12	−.05	−.16	−.18	.01	.88
.09	−.62ᵃ	.02	.07	.16	.05	.22	.57
.07	−.02	−.01	.01	−.03	.02	−.03	.99
−.01	.01	−.00	−.00	−.04	.00	−.01	.90
−.06	.04	−.06	−.04	.06	−.06	−.10	.92
−.24	−.17	.05	.00	−.10	−.01	−.08	.78
.01	−.08	−.02	−.03	.02	−.11	.01	.86
−.06	.02	.00	−.01	.15	−.02	.01	.87
.09	.07	.04	−.10	.05	−.01	.00	.86
.58ᵃ	.14	.20	.08	−.02	−.08	−.14	.51
.73ᵃ	.01	−.00	.07	.07	−.03	.03	.51
.35	−.09	−.10	−.11	−.21	−.00	−.01	.75

Table 8-1 Continued

Indices and Items		I Consensus	II Committee Formalization	III Perceived Effectiveness of Relation
FACTOR CORRELATION MATRIX		I	II	III
I	Consensus	1.00		
II	Committee Formalization	.12	1.00	
III	Perceived Effectiveness of Relation	−.43	−.12	1.00
IV	Communication Quality	.12	.01	−.10
V	Agreement Formalization	−.19	−.34	.29
VI	Personal Acquaintance	.16	−.05	−.12
VII	Communication Frequency	−.16	−.27	.41
VIII	Resource Dependence	.22	.24	−.13
IX	Agency Awareness	−.39	−.29	.34
X	Domain Similarity	.17	.21	.02

acquaintance reported by organizational boundary spanners to be highly related to how much they agree with one another on the goals and services of their respective agencies. Indeed, the perceived degree of personal acquaintance and consensus may be intractable empirically. The other, more objective measure of personal acquaintance (number of years and months boundary spanners have known each other) appears to have more discriminant validity and is used in further analysis of the instrument following.

The third departure from the hypothesized structure is the strong loading of item 19 (the frequency of committee meetings) with the items measuring the formalization of the interagency committee in factor II. As in previous chapters, the information flow index continues to break out in different ways in factor analyses, providing further evidence of the need to treat these items as indicators of different forms of communications. The data in Table 8-1 indicate that the frequency of committee meetings is highly associated with the existence of a standing interagency committee and the extent to which it follows formalized procedures and is perceived to make binding decisions. Empirical covariation among these dimensions are largely as might be expected.

Item 33 in Table 8-1, which asks about the overall quality of communications between the organizations, loads more highly on factor III with items measuring the perceived effectiveness of the relationship than it does with the other two items in the communication quality

IV Communication Quality	V Agreement Formalization	VI Personal Acquaintance	VII Communication Frequency	VIII Resource Dependence	IX Agency Awareness	X Domain Similarity	h² Item Communalities
IV	V	VI	VII	VIII	IX	X	
1.00							
.27	1.00						
.06	.03	1.00					
.14	.23	.01	1.00				
−.07	−.19	−.13	−.07	1.00			
−.01	.31	−.30	.20	−.18	1.00		
−.18	−.05	−.02	−.03	.35	−.11	1.00	

index in factor IV. Because it confounds with the perceived effectiveness index, item 33 is dropped, and the two remaining items (31 and 32), which load cleanly as factor IV, are treated as an index of communication quality.

The last departures from the hypothesized structure in Table 8-1 are the weakness of loadings of the domain similarity index on factor X and the confounding of one item (13) from this index with the resource dependence items on factor VIII. Domain similarity was defined as a very broad construct of the extent to which organizations in a relationship have the same goals, personnel skills, services, clients, and funding sources. Hence, although somewhat greater empirical convergence among these items was expected, it is not surprising to observe that the loadings of the domain similarity index are relatively weak. The significant loading of item 13 on factor VIII indicates that organizations with similar goals tend to be dependent upon each other for resources. However, since our intentions are to empirically examine relationships between resource dependence and domain similarity in a nontautological way, as well as to minimize multicollinearity among these and other indices used as independent variables in a regression analysis to predict resource flows among agencies, item 13 is eliminated from the domain similarity index.

In summary, this evaluation of the factor analysis results in Table 8-1 has detected three items that confound significantly with indices they were not intended to measure. Items 6, 33, and 13 are therefore deleted from the personal acquaintance, quality of communications, and domain similarity indices, respectively, in the analysis following. Revision of these items is necessary in future applications of the instrument.

Other Criteria of the Intrinsic Validity of IR Measures

Table 8-2 presents the reliabilities of the IR indices in terms of expected and observed coefficient alpha and the median correlations of items with other indices. As described in Chapter 3, the expected ranges of coefficient alpha are a function of the number of different conceptual elements used to define each construct.

Table 8-2 shows that the observed coefficient alphas fall well within the expected ranges for the agency awareness, communication frequency, and perceived effectiveness indices. The internal consistencies for four indices (resource dependence, domain similarity, agreement formalization, and communication quality) are slightly lower than desired but acceptable, given our rough rules of thumb on expected ranges for coefficient alpha. Finally the consensus and committee formalization indices obtained coefficient alphas somewhat higher than expected, suggesting there is a little too much redundancy among the items in these two indices.

Table 8-2   Reliabilities of Dyadic Interorganizational Dimensions

Indices	No. of Items in Each Index	Coefficient Expected	Alpha Observed	Median Correlation with Other Indices
1. Resource Dependence	2	.55–.70	.53	.49
2. Agency Awareness	2	.70–.90	.89	.33
3. Personal Acquaintance	1	—	—	.02
4. Consensus	4	.55–.70	.87	.27
5. Domain Similarity	4	.35–.55	.31	.30
6. Freq. of Communications (Composite)	4	.35–.55	.45	.33
a. Written reports, letters	1	—	—	—
b. Face-to-face discussions	1	—	—	—
c. Telephone calls	1	—	—	—
d. Committee meetings	1	—	—	—
7. Agreement Formalization	4	.70–.90	.64	.27
8. Committee Formalization	3	.70–.90	.94	.24
9. Perceived Effectiveness of Relationship	4	.70–.90	.78	.20
10. Communication Quality	2	.55–.70	.51	.03

With two exceptions, the median correlations of items in each index with all other indices are far smaller than their corresponding coefficient alphas, indicating that the discriminant validity of the indices is quite good. The average correlations between items within the resource dependence and domain similarity indices are about as large as their median correlations with the other indices. This suggests that the items in these two indices neither converge nor discriminate very well. This is corroborated by the relatively weak factor analysis loadings of the resource dependence and domain similarity items on factors VIII and X, respectively, in Table 8-1. Attempts to improve on the measurement properties of these two indices are made in the revised OAI in Appendix A.

Equally important as the intrinsic validity of the IR measures is their practical usefulness for research and organizational analysis. This was evaluated by determining: (1) if the correlations among the IR indices are consistent with the theory, (2) how well the IR indices explain variations in resource flows between organizations, and (3) how well they detect different patterns of interorganizational relationships. These three criteria of the extrinsic validity of the IR dimensions are now discussed.

Correlations among the IR Dimensions

Table 8-3 shows the correlations obtained among the IR indices. Obviously, a test of the theory developed in Section II requires longitudinal data. However, a preliminary evaluation of some of the hypotheses developed in Section II is useful for determining if the correlations among the IR dimensions are consistent with the theory.

1. Resource Dependence. Basic to the theory is the assumption that organizations do not coordinate for coordination's sake; rather, it is a rational response to a lack of resources or means to attain self-interest objectives. We therefore hypothesized that the greater the resource dependence, the greater the interorganizational activity as indicated by the frequency of communications. Table 8-3 shows that resource dependence significantly correlates with increases in the frequency of all forms of communication. Moreover, when regressing the composite frequency of all forms of communications on resource dependence, agency awareness, personal acquaintance, consensus, and domain similarity, it was found that resource dependence is the only significant predictor of communication frequency, and its standardized beta weight is .57 ($p < .01$). Thus, the preliminary evidence shows considerable support for hypothesis 1 (Figure 8-4).

Table 8-3 Correlations among Dimensions of Interorganizational Relationships[a] (n = 133 pairwise relationships among Texas child care organizations)

	Mean	SD	1	2	3	4	5	6	7	8	9	10	11	12	13	14	15	16	17	18
1. Resource Dependence	3.75	1.00	—																	
2. Agency Awareness	3.98	1.16	.22	—																
3. Personal Acquaintance	1 yr 8 mos	2 yrs 6 mos	.24	.44	—															
4. Consensus	3.63	1.44	.26	.60	.55	—														
5. Domain Similarity	2.54	.99	.45	.33	.02	.32	—													
6. Freq. of Communications (Mean)	2.86	1.65	.64	.33	.24	.50	.30	—												
7. Written reports, letters	2.54	2.02	.41	.15	.22	.15	.11	.80	—											
8. Face-to-face discussions	3.91	2.08	.33	.33	.23	.28	.29	.80	.47	—										
9. Telephone calls	4.04	2.29	.53	.31	.24	.22	.24	.89	.69	.71	—									
10. Committee meetings	.81	2.04	.29	.18	.05	.13	.36	.59	.32	.26	.26	—								
11. Communication Quality	3.57	.68	.02	.03	.10	-.05	.11	.28	.03	.26	.15	-.09	—							
12. Agreement Formalization	2.59	1.71	.39	.27	.23	.25	.21	.56	.41	.34	.42	.34	.26	—						
13. Committee Formalization	.56	1.27	.34	.24	.02	.19	.34	.53	.37	.25	.27	.82	.02	.40	—					
14. Effectiveness of Relationship	4.03	1.03	.57	.54	.35	.53	.21	.52	.44	.52	.51	.19	.20	.45	.17	—				
15. Total Resource Flows (Sum)	20.11	8.99	.66	.47	.11	.46	.50	.59	.48	.58	.53	.40	.25	.50	.46	.53	—			
16. Money	3.62	2.31	.41	.26	-.16	.15	.15	.46	.37	.24	.32	.51	.25	.47	.52	.19	.56	—		
17. Client Referrals	4.41	2.89	.40	.21	.16	.24	.46	.32	.30	.31	.25	.08	.13	.23	.09	.24	.70	.14	—	
18. Technical Assistance	6.58	2.55	.64	.58	.03	.46	.48	.59	.47	.48	.48	.39	.15	.42	.45	.59	.81	.40	.51	—
19. Visibility and Goodwill	5.95	2.88	.47	.42	.08	.43	.29	.54	.31	.53	.46	.35	.30	.38	.41	.49	.79	.38	.35	.64

[a] Correlations greater than .25 are significant beyond .01 level.

2. Awareness and Consensus. Given a condition of resource dependence, it was next hypothesized that the greater the frequency of interorganizational communications, the greater the awareness of other agencies and consensus among the parties involved on the terms of a relationship. Table 8-3 shows support for the direction of the relationships. A more direct test of the hypothesis is available with the partial correlations shown in Table 8-4. There it shows that when controlling for resource dependence, as the frequency of communications increases, there are significant increases in agency awareness (.25) and consensus (.45). However, when controlling for the frequency of communications, the partial correlations of resource dependence with agency awareness (.01) and consensus (−.09) vanish. This provides some evidence for the causal sequence in hypotheses 1 and 2 in Figure 8-4. Resource dependence appears to directly affect communication frequency and is only indirectly related to awareness and consensus through communications.

3. Resource Flows. Another hypothesis was that the amount of resource flow between organizations in a pairwise relationship is a function of resource dependence, agency awareness, and consensus. Regressing the composite measure of resource flows on these factors, the following standardized regression was obtained: resource flows = constant + .61* resource dependence + .11 awareness + .35* consensus (where the asterisked beta weights are significant beyond the .01 level). With these three factors, 55 percent of the variation in total resource flows is explained. However, as is shown in the next section, dependence,

Table 8-4   Simple and Partial Correlations with Agency Awareness and Consensus

	Agency Awareness	Interorganizational Consensus
Simple Correlation with Total Communication Frequency	.33[a]	.50[a]
Partial Correlation with Total Communication Frequency when Controlling for Resource Dependence	.25[a]	.45[a]
Simple Correlation with Resource Dependence	.22	.26[a]
Partial Correlation with Resource Dependence when Controlling for Total Communication Frequency	.01	−.09

[a] Significant beyond .05 level.

awareness, and consensus are not the only factors that are important in explaining resource transactions in an IR. Furthermore, the contributions of these three factors vary considerably when one attempts to explain specific types of resource flows between organizations.

   4. Formalization of Agreement and Committee. These are indicators of structural arrangements for integrating activities in an IR. Increases in amounts of resource transactions between organizations increase problems of integration and pattern maintenance. Therefore, it was hypothesized that as resource flows increase, formalization of the interorganizational agreement and the coordinating committee will also increase. Table 8-3 shows that associated with increases in total resource flows are significant increases in the formalization of the interagency agreement ($r = .50$) and committee ($r = .46$). When partialing out the direct effects of communication frequency, the first-order correlations of resource flows with agreement formalization (.40) and committee formalization (.35) remain quite large and suggest there is a direct connection between resource transactions and structural adaptations in pairwise interagency relationships.

   Caution, of course, must be taken in drawing any firm conclusions from these results because longitudinal data are required to test the cause-and-effect hypotheses in the theory. However, the cross-sectional data examined here are sufficient to suggest that the correlations among the OAI IR dimensions are largely as the theory would expect them to be.

Concurrent Validity of the IR Indices in Explaining Resource Flows

As stated in Section II, the defining criterion of an IR is the transaction of resources of any kind between the organizations involved. Table 8-3 shows that with the exception of personal acquaintance, all the IR dimensions are significantly correlated with at least two of the following types of resource transactions: money, client referrals, technical assistance, and less tangible resources of visibility, goodwill, or prestige. Although this provides substantial evidence of the concurrent validity of the IR indices, these results are difficult to interpret because of the strong correlations among the IR dimensions.

   To examine the unique contribution that each IR dimension makes in explaining resource flows, five standard multiple regression equations were computed—one for each type of resource and the composite measure of resource flows. For each equation, the ten composite IR indices were entered as the independent variables. Only the composite frequency of all forms of communications was used in the regression analyses to minimize multicollinearity among the independent variables. Table 8-5 shows the standardized regression coefficients (betas) obtained on each interorganizational dimension to predict each type of resource flow. After controlling for the other interorganizational dimensions, the table shows that each IR dimension explains a significant proportion of the variation in at least one of the types of resource transactions between pairs of child care organizations. Overall results of the regression analyses are presented at the bottom of Table 8-5. The ten IR dimensions explain between 34 to 62 percent of the variations in the different forms of resource transactions and 65 percent of the variation in all forms of resource flows combined.

It appears that the IR indices represent a good compromise between (1) being general enough to explain a wide variety of tangible and intangible forms of resource transactions between pairs of organizations, and (2) being specific enough to be highly related to each type of resource flow. Three to nine of the ten indices are significantly correlated with the transaction of each type of resource, and multiple regression analyses show that these dimensions account for 34 to 65 percent of the variations in resource flows. We conclude that, although there is clearly room for improvement, the concurrent validity of these IR indices is adequate for assessing various types of resource transactions between organizations.

From a substantive viewpoint, it is important to note that different patterns of interorganizational coordination are associated with different types of resource transactions among organizations. Table 8-5 suggests that monetary transactions tend to occur among interdependent but dissimilar organizations and are maintained with highly formalized agreements and impersonal coordination procedures. One explanation for these findings is that transactions of monies require formalized agreements and procedures to maintain accountability in the use of public funds. Furthermore, funding agencies generally have more formal and codified procedures for allocating their money on the basis of a set of objective criteria. These public funding agencies are generally well known, and their criteria for resource allocation are generally published. As a result, mutual degrees of personal acquaintances and consensus need not be high—as long as the criteria for resource allocation are met. Overall, therefore, relationships among money grantors and grantees tend to be formalized.

In contrast, the key factors that predict client referrals among organizations are interdependence, complementarity of services, goals, and

Table 8-5 Regression Analysis of Each Type of Resource Flow on the Interorganizational Indices
(n = 133 pairwise relationships among Texas child care organizations)

	Money Transactions beta	Client Referrals beta	Technical Assistance, Consultation beta	Visibility, Goodwill, Prestige beta	Composite Dyadic Resource Flows beta
1. Resource Dependence	.39[a]	.29[a]	.09[a]	.10	.33[a]
2. Agency Awareness	.03	-.15	.25[a]	-.01	.09
3. Time Boundary Spanners Acquainted	-.06	.17[a]	-.02	.02	.10[a]
4. Consensus	-.02	.02	-.07	.22[a]	.11
5. Domain Similarity	-.22[a]	.36[a]	.24[a]	.00	.18[a]
6. Frequency of Communications	.06	.19[a]	.17[a]	.27[a]	.23[a]
a. Freq. of reports & letters	NA[b]	NA[b]	NA[b]	NA[b]	NA[b]
b. Freq. of face-to-face talks	NA	NA	NA	NA	NA
c. Freq. of telephone calls	NA	NA	NA	NA	NA
d. Freq. of committee meetings	NA	NA	NA	NA	NA
7. Communication Quality	.21[a]	.05	.00	.24[a]	.14[a]
8. Agreement Formalization	.23[a]	.08	.01	-.01	.11[a]
9. Committee Formalization	.37[a]	-.23[a]	.14[a]	.12	.10
10. Effectiveness of Relationship	-.23[a]	-.05	.29[a]	.15	.08
Results of Multiple Regression					
% Variance Explained (R^2)	48%	34%	62%	47%	65%
F-ratio for regression	5.71 $p < .01$	3.14 $p < .01$	11.22 $p < .01$	7.00 $p < .01$	11.73 $p < .01$

[a] Standardized beta coefficient significant beyond .01 level in the multiple regression equation.
[b] Not applicable. To minimize multicolinearity, only composite frequency of communications was entered in regression equations.

skills, and greater reliance on personal acquaintance and frequent communications among boundary spanners than on formalized coordination. To establish the fact that organizations will refer clients to one another, a moderate degree of formalized agreement is needed. However, the execution of this agreement need not be highly formalized. Instead, the data suggest that it is through frequent communications between boundary spanners who are personally acquainted that client referrals among organizations are worked out. Finally, client referrals occur between organizations with complementary domains because each is dependent upon the other to the extent that each organization can provide specialized services to clients which the other does not—otherwise there would be no need for referring clients to the other organization.

IRs based on the provision of technical assistance or consultation tend to occur between organizations with complementary domains (particularly staff skills) where the boundary spanners are aware of the services and goals provided by the other organization. To the extent that an organization seeking technical assistance is aware of other organizations, its boundary spanners are able to contact the appropriate organizations to identify the consultants to help with their problems. In addition, frequent communications, some formalization of committee meeting procedures, and perceptions of effective relationships are important for explaining increases in the amounts of technical assistance or consultation organizations are willing to provide each other in an IR.

Finally, organizations often enter into relationships with others for public relations purposes (i.e., to increase visibility, goodwill, or prestige). As might be expected, communication frequency, quality, and consensus are the most important factors in explaining how much of these nontangible resources parties perceive they obtain from an IR. Organizations involved in IRs for public relations purposes are not highly dependent upon others because their core functions, objectives, and budgets are usually not at stake. Instead, organizational representatives only perceive a need for being involved with other organizations to the extent that they wish to control their environment, protect their domains, and enhance their joint interests by simple exchanges of information. Since few tangible resources are exchanged between the parties involved and because such IRs generally do not penetrate into the technical or budget cores of the organizations involved, there is little reason for not having high levels of consensus on the services and goals of each organization. Generally, only verbal agreements are established among agencies about the terms of their

Table 8-6 Analyses of Variance of Relations Maintained by Texas Child Care Organizations with Three Different Types of Organizations

Pairwise Interorganization Coordination Dimensions[a]	State Early Childhood Development Agency		Regional Dept. of Public Welfare		Local County Dept. of Public Health		F-Test for Significant Differences	
	$\bar{x}$	σ	$\bar{x}$	σ	$\bar{x}$	σ	F-ratio	$p <$
1. Resource Dependence	4.47	.45	4.56	.39	2.60	.93	25.083	.0000
2. Agency Awareness	4.54	.54	4.45	.69	2.58	1.54	14.594	.0000
3. Months Boundary Spanners Acquainted	6.79	4.56	11.00	11.35	10.17	9.11	.878	ns
4. Consensus	3.84	.94	3.90	.77	2.44	1.91	4.813	.02
5. Domain Similarity	2.53	1.23	2.72	.89	2.31	.81	.477	ns
6. Composite Freq. of Communications[b]	3.37	1.27	4.37	1.14	1.69	1.45	13.025	.0001
a. Freq. of reports & letters[b]	3.00	1.47	4.10	1.20	2.14	2.43	3.355	.05
b. Freq. of face-to-face talks[b]	3.57	.65	5.00	1.94	2.36	1.78	8.866	.001
c. Freq. of telephone calls[b]	4.36	1.78	5.80	.92	2.21	2.29	11.758	.0001
d. Freq. of committee meetings[b]	2.62	2.75	2.50	3.24	0.00	0.00	5.253	.01
7. Communication Quality	3.55	.75	3.50	.75	3.84	.87	.698	ns
8. Agreement Formalization	3.93	.83	2.87	1.07	.87	1.09	20.969	.0000
9. Committee Formalization	2.07	1.82	1.37	1.78	.00	.00	7.546	.002
10. Effectiveness of Relationship	4.42	.44	4.47	.56	3.34	1.26	7.267	.003
11. Total Resource Flows to Organization from this Agency	17.21	3.64	18.50	4.60	8.50	3.23	26.905	.0000
a. Money Flows to project	4.71	.83	3.60	1.90	.93	.27	43.469	.0000
b. Client referrals to project	.86	.36	3.40	1.65	1.36	.84	20.055	.0000
c. Technical assistance to project	4.43	1.02	4.40	.84	2.29	1.14	19.156	.0000
d. Visibility, goodwill, prestige	4.07	1.54	3.40	1.43	1.43	.94	14.979	.0000

[a] Unless otherwise indicated the basic response scale was: 0 = to no extent; 1 = to very little extent; 2 = to little extent; 3 = to some extent; 4 = to much extent; 5 = to great extent.

[b] The frequency of communication scale was: 0, 1, 2, 3 = zero to three times in past six months; 4 = about every month; 5 = about every two weeks; 6 = about every week; 7 = about every 2–3 days; 8 = about every day.

relations, and seldom are they codified or formalized. Yet, a moderate degree of committee structuring is needed to identify the principal boundary spanners within each organization to be involved in IR activities, as well as to set agreed-upon procedures for meeting together.

The theory developed in Section II did not go into sufficient detail to explain these different coordination patterns. However, they are quite consistent with what one would expect when assessing different types of resource transactions between organizations. Similar findings were obtained by Van de Ven, Walker, and Liston (1979) in another study of interorganizational coordination. The results support the conclusion by Warren et al. (1974) from their study of model cities interorganizational networks and Hall et al. (1977) on pairwise relations among problem youth organizations: *It is important to understand the different reasons for interorganizational relationships.* As the data in Table 8-5 suggest, when organizations are dependent upon one another for different types of resources, they adopt different patterns of coordination.

Usefulness of IR Indices for Diagnosing Different IRs

The last criterion for evaluating the extrinsic validity of the IR indices is their usefulness for diagnosing relationships between different organizations. The ability of the indices to detect different IRs was examined by computing a one-way analysis of variance for each dimension across the relationships all the 14 Texas child care organizations maintained with three different types of organizations: (1) a state agency for early childhood development, (2) a regional department of public welfare, and (3) a local county department of public health. Table 8-6 compares the interorganizational relations of the child care organizations with these three organizations.

1. The *State Early Childhood Development Agency* (hereafter the Agency) sponsored the original formation of the child care organizations by providing funds and technical assistance for planning community child care programs from January to August, 1973. In addition, the Agency provided financial support to the organizations to implement their programs until August, 1976, after which they were expected to be financially self-sufficient or to obtain their resources elsewhere. Knowing this from the outset, the Agency encouraged the organizations to become integrated with existing resource allocation channels and to obtain the resources needed to operate their programs as an ongoing service to the community. During the period covered by this study (spring 1974), the organizations were still highly dependent upon the

Agency for money and technical assistance to implement their child care programs.

Table 8-6 shows the pattern of relationships between the projects and the state Agency in terms of the IR dimensions. Consistent with the preceding description and relative to the other organizations, the relationships of the organizations with the Agency exhibit the highest resource dependence and agency awareness, the most formalized agreements and committee procedures, the least domain similarity, and moderately high levels of consensus and communications by reports, face-to face discussions, and telephone calls. The organization directors reported they received the most money, technical assistance, and visibility, goodwill, or prestige from the state Agency during spring 1974. The relatively small number of months that boundary spanners were acquainted (about 7 months) is explained by the fact that the Agency reassigned a number of its staff to different child care organizations in September 1973.

2. The *departments of public welfare* (*DPW*) were organized on a regional (or territorial) basis throughout the state. The child care organizations became involved with the regional DPW offices for three major reasons: (1) to obtain licensing approval to open and operate their child care programs for the public in their communities, (2) to obtain federal and state matching funds under Title IV-A (now Title XX) legislation for child care services, and (3) to obtain client referrals and technical assistance on delivering child care services.

During the first year of program operations, Table 8-6 shows that the organizations obtained most of their client referrals from DPW, received about as much technical assistance from DPW as the state Agency, and received a moderate amount of funds from DPW which matched (roughly 30 percent) the state Agency's allocation to the organizations. The relationships with DPW were somewhat less formalized, but more written and verbal communications occurred than with the state Agency. Because DPW case coordinators are involved in the direct delivery of child care services in the community, the domains of DPW and the organizations were perceived to be more similar than with the state Agency. Most of the DPW boundary spanners became familiar with the organization directors when planning the child care programs during 1973. Thus, the empirical data are consistent with what the researchers observed in site visits to the organizations.

3. Relationships with the *county departments of public health* (*DPH*) were very embryonic in spring 1974. About half of the organizations provided a health-related service in their child care programs (e.g., health care screening and immunizations, neo- and postnatal education and nutrition advisory services) and were staffed with a registered nurse or a paramedic. These organizations periodically consulted with the public health nurse of DPH on matters related to delivering these health care services, referring children with specific physical and mental health problems to appropriate treatment agencies or physicians in the community. These consultations and referrals occurred on an informal case-by-case basis, and none of the organizations was involved in a contractual relationship with DPH in spring 1974.

Table 8-6 shows an interorganization pattern of relationships with DPH that is highly consistent with this qualitative description. Relationships with DPH reflect the lowest dependence, agency awareness, consensus, communication frequency, formalized agreements, and committee procedures relative to DPW and the state Agency. Since there was little dependence and few resources were transacted with DPH, tight coupling in terms of the other interorganizational dimensions was not needed.

The preceding qualitative and quantitative comparison of the interorganizational relationships between the child care organizations and the state Agency, regional DPW, and local DPH indicate that the IR indices accurately portray the interagency patterns that were observed qualitatively by the researchers. Furthermore, the analysis of variance results in the right column of Table 8-6 show that significant differences exist between the interorganizational relations on all but one dimension (the quality of communications). This demonstrates that the OAI IR indices can detect systematic variations in both voluntary and contractual interorganizational relationships.

CONCLUSION

This section has evaluated the measurement properties of the indices used in the OAI to assess IRs. After dropping three items from the instrument that confounded indices in the factor analysis, intrinsic validity was judged satisfactory for eight indices (agency awareness, personal acquaintance, consensus, frequency and quality of communications, formalization of agreements and committee procedures, and the perceived effectiveness of an IR), whereas improvements were found necessary for the resource dependence and domain similarity indices.

The extrinsic validity of these measures was also evaluated in three ways. First, it was found that the correlations among the IR indices are highly consistent with the theory on which they are based. Second, the IR dimensions were found to explain 34 to 65 percent of the variations in different forms of resource flows between pairs of child care organizations. However, different IR dimensions are important in explaining the transactions of money, client referrals, technical assistance, and visibility or goodwill between organizations. These results point out the importance of understanding the different reasons for IRs. When organizations are dependent upon one another for different types of resources, they adopt different patterns of coordination. Finally, the OAI indices were able to detect different patterns of relationships maintained by the Texas child care organizations with three different types of organizations.

Overall, these results suggest the IR indices can be useful for research and applied assessment of interorganization relationships. The IR indices appear to represent a good compromise between being (1) general enough to apply to a variety of different types of contractual and voluntary IRs and forms of resource transactions, and (2) specific enough to explain large proportions of the variations in each type of resource transacted between organizations.

Generalization of these findings to other settings is problematic because the evaluation here is only based on 133 pairwise relationships within a relatively narrow domain of child care organizations. Therefore, the findings should be interpreted with caution and as an exploratory attempt to develop indices that measure selected dimensions of interorganization coordination. However, the preliminary evidence obtained here is promising. Appendix A describes the modifications that were made to improve and generalize these measures in the revised OAI. Further testing of these and parallel indices in other settings is needed to evaluate the revisions made.